F

CRIC

EDI…

All statistics by the Editor unless otherwise credited

PICK-A-TEAM COMPETITION 1986

SELECT AN ENGLAND XI TO PLAY THE REST OF THE WORLD

£1400 TO BE WON

Prizes: 1st: £450 2nd: £300 3rd: £225 4th: £175
Plus twenty-five prizes of £10 each

How to enter: Select, with a particular emphasis on fielding, the best current NatWest England XI from the 54 players listed below who have already represented England in Limited-Overs Internationals and who will be available to play County Cricket in 1986. Their full England One-Day records appear on pages 208-210. All have appeared in NatWest Trophy matches. Print your team in batting order on the form opposite, mark your captain with an asterisk (*), and, in a maximum of 20 words, say what you enjoy most about one-day matches and why. Don't forget to add your name and address. Entry is free.

Your Choice: On 3 February 1986, Trevor Bailey (Chairman), Fred Titmus and Pat Pocock selected an England team to play a 60-overs match against a Rest of the World XI at Lord's this summer.

Their more difficult selections were decided by superior fielding ability. You have to guess their team. Full physical fitness of all the following 54 players was guaranteed: AGNEW, ALLOTT, AMISS, ATHEY, BAILEY (R.J.), BAIRSTOW, BARLOW, BOTHAM, BOYCOTT, BUTCHER (A.R.), BUTCHER (R.O), COOK (G.), COOK (N.G.B.), COWANS, COWDREY (C.S.), DILLEY, DOWNTON, EDMONDS, ELLISON (R.M.), EMBUREY, FLETCHER (K.W.R.), FOSTER, FOWLER (G.), FRENCH, GATTING, GIFFORD, GOOCH, GOULD, GOWER, HEMMINGS, HUMPAGE, JESTY, LAMB, LARKINS, LEVER, LLOYD (T.A.), LOVE, MARKS, MILLER (G.), MOXON, OLD, POCOCK, PRINGLE, RADLEY, RANDALL, RICHARDS (C.J.), ROBINSON (R.T.), ROSE (B.C.), SMITH (C.L.), STEVENSON (G.B.), TAVARÉ, UNDERWOOD, WELLS (C.M.), WILLEY.

Rules: All entries must be on an official form (opposite). Proof of posting is not proof of entry. Batting order and choice of the most enjoyable aspect of one-day cricket will be used in judging. The decision of the judges is final and binding; no correspondence may be entered into. Employees of Macdonald & Co (Publishers) Ltd and their families are not eligible to compete.

ENTRY FORM

Please PRINT your England team in BATTING ORDER.
Put an asterisk (*) against the name of your CAPTAIN.

1
2
3
4
5
6
7
8
9
10
11

Using no more than 20 WORDS say what you enjoy most about limited-overs cricket and why.

Closing date: 12.00 noon Wednesday, 17 September 1986

Your name and address:

....

....

....

Post to: The Editor, Playfair Cricket Annual Competition, Queen Anne Press, Macdonald & Co (Publishers) Ltd, Greater London House, Hampstead Road, London NW1 7QX.

THE 1985 PICK-A-TEAM COMPETITION

(See page 2)

THE WINNING TEAM

The following team was selected by Denis Compton, Jim Laker and the late Gordon Ross on 25 March 1985:

1 GRAHAM GOOCH
2 WAYNE LARKINS
3 DAVID GOWER (Captain)
4 MIKE GATTING
5 ALLAN LAMB
6 IAN BOTHAM
7 PAUL DOWNTON
8 JOHN EMBUREY
9 NEIL FOSTER
10 DEREK UNDERWOOD
11 JOHN LEVER

There were 1,015 entries.

WINNERS OF THE 1985 PICK-A-TEAM COMPETITION

Our congratulations to all the winners, particularly to Mr J.A. Smith who submitted the only all-correct entry.

First Prize: £450 J.A. SMITH, Bury, Lancashire
Second Prize: £300 A.E. PINNEGAR, Bromley, Kent
Third Prize: £225 Mrs O. BOWEN, Kidwelly, Dyfed
Fourth Prize: £175 P.J. CONWAY, Southport

25 Runners-up: £10 each
Russell Armstrong (12), Sawtry, Huntingdon;
P.D. Balls, Colchester, Essex;
S. Barker, Welwyn, Hertfordshire;
Hilary Blumer, Richmond, Surrey;
N. Briddon, Broughton Green, Northampton;
S. Cook, Hull;
B.S. Cowey, Fenham, Newcastle upon Tyne;
G. Crang, Buxton, Derbys;
P. Darley, Selby, Yorkshire;
S. Duffin, Bury St. Edmunds, Suffolk;
B. Edwards, Wrexham;
P. Hooper, Scartho, Grimsby;
R.A. Jepson, Somercotes, Derbyshire;
D. Jimenez, Ealing W5;
P. Kitchenham, St. Sampsons, Guernsey, C.I.;
R. Kite, Bromley, Kent;
J. Luck, King's Lynn, Norfolk;
M. Long, West Wickham, Kent;
P. Meyers, Chatham, Kent;
J. Nicolson, Malvern, Worcs;
M.A. Saunders, Wilford, Nottingham;
C.J. Shimwell, Bakewell, Derbys;
E.J. Smith, High Wycombe, Bucks;
T. Westcott, Swindon, Wiltshire;
R. Whatley, Eastleigh, Hants.

PREFACE

For the first time since 1953 the cover of this Annual does not bear the name of Gordon Ross. For 32 years he edited these pages with absolute efficiency and meticulous adherence to deadlines. He was the complete professional. Honoured and delighted though I am to become *Playfair*'s third editor – Peter West edited the first six editions – I regret that it resulted from the death of a very good friend of twenty years standing. Besides being an extremely versatile writer who upheld the traditional values of cricket and could write with equal authority on half a dozen other sports, he was a most able public relations consultant. Possibly his most important contribution to cricket involved his administration of the Gillette Cup. His expertise and attention to detail produced the basis for all subsequent cricket sponsorship. He even devised Match Awards.

Gordon's last hours were spent watching Middlesex play Worcestershire at his beloved Lord's, with Kapil Dev treating him to a vintage hundred between lunch and tea. Only a few days earlier he had written his last piece for publication* and it is good to know that he derived such pleasure from the game to which he gave so much:

> 'Of course I enjoy Test cricket, but perhaps in a strange and unrelated way I enjoy Lord's more when Middlesex are playing a three-day County game (it doesn't matter which county), when there is the peace (unhappily because of lack of supporters) that we used to know, when you can drift round the old place chatting to players, umpires, scorers, groundsmen, administrators, friends, acquaintances, even to perfect strangers. As the shadows lengthen, stumps are

*Written for *The Journal of the Cricket Society* and reproduced by kind permission of its editor. A full tribute to Gordon Ross was published in the Spring 1985 edition of *The Cricketer Quarterly Facts and Figures*.

drawn and the sun sets you are in the mood of thankfulness that it has been your great piece of luck to enjoy a lifetime of cricket as a profession. I remember thinking this vividly one morning when walking along the tow-path from the Diglis Hotel, over the bridge and into the ground at Worcester to cover a game for *The Times*, when at that moment hordes would be walking over London Bridge and spilling out of commuter trains at Victoria to earn a living in a much less appealing way. I am forever grateful to the gods for their kindness.'

After 38 editions *Playfair* has established a unique style and a readership in excess of 60,000. Rest assured that I have no intention of meddling with its basic format or in essence with its contents. What I have tried to do is to remove any errors of setting or compilation, and to clarify its presentation, particularly with regard to the Who's Who and county records sections.

The Who's Who section has been completely re-compiled. Each player's entry now follows the same format, the succession of data being in a set order, with heights included for the first time. Career bests in limited-overs matches are set at the end of each entry. Where space has permitted, details for players whose careers ended last year appear at the end of each county section rather than under a separate Valete heading. County scorers, my most helpful and dedicated allies, are also listed.

I have added a few details to the Test match scores so that they provide a supplement to *The Wisden Book of Test Cricket*. Umpires, second innings batting orders, the toss, and debutants are included, together with full averages for each series.

New items include records for limited-overs internationals, University Match records and winners, Minor Counties averages and the Second XI Championship table. All constructive comments about this volume and ideas for the next will be warmly appreciated.

I would like to thank Alan Samson of Queen Anne Press for

entrusting me with the honour of editing this edition, to his editor, Pamela Dix, for her expertise and encouragement, and to Paula Dixon for helping considerably with its preparation.

BILL FRINDALL

THE ASHES REGAINED – HIGHLIGHTS

1st Test. For the first time Leeds staged the opening Test of an Ashes series. The first Test to have a standby umpire (R. Julian) in attendance, it was also the first in England in which no-balls and wides were debited to bowlers' analyses. Botham was the second England bowler after W. Voce (Sydney 1936-37) to take three wickets in four balls against Australia. England's total of 533 was their highest against Australia at Headingley.

2nd Test. Gower lost the toss for the sixth successive time in Tests. Border (196) recorded the highest score by an Australian captain at Lord's (beating 155 by W.M. Woodfull in 1930), and completed 5,000 Test runs in the record time of 6 years 186 days. In taking five or more wickets in an innings for the 25th time, Botham gained the world Test record held by S.F. Barnes since 1914. When Wood became his 326th victim, Botham succeeded R.G.D. Willis as England's leading wicket-taker.

3rd Test. Gower's 166 was his first Test century for 23 innings, and the highest score by an England captain at Trent Bridge. Wood completed 1,000 runs against England and 3,000 runs in Tests; his 599-minute innings was the second-longest for Australia in England. Australia achieved their highest total at Trent Bridge. Robinson's 77 not out was the highest score by a Nottinghamshire batsman against Australia on his home ground.

4th Test. Border succumbed to England's first stumping in a home Test since 1980. Gower completed 5,000 runs in 74 Tests in 7 years 62 days – the fastest of England's nine instances. Gatting's first century against Australia was also his first in 40 Test innings in England. At 20 years 113 days McDermott became the youngest Australian to take eight wickets in a Test innings.

5th Test. Gower became the first England captain to put Australia into bat in successive Tests. Thomson's 200th wicket in 51 Tests was also his 100th in 21 matches against England. Gower's score of 215 was the highest against Australia at Edgbaston (beating 180 by E.R. Dexter in 1961); he exceeded D.C.S. Compton's record aggregate for a home Ashes series of 562 in 1948. The second-wicket partnership of 331 between Robinson and Gower was England's second-highest for any wicket against Australia. Botham (28 Tests) succeeded R.G.D. Willis (128 wickets in 35 matches) as the leading wicket-taker against Australia.

6th Test. Australia followed-on against England for the first time since 1977 (Headingley). On the first day, England (376-3) achieved their highest total in a single day's play against Australia since 1938 (409-5 at Lord's). Gower took his aggregate for the rubber to 732 (the fourth-highest for England against all countries), and became the ninth England batsman to complete 2,000 runs against Australia; for the second consecutive innings he shared in a triple-century stand.

(Cornhill series receipts: £2,467,030. Attendance: 373,000).

ENGLAND v AUSTRALIA (1st Test)

Played at Headingley, Leeds, on 13, 14, 15, 17, 18 June 1985
Toss: Australia. Result: England won by 5 wickets
Debuts: Australia – S.P. O'Donnell

AUSTRALIA

G.M. Wood lbw b Allott	14	(2) c Lamb b Botham	3
A.M.J. Hilditch c Downton b Gooch	119	(1) c Robinson b Emburey	80
K.C. Wessels c Botham b Emburey	36	b Emburey	64
*A.R. Border c Botham b Cowans	32	c Downton b Botham	8
D.C. Boon lbw b Gooch	14	b Cowans	22
G.M. Ritchie b Botham	46	b Emburey	1
†W.B. Phillips c Gower b Emburey	30	c Lamb b Botham	91
C.J. McDermott b Botham	18	(10) c Gooch b Emburey	6
S.P. O'Donnell lbw b Botham	0	(8) c Downton b Botham	24
G.F. Lawson c Downton b Allott	0	(9) c Downton b Emburey	15
J.R. Thomson not out	4	not out	2
Extras (LB13, W4, NB1)	18	(B4, LB3, W1)	8
Total	331		324

ENGLAND

G.A. Gooch lbw b McDermott	5	lbw b O'Donnell	28
R.T. Robinson c Boon b Lawson	175	b Lawson	21
*D.I. Gower c Phillips b McDermott	17	c Border b O'Donnell	5
M.W. Gatting c Hilditch b McDermott	53	c Phillips b Lawson	12
A.J. Lamb b O'Donnell	38	not out	31
I.T. Botham b Thomson	60	b O'Donnell	12
P. Willey c Hilditch b Lawson	36	not out	3
†P.R. Downton c Border b McDermott	54		
J.E. Emburey b Lawson	21		
P.J.W. Allott c Boon b Thomson	12		
N.G. Cowans not out	22		
Extras (B5, LB16, W5, NB14)	40	(LB7, W1, NB3)	11
Total	533	(5 wickets)	123

ENGLAND	*O*	*M*	*R*	*W*	*O*	*M*	*R*	*W*	FALL OF WICKETS				
										A	*E*	*A*	*E*
Cowans	20	4	78	1	13	2	50	1	*Wkt*	*1st*	*1st*	*2nd*	*2nd*
Allott	22	3	74	2	17	4	57	0	1st	23	14	5	44
Botham	29.1	8	86	3	33	7	107	4	2nd	155	50	144	59
Gooch	21	4	57	2	9	3	21	0	3rd	201	186	151	71
Emburey	6	1	23	2	43.4	14	82	5	4th	229	264	159	83
AUSTRALIA									5th	229	344	160	110
Lawson	26	4	117	3	16	4	51	2	6th	284	417	192	—
McDermott	32	2	134	4	4	0	20	0	7th	326	422	272	—
Thomson	34	3	166	2	3	0	8	0	8th	326	462	307	—
O'Donnell	27	8	77	1	15.4	5	37	3	9th	327	484	318	—
Border	3	0	16	0	—	—	—	—	10th	331	533	324	—
Wessels	3	2	2	0	—	—	—	—					

Umpires: B.J. Meyer and K.E. Palmer

Test No. 1017/252

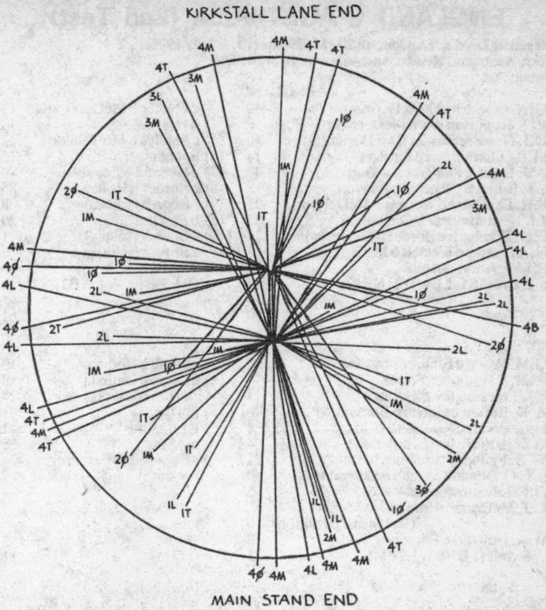

BOWLER	SYMBOL	RUNS 1	2	3	4	6	TOTAL
BORDER	B	·	·	·	1	·	4
LAWSON	L	3	7	1	7	·	48
McDERMOTT	M	8	2	3	9	·	57
O'DONNELL	Ø	8	3	1	3	·	29
THOMSON	T	7	1	-	7	·	37
TOTALS		26	13	5	27	-	175

R.T. ROBINSON at Headingley

175 RUNS
270 BALLS
413 MINUTES

TIM ROBINSON's 175 was the second highest score by an England batsman on his debut against Australia, the record being R.E. Foster's 287 at Sydney in 1903-04.

ENGLAND v AUSTRALIA (2nd Test)

Played at Lord's, London, on 27, 28, 29 June, 1, 2 July 1985
Toss: Australia. Result: Australia won by 4 wickets
Debuts: nil

ENGLAND

G.A. Gooch lbw b McDermott	30		c Phillips b McDermott	17
R.T. Robinson lbw b McDermott	6		b Holland	12
*D.I. Gower c Border b McDermott	86	(5)	c Phillips b McDermott	22
M.W. Gatting lbw b Lawson	14	(6)	not out	75
A.J. Lamb c Phillips b Lawson	47	(7)	c Holland b Lawson	9
I.T. Botham c Ritchie b Lawson	5	(8)	c Border b Holland	85
†P.R. Downton c Wessels b McDermott	21	(9)	c Boon b Holland	0
J.E. Emburey lbw b O'Donnell	33	(3)	b Lawson	20
P.H. Edmonds c Border b McDermott	21	(10)	c Boon b Holland	1
N.A. Foster c Wessels b McDermott	3	(11)	c Border b Holland	0
P.J.W. Allott not out	1	(4)	b Lawson	0
Extras (B1, LB4, W1, NB17)	23		(B1, LB12, W4, NB3)	20
Total	290			261

AUSTRALIA

G.M. Wood c Emburey b Allott	8	(2)	c Lamb b Botham	6
A.M.J. Hilditch b Foster	14	(1)	c Lamb b Botham	0
K.C. Wessels lbw b Botham	11		run out (Gower)	28
*A.R. Border c Gooch b Botham	196	(5)	not out	41
D.C. Boon c Downton b Botham	4	(6)	b Edmonds	1
G.M. Ritchie lbw b Botham	94	(4)	b Allott	2
†W.B. Phillips c Edmonds b Botham	21		c Edmonds b Emburey	29
S.P. O'Donnell c Lamb b Edmonds	48		not out	9
G.F. Lawson not out	5			
C.J. McDermott run out (Robinson/Downton)	9			
R.G. Holland b Edmonds	0			
Extras (LB10, W1, NB4)	15		(LB11)	11
Total	425		(6 wickets)	127

AUSTRALIA	*O*	*M*	*R*	*W*	*O*	*M*	*R*	*W*
Lawson	25	2	91	3	23	0	86	3
McDermott	29.2	5	70	6	20	2	84	2
O'Donnell	22	3	82	1	5	0	10	0
Holland	23	6	42	0	32	12	68	5
ENGLAND								
Foster	23	1	83	1	—	—	—	—
Allott	30	4	70	1	7	4	8	1
Botham	24	2	109	5	15	0	49	2
Edmonds	25.4	5	85	2	16	5	35	1
Gooch	3	1	11	0	—	—	—	—
Emburey	19	3	57	0	8	4	24	1

FALL OF WICKETS

Wkt	*E 1st*	*A 1st*	*E 2nd*	*A 2nd*
1st	26	11	32	0
2nd	51	24	34	9
3rd	99	80	38	22
4th	179	101	57	63
5th	184	317	77	65
6th	211	347	98	116
7th	241	398	229	—
8th	273	414	229	—
9th	283	425	261	—
10th	290	425	261	—

Umpires: H.D. Bird and D.G.L. Evans

Test No. 1018/253

ENGLAND v AUSTRALIA (3rd Test)

Played at Trent Bridge, Nottingham, on 11, 12, 13, 15, 16 July 1985
Toss: England. Result: match drawn
Debuts: England – A. Sidebottom

ENGLAND

G.A. Gooch c Wessels b Lawson	70	c Ritchie b McDermott		48
R.T. Robinson c Border b Lawson	38	not out		77
*D.I. Gower c Phillips b O'Donnell	166	c Phillips b McDermott		17
M.W. Gatting run out (Holland)	74	not out		35
A.J. Lamb lbw b Lawson	17			
I.T. Botham c O'Donnell b McDermott	38			
†P.R. Downton c Ritchie b McDermott	0			
A. Sidebottom c O'Donnell b Lawson	2			
J.E. Emburey not out	16			
P.H. Edmonds b Holland	12			
P.J.W. Allott c Border b Lawson	7			
Extras (LB12, W1, NB3)	16	(B1, LB16, NB2)		19
Total	456	(2 wickets)		196

AUSTRALIA

G.M. Wood c Robinson b Botham	172
A.M.J. Hilditch lbw b Allott	47
R.G. Holland lbw b Sidebottom	10
K.C. Wessels c Downton b Emburey	33
*A.R. Border c Botham b Edmonds	23
D.C. Boon c and b Emburey	15
G.M. Ritchie b Edmonds	146
†W.B. Phillips b Emburey	2
S.P. O'Donnell c Downton b Botham	46
G.F. Lawson c Gooch b Botham	18
C.J. McDermott not out	0
Extras (B6, LB7, W2, NB12)	27
Total	539

AUSTRALIA	*O*	*M*	*R*	*W*	*O*	*M*	*r*	*w*
Lawson	39.4	10	103	5	13	4	32	0
McDermott	35	3	147	2	16	2	42	2
O'Donnell	29	4	104	1	10	2	26	0
Holland	26	3	90	1	28	9	69	0
Ritchie	—	—	—	—	1	0	10	0
ENGLAND								
Botham	34.2	3	107	3	—	—	—	—
Sidebottom	18.4	3	65	1	—	—	—	—
Allott	18	4	55	1	—	—	—	—
Edmonds	66	18	155	2	—	—	—	—
Emburey	55	15	129	3	—	—	—	—
Gooch	8.2	2	13	0	—	—	—	—
Gatting	1	0	2	0	—	—	—	—

FALL OF WICKETS

	E	*A*	*E*
Wkt	*1st*	*1st*	*2nd*
1st	55	87	79
2nd	171	128	107
3rd	358	205	—
4th	365	234	—
5th	416	263	—
6th	416	424	—
7th	419	437	—
8th	419	491	—
9th	443	539	—
10th	456	539	—

Umpires: D.J. Constant and A.G.T. Whitehead

Test No. 1019/254

ENGLAND v AUSTRALIA (4th Test)

Played at Old Trafford, Manchester, on 1, 2, 3, 5, 6 August 1985
Toss: England. Result: match drawn
Debuts: nil

AUSTRALIA

K.C. Wessels c Botham b Emburey	34	(3) c and b Emburey	50
A.M.J. Hilditch c Gower b Edmonds	49	(1) b Emburey	40
D.C. Boon c Lamb b Botham	61	(5) b Emburey	7
*A.R. Border st Downton b Edmonds	8	not out	146
G.M. Ritchie c and b Edmonds	4	(6) b Emburey	31
†W.B. Phillips c Downton b Botham	36	(7) not out	39
G.R.J. Matthews b Botham	4	(2) c and b Edmonds	17
S.P. O'Donnell b Edmonds	45		
G.F. Lawson c Downton b Botham	4		
C.J. McDermott lbw b Emburey	0		
R.G. Holland not out	5		
Extras (LB3, W1, NB3)	7	(B1, LB6, NB3)	10
Total	257	(5 wickets)	340

ENGLAND

G.A. Gooch lbw b McDermott	74
R.T. Robinson c Border b McDermott	10
*D.I. Gower c Hilditch b McDermott	47
M.W. Gatting c Phillips b McDermott	160
A.J. Lamb run out (Matthews)	67
I.T. Botham c O'Donnell b McDermott	20
†P.R. Downton b McDermott	23
J.E. Emburey not out	31
P.H. Edmonds b McDermott	1
P.J.W. Allott b McDermott	7
J.P. Agnew not out	2
Extras (B7, LB16, NB17)	40
Total (9 wickets declared)	482

ENGLAND	*O*	*M*	*R*	*W*	*O*	*M*	*R*	*W*
Botham	23	4	79	4	15	3	50	0
Agnew	14	0	65	0	9	2	34	0
Allott	13	1	29	0	6	2	4	0
Emburey	24	7	41	2	51	17	99	4
Edmonds	15.1	4	40	4	54	12	122	1
Gatting	—	—	—	—	4	0	14	0
Lamb	—	—	—	—	1	0	10	0
AUSTRALIA								
Lawson	37	7	114	0	—	—	—	—
McDermott	36	3	141	8	—	—	—	—
Holland	38	7	101	0	—	—	—	—
O'Donnell	21	6	82	0	—	—	—	—
Matthews	9	2	21	0	—	—	—	—

FALL OF WICKETS

	A	*E*	*A*
Wkt	*1st*	*1st*	*2nd*
1st	71	21	38
2nd	97	142	85
3rd	118	148	126
4th	122	304	138
5th	193	339	213
6th	198	430	—
7th	211	448	—
8th	223	450	—
9th	224	470	—
10th	257	—	—

Umpires: H.D. Bird and D.R. Shepherd

Test No. 1020/255

ENGLAND v AUSTRALIA (5th Test)

Played at Edgbaston, Birmingham, on 15, 16, 17, 19, 20 August 1985
Toss: England. Result: England won by an innings and 118 runs
Debuts: England – L.B. Taylor

AUSTRALIA

G.M. Wood c Edmonds b Botham	19	(2) c Robinson b Ellison	10
A.M.J. Hilditch c Downton b Edmonds	39	(1) c Ellison b Botham	10
K.C. Wessels c Downton b Ellison	83	c Downton b Ellison	10
*A.R. Border c Edmonds b Ellison	45	(5) b Ellison	2
G.M. Ritchie c Botham b Ellison	8	(6) c Lamb b Emburey	20
†W.B. Phillips c Robinson b Ellison	15	(7) c Gower b Edmonds	59
S.P. O'Donnell c Downton b Taylor	1	(8) b Botham	11
G.F. Lawson run out (Gower)	53	(9) c Gower b Edmonds	3
C.J. McDermott c Gower b Ellison	35	(10) c Edmonds b Botham	8
J.R. Thomson not out	28	(11) not out	4
R.G. Holland c Edmonds b Ellison	0	(4) lbw b Ellison	0
Extras (LB4, W1, NB4)	9	(B1, LB3, NB1)	5
Total	335		142

ENGLAND

G.A. Gooch c Phillips b Thomson	19
R.T. Robinson b Lawson	148
*D.I. Gower c Border b Lawson	215
M.W. Gatting not out	100
A.J. Lamb c Wood b McDermott	46
I.T. Botham c Thomson b McDermott	18
†P.R. Downton not out	0
J.E. Emburey, R.M. Ellison, P.H. Edmonds, L.B. Taylor did not bat	
Extras (B7, LB20, NB22)	49
Total (5 wickets declared)	595

ENGLAND	*O*	*M*	*R*	*W*	*O*	*M*	*R*	*W*
Botham	27	1	108	1	14.1	2	52	3
Taylor	26	5	78	1	13	4	27	0
Ellison	31.5	9	77	6	9	3	27	4
Edmonds	20	4	47	1	15	9	13	2
Emburey	9	2	21	0	13	5	19	1
AUSTRALIA								
Lawson	37	1	135	2	–	–	–	–
McDermott	31	2	155	2	–	–	–	–
Thomson	19	1	101	1	–	–	–	–
Holland	25	4	95	0	–	–	–	–
O'Donnell	16	3	69	0	–	–	–	–
Border	6	1	13	0	–	–	–	–

FALL OF WICKETS

	A	*E*	*A*
Wkt	*1st*	*1st*	*2nd*
1st	44	38	10
2nd	92	369	32
3rd	189	463	32
4th	191	572	35
5th	207	592	36
6th	208	–	113
7th	218	–	117
8th	276	–	120
9th	335	–	137
10th	335	–	142

Umpires: D.J. Constant and D.R. Shepherd

Test No. 1021/256

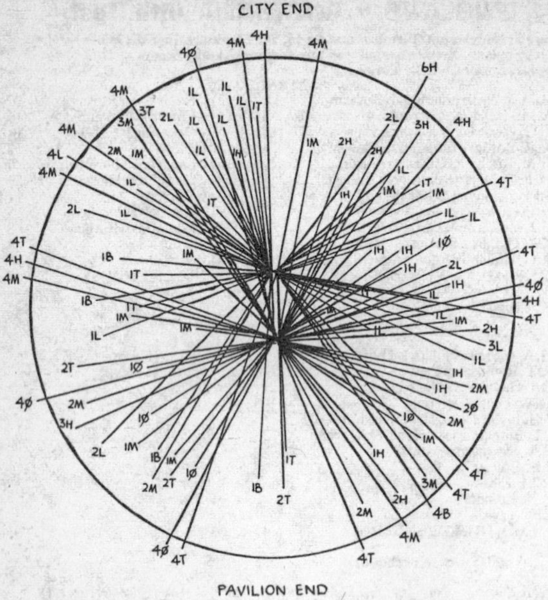

BOWLER	SYMBOL	RUNS					
		1	2	3	4	6	TOTAL
BORDER	B	4	-	-	1	-	8
HOLLAND	H	9	4	2	4	1	45
LAWSON	L	16	5	1	1	-	33
McDERMOTT	M	12	6	2	7	-	58
O'DONNELL	Ø	5	1	-	4	-	23
THOMSON	T	7	3	1	8	-	48
TOTALS		53	19	6	25	1	215

D.I. GOWER at Edgbaston

215 RUNS
314 BALLS
452 MINUTES
(Left-handed batsman)

DAVID GOWER's 215 was his highest score in first-class cricket, the highest against Australia at Edgbaston and the second-highest by an England captain against Australia after W.R. Hammond's 240 at Lord's in 1938.

ENGLAND v AUSTRALIA (6th Test)

Played at Kennington Oval, London, on 29, 30, 31 August, 2, 3 September 1985
Toss: England. Result: England won by an innings and 94 runs
Debuts: Australia – D.R. Gilbert

ENGLAND

G.A. Gooch c and b McDermott	196
R.T. Robinson b McDermott	3
*D.I. Gower c Bennett b McDermott	157
M.W. Gatting c Border b Bennett	4
J.E. Emburey c Wellham b Lawson	9
A.J. Lamb c McDermott b Lawson	1
I.T. Botham c Phillips b Lawson	12
†P.R. Downton b McDermott	16
R.M. Ellison c Phillips b Gilbert	3
P.H. Edmonds lbw b Lawson	12
L.B. Taylor not out	1
Extras (B13, LB11, NB26)	50
Total	464

AUSTRALIA

G.M. Wood lbw b Botham	22	(2) b Botham	6
A.M.J. Hilditch c Gooch b Botham	17	(1) c Gower b Taylor	9
K.C. Wessels b Emburey	12	c Downton b Botham	7
*A.R. Border b Edmonds	38	c Botham b Ellison	58
D.M. Wellham c Downton b Ellison	13	lbw b Ellison	5
G.M. Ritchie not out	64	c Downton b Ellison	6
†W.B. Phillips b Edmonds	18	c Downton b Botham	10
M.J. Bennett c Robinson b Ellison	12	c and b Taylor	11
G.F. Lawson c Botham b Taylor	14	c Downton b Ellison	7
C.J. McDermott run out (Robinson/Emburey)	25	c Botham b Ellison	2
D.R. Gilbert b Botham	1	not out	0
Extras (LB3, W2)	5	(B4, NB4)	8
Total	241		129

AUSTRALIA	*O*	*M*	*R*	*W*	*O*	*M*	*R*	*W*
Lawson	29.2	6	101	4	—	—	—	—
McDermott	31	2	108	4	—	—	—	—
Gilbert	21	2	96	1	—	—	—	—
Bennett	32	8	111	1	—	—	—	—
Border	2	0	8	0	—	—	—	—
Wessels	3	0	16	0	—	—	—	—
ENGLAND								
Botham	20	3	64	3	17	3	44	3
Taylor	13	1	39	1	11.3	1	34	2
Ellison	18	5	35	2	17	3	46	5
Emburey	19	7	48	1	1	0	1	0
Edmonds	14	2	52	2	—	—	—	—

FALL OF WICKETS

	E	*A*	*A*
Wkt	*1st*	*1st*	*2nd*
1st	20	35	13
2nd	371	52	16
3rd	376	56	37
4th	403	101	51
5th	405	109	71
6th	418	144	96
7th	425	171	114
8th	447	192	127
9th	452	235	129
10th	464	241	129

Umpires: H.D. Bird and K.E. Palmer

Test No. 1022/257

ENGLAND v AUSTRALIA AVERAGES

ENGLAND – BATTING AND FIELDING

	M	*I*	*NO*	*HS*	*Runs*	*Avge*	*100*	*50*	*Ct/St*
M.W. Gatting	6	9	3	160	527	87.83	2	3	—
D.I. Gower	6	9	0	215	732	81.33	3	1	6
R.T. Robinson	6	9	1	175	490	61.25	2	1	5
G.A. Gooch	6	9	0	196	487	54.11	1	2	4
A.J. Lamb	6	8	1	67	256	36.57	—	1	7
J.E. Emburey	6	6	2	33	130	32.50	—	—	3
I.T. Botham	6	8	0	85	250	31.25	—	2	8
P.R. Downton	6	7	1	54	114	19.00	—	1	19/1
P.H. Edmonds	5	5	0	21	47	9.40	—	—	8
P.J.W. Allott	4	5	1	12	27	6.75	—	—	—

Also batted (2 matches): R.M. Ellison 3 (1 ct); L.B. Taylor 1* (1 ct); (1 match): J.P. Agnew 2*; N.G. Cowans 22*; N.A. Foster 3,0; A. Sidebottom 2; P. Willey 36,3*.

ENGLAND – BOWLING

	Overs	*Mdns*	*Runs*	*Wkts*	*Avge*	*Best*	*5 wI*	*10 wM*
R.M. Ellison	75.5	20	185	17	10.88	6-77	2	1
I.T. Botham	251.4	36	855	31	27.58	5-109	1	—
J.E. Emburey	248.4	75	544	19	28.63	5-82	1	—
P.H. Edmonds	225.5	59	549	15	36.60	4-40	—	—
P.J.W. Allott	113	22	297	5	59.40	2-74	—	—

Also bowled: J.P. Agnew 23-2-99-0; N.G. Cowans 33-6-128-2; N.A. Foster 23-1-83-1; M.W. Gatting 5-0-16-0; G.A. Gooch 41.2-10-102-2; A.J. Lamb 1-0-10-0; A. Sidebottom 18.4-3-65-1; L.B. Taylor 63.3-11-178-4.

AUSTRALIA – BATTING AND FIELDING

	M	*I*	*NO*	*HS*	*Runs*	*Avge*	*100*	*50*	*Ct/St*
A.R. Border	6	11	2	196	597	66.33	2	1	11
G.M. Ritchie	6	11	1	146	422	42.20	1	2	3
A.M.J. Hilditch	6	11	0	119	424	38.54	1	1	3
W.B. Phillips	6	11	1	91	350	35.00	—	2	11
K.C. Wessels	6	11	0	83	368	33.45	—	3	3
G.M. Wood	5	9	0	172	260	28.88	1	—	1
S.P. O'Donnell	5	8	1	48	184	26.28	—	—	3
D.C. Boon	4	7	0	61	124	17.71	—	1	4
G.F. Lawson	6	9	1	53	119	14.87	—	1	—
C.J. McDermott	6	9	1	35	103	12.87	—	—	2
R.G. Holland	4	5	1	10	15	3.75	—	—	1
J.R. Thomson	2	4	4	28*	38	—	—	—	1

Also batted (1 match): M.J. Bennett 12,11 (1 ct); D.R. Gilbert 1,0*; G.R.J. Matthews 4,17; D.M. Wellham 13,5 (1 ct).

AUSTRALIA – BOWLING

	Overs	*Mdns*	*Runs*	*Wkts*	*Avge*	*Best*	*5 wI*	*10 wM*
C.J. McDermott	234.2	21	901	30	30.03	8.141	2	—
G.F. Lawson	246	38	830	22	37.72	5.103	1	—
R.G. Holland	172	41	465	6	77.50	5.68	1	—
S.P. O'Donnell	145.4	31	487	6	81.16	3.37	—	—

Also bowled: M.J. Bennett 32-8-111-1; A.R. Border 11-1-37-0; D.R. Gilbert 21-2-96-1; G.R.J. Matthews 9-2-21-0; G.M. Ritchie 1-0-10-0; J.R. Thomson 56-4-275-3; K.C. Wessels 6-2-18-0.

LLOYD ENDS TEST CAREER

After leading West Indies to an emphatic 3-1 victory in Australia in 1984-85, Clive Lloyd confirmed his retirement from Test cricket. His decision brought to an end the most successful captaincy career at Test level.

Lloyd's record as CAPTAIN stands supreme:

Most Tests	74
Most victories	36
Most successive victories	11
Most consecutive matches without defeat	26†

† West Indies achieved a sequence of 27 Tests without defeat but Lloyd did not play in the 2nd Test v Australia in 1983-84.

Under his captaincy West Indies were undefeated in 18 matches against England (11 wins and 7 draws).

West Indies were defeated in just two of the 18 rubbers during Lloyd's reign: in Australia 1975-76 and in New Zealand 1979-80.

At the time of his retirement, Lloyd had appeared in more Test matches than anyone except Colin Cowdrey (114), and only Boycott, Cowdrey and Gavaskar had played more innings in Tests.

His aggregate of 7,515 runs was the second-highest for West Indies and had then been exceeded only by Gavaskar, Boycott, Sobers and Cowdrey. Only Sobers (26) had scored more hundreds for West Indies. Curiously, although he scored centuries against England (5), Australia (6), India (7) and Pakistan (1), his highest score in eight Tests against New Zealand was only 44.

Only Sobers (109) had exceeded Lloyd's total of 89 catches in the field for West Indies.

LLOYD'S TEST CAREER

	M	*I*	*NO*	*HS*	*Runs*	*Avge*	*100*
As player	36	64	5	178	2282	38.67	5
As captain	74	111	9	242*	5233	51.30	14
Totals	110	175	14	242*	7515	46.67	19

CAPTAINCY RECORD: Played 74; Won 36; Lost 12; Drawn 26

Although Clive Lloyd has retired from Test cricket he has been reappointed captain of Lancashire for 1986.

NEW ZEALAND v PAKISTAN (1st Test)

Played at Basin Reserve, Wellington, on 18, 19, 20, 21, 22 (no play) January 1985
Toss: New Zealand. Result: match drawn
Debuts: nil

NEW ZEALAND

*G.P. Howarth run out	33	c Anil b Azeem	17
J.G. Wright c Shoaib b Azeem	11	lbw b Mudassar	11
J.F. Reid b Azeem	148	c Qadir b Iqbal Qasim	3
M.D. Crowe c Anil b Iqbal Qasim	37	c Qadir b Iqbal Qasim	33
J.J. Crowe c Shoaib b Iqbal Qasim	4	not out	19
J.V. Coney b Qadir	48	not out	18
R.J. Hadlee c Miandad b Azeem	89		
†I.D.S. Smith c and b Mudassar	65		
B.L. Cairns b Azeem	36		
S.L. Boock c Anil b Azeem	0		
E.J. Chatfield not out	3		
Extras (B5, LB12, NB1)	18	(LB2)	2
Total	492	(4 wickets)	103

PAKISTAN

Mudassar Nazar c and b Boock	38
Mohsin Khan c Wright b Boock	40
Shoaib Mohammad run out	7
Qasim Omar b Boock	8
*Javed Miandad c Smith b Boock	30
Salim Malik c Cairns b Hadlee	66
Wasim Raja c M.D. Crowe b Boock	14
Abdul Qadir c Smith b Hadlee	54
†Anil Dalpat c Smith b Chatfield	15
Iqbal Qasim not out	27
Azeem Hafeez c Boock b Cairns	3
Extras (B9, LB9, NB2)	20
Total	322

PAKISTAN	*O*	*M*	*R*	*W*	*O*	*M*	*R*	*W*	FALL OF WICKETS			
										NZ	*P*	*NZ*
									Wkt	*1st*	*1st*	*2nd*
Mudassar	29	5	80	1	6	3	13	1	1st	24	62	24
Azeem	48	12	127	5	15	3	51	1	2nd	61	85	30
Qadir	51	13	142	1	8	1	18	0	3rd	126	95	42
Iqbal Qasim	41	5	105	2	16	8	19	2	4th	138	102	73
Wasim	2	0	10	0	—	—	—	—	5th	230	161	—
Shoaib	1	0	4	0	—	—	—	—	6th	375	187	—
Miandad	3	1	7	0	—	—	—	—	7th	414	223	—
N. ZEALAND									8th	488	288	—
Hadlee	32	11	70	2	—	—	—	—	9th	488	309	—
Cairns	27.3	5	65	1	—	—	—	—	10th	492	322	—
Chatfield	25	10	52	1	—	—	—	—				
Boock	45	18	117	5	—	—	—	—				

Umpires: G.C. Morris and S.J. Woodward — Test No. 1010/25

NEW ZEALAND v PAKISTAN (2nd Test)

Played at Eden Park, Auckland, on 25, 26, 27, 28 January 1985
Toss: New Zealand. Result: New Zealand won by an innings and 99 runs
Debuts: Pakistan – Wasim Akram

J.F. Reid (123) retired hurt at 322 and resumed at 359.

PAKISTAN

Mudassar Nazar lbw b Hadlee	12		b Cairns	89
Mohsin Khan c Coney b Cairns	26		c Coney b Hadlee	1
Qasim Omar c M.D. Crowe b Cairns	33		c Cairns b Chatfield	22
*Javed Miandad c Smith b Chatfield	26	(5)	c Smith b Chatfield	1
Zaheer Abbas c J.J. Crowe b Cairns	6	(6)	c sub (J.G. Bracewell) b Hadlee	12
Salim Malik not out	41	(4)	c Cairns b Chatfield	0
Wasim Raja c Smith b Chatfield	4		c Wright b Boock	11
Abdul Qadir run out	0		lbw b Cairns	10
†Anil Dalpat c J.J. Crowe b Hadlee	7		lbw b Cairns	6
Wasim Akram c M.D. Crowe b Hadlee	0	(11)	not out	0
Azeem Hafeez c Boock b Hadlee	6	(10)	lbw b Cairns	17
Extras (LB5, NB3)	8		(LB11, NB3)	14
Total	169			183

NEW ZEALAND

*G.P. Howarth c Miandad b Mudassar	13
J.G. Wright c Salim b Wasim Akram	66
J.F. Reid not out	158
M.D. Crowe c sub (Shoaib Mohammad) b Qadir	84
S.L. Boock c Wasim Raja b Azeem	10
J.J. Crowe run out	30
J.V. Coney c Anil b Mudassar	25
R.J. Hadlee c Mohsin b Azeem	13
†I.D.S. Smith c Miandad b Wasim Akram	7
B.L. Cairns b Azeem	23
E.J. Chatfield not out	1
Extras (B6, LB9, NB6)	21
Total (9 wickets declared)	451

N. ZEALAND	O	M	R	W	O	M	R	W	FALL OF WICKETS	P	NZ	P
Hadlee	19.5	3	60	4	17	1	66	2	*Wkt*	*1st*	*1st*	*2nd*
Cairns	29	10	73	3	19.5	8	49	4	1st	33	60	13
Chatfield	14	5	24	2	19	5	47	3	2nd	58	108	54
Coney	4	1	7	0	—	—	—	—	3rd	93	245	54
Boock	—	—	—	—	4	2	10	1	4th	105	278	57
PAKISTAN									5th	111	359	79
Azeem	47	10	157	3	—	—	—	—	6th	115	366	122
Wasim Akram	34.4	4	105	2	—	—	—	—	7th	123	387	140
Mudassar	34	5	85	2	—	—	—	—	8th	147	411	152
Wasim Raja	1	0	3	0	—	—	—	—	9th	151	447	178
Qadir	22	5	52	1	—	—	—	—	10th	169	—	183
Salim	8.2	3	34	0	—	—	—	—				

Umpires: F.R. Goodall and S.J. Woodward — Test No. 1011/26

NEW ZEALAND v PAKISTAN (3rd Test)

Played at Carisbrook, Dunedin, on 9, 10, 11, 13, 14 February 1985
Toss: New Zealand. Result: New Zealand won by 2 wickets
Debuts: nil

B.L. Cairns retired hurt at 217.

PAKISTAN

Mudassar Nazar c J.J. Crowe b Hadlee	18	c Coney b Bracewell	5
Mohsin Khan run out	39	c M.D. Crowe b Hadlee	27
Qasim Omar c J.J. Crowe b Coney	96	c Smith b Chatfield	89
*Javed Miandad c Smith b Hadlee	79	c Reid b Hadlee	2
Zaheer Abbas c Reid b Hadlee	6	lbw b Cairns	0
Rashid Khan c M.D. Crowe b Hadlee	0	(9) b Bracewell	37
†Anil Dalpat b Bracewell	16	b Chatfield	21
Salim Malik lbw b Hadlee	0	(6) b Cairns	9
Tahir Naqqash c Wright b Hadlee	0	(8) run out	1
Azeem Hafeez c Smith b Bracewell	4	b Chatfield	7
Wasim Akram not out	1	not out	8
Extras (B1, LB2, NB12)	15	(B1, LB9, NB7)	17
Total	274		223

NEW ZEALAND

*G.P. Howarth b Wasim	23	c Mohsin b Wasim	17
J.G. Wright c Omar b Azeem	32	c Mohsin b Azeem	1
J.F. Reid b Wasim	24	c Anil b Wasim	0
M.D. Crowe c Miandad b Wasim	57	c Mudassar b Tahir	84
J.J. Crowe lbw b Wasim	6	lbw b Wasim	0
J.V. Coney c Anil b Rashid	24	not out	111
R.J. Hadlee c Anil b Rashid	18	b Azeem	11
†I.D.S. Smith lbw b Tahir	12	c Miandad b Wasim	6
B.L. Cairns c Anil b Wasim	6	retired hurt	0
B.P. Bracewell c Rashid b Tahir	3	c Tahir b Wasim	4
E.J. Chatfield not out	2	not out	21
Extras (B7, LB5, NB1)	13	(B5, LB6, W1, NB11)	23
Total	220	(8 wickets)	278

N. ZEALAND	*O*	*M*	*R*	*W*	*O*	*M*	*R*	*W*
Hadlee	24	5	51	6	26	9	59	2
Bracewell	18.2	1	81	2	14.4	2	48	2
Cairns	22	0	77	0	22	4	41	2
Chatfield	24	6	46	0	26	5	65	3
Coney	6	1	16	1	—	—	—	—
PAKISTAN								
Rashid	23	7	64	2	9	2	33	0
Azeem	20	6	65	1	32	9	84	2
Wasim	26	7	56	5	33	10	72	5
Tahir	16.4	4	23	2	16.4	1	58	1
Mudassar	—	—	—	—	9	2	20	0

FALL OF WICKETS

Wkt	*P 1st*	*NZ 1st*	*P 2nd*	*NZ 2nd*
1st	25	41	5	4
2nd	100	81	72	5
3rd	241	84	75	23
4th	243	92	76	23
5th	245	149	103	180
6th	251	185	157	208
7th	251	203	166	217
8th	255	205	169	228
9th	273	216	181	—
10th	274	220	223	—

Umpires: F.R. Goodall and G.C. Morris

Test No. 1012/27

NEW ZEALAND v PAKISTAN AVERAGES

NEW ZEALAND – BATTING AND FIELDING

	M	I	NO	HS	Runs	Avge	100	50	Ct/St
J.F. Reid	3	5	1	158*	333	83.25	2	—	2
J.V. Coney	3	5	2	111*	226	75.33	1	—	3
M.D. Crowe	3	5	0	84	295	59.00	—	3	5
R.J. Hadlee	3	4	0	89	131	32.75	—	1	5
E.J. Chatfield	3	4	4	21*	27	—	—	—	—
J.G. Wright	3	5	0	66	121	24.20	—	1	3
I.D.S. Smith	3	4	0	65	90	22.50	—	1	9
B.L. Cairns	3	4	1	36	65	21.66	—	—	3
G.P. Howarth	3	5	0	33	103	20.60	—	—	—
J.J. Crowe	3	5	1	30	59	14.75	—	—	4
S.L. Boock	2	2	0	10	10	5.00	—	—	3

Also batted (1 Test): B.P. Bracewell 3, 4.

NEW ZEALAND – BOWLING

	O	M	R	W	Avge	Best	5 wI	10 wM
R.J. Hadlee	118.5	29	306	16	19.12	6-51	1	—
S.L. Boock	49	20	127	6	21.16	5-117	1	—
E.J. Chatfield	108	31	234	9	26.00	3-47	—	—
B.L. Cairns	120.2	28	305	10	30.50	4-49	—	—

Also bowled: B.P. Bracewell 33-3-129-4; J.V. Coney 10-2-23-1.

PAKISTAN – BATTING AND FIELDING

	M	I	NO	HS	Runs	Avge	100	50	Ct/St
Qasim Omar	3	5	0	96	248	49.60	—	2	1
Mudassar Nazar	3	5	0	89	162	32.40	—	1	2
Salim Malik	3	5	1	66	116	29.00	—	1	1
Javed Miandad	3	5	0	79	138	27.60	—	1	5
Mohsin Khan	3	5	0	40	133	26.60	—	—	3
Abdul Qadir	2	3	0	54	64	21.33	—	1	2
Anil Dalpat	3	5	0	21	65	13.00	—	—	8
Wasim Raja	2	3	0	14	29	9.66	—	—	1
Wasim Akram	2	4	3	8*	9	9.00	—	—	—
Azeem Hafeez	3	5	0	17	37	7.40	—	—	—
Zaheer Abbas	2	4	0	12	24	6.00	—	—	—

Also batted (1 Test): Iqbal Qasim 27*; Rashid Khan 0, 37 (1 ct); Shoaib Mohammad 7 (2 ct); Tahir Naqqash 0, 1 (1 ct).

PAKISTAN – BOWLING

	O	M	R	W	Avge	Best	5 wI	10 wM
Wasim Akram	93.4	21	233	12	19.41	5-56	2	1
Azeem Hafeez	162	40	484	12	40.33	5-127	1	—

Also bowled: Abdul Qadir 81-19-212-2; Iqbal Qasim 57-13-124-4; Javed Miandad 3-1-7-0; Mudassar Nazar 78-15-198-4; Rashid Khan 32-9-97-2; Salim Malik 8.2-2-34-0; Shoaib Mohammad 1-0-4-0; Tahir Naqqash 33.2-5-81-3; Wasim Raja 3-0-13-0.

WEST INDIES v NEW ZEALAND (1st Test)

Played at Queen's Park Oval, Port-of-Spain, Trinidad, on 29, 30, 31 March, 2, 3 April 1985
Toss: West Indies. Result: match drawn
Debuts: New Zealand – K.R. Rutherford

WEST INDIES

C.G. Greenidge b Boock		100		
D.L. Haynes c Rutherford b Hadlee		0	(1) c M.D. Crowe b Chatfield	78
H.A. Gomes c Smith b Hadlee		0	c and b Chatfield	25
R.B. Richardson c Hadlee b Coney		78	(2) c Smith b Chatfield	3
*I.V.A. Richards b Hadlee		57	(4) b Cairns	78
A.L. Logie b Chatfield		24	(5) b Cairns	42
†P.J.L. Dujon b Chatfield		15	(6) b Chatfield	5
M.D. Marshall c sub (J.G. Bracewell) b Chatfield		0	(7) c Coney b Chatfield	1
R.A. Harper c Howarth b Chatfield		0	(8) not out	11
M.A. Holding lbw b Hadlee		12	(9) c J.J. Crowe b Chatfield	8
J. Garner not out		0		
Extras	(B1, LB16, NB4)	21	(LB3, NB7)	10
Total		307	(8 wickets declared)	261

NEW ZEALAND

J.G. Wright c Richardson b Harper		40	lbw b Holding	19
K.R. Rutherford c Haynes b Marshall		0	run out	0
J.J. Crowe c and b Harper		64	c Garner b Marshall	27
M.D. Crowe lbw b Holding		3	c Haynes b Marshall	2
*G.P. Howarth c sub (P.V. Simmons) b Holding		45	b Marshall	14
J.V. Coney lbw b Marshall		25	c Dujon b Marshall	44
R.J. Hadlee c Garner b holding		18	not out	39
†I.D.S. Smith c Logier b Holding		10	not out	11
B.L. Cairns c Harper b Garner		8		
S.L. Boock c sub (P.V. Simmons) b Garner		3		
E.J. Chatfield not out		4		
Extras	(B12, LB11, NB19)	42	(B17, LB6, NB8)	31
Total		262	(6 wickets)	187

N. ZEALAND	O	M	R	W	O	M	R	W
Hadlee	24.3	6	82	4	17	2	58	0
Chatfield	28	11	51	4	22	4	73	6
Cairns	26	3	93	0	19	2	70	2
Boock	19	5	47	1	14	4	57	0
Coney	9	3	17	1	—	—	—	—
WEST INDIES								
Marshall	25	3	78	2	26	4	65	4
Garner	21.3	8	41	2	18	2	41	0
Holding	29	8	79	4	17	6	36	1
Harper	22	11	33	2	14	7	19	0
Richards	2	0	7	0	2	1	1	0
Gomes	1	0	1	0	2	1	2	0
Richardson	—	—	—	—	1	1	0	0
Logie	—	—	—	—	1	1	0	0

FALL OF WICKETS

Wkt	WI 1st	NZ 1st	WI 2nd	NZ 2nd
1st	51	1	10	0
2nd	9	110	58	40
3rd	194	113	172	59
4th	196	132	226	76
5th	236	182	239	83
6th	267	223	240	158
7th	267	225	241	—
8th	269	248	261	—
9th	302	250	—	—
10th	307	262	—	—

Umpires: D.M. Archer and C.E. Cumberbatch

Test No. 1013/18

WEST INDIES v NEW ZEALAND (2nd Test)

Played at Bourda, Georgetown, Guyana, on 6, 7, 8, 10, 11 April 1985
Toss: West Indies. Result: match drawn
Debuts: West Indies – C.G. Butts

WEST INDIES

C.G. Greenidge b Chatfield	10	c and b Coney	69
D.L. Haynes b Hadlee	90	c Smith b Hadlee	9
R.B. Richardson run out	185	(4) c J.J. Crowe b Cairns	60
H.A. Gomes lbw b Cairns	53	(5) c sub (J.G. Bracewell) b Rutherford	35
*I.V.A. Richards st Smith b Coney	40	(8) not out	7
A.L. Logie c Howarth b Hadlee	52	not out	41
†P.J.L. Dujon not out	60	b Cairns	3
C.G. Butts } did not bat		(3) c Smith b Hadlee	3
M.D. Marshall } did not bat			
M.A. Holding } did not bat			
J. Garner } did not bat			
Extras (B1, LB16, W1, NB3)	21	(B7, LB25, W1, NB2)	35
Total (6 wickets declared)	511	(6 wickets declared)	268

NEW ZEALAND

J.G. Wright run out	27
K.R. Rutherford c Dujon b Garner	4
J.J. Crowe b Marshall	22
M.D. Crowe lbw b Garner	188
*G.P. Howarth c Haynes b Marshall	4
J.V. Coney c Richards b Holding	73
R.J. Hadlee c Dujon b Marshall	16
†I.D.S. Smith lbw b Marshall	53
B.L. Cairns b Holding	3
S.L. Boock b Holding	0
E.J. Chatfield not out	3
Extras (B12, LB2, W6, NB27)	47
Total	440

N. ZEALAND	*O*	*M*	*R*	*W*	*O*	*M*	*R*	*W*	FALL OF WICKETS			
										WI	*NZ*	*WI*
Hadlee	25.5	5	83	2	16	3	32	2	*Wkt*	*1st*	*1st*	*2nd*
Chatfield	30	3	122	1	16	3	43	0	1st	30	8	22
Cairns	32	5	105	1	18	4	47	2	2nd	221	45	46
Boock	43	11	107	0	18	3	52	0	3rd	327	81	150
Coney	18	2	62	1	10	3	20	1	4th	394	98	191
Howarth	4	1	15	0	5	4	2	0	5th	407	240	207
Rutherford	—	—	—	—	9	1	38	1	6th	511	261	225
Wright	—	—	—	—	3	1	2	0	7th	—	404	—
WEST INDIES									8th	—	415	—
Marshall	33	3	110	4	—	—	—	—	9th	—	415	—
Garner	27.5	5	72	2	—	—	—	—	10th	—	440	—
Holding	28	6	89	3	—	—	—	—				
Butts	47	12	113	0	—	—	—	—				
Richards	8	1	22	0	—	—	—	—				
Gomes	8	2	20	0	—	—	—	—				

Umpires: L.H. Barker and D.J. Narine

Test No. 1014/19

WEST INDIES v NEW ZEALAND (3rd Test)

Played at Kensington Oval, Bridgetown, Barbados, on 26, 27, 28, 30 April, 1 May 1985
Toss: West Indies. Result: West Indies won by 10 wickets
Debuts: nil
In the second innings, I.D.S. Smith (14) retired hurt at 132-5 and resumed at 235-9.

NEW ZEALAND

*G.P. Howarth c Greenidge b Garner	1	c Haynes b Marshall	5
J.G. Wright c Dujon b Marshall	0	c Richardson b Davis	64
K.R. Rutherford c Richards b Marshall	0	c Holding b Marshall	2
M.D. Crowe hit wkt b Holding	14	c Dujon b Marshall	2
J.J. Crowe c Dujon b Davis	21	b Davis	4
J.V. Coney c Richardson b Marshall	12	c Logie b Marshall	83
†I.D.S. Smith c Greenidge b Marshall	2	c and b Marshall	26
R.J. Hadlee c Logie b Davis	29	c Greenidge b Davis	3
D.A. Stirling c Logie b Davis	6	b Marshall	3
S.L. Boock c Dujon b Garner	1	c Haynes b Marshall	22
E.J. Chatfield not out	0	not out	4
Extras (NB8)	8	(B8, LB1, W2, NB19)	30
Total	94		248

WEST INDIES

C.G. Greenidge c J.J. Crowe b Hadlee	2	not out	4
D.L. Haynes c Smith b Hadlee	62	not out	5
R.B. Richardson lbw b M.D. Crowe	22		
H.A. Gomes c J.J. Crowe b M.D. Crowe	0		
W.W. Davis c Smith b Stirling	16		
*I.V.A. Richards c M.D. Crowe b Boock	105		
A.L. Logie c J.J. Crowe b Chatfield	7		
†P.J.L. Dujon b Hadlee	3		
M.D. Marshall c J.J. Crowe b Chatfield	63		
J. Garner not out	37		
M.A. Holding c Smith b Stirling	1		
Extras (B2, LB8, W6, NB2)	18	(W1)	1
Total	336	(0 wickets)	10

WEST INDIES	*O*	*M*	*R*	*W*	*O*	*M*	*R*	*W*
Marshall	15	3	40	4	25.3	6	80	7
Garner	15	9	14	2	19	5	56	0
Holding	7	4	12	1	1	0	2	0
Davis	10.4	5	28	3	18	0	66	3
Richards	—	—	—	—	13	3	25	0
Gomes	—	—	—	—	4	0	10	0
N. ZEALAND								
Hadlee	26	5	86	3	—	—	—	—
Chatfield	28	10	57	2	—	—	—	—
Stirling	14.1	0	82	2	—	—	—	—
M.D. Crowe	10	2	25	2	—	—	—	—
Boock	15	1	76	1	1	1	0	0
Rutherford	—	—	—	—	0.4	0	10	0

FALL OF WICKETS

Wkt	*NZ 1st*	*WI 1st*	*NZ 2nd*	*WI 2nd*
1st	1	12	26	—
2nd	1	91	35	—
3rd	1	91	45	—
4th	18	95	60	—
5th	37	142	108	—
6th	44	161	141	—
7th	80	174	149	—
8th	87	257	226	—
9th	90	327	235	—
10th	94	336	248	—

Umpires: D.M. Archer and L.H. Barker

Test No. 1015/20

WEST INDIES v NEW ZEALAND (4th Test)

Played at Sabina Park, Kingston, Jamaica, on 4, 5, 6, 8 May 1985
Toss: New Zealand. Result: West Indies won by 10 wickets
Debuts: nil
J.V. Coney retired hurt at 51-3.

WEST INDIES

C.G. Greenidge c J.J. Crowe b M.D. Crowe	46	not out	33
D.L. Haynes c J.J. Crowe b Coney	76	not out	24
R.B. Richardson c M.D. Crowe b Coney	30		
H.A. Gomes c Wright b Hadlee	45		
*I.V.A. Richards lbw b Hadlee	23		
A.L. Logie c M.D. Crowe b Hadlee	0		
†P.J.L. Dujon c Bracewell b Troup	70		
M.D. Marshall lbw b Bracewell	26		
W.W. Davis c M.D. Crowe b Troup	0		
J. Garner c M.D. Crowe b Hadlee	12		
C.A. Walsh not out	12		
Extras (B7, LB9, W1, NB6)	23	(B1, LB1)	2
Total	363	(0 wickets)	59

NEW ZEALAND

*G.P. Howarth c Gomes b Marshall	5		c Garner b Walsh	84
J.G. Wright b Davis	53		c Dujon b Garner	10
J.J. Crowe c Richardson b Garner	2		c Marshall b Richards	112
M.D. Crowe c Davis b Walsh	6		c Dujon b Walsh	1
J.V. Coney retired hurt	4		absent hurt	—
K.R. Rutherford c Dujon b Marshall	1	(5)	lbw b Marshall	5
†I.D.S. Smith b Garner	0	(6)	b Marshall	9
R.J. Hadlee c Dujon b Davis	18	(7)	c Walsh b Marshall	14
J.G. Bracewell not out	25	(8)	c Gomes b Marshall	27
G.B. Troup c Marshall b Davis	0	(9)	c Richardson b Garner	2
E.J. Chatfield b Davis	2	(10)	not out	0
Extras (B4, LB1, W2, NB15)	22		(B7, LB4, NB8)	19
Total	138			283

N. ZEALAND	*O*	*M*	*R*	*W*	*O*	*M*	*R*	*W*
Hadlee	28.4	11	53	4	5	1	15	0
Troup	17	1	87	2	3	0	13	0
Chatfield	26	5	85	0	2	0	10	0
M.D. Crowe	10	2	30	1	—	—	—	—
Bracewell	21	5	54	1	4	0	14	0
Coney	14	3	38	2	—	—	—	—
Smith	—	—	—	—	3	1	5	0
WEST INDIES								
Marshall	17	3	47	2	28.4	8	66	4
Garner	16	0	37	2	19	8	41	2
Davis	13.5	5	19	4	21	1	75	0
Walsh	9	1	30	1	16	4	45	2
Richards	—	—	—	—	14	2	34	1
Gomes	—	—	—	—	3	0	11	0
Richardson	—	—	—	—	1	1	0	0

FALL OF WICKETS

Wkt	*WI 1st*	*NZ 1st*	*NZ 2nd*	*WI 2nd*
1st	82	11	13	—
2nd	144	15	223	–
3rd	164	37	223	—
4th	207	65	228	—
5th	207	68	238	—
6th	273	106	242	—
7th	311	113	259	—
8th	311	122	281	—
9th	339	138	283	—
10th	363	—	—	—

Umpires: D.M. Archer and J.R. Gayle

Test No. 1016/21

WEST INDIES v NEW ZEALAND AVERAGES

WEST INDIES – BATTING AND FIELDING

	M	I	NO	HS	Runs	Avge	100	50	Ct/St
R.B. Richardson	4	6	0	185	378	63.00	1	2	5
I.V.A. Richards	4	6	1	105	310	62.00	1	2	2
D.L. Haynes	4	8	2	90	344	57.33	—	4	5
C.G. Greenidge	4	7	2	100	264	52.80	1	1	3
J. Garner	4	3	2	37*	49	49.00	—	—	3
A.L. Logie	4	6	1	52	166	33.20	—	1	4
P.J.L. Dujon	4	6	1	70	156	31.20	—	2	11
H.A. Gomes	4	6	0	53	158	26.33	—	1	2
M.D. Marshall	4	4	0	63	90	22.50	—	1	3
M.A. Holding	3	3	0	12	21	7.00	—	—	1

Also batted (2 Tests): W.W. Davis 16,0 (1 ct);
(1 Test): C.G. Butts 9; R.A. Harper 0,11* (2 ct); C.A. Walsh 12* (1 ct).

WEST INDIES – BOWLING

	O	M	R	W	Avge	Best	5 wI	10 wM
M.D. Marshall	170.1	30	486	27	18.00	7-80	1	1
W.W. Davis	63.3	11	188	10	18.80	4-19	—	—
M.A. Holding	82	24	218	9	24.22	4-79	—	—
J. Garner	136.1	37	302	10	30.20	2-14	—	—

Also bowled: C.G. Butts 47-12-113-0; H.A. Gomes 18-3-44-0; R.A. Harper 36-18-52-2; A.L. Logie 1-1-0-0; I.V.A. Richards 39-7-1-89; R.B. Richardson 2-2-0-0; C.A. Walsh 25-5-75-3.

NEW ZEALAND – BATTING AND FIELDING

	M	I	NO	HS	Runs	Avge	100	50	Ct/St
J.V. Coney	4	6	1	83	241	48.20	—	2	2
J.J. Crowe	4	7	0	112	252	36.00	1	1	8
M.D. Crowe	4	7	0	188	216	30.85	1	—	6
J.G. Wright	4	7	0	64	213	30.42	—	2	1
R.J. Hadlee	4	7	1	39*	137	22.83	—	—	1
G.P. Howarth	4	7	0	84	158	22.57	—	1	2
I.D.S. Smith	4	7	1	53	111	18.50	—	1	7/1
E.J. Chatfield	4	6	5	4*	13	13.00	—	—	1
S.L. Boock	3	4	0	22	26	6.50	—	—	—
K.R. Rutherford	4	7	0	5	12	1.71	—	—	1

Also batted (2 Tests): B.L. Cairns 8,3;
(1 Test): J.G. Bracewell 25*, 27 (1 ct); D.A. Stirling 6, 3; G.B. Troup 0, 2.

NEW ZEALAND – BOWLING

	O	M	R	W	Avge	Best	5 wI	10 wM
R.J. Hadlee	143	31	409	15	27.26	4-53	—	—
J.V. Coney	51	11	137	5	27.40	2-38	—	—
E.J. Chatfield	152	35	441	13	33.92	6-73	1	1
B.L. Cairns	95	14	315	5	63.00	2-47	—	—

Also bowled: S.L. Boock 110-25-339-2; J.G. Bracewell 25-5-68-1; M.D. Crowe 20-4-55-3; G.P. Howarth 9-5-17-0; K.R. Rutherford 9.4-1-48-1; I.D.S. Smith 3-1-5-0; D.A. Stirling 14.1-0-2-82-2; G.B. Troup 20-1-100-2; J.G. Wright 3-1-2-0.

SRI LANKA v INDIA (1st Test)

Played at Sinhalese Sports Club Ground, Colombo, on 30, 31 August, 1, 3, 4 September 1985
Toss: India. Result: match drawn
Debuts: Sri Lanka – F.S. Ahangama, E.A.R. De Silva; India – L.S. Rajput, S. Viswanath

INDIA

L.S. Rajput c Silva b Ahangama	32	c Silva b Ratnayake	61
K. Srikkanth b Ratnayake	2	c Silva b Ratnayake	9
M. Azharuddin c Silva b Ahangama	3	lbw b Ahangama	16
D.B. Vengsarkar c Silva b De Mel	6	not out	98
S.M. Gavaskar run out	51	c De Mel b Ratnayake	0
R.J. Shastri c Silva b De Mel	9	lbw b Ratnayake	40
*Kapil Dev c Silva b De Mel	36	c sub (S.D. Anurasiri) b Ratnayake	6
†S. Viswanath c E.A.R. De Silva b De Mel	20	c Silva b Ratnayake	0
C. Sharma c Silva b De Mel	38	run out	4
G. Sharma not out	10	lbw b Ahangama	1
Maninder Singh lbw b Ratnayake	0	b Ahangama	3
Extras (LB5, W1, NB5)	11	(B4, LB3, NB6)	13
Total	218		251

SRI LANKA

S. Wettimuny c Viswanath b C. Sharma	13		
†S.A.R. Silva c Azharuddin b C. Sharma	7	(6) not out	1
R.S. Madugalle c and b Maninder	103	(5) not out	5
R.L. Dias c Azharuddin b C. Sharma	4	(3) c Srikkanth b Kapil Dev	0
*L.R.D. Mendis c Gavaskar b Maninder	51	(2) c Kapil Dev b C. Sharma	18
A. Ranatunga b Shastri	111	(4) run out	15
P.A. De Silva c Azharuddin b Shastri	33	(1) c Maninder b Kapil Dev	21
A.L.F. De Mel c Viswanath b Kapil Dev	16		
R.J. Ratnayake lbw b Kapil Dev	2		
E.A.R. De Silva not out	1		
F.S. Ahangama c Viswanath b Kapil Dev	0		
Extras (LB5, NB1)	6	(LB1)	1
Total	347	(4 wickets)	61

SRI LANKA	*O*	*M*	*R*	*W*	*O*	*M*	*R*	*W*
De Mel	28	8	64	5	30	3	84	0
Ratnayake	24.2	7	64	2	41	10	85	6
Ahangama	23	3	60	2	27.3	10	49	3
E. De Silva	12	5	18	0	15	6	20	0
Ranatunga	10	8	7	0	6	2	6	0
INDIA								
Kapil Dev	30.4	8	74	3	4	0	36	2
C. Sharma	25	3	81	3	4	0	24	1
Shastri	34	9	70	2	—	—	—	—
Maninder	40	12	82	2	—	—	—	—
G. Sharma	15	6	35	0	—	—	—	—

FALL OF WICKETS

Wkt	*I* *1st*	*SL* *1st*	*I* *2nd*	*SL* *2nd*
1st	19	18	23	38
2nd	30	29	54	39
3rd	47	33	130	44
4th	49	118	130	58
5th	65	262	188	—
6th	101	317	206	—
7th	143	342	206	—
8th	202	346	220	—
9th	218	346	229	—
10th	218	347	251	—

Umpires: H.C. Felsinger and K.T. Francis

Test No. 1023/2

SRI LANKA v INDIA (2nd Test)

Played at P. Saravanamuttu Stadium, Colombo, on 6, 7, 8, 10, 11 September 1985
Toss: Sri Lanka. Result: Sri Lanka won by 149 runs
Debuts: Sri Lanka – C.D.U.S. Weerasinghe

SRI LANKA

S. Wettimuny run out	19	c Rajput b Sharma	32
†S.A.R. Silva c Viswanath b Shastri	111	c Vengsarkar b Kapil Dev	11
R.S. Madugalle lbw b Sharma	54		
R.L. Dias c Viswanath b Sharma	95	not out	60
*L.R.D. Mendis c Shastri b Amarnath	51	not out	13
A. Ranatunga lbw b Sharma	21		
P.A. De Silva c Azharuddin b Sharma	2	(3) b Shastri	75
A.L.F. De Mel lbw b Shastri	0		
R.J. Ratnayake c Sivaramakrishnan b Shastri	7		
C.D.U.S. Weerasinghe b Sharma	3		
F.S. Ahangama not out	0		
Extras (LB3, W4, NB15)	22	(B4, LB6, NB5)	15
Total	385	(3 wickets declared)	206

INDIA

L.S. Rajput c Silva b De Mel	0	lbw b De Mel	12
K. Srikkanth c Mendis b Ahangama	64	lbw b Ratnayake	25
M. Azharuddin c Silva b Ratnayake	0	c Silva b De Mel	25
D.B. Vengsarkar c Ranatunga b Ratnayake	1	c Silva b Ratnayake	0
L. Sivaramakrishnan c Wettimuny b Ratnayake	18	(9) c Silva b De Mel	21
S.M. Gavaskar st Silva b Ranatunga	52	(5) c Silva b Ratnayake	19
M. Amarnath c Ahangama b De Mel	60	(6) c De Silva b Ratnayake	10
R.J. Shastri c Silva b Ahangama	17	(7) c Silva b Ahangama	4
*Kapil Dev c Ratnayake b Ahangama	6	(8) c and b Ratnayake	78
†S. Viswanath c Wettimuny b Ratnayake	7	lbw b Ahangama	0
C. Sharma not out	4	not out	0
Extras (B4, LB6, W1, NB4)	15	(LB2, NB2)	4
Total	244		198

INDIA	*O*	*M*	*R*	*W*	*O*	*M*	*R*	*W*
Kapil Dev	32	10	69	0	20	4	73	1
Sharma	33	3	118	5	13	1	55	1
Shastri	45.3	11	74	3	13	4	41	1
Siva	31	4	90	0	7	1	27	0
Amarnath	15	2	31	1	—	—	—	—
SRI LANKA								
De Mel	31	8	63	2	22	4	64	3
Ratnayake	25.1	5	76	4	23.2	6	49	5
Ahangama	18	3	59	3	14	3	56	2
Weerasinghe	16	7	28	0	3	1	8	0
Ranatunga	5	1	8	1	4	0	19	0

FALL OF WICKETS

Wkt	*SL 1st*	*I 1st*	*SL 2nd*	*I 2nd*
1st	74	0	46	39
2nd	169	1	48	39
3rd	229	3	180	41
4th	328	79	—	84
5th	368	88	—	84
6th	372	178	—	98
7th	375	218	—	98
8th	375	229	—	168
9th	379	238	—	169
10th	385	244	—	198

Umpires: S. Ponnadurai and P.W. Vidanagamage — Test No. 1024/3

SRI LANKA v INDIA (3rd Test)

Played at Asgiriya Stadium, Kandy, on 14, 15, 16, 18, 19 September 1985
Toss: India. Result: match drawn
Debuts: Sri Lanka – B.R. Jurangpathy
In India's first innings, C. Sharma (4) retired hurt at 237 and resumed at 242.

INDIA

R.J. Shastri c Madugalle b De Mel	6		c Silva b Ahangama	81
K. Srikkanth b Ahangama	40		lbw b Ahangama	47
M. Amarnath lbw b Ahangama	30		not out	116
D.B. Vengsarkar run out	62		lbw b Ahangama	10
M. Azharuddin c Silva b Ahangama	25	(6)	b Ratnayake	43
S.M. Gavaskar c Silva b Ratnayake	49	(7)	not out	15
*Kapil Dev lbw b Ahangama	0	(5)	b Ranatunga	2
R.M.H. Binny c De Mel b Ahangama	19			
C. Sharma c Wettimuny b De Mel	11			
†S. Viswanath c Silva b Ratnayake	4			
Maninder Singh not out	0			
Extras (LB1, W1, NB1)	3		(LB5, W4, NB2)	11
Total	249		(5 wickets declared)	325

SRI LANKA

S. Wettimuny c Viswanath b Kapil Dev	34		c Vengsarkar b Sharma	5
†S.A.R. Silva lbw Binny	19		c Viswanath b Kapil Dev	2
R.S. Madugalle c and b Binny	5		c Viswanath b Kapil Dev	10
R.L. Dias c Viswanath b Sharma	8		run out	106
*L.R.D. Mendis c sub (L. Sivaramakrishnan b Maninder	53		c Gavaskar b Sharma	124
A. Ranatunga c Vengsarkar b Maninder	38		b Sharma	0
F.S. Ahangama c Gavaskar b Maninder	11			
P.A. De Silva run out	8	(7)	not out	29
B.R. Jurangpathy c Viswanath b Kapil Dev	1	(8)	lbw b Kapil Dev	0
A.L.F. De Mel c Viswanath b Maninder	1	(9)	not out	9
R.J. Ratnayake not out	0			
Extras (LB4, NB16)	20		(B8, LB4, W4, NB6)	22
Total	198		(7 wickets)	307

	O	*M*	*R*	*W*	*O*	*M*	*R*	*W*
SRI LANKA								
De Mel	26.3	5	97	2	13	2	66	0
Ratnayake	26	5	88	2	23	2	97	1
Ahangama	24	7	52	5	27	6	72	3
Ranatunga	8	5	11	0	16	4	51	1
Jurangpathy	—	—	—	—	4	0	24	0
Madugalle	—	—	—	—	1	0	10	0
INDIA								
Kapil Dev	19	4	46	2	24	4	74	3
Binny	12	0	49	2	—	—	—	—
Sharma	14	1	40	1	20	4	65	3
Shastri	6	2	28	0	24	5	57	0
Maninder	12.3	4	31	4	34	11	99	0

FALL OF WICKETS

	I	*SL*	*I*	*SL*
Wkt	*1st*	*1st*	*2nd*	*2nd*
1st	10	36	74	5
2nd	66	44	178	8
3rd	111	68	206	34
4th	161	80	211	250
5th	180	153	289	250
6th	180	173	—	266
7th	212	196	—	267
8th	241	197	—	—
9th	242	198	—	—
10th	249	198	—	—

Test No. 1025/4

Umpires: D.P. Buultjens and M.D.D.N. Gooneratne

SRI LANKA v INDIA AVERAGES

SRI LANKA – BATTING AND FIELDING

	M	*I*	*NO*	*HS*	*Runs*	*Avge*	*100*	*50*	*Ct/St*
L.R.D. Mendis	3	6	1	124	310	62.00	1	3	1
R.L. Dias	3	6	1	106	273	54.60	1	2	—
R.S. Madugalle	3	5	1	103	177	44.25	1	1	1
A. Ranatunga	3	5	0	111	185	37.00	1	—	1
P.A. De Silva	3	6	1	75	168	33.60	—	1	1
S.A.R. Silva	3	6	1	111	151	30.20	1	—	21/1
S. Wettimuny	3	5	0	34	103	20.60	—	—	3
A.L.F. De Mel	3	4	1	16	26	8.66	—	—	2
F.S. Ahangama	3	3	1	11	11	5.50	—	—	1
R.J. Ratnayake	3	3	1	7	9	4.40	—	—	2

Also batted (1 match): E.A.R. De Silva 1* (1ct); B.R. Jurangpathy 1,0; C.D.U.S. Weerasinghe 3.

SRI LANKA – BOWLING

	Overs	*Mdns*	*Runs*	*Wkts*	*Avge*	*Best*	*5 wI*	*10 wM*
F.S. Ahangama	133.3	32	348	18	19.33	5-52	1	—
R.J. Ratnayake	162.5	35	459	20	22.95	6-85	2	—
A.L.F. De Mel	150.3	30	438	12	36.50	5-64	1	—

Also bowled: E.A.R. De Silva 27-11-38-0; B.R. Jurangpathy 4-0-24-0; R.S. Madugalle 1-0-10-0; A. Ranatunga 49-20-102-2; C.D.U.S. Weerasinghe 19-8-36-0.

INDIA – BATTING AND FIELDING

	M	*I*	*NO*	*HS*	*Runs*	*Avge*	*100*	*50*	*Ct/St*
M. Amarnath	2	4	1	116*	216	72.00	1	1	—
S.M. Gavaskar	3	6	1	52	186	37.20	—	2	3
D.B. Vengsarkar	3	6	1	98*	177	35.40	—	2	3
K. Srikkanth	3	6	0	64	187	31.16	—	1	1
L.S. Rajput	2	4	0	61	105	26.25	—	1	1
R.J. Shastri	3	6	0	81	157	26.16	—	1	1
Kapil Dev	3	6	0	78	128	21.33	—	1	1
C. Sharma	3	5	2	38	57	19.00	—	—	—
M. Azharuddin	3	6	0	43	112	18.66	—	—	4
S. Viswanath	3	5	0	20	31	6.20	—	—	11
Maninder Singh	2	3	1	3	3	1.50	—	—	2

Also batted (1 match): R.M.H. Binny 19 (1ct); G. Sharma 10*,1; L. Sivaramakrishnan 18,21 (1ct).

INDIA – BOWLING

	Overs	*Mdns*	*Runs*	*Wkts*	*Avge*	*Best*	*5 wI*	*10 wM*
C. Sharma	109	12	383	14	27.35	5-118	1	—
Kapil Dev	129.4	30	372	11	33.81	3-74	—	—
Maninder Singh	86.3	27	212	6	35.33	4-31	—	—
R.J. Shastri	122.3	31	270	6	45.00	3-74	—	—

Also bowled: M. Amarnath 15-2-31-1; R.M.H. Binny 12-0-49-2; G. Sharma 15-6-35-0; L. Sivaramakrishnan 38-5-117-0.

PAKISTAN v SRI LANKA (1st Test)

Played at Iqbal Stadium, Faisalabad, on 16, 17, 18, 20, 21 October 1985
Toss: Sri Lanka. Result: match drawn
Debuts: Nil

SRI LANKA

S. Wettimuny lbw b Qadir	52
†S.A.R. Silva c Shoaib b Imran	17
R.S. Madugalle b Mudassar	5
R.L. Dias c Ashraf b Jalaluddin	48
*L.R.D. Mendis lbw b Imran	15
A. Ranatunga c Shoaib b Qadir	79
P.A. De Silva c Ashraf b Imran	122
J.R. Ratnayeke run out	34
A.L.F. De Mel c Ashraf b Wasim	17
R.J. Ratnayake lbw b Qadir	56
R.G.C.E. Wijesuriya not out	7
Extras (B4, LB11, W2, NB10)	27
Total	479

PAKISTAN

Mudassar Nazar lbw b Ratnayake	78
Shoaib Mohammad c Silva b Ratnayake	33
Qasim Omar b Ratnayeke	206
*Javed Miandad not out	203
Zaheer Abbas, Salim Malik, Imran Khan, †Ashraf Ali, Abdul Qadir, Wasim Akram, Jalaluddin did not bat	
Extras (B6, LB17, W1, NB11)	35
Total (3 wickets)	555

PAKISTAN	*O*	*M*	*R*	*W*
Imran	49	15	112	3
Wasim	42.3	12	98	1
Jalaluddin	39	12	89	1
Mudassar	13.3	3	29	1
Qadir	54.3	17	132	3
Shoaib	2	1	4	0
SRI LANKA				
De Mel	27	3	106	0
Ratnayake	32	4	93	2
Ratnayeke	29.5	3	117	1
Wijesuriya	44	13	102	0
Ranatunga	18	1	74	0
Madugalle	7	1	18	0
De Silva	5	0	22	0

FALL OF WICKETS

	SL	*P*
Wkt	*1st*	*1st*
1st	23	86
2nd	40	158
3rd	125	555
4th	129	—
5th	165	—
6th	286	—
7th	352	—
8th	391	—
9th	443	—
10th	479	—

Umpires: Khizar Hayat and Mahboob Shah

Test No. 1026/4

PAKISTAN v SRI LANKA (2nd Test)

Played at Jinnah Park, Sialkot, on 27, 28, 29, 31 October 1985
Toss: Pakistan. Result: Pakistan won by 8 wickets
Debuts: Nil
In Sri Lanka's first innings, R.L. Dias (5) retired hurt at 49-2 and resumed at 170-7.

SRI LANKA

S. Wettimuny c Salim Yousuf b Imran	45	lbw b Imran	0
†S.A.R. Silva c Qasim b Mudassar	12	c Wasim b Mudassar	35
R.S. Madugalle c Salim Yousuf b Mohsin Kamal	0	c Miandad b Mohsin Kamal	65
R.L. Dias c Qasim b Mohsin Kamal	21	lbw b Mudassar	7
*L.R.D. Mendis c Mudassar b Mohsin Kamal	20	c Salim Yousuf b Wasim	3
A. Ranatunga not out	25	c Salim Malik b Imran	28
P.A. De Silva hit wkt b Imran	2	c Salim Yousuf b Wasim	8
J.R. Ratnayeke c Salim Yousuf b Imran	0	not out	17
A.L.F. De Mel lbw b Wasim	1	b Imran	0
R.J. Ratnayake b Imran	1	c sub (Ramiz Raja) b Imran	2
R.G.C.E. Wijesuriya lbw b Wasim	8	lbw b Imran	0
Extras (B6, LB2, W3, NB11)	22	(B9, LB10, NB16)	35
Total	157		200

PAKISTAN

Mudassar Nazar c Silva b Ratnayake	78	not out	24
Mohsin Khan lbw b Ratnayake	50	run out	44
Qasim Omar c Wijesuriya b Ratnayeke	1	c Ranatunga b De Mel	3
*Javed Miandad lbw b Ratnayeke	40		
Zaheer Abbas b Ratnayeke	4		
Salim Malik lbw b Ratnayeke	22		
Imran Khan c sub (A.P. Gurusinghe) b Ratnayeke	6		
†Salim Yousuf lbw b Ratnayeke	23	(4) not out	13
Abdul Qadir c Silva b Ratnayeke	10		
Wasim Akram c Silva b Ratnayeke	4		
Mohsin Kamal not out	4		
Extras (B5, LB3, W1, NB8)	17	(B4, LB4, NB8)	16
Total	259	(2 wickets)	100

PAKISTAN	O	M	R	W	O	M	R	W
Imran	19	3	55	4	18.3	5	40	5
Wasim	14.2	4	38	2	19	4	74	2
Mohsin Kamal	17	3	50	3	12	2	38	1
Mudassar	6	1	6	1	11.5	1	28	2
Qadir	—	—	—	—	1.1	0	1	0
SRI LANKA								
De Mel	15	3	63	0	10	1	43	1
Ratnayake	18	2	77	2	6	0	24	0
Ratnayeke	23.2	5	83	8	7.4	1	25	0
Ranatunga	3	0	18	0	—	—	—	—
Wijesuriya	4	1	10	0	—	—	—	—

FALL OF WICKETS

Wkt	*SL 1st*	*P 1st*	*SL 2nd*	*P 2nd*
1st	41	88	110	76
2nd	41	93	98	82
3rd	81	181	111	—
4th	99	185	121	—
5th	101	209	147	—
6th	101	216	163	—
7th	110	216	188	—
8th	130	245	188	—
9th	131	252	200	—
10th	157	259	200	—

Umpires: Javed Akhtar and Mian Aslam   Test No. 1027/5

PAKISTAN v SRI LANKA (3rd Test)

Played at National Stadium, Karachi, on 7, 8, 9, 11 November 1985
Toss: Sri Lanka. Result: Pakistan won by 10 wickets
Debuts: Sri Lanka – A.P. Gurusinghe

SRI LANKA

S. Wettimuny b Wasim	17		c Salim Yousuf b Imran	10
J.R. Ratnayeke b Qadir	36		c Salim Yousuf b Imran	3
R.S. Madugalle lbw b Wasim	0	(8)	b Tausif	5
R.L. Dias c Salim Yousuf b Imran	7		c Salim Malik b Qadir	4
*L.R.D. Mendis c Miandad b Qadir	15	(7)	b Imran	2
A. Ranatunga c Miandad b Tausif	12	(5)	c Salim Yousif b Wasim	25
P.A. De Silva c and b Qadir	13	(3)	c Salim Yousuf b Tausif	105
†A.P. Gurusinghe lbw b Imran	17	(6)	c Salim Yousuf b Tausif	12
A.L.F. De Mel st Salim Yousuf b Qadir	3		b Tausif	18
R.J. Ratnayake not out	21		c Qasim b Tausif	22
R.G.C.E. Wijesuriya lbw b Qadir	2		not out	2
Extras (B5, LB10, W1, NB3)	19		(B5, LB11, NB6)	22
Total	162			230

PAKISTAN

Mudassar Nazar c Gurusinghe b De Mel	16	not out	57
Mohsin Khan c Gurusinghe b De Mel	13	not out	36
Qasim Omar c Ranatunga b De Mel	8		
*Javed Miandad lbw b De Mel	63		
Ramiz Raja c and b De Mel	52		
Salim Malik b De Mel	4		
Imran Khan c Ratnayake b Ratnayeke	63		
†Salim Yousuf lbw b Ratnayake	27		
Abdul Qadir c Wettimuny b Wijesuriya	19		
Tausif Ahmed b Ratnayake	1		
Wasim Akram not out	5		
Extras (B13, LB8, W2, NB1)	24	(B1, LB3, NB1)	5
Total	295	(0 wickets)	98

PAKISTAN	*O*	*M*	*R*	*W*	*O*	*M*	*R*	*W*
Imran	20	9	36	2	14.1	5	28	3
Wasim	14	7	17	2	14	4	24	1
Tausif	22	10	50	1	23.2	8	54	5
Qadir	20.5	5	44	5	25.5	4	102	1
Mudassar	—	—	—	—	3	0	6	0
SRI LANKA								
De Mel	22	1	109	6	3	0	28	0
Ratnayake	15	2	48	2	4	0	33	0
Ratnayeke	15	4	48	1	6	1	24	0
Wijesuriya	22	5	68	1	3.4	2	9	0
Ranatunga	1	0	1	0	—	—	—	—

FALL OF WICKETS

Wkt	*SL 1st*	*P 1st*	*SL 2nd*	*P 2nd*
1st	27	27	14	—
2nd	28	43	15	—
3rd	60	60	57	—
4th	89	68	104	—
5th	90	153	132	—
6th	106	228	139	—
7th	122	259	157	—
8th	125	288	191	—
9th	151	290	221	—
10th	162	295	230	—

Test No. 1028/6

Umpires: Khizar Hayat and Mahboob Shah

PAKISTAN v SRI LANKA
TEST AVERAGES

PAKISTAN – BATTING AND FIELDING

	M	I	NO	HS	Runs	Avge	100	50	Ct/St
Javed Miandad	3	3	1	203*	306	153.00	1	1	3
Mudassar Nazar	3	5	2	78	253	84.33	—	3	1
Qasim Omar	3	4	0	206	218	54.50	1	—	3
Mohsin Khan	2	4	1	50	143	47.66	—	1	—
Imran Khan	3	2	0	63	69	34.50	—	1	—
Salim Yousuf	2	3	1	27	63	31.50	—	—	11/1
Abdul Qadir	3	2	0	19	29	14.50	—	—	1
Salim Malik	3	2	0	22	26	13.00	—	—	2
Wasim Akram	3	2	1	5*	9	9.00	—	—	1

Also batted: Ashraf Ali (1 match) did not bat (3 ct); Jalaluddin (1 match) did not bat; Mohsin Kamal (1 match) 4*; Ramiz Raja (1 match) 52; Shoaib Mohammad (1 match) 33 (2 ct); Tausif Ahmed (1 match) 1; Zaheer Abbas (2 matches) 4.

PAKISTAN – BOWLING

	Overs	Mdns	Runs	Wkts	Avge	Best	5 wI	10 wM
Imran Khan	120.4	37	271	17	15.94	5-40	1	—
Tausif Ahmed	45.2	18	104	6	17.33	5-54	1	—
Abdul Qadir	102.2	26	279	9	31.00	5-44	1	—
Wasim Akram	103.5	31	251	8	31.37	2-17	—	—

Also bowled: Jalaluddin 39-12-89-1; Mohsin Kamal 29-5-88-4; Mudassar Nazar 34.2-5-69-4; Shoaib Mohammad 2-1-4-0.

SRI LANKA – BATTING AND FIELDING

	M	I	NO	HS	Runs	Avge	100	50	Ct/St
P.A. De Silva	3	5	0	122	250	50.00	2	—	—
A. Ranatunga	3	5	1	79	169	42.25	—	1	2
R.J. Ratnayake	3	5	1	56	102	25.50	—	1	1
S. Wettimuny	3	5	0	52	124	24.80	—	1	1
J.R. Ratnayeke	3	5	1	36	90	22.50	—	—	—
S.A.R. Silva	2	3	0	35	64	21.33	—	—	4
R.L. Dias	3	5	0	48	87	17.40	—	—	—
R.S. Madugalle	3	5	0	65	75	15.00	—	1	—
L.R.D. Mendis	3	5	0	20	55	11.00	—	—	—
A.L.F. De Mel	3	5	0	18	39	7.80	—	—	1
R.G.C.E. Wijesuriya	3	5	2	8	19	6.33	—	—	1

Played in one match: A.P. Gurusinghe 17,12 (2 ct).

SRI LANKA – BOWLING

	Overs	Mdns	Runs	Wkts	Avge	Best	5 wI	10 wM
J.R. Ratnayeke	81.5	14	297	10	29.70	8-83	1	—
R.J. Ratnayake	75	8	275	6	45.83	2-48	—	—
A.L.F. De Mel	77	8	349	7	49.85	6-109	1	—

Also bowled: P.A. De Silva 5-0-22-0; R.S. Madugalle 7-1-18-0; A. Ranatunga 22-1-93-0; R.G.C.E. Wijesuriya 73.4-21-189-1.

AUSTRALIA v NEW ZEALAND (1st Test)

Played at Woolloongabba, Brisbane, on 8, 9, 10, 11, 12 November 1985
Toss: New Zealand. Result: New Zealand won by an innings and 41 runs
Debuts: New Zealand – V.R. Brown

AUSTRALIA

K.C. Wessels lbw b Hadlee	70	(2) c Brown b Chatfield	3
A.M.J. Hilditch c Chatfield b Hadlee	0	(1) c Chatfield b Hadlee	12
D.C. Boon c Coney b Hadlee	31	c Smith b Chatfield	1
*A.R. Border c Edgar b Hadlee	1	not out	152
G.M. Ritchie c M.D. Crowe b Hadlee	8	c Coney b Sneddon	20
†W.B. Phillips b Hadlee	34	b Hadlee	2
G.R.J. Matthews b Hadlee	2	c Cooney b Hadlee	115
G.F. Lawson c Hadlee b Brown	8	(9) c Brown b Chatfield	7
C.J. McDermott c Coney b Hadlee	9	(8) c and b Hadlee	5
D.R. Gilbert not out	0	c Chatfield b Hadlee	10
R.G. Holland c Brown b Hadlee	0	b Hadlee	0
Extras (B9, LB5, NB2)	16	(LB3, NB3)	6
Total	179		333

NEW ZEALAND

B.A. Edgar c Phillips b Gilbert	17
J.G. Wright lbw b Matthews	46
J.F. Reid c Border b Gilbert	108
M.D. Crowe b Matthews	188
*J.V. Coney c Phillips b Lawson	22
J.J. Crowe c Holland b Matthews	35
V.R. Brown not out	36
R.J. Hadlee c Phillips b McDermott	54
†I.D.S. Smith not out	2
M.C. Sneddon, E.J. Chatfield } did not bat	
Extras (B2, LB11, NB32)	45
Total 7 wickets declared	553

BOWLING

N. ZEALAND	O	M	R	W	O	M	R	W
Hadlee	23.4	4	52	9	28.5	9	71	6
Chatfield	18	6	29	0	32	9	75	3
Sneddon	11	1	45	0	19	3	66	1
M.D. Crowe	5	0	14	0	9	2	19	0
Brown	12	5	17	1	25	5	96	0
Coney	7	5	8	0	3	1	3	0
AUSTRALIA								
Lawson	36.5	8	96	1	–	–	–	–
McDermott	31	3	119	1	–	–	–	–
Gilbert	39	9	102	2	–	–	–	–
Matthews	31	5	110	3	–	–	–	–
Holland	22	3	106	0	–	–	–	–
Border	0.1	0	0	0	–	–	–	–
Wessels	1	0	7	0	–	–	–	–

FALL OF WICKETS

Wkt	*A 1st*	*NZ 1st*	*A 2nd*
1st	1	36	14
2nd	70	85	16
3rd	72	309	16
4th	82	362	47
5th	148	427	67
6th	150	471	264
7th	159	549	272
8th	175	–	291
9th	179	–	333
10th	179	–	333

Umpires: A.R. Crafter and R.A. French

Test No. 1029/16

AUSTRALIA v NEW ZEALAND (2nd Test)

Played at Sydney Cricket Ground, Sydney, on 22, 23, 24, 25, 26 November 1985
Toss: Australia. Result: Australia won by 4 wickets
Debut: Australia – R.B. Kerr

NEW ZEALAND

J.G. Wright c O'Donnell b Bright	38	c and b Matthews	43
B.A. Edgar c Border b Holland	50	c and b Holland	52
J.F. Reid c Kerr b Holland	7	b Matthews	19
M.D. Crowe run out	8	b Holland	0
*J.V. Coney c Border b Holland	8	b Holland	7
J.J. Crowe b Holland	13	c and b Holland	6
V.R. Brown lbw b Holland	0	b Bright	15
†I.D.S. Smith c Hookes b Bright	28	c and b Bright	12
R.J. Hadlee lbw b Holland	5	lbw b Gilbert	26
J.G. Bracewell not out	83	not out	2
S.L. Boock lbw b Gilbert	37	c Boon b Bright	3
Extras (B6, LB8, NB2)	16	(B1, LB4, NB3)	8
Total	293		193

AUSTRALIA

†W.B. Phillips b Bracewell	31	c Bracewell b Boock	63
R.B. Kerr lbw b Hadlee	7	c Wright b Bracewell	7
D.C. Boon lbw b Hadlee	0	c Reid b Bracewell	81
*A.R. Border b Bracewell	20	st Smith b Bracewell	11
G.M. Ritchie c J.J. Crowe b Hadlee	89	c M.D. Crowe b Hadlee	13
D.W. Hookes run out	0	not out	38
G.R.J. Matthews c Smith b Hadlee	50	lbw b Hadlee	32
S.P. O'Donnell not out	20	not out	2
R.J. Bright lbw b Boock	1		
D.R. Gilbert c Smith b Hadlee	0		
R.G. Holland st Smith b Boock	0		
Extras (B5, LB2, Nb2)	9	(B3, LB9, NB1)	13
Total	227	(6 wickets)	260

AUSTRALIA	*O*	*M*	*R*	*W*	*O*	*M*	*R*	*W*	FALL OF WICKETS				
										NZ	*A*	*NZ*	*A*
Gilbert	20.3	6	41	1	9	2	22	1	*Wkt*	*1st*	*1st*	*2nd*	*2nd*
O'Donnell	6	2	13	0	5	4	4	0	1st	79	19	100	27
Bright	34	12	87	2	17.5	3	39	3	2nd	92	22	106	132
Matthews	17	3	32	0	30	11	55	2	3rd	109	48	107	144
Holland	47	19	106	6	41	16	68	4	4th	112	71	119	163
N. ZEALAND									5th	128	71	131	192
Hadlee	24	2	65	5	27.1	10	58	2	6th	128	186	137	258
M.D. Crowe	5	2	15	0	2	1	7	0	7th	161	224	162	—
Bracewell	25	9	51	2	30	7	91	3	8th	166	225	163	—
Boock	29.5	14	53	2	22	4	49	1	9th	169	226	190	—
Brown	13	3	35	0	7	0	28	0	10th	293	227	193	—
Coney	1	0	1	0	9	1	15	0					

Umpires: M.J. Johnson and B.E. Martin   Test No. 1030/17

AUSTRALIA v NEW ZEALAND (3rd Test)

Played at W.A.C.A. Ground, Perth, on 30 November, 1, 2, 3, 4 December 1985
Toss: New Zealand. Result: New Zealand won by 6 wickets
Debut: Nil

AUSTRALIA

†W.B. Phillips c Smith b Chatfield	37	c Smith b Chatfield	10
R.B. Kerr c Smith b Chatfield	17	b Hadlee	0
D.C. Boon c Bracewell b Hadlee	12	b Hadlee	50
*A.R. Border c Smith b Hadlee	12	b Hadlee	83
G.M. Ritchie lbw b Coney	6	c M.D. Crowe b Coney	44
D.W. Hookes c Bracewell b Coney	14	b Bracewell	7
G.R.J. Matthews b Hadlee	34	lbw b Hadlee	14
G.F. Lawson c J.J. Crowe b Hadlee	11	c J.J. Crowe b Hadlee	21
C.J. McDermott b Chatfield	36	lbw b Bracewell	11
D.R. Gilbert not out	12	b Hadlee	3
R.G. Holland c M.D. Crowe b Hadlee	4	not out	0
Extras (LB6, NB2)	8	(B2, LB5, NB9)	16
Total	203		259

NEW ZEALAND

J.G. Wright c Phillips b Lawson	20	(2) b Gilbert	35
B.A. Edgar c Hookes b McDermott	74	(1) c Border b Matthews	16
J.F. Reid b Gilbert	7	c Phillips b Gilbert	28
M.D. Crowe lbw b Holland	71	not out	42
*J.V. Coney c Phillips b Lawson	19	b Gilbert	16
J.J. Crowe lbw b Holland	17	not out	2
R.J. Hadlee c Hookes b Holland	26		
†I.D.S. Smith c Matthews b Lawson	12		
J.G. Bracewell not out	28		
B.L. Cairns c Ritchie b Holland	0		
E.J. Chatfield c Phillips b Lawson	3		
Extras (B1, LB7, NB14)	22	(B7, LB7, NB11)	25
Total	299	(4 wickets)	164

N. ZEALAND	*O*	*M*	*R*	*W*	*O*	*M*	*R*	*W*
Hadlee	26.5	6	65	5	39	11	90	6
Cairns	14	1	50	0	26	6	59	0
Chatfield	16	6	33	3	30	9	47	1
Coney	21	11	43	2	8	5	9	1
Bracewell	6	3	6	0	28.5	8	47	2
AUSTRALIA								
Lawson	47	12	79	4	21	7	35	0
McDermott	33	9	66	2	13	1	27	0
Gilbert	31	9	75	1	23	5	48	3
Holland	40	12	63	3	8	1	27	0
Matthews	5	3	6	0	9	3	13	1
Hookes	1	0	2	0	—	—	—	—

FALL OF WICKETS

Wkt	*A 1st*	*NZ 1st*	*A 2nd*	*NZ 2nd*
1st	38	43	3	47
2nd	63	55	28	77
3rd	78	184	109	121
6th	114	253	214	—
5th	85	215	207	—
6th	114	253	214	—
7th	131	256	234	—
8th	159	273	251	—
9th	190	276	255	—
10th	203	299	259	—

Umpires: R.C. Isherwood and P.J. McConnell

Test No. 1031/18

AUSTRALIA v NEW ZEALAND

TEST AVERAGES

AUSTRALIA – BATTING AND FIELDING

	M	I	NO	HS	Runs	Avge	100	50	Ct/St
A.R. Border	3	6	1	152*	279	55.80	1	1	4
G.R.J. Matthews	3	6	0	115	247	41.16	1	1	2
G.M. Ritchie	3	6	0	89	180	30.00	—	1	1
W.B. Phillips	3	6	0	63	177	29.50	—	1	7
D.C. Boon	3	6	0	81	175	29.16	—	2	1
D.W. Hookes	2	4	1	38*	59	19.66	—	—	3
C.J. McDermott	2	4	0	36	61	15.25	—	—	—
G.F. Lawson	2	4	0	21	47	11.75	—	—	—
D.R. Gilbert	3	5	2	12*	25	8.33	—	—	—
R.B. Kerr	2	4	0	17	31	7.75	—	—	1
R.G. Holland	3	5	1	4	4	1.00	—	—	3

Played in one match: R.J. Bright 1 (1 ct); A.M.J. Hilditch 0,12; S.P. O'Donnell 20*,2* (1 ct); K.C. Wessels 70,3.

AUSTRALIA – BOWLING

	Overs	Mdns	Runs	Wkts	Avge	Best	5 wI	10 wM
R.J. Bright	51.5	15	126	5	25.20	3-39	—	—
R.G. Holland	158	51	370	13	28.46	6-106	1	1
D.R. Gilbert	122.3	31	288	8	36.00	3-48	—	—
G.R.J. Matthews	92	25	216	6	36.00	3-110	—	—
G.F. Lawson	104.5	27	210	5	42.00	4-79	—	—

Also bowled: A.R. Border 0.1-0-0-0; D.W. Hookes 1-0-2-0; C.J. McDermott 77-13-212-3; S.P. O'Donnell 11-6-17-0; K.C. Wessels 1-0-7-0.

NEW ZEALAND – BATTING AND FIELDING

	M	I	NO	HS	Runs	Avge	100	50	Ct/St
M.D. Crowe	3	5	1	188	309	77.25	1	1	4
B.A. Edgar	3	5	0	74	209	41.80	—	3	1
J.G. Wright	3	5	0	46	182	36.40	—	—	1
J.F. Reid	3	5	0	108	169	33.80	1	—	1
R.J. Hadlee	3	4	0	54	111	27.75	—	1	2
V.R. Brown	2	3	1	36*	51	25.50	—	—	3
J.J. Crowe	3	5	1	35	73	18.25	—	—	3
I.D.S. Smith	3	4	1	28	54	18.00	—	—	7/2
J.V. Coney	3	5	0	22	72	14.40	—	—	4

Also batted: S.L. Boock (1 match) 37,3; B.P. Bracewell (2 matches) 83*,2*,28* (3 ct); B.L. Cairns (1 match) 0; E.J. Chatfield (2 matches) 3 (3 ct). M.C. Snedden (1 match) did not bat.

NEW ZEALAND – BOWLING

	Overs	Mdns	Runs	Wkts	Avge	Best	5 wI	10 wM
R.J. Hadlee	169.3	42	401	33	12.15	9-52	5	2
E.J. Chatfield	96	30	184	7	26.28	3-33	—	—
J.G. Bracewell	89.5	27	195	7	27.85	3-91	—	—

Also bowled: S.L. Boock 51.5-18-102-3; V.R. Brown 57-13-176-1; B.L. Cairns 40-7-109-0; J.V. Coney 49-23-79-3; M.D. Crowe 21-5-55-0; M.C. Snedden 30-4-111-1.

AUSTRALIA v INDIA (1st TEST)

Played at Adelaide Oval on 13, 14, 15, 16, 17 December 1985
Toss: Australia. Result: match drawn
Debuts: Australia – M.G. Hughes, G.R. Marsh, B.A. Reid
Close of play scores: 1st day – A 4-248 (Ritchie 55; Hookes 2); 2nd – I 1-97 (Gavaskar 39, Sharma 1); 3rd – I 3-176 (Azharuddin 12, Amarnath 4); 4th – I 7-391 (Gavaskar 94, Binney 34)
S.M. Gavaskar retired hurt at 97 and resumed at 247.

AUSTRALIA			
†W.B. Phillips c Yadav b Kapil Dev	11		
D.C. Boon c Vengsarkar b Kapil Dev	123	(1) not out	11
G.R. Marsh c Sharma b Binny	5	(2) not out	2
*A.R. Border b Kapil Dev	49		
G.M. Ritchie c Kirmani b Kapil Dev	128		
D.W. Hookes b Yadav	34		
G.R.J. Matthews lbw b Kapil Dev	18		
R.J. Bright not out	5		
C.J. McDermott lbw b Kapil Dev	0		
B.A. Reid c Gavaskar b Kapil Dev	2		
M.G. Hughes c Vengsarkar b Kapil Dev	0		
Extras (LB4, NB2)	6	(LB3, NB1)	4
Total	381	(0 wickets)	17

INDIA	
S.M. Gavaskar not out	166
K. Srikkanth c Ritchie b McDermott	51
C. Sharma c Phillips b Reid	54
D.B. Vengsarkar c Phillips b Hughes	7
M. Azharuddin c Phillips b Reid	17
M. Amarnath c Marsh b McDermott	37
R.J. Shastri b Reid	42
*Kapil Dev lbw b Bright	38
R.M.H. Binny c Phillips b McDermott	38
†S.M.H. Kirmani c Boon b Reid	7
N.S. Yadav c Hughes b Hookes	41
Extras (B2, LB7, W1, NB12)	22
Total	520

INDIA	*O*	*M*	*R*	*W*	*O*	*M*	*R*	*W*	FALL OF WICKETS			
										A	*I*	*A*
Kapil Dev	38	6	106	8	3	1	3	0				
Binny	24	7	56	1	—	—	—	—	*Wkt*	*1st*	*1st*	*2nd*
Sharma	19	3	70	0	2	0	9	0	1st	19	95	—
Yadav	27	6	66	1	2	1	2	0	2nd	33	131	—
Shastri	38	11	70	0	1	1	0	0	3rd	124	171	—
Armanath	3	0	9	0	—	—	—	—	4th	241	187	—
AUSTRALIA									5th	318	247	—
McDermott	48	14	131	3	—	—	—	—	6th	374	273	—
Hughes	38	6	123	1	—	—	—	—	7th	375	333	—
Reid	53	22	113	4	—	—	—	—	8th	375	409	—
Bright	44	15	80	1	—	—	—	—	9th	381	426	—
Matthews	17	2	60	0	—	—	—	—	10th	381	520	—
Hookes	2	0	4	1	—	—	—	—				

Umpires: A.R. Crafter and S.G. Randell. Test No. 1032/40

AUSTRALIA v INDIA (2nd TEST)

Played at Melbourne Cricket Ground on 26, 27, 28, 29, 30 December 1985
Toss: India. Result: match drawn
Debut: Australia – S.R. Waugh
Close of play scores: 1st day – A 8-210 (Matthews 54; Reid 0); 2nd – I 3-187 (Vengsarkar 38; Azharuddin 5); 3rd – I 9-431 (Sivaramakrishnan 6; Yadav 2); 4th – A 8-228 (Border 98; Reid 11)

AUSTRALIA

*W.B. Phillips b Yadav	7	(7) c Srikkanth b Yadav	13
D.C. Boon lbw b Shastri	14	c and b Kapil Dev	19
G.R. Marsh c Siva b Yadav	30	(1) c Siva b Shastri	19
*A.R. Border c and b Siva	11	(3) st Kirmani b Yadav	163
D.W. Hookes b Shastri	42	(4) c Srikkanth b Shastri	0
S.R. Waugh c Kapil Dev b Siva	13	(5) b Shastri	5
G.R.J. Matthews not out	100	(6) c Azharuddin b Siva	16
R.J. Bright b Shastri	28	lbw b Kapil Dev	20
C.J. McDermott c Kapil Dev b Shastri	1	c and b Shastri	2
B.A. Reid c Srikkanth b Kapil Dev	1	c Siva b Yadav	13
D.R. Gilbert c Kirmani b Yadav	4	not out	10
Extras (B5, LB6)	11	(B11, LB16, NB1)	28
Total	262		308

INDIA

S.M. Gavaskar b Gilbert	6	b Reid	8
K. Srikkanth lbw b Gilbert	86	c Bright b Reid	38
M. Amarnath c Phillips b Reid	45	not out	3
D.B. Vengsarkar c and b Matthews	75	not out	1
M. Azharuddin b Matthews	37		
R.J. Shastri c Phillips b Waugh	49		
*Kapil Dev c Hookes b Reid	55		
R.M.H. Binny c Matthews b Reid	0		
†S.M.H. Kirmani c Phillips b Waugh	35		
L. Sivaramakrishnan c Phillips b Reid	15		
N.S. Yadav not out	6		
Extras (B4, LB15, NB17)	36	(B4, LB1, NB4)	9
Total	445	(2 wickets)	59

INDIA	*O*	*M*	*R*	*W*	*O*	*M*	*R*	*W*
Kapil Dev	23	6	38	1	22	7	53	2
Binny	3	0	11	0	—	—	—	—
Shastri	37	13	87	4	47	13	92	4
Yadav	27.5	10	64	3	38.5	15	84	3
Siva	13	2	51	2	13	1	43	1
Amarnath	—	—	—	—	3	0	9	0
AUSTRALIA								
McDermott	15	5	52	0	6	1	17	0
Gilbert	22	1	81	2	4	0	9	0
Reid	38.2	11	100	4	8	1	23	2
Bright	31	8	76	0	7	4	5	0
Matthews	31	7	81	2	—	—	—	—
Waugh	11	5	36	2	—	—	—	—

FALL OF WICKETS

	A	*I*	*A*	*I*
Wkt	*1st*	*1st*	*2nd*	*2nd*
1st	22	15	32	39
2nd	26	116	54	57
3rd	41	172	54	—
4th	90	246	84	—
5th	109	291	126	—
6th	127	370	161	—
7th	193	372	202	—
8th	195	420	205	—
9th	216	425	231	—
10th	262	445	308	—

Umpires: R.A. French and R.C. Isherwood

Test No. 1033/41

AUSTRALIA v INDIA (3rd TEST)

Played at Sydney Cricket Ground on 2, 3, 4, 5, 6 January 1986
Toss: India. Result: match drawn
Debuts: nil

INDIA

S.M. Gavaskar b Holland	172
K. Srikkanth b Reid	116
M. Amarnath c Bright b Gilbert	138
*Kapil Dev b Gilbert	42
D.B. Vengsarkar not out	37
M. Azharuddin not out	59
R.J. Shastri, C. Sharma, †S.M.H. Kirmani, N.S. Yadav, L. Sivaramakrishnan — did not bat	
Extras (B5, LB9, NB22)	36
Total (4 wickets declared)	600

AUSTRALIA

D.C. Boon b Kapil Dev	131	(2) run out	25
G.R. Marsh c Gavaskar b Shastri	92	(1) c Azharuddin b Yadav	28
*A.R. Border c Sharma b Shastri	71	(7) c Siva b Yadav	4
G.M. Ritchie c Kapil Dev b Yadav	14	(3) not out	17
†W.B. Phillips c Srikkanth b Shastri	14	c Srikkanth b Shastri	22
G.R.J. Matthews c Amarnath b Yadav	40	c Kapil Dev b Yadav	17
S.J. Waugh c Siva b Yadav	8	(4) lbw b Shastri	0
R.J. Bright c Kirmani b Shastri	3	not out	0
D.R. Gilbert c Azharuddin b Yadav	1		
B.R. Reid st Kirmani b Yadav	4		
R.G. Holland not out	1		
Extras (LB14, NB3)	17	(B3, LB2, NB1)	6
Total	396	(6 wickets)	119

AUSTRALIA	O	M	R	W	O	M	R	W	FALL OF WICKETS	I	A	A
Gilbert	37	3	135	2	—	—	—	—	*Wkt*	*1st*	*1st*	*2nd*
Reid	34	8	89	1	—	—	—	—	1st	191	217	57
Bright	41	7	121	0	—	—	—	—	2nd	415	258	57
Holland	21	6	113	1	—	—	—	—	3rd	485	277	60
Matthews	29	2	95	0	—	—	—	—	4th	510	302	87
Waugh	7	0	33	0	—	—	—	—	5th	—	369	111
INDIA									6th	—	387	115
Kapil Dev	25	8	65	1	7	3	11	0	7th	—	388	—
Shastri	57	21	101	4	25	12	36	2	8th	—	390	—
Yadav	62.3	20	99	5	33	22	19	3	9th	—	395	—
Siva	22	2	79	0	9	0	37	0	10th	—	396	—
Sharma	13	2	38	0	3	0	11	0				

Umpires: P.J. McConnell and S.G. Randell — Test No. 1034/42

AUSTRALIA v INDIA

TEST AVERAGES

AUSTRALIA – BATTING AND FIELDING

	M	*I*	*NO*	*HS*	*Runs*	*Avge*	*100*	*50*	*Ct/St*
G.M. Ritchie	2	3	1	128	159	79.50	1	—	1
D.C. Boon	3	6	1	131	323	64.60	2	—	1
A.R. Border	3	5	0	163	298	59.60	1	1	—
G.R.J. Matthews	3	5	1	100*	191	47.75	1	—	2
G.R. Marsh	3	6	1	92	176	35.20	—	1	1
D.W. Hookes	2	3	0	42	76	25.33	—	—	1
R.J. Bright	3	5	2	28	56	18.66	—	—	2
W.B. Phillips	3	5	0	22	67	13.40	—	—	8
D.R. Gilbert	2	3	1	10*	15	7.50	—	—	—
S.R. Waugh	2	4	0	13	26	6.50	—	—	—
B.A. Reid	3	4	0	13	20	5.00	—	—	—
C.J. McDermott	2	3	0	2	3	1.00	—	—	—

Played in 1 match: R.G. Holland 1*; M.G. Hughes 0.

AUSTRALIA – BOWLING

	Overs	*Mdns*	*Runs*	*Wkts*	*Avge*	*Best*	*5 wI*	*10 wM*
B.A. Reid	133.2	42	325	11	29.54	4-100	—	—
D.R. Gilbert	63	4	225	4	56.25	2-81	—	—
C.J. McDermott	69	20	200	3	66.66	3-131	—	—

Also bowled: R.J. Bright 123-34-282-1; R.G. Holland 21-6-113-1; D.W. Hookes 2-0-4-1; M.G. Hughes 38-6-123-1; G.R.J. Matthews 77-11-236-2; S.R. Waugh 18-5-69-2.

INDIA – BATTING AND FIELDING

	M	*I*	*NO*	*HS*	*Runs*	*Avge*	*100*	*50*	*Ct/St*
S.M. Gavaskar	3	4	1	172	352	117.33	2	—	2
M. Amarnath	3	4	1	138	223	74.33	1	—	1
K. Srikkanth	3	4	0	116	291	72.75	1	2	5
D.B. Vengsarkar	3	4	2	75	120	60.00	—	1	2
M. Azharuddin	3	3	1	59*	113	56.50	—	1	3
N.S. Yadav	3	2	1	41	47	47.00	—	—	1
R.J. Shastri	3	2	0	49	91	45.50	—	—	1
Kapil Dev	3	3	0	55	135	45.00	—	1	5
S.M.H. Kirmani	3	2	0	35	42	21.00	—	—	3/2
R.M.H. Binny	2	2	0	38	38	19.00	—	—	—

Played in 2 matches: C. Sharma 54 (2 ct); L. Sivaramakrishnan 15 (6 ct).

INDIA – BOWLING

	Overs	*Mdns*	*Runs*	*Wkts*	*Avge*	*Best*	*5 wI*	*10 wM*
N.S. Yadav	191.4	74	334	15	22.66	5-99	1	—
Kapil Dev	118	31	276	12	23.00	8-106	1	—
R.J. Shastri	205	71	386	14	27.57	4-87	—	—

Also bowled: M. Amarnath 6-0-18-0; R.M.H. Binny 27-7-67-1; C. Sharma 37-5-128-0; L. Sivaramakrishnan 57-5-210-3.

Your flexible friend – a big hit wherever he goes.
NatWest Access

RESULTS SUMMARY OF ALL TEST MATCHES 1876-77 to 1985-86†

†up to and including 6 January 1986

		Tests	*Won by*								*Tied*	*Drawn*
			E	*A*	*SA*	*WI*	*NZ*	*I*	*P*	*SL*		
England	v Australia	257	86	96	—	—	—	—	—	—	—	75
	v South Africa	102	46	—	18	—	—	—	—	—	—	38
	v West Indies	85	21	—	—	30	—	—	—	—	—	34
	v New Zealand	60	30	—	—	—	3	—	—	—	—	27
	v India	72	30	—	—	—	—	9	—	—	—	33
	v Pakistan	39	13	—	—	—	—	—	3	—	—	23
	v Sri Lanka	2	1	—	—	—	—	—	—	—	—	1
Australia	v South Africa	53	—	29	11	—	—	—	—	—	—	13
	v West Indies	62	—	27	—	19	—	—	—	—	1	15
	v New Zealand	18	—	9	—	—	4	—	—	—	—	5
	v India	42	—	20	—	—	—	8	—	—	—	14
	v Pakistan	28	—	11	—	—	—	—	8	—	—	9
	v Sri Lanka	1	—	1	—	—	—	—	—	—	—	—
South Africa	v New Zealand	17	—	—	9	—	2	—	—	—	—	6
West Indies	v New Zealand	21	—	—	—	7	3	—	—	—	—	11
	v India	54	—	—	—	22	—	5	—	—	—	27
	v Pakistan	19	—	—	—	7	—	—	4	—	—	8
New Zealand	v India	25	—	—	—	—	4	10	—	—	—	11
	v Pakistan	27	—	—	—	—	3	—	10	—	—	14
	v Sri Lanka	5	—	—	—	—	4	—	—	—	—	1
India	v Pakistan	35	—	—	—	—	—	4	6	—	—	25
	v Sri Lanka	4	—	—	—	—	—	—	—	1	—	3
Pakistan	v Sri Lanka	6	—	—	—	—	—	—	4	—	—	2
		1034	227	193	38	85	23	36	35	1	1	395

	Tests	*Won*	*Lost*	*Drawn*	*Tied*	*Toss Won*
England	617	227	159	231	—	303
Australia	461	193	136	131	1	230
South Africa	172	38	77	57	—	80
West Indies	241	85	60	95	1	130
New Zealand	173	23	75	75	—	85
India	232	36	83	113	—	117
Pakistan	154	35	38	81	—	81
Sri Lanka	18	1	10	7	—	8

THE 1985 FIRST-CLASS SEASON STATISTICAL HIGHLIGHTS

HIGHEST INNINGS TOTALS

595-5d	England v Australia (5th Test)	Birmingham
567-8d	Middlesex v Northamptonshire	Uxbridge
566-5d	Somerset v Warwickshire	Taunton
539	Australia v England (3rd Test)	Nottingham
533	England v Australia (1st Test)	Leeds

LOWEST INNINGS TOTALS

24	Oxford University v Leicestershire	Oxford
47	Oxford University v Lancashire	Oxford
58	Glamorgan v Sussex	Hove
63	Warwickshire v Surrey	The Oval
76	Australians v Hampshire	Southampton
77	Lancashire v Surrey	The Oval

HIGHEST MATCH AGGREGATE

1415 (Avge 67.38)	Somerset v Warwickshire	Taunton

USING ELEVEN BOWLERS IN AN INNINGS

Middlesex v Glamorgan (478-5d)	Cardiff

MOST EXTRAS IN AN INNINGS

53	Essex v Australians	Chelmsford
52	Leicestershire v Australians	Leicester
52	Derbyshire v Leicestershire	Chesterfield
50	England v Australia (6th Test)	The Oval

FIRST TO INDIVIDUAL TARGETS

1000 RUNS	C.L. Smith	Hampshire	June 13
2000 RUNS	G.A. Gooch	Essex	September 12
100 WICKETS	N.V. Radford	Worcestershire	September 17

TRIPLE HUNDRED AND 300 RUNS IN A DAY

I.V.A. Richards	322	Somerset v Warwickshire	Taunton

The most in a day in England since 1949 (J.D.B. Robertson 331)*

DOUBLE HUNDREDS

D.C. Boon	206*	Australians v Northants	Northampton
G.A. Gooch	202	Essex v Nottinghamshire	Nottingham
D.I. Gower	215	England v Australia (5th Test)	Birmingham
C.G. Greenidge	204	Hampshire v Warwickshire	Birmingham
G.A. Hick	230	Zimbabweans v Oxford U.	Oxford
Javed Miandad	200*	Glamorgan v Australians	Neath
C.T. Radley	200	Middlesex v Northants	Uxbridge
W.N. Slack	201*	Middlesex v Australians	Lord's

HUNDRED IN EACH INNINGS

G.D. Mendis	103	100*	Sussex v Lancashire	Hastings
R.T. Robinson	103	130*	Nottinghamshire v Glamorgan	Swansea
C.L. Smith	110	100	Hampshire v Oxford U.	Oxford

FOUR HUNDREDS IN SUCCESSIVE INNINGS

A.R. Border (Australians) 106 v Sm. 135 v Wo. 125 v MCC. 100 v D

THREE HUNDREDS IN SUCCESSIVE INNINGS

I.V.A. Richards (Somerset) 120 v La. 123 v D. 112 v Sx

FASTEST HUNDRED (WALTER LAWRENCE TROPHY)

I.T. Botham	50 balls	Somerset v Warwickshire	Birmingham

In 49 minutes and from 26 scoring strokes – 94 in boundaries.

HUNDRED BEFORE LUNCH

				Day
D.L. Bairstow	100*	Yorkshire v Leicestershire	Bradford	3
K.S. McEwan	110	Essex v Cambridge U.	Cambridge	3
A. Needham	124	Surrey v Zimbabweans	The Oval	2

HUNDRED ON FIRST-CLASS DEBUT

A.C. Storie	106	Northamptonshire v Hampshire	Northampton
M.P. Maynard	102	Glamorgan v Yorkshire	Swansea

In 87 minutes, out of 117, and including 5 sixes and 13 fours.

CARRYING BAT THROUGH COMPLETED INNINGS

G. Boycott	55*	(131)	Yorkshire v Surrey	Sheffield
P.M. Roebuck†	33*	(125)	Somerset v Australians	Taunton
W.N. Slack	72*	(195)	Middlesex v Worcestershire	Lord's

†one man absent

MOST RUNS OFF ONE OVER

30 (662664)	G.A. Gooch (off S.R. Gorman)	Essex v CU	Cambridge

FIFTY BOUNDARIES IN AN INNINGS

I.V.A. Richards	42×4 8×6	Somerset v Warwickshire	Taunton

TWELVE SIXES IN AN INNINGS

I.T. Botham	Somerset v Warwickshire	Birmingham

THREE SIXES OFF SUCCESSIVE BALLS

M.A. Lynch (off J.W. Lloyds)	Surrey v Gloucestershire	The Oval
M.P. Maynard (off P. Carrick)	Glamorgan v Yorkshire	Swansea

To complete his hundred on debut.

MOST SIXES IN A SEASON

I.T. Botham	80	Somerset and England	**WORLD RECORD**

NOTABLE PARTNERSHIPS

First Wicket

351 G. Boycott/M.D. Moxon, Yorkshire v Worcs	Worcester
250* J.A. Hopkins/G.C. Holmes, Glamorgan v Worcs	Abergavenny

Second Wicket

351 G.A. Gooch/D.I. Gower, England v Australia	The Oval
331 R.T. Robinson/D.I. Gower, England v Australia	Birmingham
263 N.R. Taylor/D.G. Aslett, Kent v Oxford U	Oxford
255 W. Larkins/R.J. Boyd-Moss, Northants v Worcs	Worcester
253 J.C. Balderstone/D.I. Gower, Leics v Australians	Leicester

Third Wicket

305 C.W.J. Athey/P. Bainbridge, Glos v Derbyshire	Derby

Fourth Wicket

306*† Javed Miandad/Younis Ahmed, Glam v Australians	Neath
277 G.A. Hick/D.L. Houghton, Zimbabweans v OU	Oxford
259 M.C.J. Nicholas/R.A. Smith, Hampshire v Leics	Bournemouth

Fifth Wicket

289 C.T. Radley/P.R. Downton, Middlesex v Northants	Uxbridge
252 A.J. Stewart/M.A. Lynch, Surrey v Kent	Canterbury
227 T.S. Curtis/M.J. Weston, Worcs v Surrey	Worcester

Eighth Wicket

227† K.D. James/T.M. Tremlett, Hampshire v Somerset	Taunton
186 K.W.R. Fletcher/D.E. East, Essex v Glos	Southend

Tenth Wicket

115 J. Stanworth/P.J.W. Allott, Lancashire v Glos	Bristol

†*County record*

FAST PARTNERSHIP

152 (29 min) J.D. Love/P.E. Robinson, Yorkshire v Sussex	Hove

NINE WICKETS IN AN INNINGS

J.P. Agnew	9-70	Leicestershire v Kent	Leicester

EIGHT WICKETS IN AN INNINGS

A.H. Gray 8-40, Surrey v Yorkshire	Sheffield
R.J. Hadlee 8-41, Nottinghamshire v Lancashire	Nottingham
C.J. McDermott 8-141, Australia v England (4th Test)	Manchester
V.J. Marks 8-17, Somerset v Lancashire	Bath
R.C. Ontong 8-67, Glamorgan v Nottinghamshire	Nottingham
G.J. Toogood 8-52, Oxford U. v Cambridge U.	Lord's

TEN OR MORE WICKETS IN A MATCH

J.P. Agnew	11-118	Leics v Kent	Leicester
P. Carrick	10-105	Yorks v Derbys	Chesterfield
R.M. Ellison (2)	11-164	Kent v Northants	Maidstone
	10-104	England v Aus. (5th Test)	Birmingham
A.M. Ferreira	10-84	Warwicks v Lancs	Manchester
A.H. Gray	10-119	Surrey v Yorks	Sheffield
M.A. Holding	10-118	Derbys v Warwicks	Chesterfield
R.K. Illingworth	13-59	Worcs v Oxford U.	Oxford
V.J. Marks (2)	11-73	Somerset v Lancs	Bath
	11-208	Somerset v Leics	Taunton
R.C. Ontong	13-106	Glam v Notts	Nottingham
B.P. Patterson	10-112	Lancs v Essex	Ilford
K. Saxelby	10-113	Notts v Kent	Tunbridge Wells
G.J. Toogood	10-93	Oxford U. v Camb U.	Lord's
D.L. Underwood	10-136	Kent v Essex	Dartford
C.A. Walsh	13-128	Glos v Warwicks	Cheltenham

FOUR WICKETS IN FIVE BALLS

A.H. Gray	Surrey v Yorkshire	Sheffield

HAT-TRICKS

P.B. Clift	Leicestershire v Derbyshire	Chesterfield
G.R. Dilley	Kent v Surrey	The Oval
A.H. Gray	Surrey v Yorkshire	Sheffield
P.W. Jarvis	Yorkshire v Derbyshire	Chesterfield

Youngest (20 yrs 25 days) to achieve hat-trick for Yorkshire.

MATCH DOUBLES (100 RUNS AND 10 WICKETS)

R.C. Ontong	130	13-106	Glam v Notts	Nottingham
G.J. Toogood	149	10-93	Oxford U. v Cambridge U.	Lord's

SIX OR MORE WICKET-KEEPING DISMISSALS IN AN INNINGS

8	D.E. East	(8 ct)	Essex v Somerset	Taunton

On his 26th birthday, the first 8 wickets to fall. **WORLD RECORD**

6	B.N. French	(6 ct)	Notts v Derbys	Nottingham

STUMPED BY A SUBSTITUTE

R.B. Phillips (2)	Australians v Somerset	Taunton

MIDDLESEX WIN BRITANNIC ASSURANCE CHAMPIONSHIP

Middlesex won the 1985 Britannic Assurance County Championship by 18 points at 3.01 on the final afternoon of the season. In doing so they overcame the loss of half their side to Test calls (not to mention the pre-season doubts of their captain), but were greatly helped in the wettest of summers by losing only 59 hours of play, the equivalent of nine complete days. Only Nottinghamshire (42 hours) lost less, whereas Northamptonshire (160 hours) and Gloucestershire (143.5) suffered most.

Congratulations to Middlesex must be tempered by revealing that they won only a third of their matches, their total of eight victories being the lowest by any champion county since 1903. Only 37% of matches produced positive results, the lowest in the entire history of the Championship. The obscene weather was mostly to blame but the current bonus points system places too great an emphasis on the first innings of matches. In each of the last 18 seasons the combined total of bonus points has exceeded that of points awarded for victory. In 1985 only 1,216 points were gained by winning matches compared with 2,054 bonus points.

Middlesex were alone in boasting four bowlers with over fifty wickets: Daniel 79, Cowans 60, Williams 54, Edmonds 51. Wayne Daniel's form, fitness, and recovery of a yard of pace were crucial factors in this unexpected success. Nor were their batsmen idle; Graham Barlow scored hundreds in each of five successive mid-season matches, Wilf Slack carried his bat through the first innings of his most successful season, Clive Radley marked his 22nd Championship year with his first double century, and Paul Downton contributed his maiden first-class hundred.

By August only Hampshire and Gloucestershire, 15th and last respectively in 1984, were serious challengers to Gatting's surprised team. Hampshire, although excitingly led by Mark Nicholas and reinforced by Greenidge and Marshall, failed to win a match between July 9 and August 27. Gloucestershire owed much to their influx of new and borrowed talent. By awarding seven caps they equalled the post-war record set by Lancashire and Warwickshire in 1946. Three of them – Walsh, Lawrence and Curran – shared 213 Championship wickets at 22.49 runs apiece.

Somerset's abject failure was as startling as the triumph of Middlesex.

Despite the services of three world-class players, they finished last for the first time since 1969. Although they gained the most batting bonus points (70), they could manage only a paltry 45 for bowling, 40 fewer than the champions. Botham and Richards jointly amassed 3,047 runs (avge 84.63), with 14 hundreds and 123 sixes in the competition. Botham scored 1,211 runs and averaged an incredible 100.91 per innings. His century off 50 balls with just 26 scoring strokes in 49 minutes against Warwickshire comfortably won the Walter Lawrence Trophy. In all first-class matches he averaged 124.8 runs/100 balls, 60.4 runs/hour and 2.96 sixes per innings. His 80 sixes easily exceeded the world record set by Arthur Wellard 50 years earlier. Richards enjoyed the rare privilege of earning three batting bonus points on his own on the first day, his 322 against Warwickshire being the highest innings for Somerset and by a West Indian in Britain.

BRITANNIC ASSURANCE COUNTY CHAMPIONSHIP FINAL TABLE

Win = 16 points*					*1st Inns Points*		*Total*
	P	*W*	*L*	*D*	*Bt*	*Bw*	*Pts*
1 Middlesex (3)	24	8	4	12	61	85	274
2 Hampshire (15)	24	7	2	15	66	78	256
3 Gloucestershire (17)	23	7	3	13	51	78	241
4 Essex (1)	23	7	2	14	42	70	224
5 Worcestershire (10)	24	5	6	13	65	68	221
6 Surrey (8)	24	5	5	14	62	76	218
7 Sussex (6)	23	6	1	16	52	57	205
8 Nottinghamshire (2)	24	4	2	18	66	69	199
9 Kent (5)	24	4	5	15	51	71	186
10 Northamptonshire (11)	24	5	4	15	52	51	183
11 Yorkshire (14)	23	3	4	16	58	59	165
12 Glamorgan (13)	24	4	4	16	41	50	163
13 Derbyshire (12)	24	3	9	12	46	69	163
14 Lancashire (16)	24	3	7	14	44	67	159
15 Warwickshire (9)	24	2	8	14	47	74	153
16 Leicestershire (4)	24	2	3	19	48	65	145
17 Somerset (7)	24	1	7	16	70	45	131

1984 final positions are shown in brackets.

*The totals for Worcestershire and Glamorgan include eight points for levelling the scores in drawn matches. Where sides are equal on points, the one with the most wins has priority.

The following two matches were abandoned and are not included in the above table: May 22, 23, 24 – Yorkshire v Essex at Sheffield; June 22, 24, 25 – Gloucestershire v Sussex at Bristol.

COUNTY CHAMPIONS

The English County Championship was not officially constituted until December 1889. Prior to that date there was no generally accepted method of awarding the title; although the 'least matches lost' method existed, it was not consistently applied. Rules governing playing qualifications were not agreed until 1873, and the first unofficial points system was not introduced until 1888. Recent research has produced a list of champions dating back to 1826, but at least seven different versions exist for the period from 1864 to 1889 (see *The Wisden Book of Cricket Records*). Only from 1890 can any authorised list of county champions commence. From 1977 to 1983 the Championship was sponsored by Schweppes, and since 1984 by Britannic Assurance.

1890	Surrey
1891	Surrey
1892	Surrey
1893	Yorkshire
1894	Surrey
1895	Surrey
1896	Yorkshire
1897	Lancashire
1898	Yorkshire
1899	Surrey
1900	Yorkshire
1901	Yorkshire
1902	Yorkshire
1903	Middlesex
1904	Lancashire
1905	Yorkshire
1906	Kent
1907	Nottinghamshire
1908	Yorkshire
1909	Kent
1910	Kent
1911	Warwickshire
1912	Yorkshire
1913	Kent
1914	Surrey
1919	Yorkshire
1920	Middlesex
1921	Middlesex
1922	Yorkshire
1923	Yorkshire
1924	Yorkshire
1925	Yorkshire
1926	Lancashire
1927	Lancashire
1928	Lancashire
1929	Nottinghamshire
1930	Lancashire
1931	Yorkshire
1932	Yorkshire
1933	Yorkshire
1934	Lancashire
1935	Yorkshire
1936	Derbyshire
1937	Yorkshire
1938	Yorkshire
1939	Yorkshire
1946	Yorkshire
1947	Middlesex
1948	Glamorgan
1949	Middlesex
	Yorkshire
1950	Lancashire
	Surrey
1951	Warwickshire
1952	Surrey
1953	Surrey
1954	Surrey
1955	Surrey
1956	Surrey
1957	Surrey
1958	Surrey
1959	Yorkshire
1960	Yorkshire
1961	Hampshire
1962	Yorkshire
1963	Yorkshire
1964	Worcestershire
1965	Worcestershire
1966	Yorkshire
1967	Yorkshire
1968	Yorkshire
1969	Glamorgan
1970	Kent
1971	Surrey
1972	Warwickshire
1973	Hampshire
1974	Worcestershire
1975	Leicestershire
1976	Middlesex
1977	Kent
	Middlesex
1978	Kent
1979	Essex
1980	Middlesex
1981	Nottinghamshire
1982	Middlesex
1983	Essex
1984	Essex
1985	Middlesex

ESSEX WIN NATWEST TROPHY

For the third time in its five-year existence the NatWest Trophy Final was decided off the very last ball. Essex won a most memorable match by a single run to claim their first 60-overs match title. When the last over began Nottinghamshire, needing 18 to win, seemed completely out of the hunt. Such situations have always brought the best out of Derek Randall and he plundered 16 runs off Derek Pringle's first five offerings (24244). Fletcher took a full minute to calm and set his fielders for the final ball. Randall again moved outside his leg stump to hit it on the off, was tucked up, and could only clip it to Paul Prichard who pulled down a difficult catch at mid-wicket. Put in, Gooch and Hardie opted for the steady start, the first six overs yielding just six runs. Then Brian Hardie took control and played the innings of his life, reaching 40 before Gooch could advance from 10. His audacity undermined Notts and richly deserved the match award. Their stand of 202 was a record for any wicket in an English final and provided a perfect springboard for a farewell cameo of deftly timed strokes by Ken McEwan. Undaunted by the fact that no side batting second had scored 281 in a final at Lord's, Robinson, Broad and Hadlee kept Notts on schedule. Lever's accuracy and some inspired fielding set them back before Randall, abetted by an impressive first limited-overs innings by Duncan Martindale, almost snatched a most improbable victory. An extremely relieved Fletcher thus became the first captain to lead his side to all four county titles.

GILLETTE CUP WINNERS

1963	Sussex	1969	Yorkshire	1975	Lancashire
1964	Sussex	1970	Lancashire	1976	Northamptonshire
1965	Yorkshire	1971	Lancashire	1977	Middlesex
1966	Warwickshire	1972	Lancashire	1978	Sussex
1967	Kent	1973	Gloucestershire	1979	Somerset
1968	Warwickshire	1974	Kent	1980	Middlesex

NATWEST BANK TROPHY WINNERS

1981	Derbyshire	1983	Somerset	1985	Essex
1982	Surrey	1984	Middlesex		

THE NATWEST BANK TROPHY 1985

FIRST ROUND 3 July	SECOND ROUND 17, 18 July	QUARTER-FINALS 7,8,9 August	SEMI-FINALS 21, 22 August	FINAL 7 September	
ESSEX†	ESSEX†	ESSEX†	ESSEX	ESSEX	ESSEX (£17,000)
Oxfordshire					
Cumberland	Middlesex				
MIDDLESEX†					
Derbyshire†	Durham	Kent (£2,125)			
DURHAM					
KENT†	KENT†				
Surrey					
Berkshire	HAMPSHIRE†	HAMPSHIRE	Hampshire† (£4,250)		
HAMPSHIRE†					
LEICESTERSHIRE	Leicestershire				
Norfolk†					
Buckinghamshire	SOMERSET	Somerset† (£2,125)			
SOMERSET†					
Cheshire†	Yorkshire†				
YORKSHIRE					
Bedfordshire†	GLOUCESTERSHIRE†	Gloucestershire† (£2,125)	NOTTS	Notts (£8,500)	
GLOUCESTERSHIRE					
NORTHAMPTONSHIRE	Northamptonshire				
Shropshire†					
NOTTINGHAMSHIRE†	NOTTINGHAMSHIRE†	NOTTINGHAMSHIRE			
Staffordshire					
Devon	Warwickshire				
WARWICKSHIRE†					
GLAMORGAN	GLAMORGAN†	Glamorgan† (£2,125)	Worcestershire† (£4,250)		
Scotland†					
Ireland	Sussex				
SUSSEX†					
LANCASHIRE	Lancashire†	WORCESTERSHIRE			
Suffolk†					
Hertfordshire†	WORCESTERSHIRE				
WORCESTERSHIRE					

Home team† Winning teams are shown in capitals. Amounts in brackets show prize-money won by that county.

1985 NATWEST TROPHY FINAL

Played at Lord's, London, on 7 September
Toss: Nottinghamshire. Result: Essex won by 1 run
Man of the Match: B.R. Hardie **Adjudicator:** P.B.H. May

ESSEX	**RUNS**	**MINS**	**BALLS**	**6s**	**4s**
G.A. Gooch b Pick	91	169	142	1	8
B.R. Hardie run out (Hemmings)	110	176	149	—	15
K.S. McEwan not out	46	47	39	1	4
D.R. Pringle not out	29	40	30	—	2
P.J. Prichard, *K.W.R. Fletcher, A.W. Lilley, †D.E. East, S. Turner, I.L. Pont, J.K. Lever — did not bat					
Extras (B1, LB3, W—, NB—)	4				
Total (60 overs – 217 minutes)	280-2				

NOTTINGHAMSHIRE	**RUNS**	**MINS**	**BALLS**	**6s**	**4s**
R.T. Robinson c Hardie b Turner	80	149	142	1	4
B.C. Broad run out (Pont/East)	64	137	107	—	6
*C.E.B. Rice c Hardie b Turner	12	26	19	—	1
D.W. Randall c Prichard b Pringle	66	72	54	—	6
R.J. Hadlee b Pont	22	20	17	1	2
D.J.R. Martindale not out	20	33	22	—	—
†B.N. French, E.E. Hemmings, R.A. Pick, K. Saxelby, K.E. Cooper — did not bat					
Extras (B—, LB14, W—, NB1)	15				
Total (60 overs – 222 minutes)	279-5				

NOTTINGHAMSHIRE	*O*	*M*	*R*	*W*
Hadlee	12	4	48	0
Cooper	9	3	27	0
Saxelby	12	0	73	0
Rice	7	0	38	0
Pick	8	0	36	1
Hemmings	12	1	54	0
ESSEX				
Lever	12	2	53	0
Pont	12	0	54	1
Turner	12	1	43	2
Gooch	12	0	47	0
Pringle	12	1	68	1

FALL OF WICKETS

Wkt	*E*	*Nt*
1st	202	143
2nd	203	153
3rd	—	173
4th	—	214
5th	—	279
6th	—	—
7th	—	—
8th	—	—
9th	—	—
10th	—	—

Umpires: D.J. Constant and B.J. Meyer

*Captain †Wicket-keeper

NATWEST BANK TROPHY
PRINCIPAL RECORDS 1963-1985
(Including The Gillette Cup)

Highest Total: 392-5 Warwicks v Oxon; Birmingham 1984
Highest Total in a Final: 317-4 Yorkshire v Surrey; Lord's 1965
Highest Total by a Minor County: 256 Oxon v Warwicks; Birmingham 1983
Highest Total Batting Second: 306-6 Glos v Leics; Leicester 1983
Highest Losing Total: 302-5 Leics v Glos; Leicester 1983
Lowest Total: 39 Ireland v Sussex; Hove 1985
Lowest Total in a Final: 118 Lancashire v Kent; Lord's 1974
Lowest Total to Win Batting First: 98 Worcs v Durham; Chester-le-Street 1968
Highest Score: 206 A.I. Kallicharran, Warwicks v Oxon; Birmingham 1984
HS (Minor County): 132 G. Robinson, Lincolnshire v Northumberland; Jesmond 1971
Hundreds: 137 have been scored in GC (93) and NWT (44) matches
Fastest Hundred: 77 min – R.E. Marshall, Hampshire v Bedfordshire; Goldington 1967

Highest Partnerships for Each Wicket

1st	227	R.E. Marshall/B.L. Reed, Hampshire v Beds; Goldington	1981
2nd	223	M.J. Smith/C.T. Radley, Middlesex v Hants; Lord's	1977
3rd	179	G.A. Gooch/K.S. McEwan, Essex v Scotland; Chelmsford	1984
4th	234*	D. Lloyd/C.H. Lloyd, Lancs v Glos; Manchester	1978
5th	166	M.A. Lynch/G.R.J. Roope, Surrey v Durham; The Oval	1982
6th	105	G. St A. Sobers/R.A. White, Notts v Worcs; Worcester	1974
7th	160*	C.J. Richards/I.R. Payne, Surrey v Lincs; Sleaford	1983
8th	69	S.J. Rouse/D.J. Brown, Warwicks v Middx; Lord's	1977
9th	87	M.A. Nash/A.E. Cordle, Glamorgan v Lincs; Swansea	1974
10th	81	S. Turner/R.E. East, Essex v Yorkshire; Leeds	1982

Most Wickets	7-15 A.L. Dixon, Kent v Surrey; Oval	1967
	7-30 P.J. Sainsbury, Hants v Norfolk; Southampton	1965
	7-32 S.P. Davis, Durham v Lancs; Chester-le-Street	1983
	7-33 R.D. Jackman, Surrey v Yorkshire; Harrogate	1970
	7-37 N.A. Mallender, Northants v Worcs; Northampton	1984
Hat Tricks	J.D.F. Larter, Northants v Sussex; Northampton	1963
	D.A.D. Sydenham, Surrey v Cheshire; Hoylake	1964
	R.N.S. Hobbs, Essex v Middlesex; Lord's	1968
	N.M. McVicker, Warwicks v Lincs; Birmingham	1971
	G.S. Le Roux, Sussex v Ireland; Hove	1985

Most Wicket-Keeping Dismissals

6 (5 ct, 1 st) R.W. Taylor, Derbys v Essex; Derby 1981

Most Catches in the Field

4	A.S. Brown, Glos v Middlesex; Bristol	1963
4	G. Cook, Northants v Glam; Northampton	1972
4	C.G. Greenidge, Hants v Cheshire; Southampton	1981
4	D.C. Jackson, Durham v Northants; Darlington	1984
4	T.S. Smith, Herts v Somerset; St Albans	1984

Most Match Awards: 8 C.H. Lloyd (Lancashire); 6 B.L. D'Oliveira (Worcestershire) and B. Wood (Lancashire); 5 G. Cook (Northamptonshire), M.C. Cowdrey (Kent), G.A. Gooch (Essex), A.W. Greig (Sussex), T.E. Jesty (Hampshire) and R.D.V. Knight (Gloucestershire and Surrey).

NATWEST BANK TROPHY

PRINCIPAL RECORDS 1981-1985

Highest Total: 392-5 Warwicks v Oxon; Birmingham 1984
Highest Total by a Minor County: 256 Oxon v Warwicks; Birmingham 1983
Highest Total Batting Second: 306-6 Glos v Leics; Leicester 1983
Highest Losing Total: 302-5 Leics v Glos; Leicester 1983
Lowest Total: 39 Ireland v Sussex; Hove 1985
Highest Score: 206 A.I. Kallicharran, Warwicks v Oxon; Birmingham 1984
HS (Minor County): 119 P.A. Fowler, Oxon v Warwicks; Birmingham 1983
Hundreds: 44 have been scored in NatWest Trophy matches

Highest Partnerships for Each Wicket

1st	202	G.A. Gooch/B.R. Hardie, Essex v Notts; Lord's	1985
2nd	197	K.D. Smith/A.I. Kallicharran, Warwicks v Oxon; Birmingham	1984
3rd	179	G.A. Gooch/K.S. McEwan, Essex v Scotland; Chelmsford	1984
4th	154	P.W.G. Parker/C.M. Wells, Sussex v Ireland; Hove	1985
5th	166	M.A. Lynch/G.R.J. Roope, Surrey v Durham; The Oval	1982
6th	104	I.T. Botham/N.F.M. Popplewell, Somerset v Middx; Lord's	1983
	104	C.H. Lloyd/M. Watkinson, Lancashire v Worcs; Manchester	1985
7th	160*	C.J. Richards/I.R. Payne, Surrey v Lincs; Sleaford	1983
8th	54	C.S. Cowdrey/R.M. Ellison, Kent v Essex; Chelmsford	1983
9th	62	Asif Din/G.C. Small, Warwicks v Surrey; Lord's	1982
10th	81	S. Turner/R.E. East, Essex v Yorkshire; Leeds	1982

Most Wickets 7-32 S.P. Davis, Durham v Lancs; Chester-le-Street 1983

Hat Trick G.S. Le Roux, Sussex v Ireland; Hove 1985

Most Economical Analyses (12 overs)

O	*M*	*R*	*W*		
12	9	3	1	J. Simmons, Lancs v Suffolk; Bury St. Edmunds	1985
12	8	4	2	P. Willey, Leics v Norfolk; Norwich	1985

Most Expensive Analyses

O	*M*	*R*	*W*		
12	0	106	2	D.A. Gallop, Oxon v Warwicks; Birmingham	1984
12	0	105	1	S.R. Porter, Oxon v Warwicks; Birmingham	1984

Most Wicket-Keeping Dismissals

6 (5 ct, 1 st) R.W. Taylor, Derbys v Essex; Derby 1981

Most Catches in the Field

4	C.G. Greenidge, Hants v Cheshire; Southampton	1981
4	D.C. Jackson, Durham v Northants; Darlington	1984
4	T.S. Smith, Herts v Somerset; St. Albans	1984

LEICESTERSHIRE OUST FAVOURITES TO WIN BENSON AND HEDGES CUP

Guided by the determined professionalism of Peter Willey, Leicestershire won the Benson and Hedges Cup for the third time. In doing so they recorded the highest total to win the final of this competition by a team batting second, beating Essex, the undoubted favourites, by three wickets with 18 balls to spare.

Scheduled for the middle of the wettest portion of one of the more miserable apologies for any English summer, the final was blessed with that rare surprise, a fine day. An inevitably sluggish pitch made for a dour and predictable match until Peter Willey, perhaps inspired by the Randallesque impetuosity of Garnham's running between the wickets, accelerated the end by forcing boundaries off four of the last ten balls he faced. Willey's calmness, allied to the immense strength of forearm which brought him half his side's boundaries, steered the Cup back to Grace Road after a ten-year absence and eased Denis Compton's adjudication worries.

Psychologically Essex probably never atoned for the loss of both their injured captain and the toss. Although the absence of their canny old gnome thrust extra pressure on Graham Gooch, he led the side most ably, contributed his 25th fifty in 60 innings in this competition, and temporarily recovered the initiative for Essex with a dramatic spell of swing bowling which claimed two wickets at a cost of only five runs in 14 balls, and earned him the accolade of an umpire's warning for damaging the pitch.

BENSON AND HEDGES CUP WINNERS

1972	Leicestershire	1977	Gloucestershire	1982	Somerset
1973	Kent	1978	Kent	1983	Middlesex
1974	Surrey	1979	Essex	1984	Lancashire
1975	Leicestershire	1980	Northamptonshire	1985	Leicestershire
1976	Kent	1981	Somerset		

1985 BENSON AND HEDGES CUP

GROUP A	*P*	*W*	*L*	*NR*	*Pts*
NORTHAMPTONSHIRE	4	2	0	2	6
DERBYSHIRE	4	2	1	1	5
Nottinghamshire	4	2	1	1	5
Gloucestershire	4	2	2	—	4
Scotland	4	0	4	—	0
GROUP B	*P*	*W*	*L*	*NR*	*Pts*
WORCESTERSHIRE	4	3	1	—	6
LEICESTERSHIRE	4	3	1	—	6
Yorkshire	4	2	2	—	4
Warwickshire	4	1	3	—	2
Lancashire	4	1	3	—	2
GROUP C	*P*	*W*	*L*	*NR*	*Pts*
ESSEX	4	4	0	—	8
MIDDLESEX	4	2	2	—	4
Surrey	4	2	2	—	4
Sussex	4	2	2	—	4
Combined Univ.	4	0	4	—	0
GROUP D	*P*	*W*	*L*	*NR*	*Pts*
HAMPSHIRE	4	4	0	—	8
KENT	4	3	1	—	6
Glamorgan	4	2	2	—	4
Somerset	4	1	3	—	2
Minor Counties	4	0	4	—	0

Note: where two or more teams in a group have equal points, their positions are determined by the faster rate of taking wickets in all zonal matches (total balls bowled divided by wickets taken).

FINAL ROUNDS

QUARTER-FINALS 5, 6, 7 June	SEMI-FINALS 19, 20 June	FINAL 20 July	
ESSEX† Derbyshire (£2,125)	ESSEX†	Essex (£8,500)	LEICESTERSHIRE (£17,000)
MIDDLESEX Worcestershire† (£2,125)	Middlesex (£4,250)		
KENT Northamptonshire† (£2,125)	Kent (£4,250)	LEICESTERSHIRE	
Hampshire† (£2,125) LEICESTERSHIRE	LEICESTERSHIRE†		

Home team† Winning teams in capitals. Prize-money in brackets.

1985 BENSON AND HEDGES CUP FINAL

Played at Lord's, London, on 20 July
Toss: Leicestershire. Result: Leicestershire won by 5 wickets
Man of the Match: P. Willey **Adjudicator:** D.C.S. Compton

ESSEX	RUNS	MINS	BALLS	6s	4s
*G.A. Gooch b Willey	57	122	105	—	3
B.R. Hardie c & b Clift	25	98	76	—	1
P.J. Prichard b Taylor	32	55	46	—	4
K.S. McEwan c Garnham b Taylor	29	50	38	—	2
D.R. Pringle c Agnew b Taylor	10	13	15	—	1
C. Gladwin b Clift	14	23	17	—	2
A.W. Lilley b Agnew	12	27	17	—	1
†D.E. East not out	7	17	10	—	1
S. Turner run out (Balderstone)	3	2	4	—	—
N.A. Foster not out	6	7	4	—	1
J.K. Lever did not bat					
Extras (B1, LB15, W1, NB1)	18				
Total (55 overs, 214 minutes)	213-8				

LEICESTERSHIRE	RUNS	MINS	BALLS	6s	4s
†I.P. Butcher c Prichard b Turner	19	63	49	—	2
J.C. Balderstone c Prichard b Pringle	12	49	38	—	—
*D.I. Gower c Lilley b Foster	43	77	61	—	5
P. Willey not out	86	144	96	—	12
J.J. Whitaker b Gooch	1	8	9	—	—
N.E. Briers lbw b Gooch	6	16	16	—	1
M.A. Garnham not out	34	54	45	—	4
P.B. Clift, G.J. Parsons, J.P. Agnew, L.B. Taylor did not bat					
Extras (B2, LB9, W2, NB1)	14				
Total (52 overs, 209 minutes)	215-5				

LEICESTERSHIRE	*O*	*M*	*R*	*W*
Agnew	11	1	51	1
Taylor	11	3	26	3
Parsons	11	0	39	0
Clift	11	1	40	2
Willey	11	0	41	1
ESSEX				
Lever	11	0	50	0
Foster	11	2	32	1
Pringle	10	0	42	1
Turner	10	1	40	1
Gooch	10	1	40	2

FALL OF WICKETS

Wkt	*Ex*	*Le*
1st	71	33
2nd	101	37
3rd	147	120
4th	163	123
5th	164	135
6th	191	—
7th	195	—
8th	198	—
9th	—	—
10th	—	—

Umpires: H.D. Bird and K.E. Palmer

*Captain †Wicket-keeper

BENSON AND HEDGES CUP

PRINCIPAL RECORDS 1972-1985

Highest Total: 350-3 Essex v Comb Univs; Chelmsford	1979
Highest Total Batting Second: 291-5 Warwicks v Lancs; Manchester	1981
Highest Losing Total: 294-7 Glos v Somerset; Taunton	1982
Lowest Total: 56 Leics v Minor C; Wellington	1982
Highest Score: 198* G.A. Gooch, Essex v Sussex; Hove	1982
Hundreds: 118 have been scored in Benson and Hedges Cup matches	

Highest Partnerships for Each Wicket

1st	241	S.M. Gavaskar/B.C. Rose, Somerset v Kent; Canterbury	1980
2nd	285*	C.G. Greenidge/D.R. Turner, Hants v Minor C (S); Amersham	1973
3rd	268*	G.A. Gooch/K.W.R. Fletcher, Essex v Sussex; Hove	1982
4th	184*	D. Lloyd/B.W. Reidy, Lancashire v Derbys; Chesterfield	1980
5th	134	M. Maslin/D.N.F. Slade, Minor C (E) v Notts; Nottingham	1976
6th	114	Majid Khan/G.P. Ellis, Glamorgan v Glos; Bristol	1975
7th	149*	J.D. Love/C.M. Old, Yorks v Scotland; Bradford	1981
8th	109	R.E. East/N. Smith, Essex v Northants; Chelmsford	1977
9th	85	P.G. Newman/M.A. Holding, Derbyshire v Notts; Nottingham	1985
10th	80*	D.L. Bairstow/M. Johnson, Yorkshire v Derbys; Derby	1981

Most Wickets	7-12 W.W. Daniel, Middx v Minor C (E); Ipswich	1978
	7-22 J.R. Thomson, Middx v Hampshire; Lord's	1981
	7-32 R.G.D. Willis, Warwicks v Yorks; Birmingham	1981

Hat Tricks	G.D. McKenzie, Leics v Worcs; Worcester	1972
	K. Higgs, Leics v Surrey; Lord's	1974
	A.A. Jones, Middlesex v Essex; Lord's	1977
	M.J. Procter, Glos v Hampshire; Southampton	1977
	W. Larkins, Northants v Comb Univs; Northampton	1980
	E.A. Moseley, Glamorgan v Kent; Cardiff	1981
	G.C. Small, Warwicks v Leics; Leicester	1984

Most Wicket-Keeping Dismissals

8 (8 ct)	D.J.S. Taylor, Somerset v Comb Univs; Taunton	1982

Most Catches in the Field

5	V.J. Marks, Comb Univs v Kent; Oxford	1976

Most Match Awards: 12 G.A. Gooch (Essex); 11 B. Wood (Lancashire and Derbyshire); 10 J.C. Balderstone (Leicestershire); G. Boycott (Yorkshire) and J.H. Edrich (Surrey); 8 T.E. Jesty (Hampshire and Surrey) and C.E.B. Rice (Nottinghamshire).

JOHN PLAYER LEAGUE 1985

ESSEX COMPLETE UNIQUE DOUBLE

Essex emulated Lancashire and Kent by retaining the John Player League title. On the final evening of the competition and only eight days after their last-ball NatWest Trophy triumph, they achieved a unique double in a similarly desperate finish. A capacity Chelmsford crowd saw Foster secure a two-wicket win against Yorkshire with an on-drive off the penultimate ball of the match. It completed a sequence of eight wins in nine matches, gained the Sunday trophy for the third time (equalling Kent's record), and was a fitting reward for the team. It is hard to believe that, until 1979, Essex had failed to claim a single title in 103 years of existence. This success was their eighth in seven years (three Championships, two Cup Finals and three Sunday Leagues), and it brought their winnings for the season to £50,000. What a marvellous finale to Keith Fletcher's reign as captain and to Ken McEwan's career in England. Had Essex failed to reach their target of 232, Sussex would have gained their Sunday title. After comfortably defeating Glamorgan to earn a temporary two-point lead, they could only watch their dressing-room television in disbelief as Paul Prichard's inspired strokeplay yielded 14 runs during the 39th over to virtually seal their fate.

JOHN PLAYER LEAGUE FINAL TABLE

		P	*W*	*L*	*T*	*NR*	*Pts*	*6s*	*4w*
1	ESSEX (1)	16	9	3	1	3	44	21	4
2	Sussex (3)	16	10	5	—	1	42	41	6
3	Hampshire (9)	16	8	4	—	4	40	27	2
4	Derbyshire (17)	16	8	5	—	3	38	39	3
5	Northamptonshire (12)	16	7	4	1	4	38	33	2
6	Gloucestershire (13)	16	8	8	—	0	32	39	3
	Warwickshire (7)	16	7	7	—	2	32	30	2
	Yorkshire (13)	16	6	6	—	4	32	26	—
	Leicestershire (13)	16	5	5	1	5	32	11	—
10	Kent (9)	16	6	7	—	3	30	16	2
	Somerset (13)	16	5	6	—	5	30	32	3
12	Nottinghamshire (2)	16	6	8	—	2	28	24	—
	Middlesex (5)	16	5	7	—	4	28	20	—
14	Glamorgan (9)	16	4	7	1	4	26	14	2
	Lancashire (4)	16	3	6	2	5	26	22	2
16	Worcestershire (5)	16	5	9	—	2	24	28	1
17	Surrey (8)	16	4	9	—	3	22	37	1

For the first four places only, the final positions for teams finishing with equal points are decided by the most wins.
1984 final positions are shown in brackets.

JOHN PLAYER LEAGUE

PRINCIPAL RECORDS 1969-1985

Highest Total: 310-5 Essex v Glamorgan; Southend 1983
Highest Total Batting Second: 301-6 Warwicks v Essex; Colchester 1982
Lowest Total: 23 Middlesex v Yorks; Leeds 1974
Highest Score: 176 G.A. Gooch, Essex v Glamorgan; Southend 1983
Hundreds: 253 have been scored in John Player League matches

Highest Partnerships for Each Wicket

1st	239	G.A. Gooch/B.R. Hardie, Essex v Notts; Nottingham	1985
2nd	273	G.A. Gooch/K.S. McEwan, Essex v Notts; Nottingham	1983
3rd	215	W. Larkins/R.G. Williams, Northants v Worcs; Luton	1982
4th	178	J.J. Whitaker/P. Willey, Leics v Glamorgan; Swansea	1984
5th	179	I.T. Botham/I.V.A. Richards, Somerset v Hants; Taunton	1981
6th	121	C.P. Wilkins/A.J. Borrington, Derbys v Warwicks; Chesterfield	1972
7th	101	S.J. Windaybank/D.A. Graveney, Glos v Notts; Nottingham	1981
8th	95*	D. Breakwell/K.F. Jennings, Somerset v Notts; Nottingham	1976
9th	105	D.G. Moir/R.W. Taylor, Derbyshire v Kent; Derby	1984
10th	57	D.A. Graveney/J.B. Mortimore, Glos v Lancs; Tewkesbury	1973

Most Wickets	8-26	K.D. Boyce, Essex v Lancashire; Manchester	1971
	7-15	R.A. Hutton, Yorkshire v Worcs; Leeds	1969
	7-39	A. Hodgson, Northants v Somerset; Northampton	1976

Four Wickets in Four Balls: A. Ward, Derbyshire v Sussex; Derby 1970

Hat Tricks: 16 bowlers have achieved this feat in League matches: Derbyshire – A. Ward (1970), C.J. Tunnicliffe (1979); Essex – K.D. Boyce (1971); Glamorgan – M.A. Nash (1975), A.E. Cordle (1979); Hampshire – J.M. Rice (1975), M.D. Marshall (1981); Kent – R.M. Ellison (1983); Leicestershire – G.D. McKenzie (1972); Northamptonshire – A. Hodgson (1976); Somerset – R. Palmer (1970), I.V.A. Richards (1982); Sussex – A. Buss (1974); Warwickshire – R.G.D. Willis (1973), W. Blenkiron (1974); Yorkshire – P.W. Jarvis (1982).

Most Economical Analysis

O	*M*	*R*	*W*		
8	8	0	0	B.A. Langford, Somerset v Essex; Yeovil	1969

Most Expensive Analyses

O	*M*	*R*	*W*		
7.5	0	89	3	G. Miller, Derbys v Glos; Gloucester	1984
8	0	88	1	E.E. Hemmings, Notts v Somerset; Nottingham	1983

Most Wicket-Keeping Dismissals

7 (6 ct, 1 st) R.W. Taylor, Derbyshire v Lancs; Manchester 1975

Most Catches in the Field

5 J.M. Rice, Hants v Warwicks; Southampton 1978

JOHN PLAYER LEAGUE CHAMPIONS

1969	Lancashire	1975	Hampshire	1981	Essex
1970	Lancashire	1976	Kent	1982	Sussex
1971	Worcestershire	1977	Leicestershire	1983	Yorkshire
1972	Kent	1978	Hampshire	1984	Essex
1973	Kent	1979	Somerset	1985	Essex
1974	Leicestershire	1980	Warwickshire		

MINOR COUNTIES CRICKET

UNITED FRIENDLY INSURANCE COUNTY CHAMPIONSHIP 1985
FINAL TABLE

EASTERN DIVISION (Points:)		*Played*	*Won* (10)	*Lost*	*w 1st Inns* (3)	*t 1st Inns* (2)	*l 1st Inns* (1)	*no Result* (2)	*Points*
Suffolk	NW	9	3	1*	1	1	3	—	41
Staffordshire	NW	9	3	3*	1	—	1	1	39
Cumberland	NW	9	2	1*	1	—	3	2	33
Durham	NW	9	2	1	3	1	2	—	33
Hertfordshire	NW	9	2	—	1	—	4	2	31
Northumberland	NW	9	1	1†	4	2	—	1	30
Cambridgeshire	NW	9	2	2	2	—	3	1	29
Norfolk		9	1	1*	2	2	1	2	28
Lincolnshire		9	—	3*	3	—	1	2	17
Bedfordshire		9	—	3	2	2	2	—	12

WESTERN DIVISION		*Played*	*Won*	*Lost*	*W 1st Inns*	*T 1st Inns*	*L 1st Inns*	*No Result*	*Points*
Cheshire	NW	9	5	—	2	—	2	—	58
Devon	NW	9	1	—	3	1	4	—	25
Berkshire	NW	9	1	2*	1	1	2	2	24
Cornwall	NW	9	1	1	2	1	2	2	24
Dorset	NW	9	—	1*	5	—	3	—	21
Oxfordshire	NW	9	—	—	4	2	2	1	20
Somerset II		9	—	—	3	1	3	2	18
Buckinghamshire		9	—	2*	3	1	3	—	17
Shropshire		9	—	2*	2	—	2	3	17
Wiltshire		9	—	—	2	1	4	2	16

* 1st Innings points in 1 match lost
† Tie on 1st Innings in 1 match lost
NW Qualified for 1986 NatWest Trophy
Where sides finished equal on points and wins, the one with a superior nett batting average took precedence.

UNITED FRIENDLY INSURANCE CHAMPIONSHIP FINAL 1985

Played at The County Ground, Worcester, on 7 September 1985
Toss: Suffolk. Result: Cheshire won by 58 runs

CHESHIRE		
I. Tansley	c McEvoy b Wright	0
J.J. Hitchmough	c Brown b Hayes	32
I. Cockbain	b Hayes	45
N.T. O'Brien	c McEvoy b Bailey	21
S.C. Yates	c Green b Wright	21
S.T. Crawley	lbw b Herbert	1
*J.A. Sutton	run out	24
K. Teasdale	not out	17
K.B.K. Ibadulla	b Green	2
†J.K. Pickup	lbw b Green	0
A.J. Murphy	run out	1
Extras		30
Total		194
SUFFOLK		
P.D. Barker	c Teasdale b Murphy	1
*M.S.A. McEvoy	run out	5
R. Herbert	c Teasdale b Murphy	16
G. Morgan	b Sutton	31
P.J. Caley	b O'Brien	27
R. Bond	lbw b Sutton	14
P.J. Hayes	c Yates b Sutton	2
H. Wright	b O'Brien	2
R. Green	b Murphy	9
M.D. Bailey	not out	8
†A.D. Brown	not out	4
Extras		17
Total (9 wickets)		136

CHESHIRE	*O*	*M*	*R*	*W*
Green	10	1	43	2
Wright	10.2	2	44	2
Hayes	11	3	16	2
Bailey	11	3	35	1
Herbert	11	0	33	1
SUFFOLK				
Murphy	11	1	29	3
Crawley	11	2	22	0
Sutton	11	1	27	3
Teasdale	11	1	33	0
O'Brien	11	4	15	2

FALL OF WICKETS

Wkt	*Ches*	*Suff*
1st	1	3
2nd	85	26
3rd	94	28
4th	131	79
5th	140	102
6th	145	107
7th	183	110
8th	189	110
9th	189	122
10th	—	—

Man of the Match: J.A. Sutton **Adjudicator:** D. Humphries
Umpires: K.S. Shenton & T.G. Wilson

LEADING AVERAGES 1985

Qualifications: Batting – 8 Innings, Average 25
Bowling – 20 Wickets, Average 25

BATTING

		I	*NO*	*Runs*	*HS*	*Avge*
Parvez Mir	Norfolk	9	4	332	126*	66.40
A. Fordham	Beds	8	0	454	123	56.75
G.S. Warner	Staffs	9	4	272	82*	54.40
Mudassar Nazar	Cheshire	12	3	488	112*	54.22
S.J. Halliday	Dorset	13	3	526	96*	52.60
N.J. Archer	Staffs	12	7	260	63*	52.00
N. Priestley	Lincs	15	4	551	126*	50.09
R.J. Harden	Som II	8	4	190	43	47.50
R.L. Ollis	Som II	9	2	330	170*	47.14
J.R. Moyes	Cumb	12	4	356	129	44.50
D.R. Parry	Cambs	14	3	486	108	44.18
G.R.J. Roope	Berks	15	4	483	76*	43.91
N.A. Riddell	Durham	17	3	594	91	42.43
A. Kennedy	Dorset	16	2	589	171*	42.07
K. Gentle	Beds	18	2	627	104*	39.19
I. Tansley	Cheshire	16	2	541	118*	38.64
D. Lloyd	Cumb	11	1	382	93	38.20
J.A. Waterhouse	Staffs	9	4	187	50*	37.40
M.S.T. Dunstan	Cornwall	8	2	218	72	36.33
S.G. Plumb	Norfolk	12	4	286	58*	35.75
J. Foster	Shrops	11	1	356	65	35.60
S.R. Atkinson	Durham	11	0	380	94	34.55
A.S. Patel	Durham	17	3	480	106	34.29
D. Cartledge	Staffs	14	1	445	78	34.23
D.S. Steele	Beds	10	3	239	39	34.14
R.P. Twose	Devon	8	0	272	91	34.00
W.M. Osman	Herts	8	0	271	88	33.88
P.A. Marshall	Staffs	17	4	438	133*	33.69
K. Pearson	N'land	15	3	392	115*	32.67
M.D. Nurton	Oxon	17	5	390	72*	32.50
J.F. Harvey	Berks	12	5	226	48*	32.29
P.G. Ingham	N'land	9	3	190	63	31.67
S.C. Yates	Cheshire	11	2	284	83	31.56
C.J. Edwards	Devon	16	7	283	53*	31.44
M.S.A. McEvoy	Suffolk	14	1	403	70	31.00
P.J. Caley	Suffolk	13	3	307	67	30.70
M.G. Lickley	Berks	15	2	381	78*	29.31
K.C. Williams	N'land	9	2	204	57*	29.14
S. Greensword	Durham	15	3	346	69	28.83
S.J. Lines	Beds	15	2	368	67	28.31
J.R. Carter	Norfolk	10	2	224	81	28.00
G.R. Morris	N'land	9	2	195	75*	27.86
C.S. Bannister	Herts	8	0	221	58	27.63
N.T. Gadsby	Cambs	14	1	357	83*	27.46
R.J. Lanchbury	Wilts	11	1	274	72	27.40
B.H. White	Wilts	9	0	246	67	27.33

Batting (*cont.*)		*I*	*NO*	*Runs*	*HS*	*Avge*
N.T. O'Brien	Cheshire	14	1	353	64	27.15
M.A. Fell	Lincs	11	0	297	67	27.00
B.W. Reidy	Cumb	8	0	216	70	27.00
M.E. Younger	N'land	11	3	216	59*	27.00
P.J. Hayes	Suffolk	12	6	161	43*	26.83
D. Halliwell	Cumb	8	5	80	42*	26.67
G.R. Black	Bucks	15	3	319	68	26.58
R.D. Huggins	Norfolk	14	6	209	45	26.13
K.G. Rice	Devon	12	0	313	82	26.08
J.J. Hitchmough	Cheshire	15	1	360	74	25.71
G. Clarke	Cumb	13	1	306	91	25.50
A. Zahid	Devon	11	0	278	83	25.27
E.P. Neal	Herts	10	1	227	54	25.22
M. Woods	Cumb	15	1	351	64	25.07

BOWLING

		O	*M*	*R*	*W*	*Avge*
G.R. Black	Bucks	105.4	26	252	22	11.45
M. Woods	Cumb	85.4	28	236	20	11.80
S. Burrow	Bucks	141.2	54	284	21	13.52
D.R. Parry	Cambs	329	84	753	53	14.21
J.A. Sutton	Cheshire	203	70	555	38	14.61
H.A. Page	Staffs	144	36	369	25	14.76
Mudassar Nazar	Cheshire	129	32	305	20	15.25
A.R. Wingfield-Digby	Dorset	166.4	49	518	33	15.70
M.A. Watts	Wilts	187	44	489	31	15.77
P.C. Graham	N'land	152.1	42	402	25	16.08
S.R. Porter	Oxon	110.1	13	436	26	16.77
D.C. Blank	Staffs	163.3	38	425	25	17.00
A.J. Buzza	Cornwall	167	43	522	29	18.00
D. Halliwell	Cumb	180.2	46	476	26	18.31
I.E.W. Sanders	Dorset	135.1	41	385	21	18.33
D.A. Toseland	Cornwall	201.3	83	390	21	18.57
R.C. Green	Suffolk	199.3	41	578	31	18.65
J.P. Dawson	Shrops	154	41	394	21	18.76
Mushtaq Mohammed	Shrops	148	45	378	20	18.90
P.J. Kippax	Durham	207.3	58	496	26	19.08
D.S. Steele	Beds	160.4	43	490	25	19.60
A.W. Scott	Durham	160.5	23	543	27	20.11
G.V. Palmer	Som II	107	21	403	20	20.15
D.I. Yeabsley	Devon	215	57	551	27	20.41
P.J. Lewington	Berks	199.3	61	525	25	21.00
M.D. Harman	Som II	171.4	33	459	21	21.86
Parvez Mir	Norfolk	196	65	447	20	22.35
R. Herbert	Suffolk	182.4	38	512	22	23.27
R.W. Flower	Staffs	186.3	58	532	22	24.18
A.W. Allin	Devon	238.1	76	608	25	24.32
A.J. Webster	Staffs	162	33	511	21	24.33

SECOND XI CHAMPIONSHIP
FINAL TABLE

Position	P	W	L	D	Bt	Bw	Total	Avge Points Played
		Results			*Bonus Points*			
1 Nottinghamshire	15	7	2	6	21	46	171†	11.40
2 Surrey	13	6	2	5	29	38	147‡	11.30
3 Middlesex	14	5	2	7	33	44	157	11.21
4 Sussex	12	4	4	4	22	39	125	10.41
5 Lancashire	16	4	3	9	35	50	149	9.31
6 Essex	13	3	5	5	23	43	114	8.76
7 Warwickshire	18	4	3	11	39	46	149	8.27
8 Kent	15	2	3	10	38	44	114	7.60
9 Glamorgan	14	3	2	9	22	35	105	7.50
10 Worcestershire	11	2	1	8	20	29	81	7.36
11 Leicestershire	14	2	2	10	29	40	101	7.21
12 Yorkshire	14	3	3	8	25	26	95*	6.87
13 Hampshire	12	1	4	7	24	41	81	6.75
14 Somerset	11	1	2	8	27	24	63*	5.72
15 Derbyshire	12	1	3	8	24	25	61*	5.08
16 Northamptonshire	13	0	3	10	23	35	58	4.46
17 Gloucestershire	9	0	4	5	6	23	29	3.22

*includes 12 points for 1 win in 1 innings match.
†includes 24 points for 2 wins in 1 innings match.
‡includes 24 points (16 win/4 bat/4 bowl) deducted from Surrey by TCCB Discipline Committee for playing an ineligible cricketer in the Sussex v Surrey match on 31 July, 1, 2 August.

SECOND XI CHAMPIONS

1959	Gloucestershire	1968	Surrey	1977	Yorkshire
1960	Northamptonshire	1969	Kent	1978	Sussex
1961	Kent	1970	Kent	1979	Warwickshire
1962	Worcestershire	1971	Hampshire	1980	Glamorgan
1963	Worcestershire	1972	Nottinghamshire	1981	Hampshire
1964	Lancashire	1973	Essex	1982	Worcestershire
1965	Glamorgan	1974	Middlesex	1983	Leicestershire
1966	Surrey	1975	Surrey	1984	Yorkshire
1967	Hampshire	1976	Kent	1985	Nottinghamshire

Abbreviations cont. from p. 72

Teams/Countries Toured

Cav	Cavaliers	ND	Northern Districts
DHR	D.H. Robins' XI	NSW	New South Wales
DN	Duke of Norfolk's XI	OFS	Orange Free State
Eng Co	English Counties XI	PIA	Pakistan International Airlines
GW	Griqualand West		
Int XI	International XI	RW	Rest of the World XI
IW	International Wanderers	SAB	South African Breweries XI
		Zim	Zimbabwe (Rhodesia)

THE FIRST-CLASS COUNTIES HONOURS, WHO'S WHO, RECORDS AND 1985 AVERAGES

Records are complete to the end of the 1985 English season and do not include the Indian tour of Sri Lanka which began on 21 August.

ABBREVIATIONS

General

*	not out/unbroken partnership		
b	born	f-c	first-class
BB	Best innings bowling analysis	HS	Highest Score
		LOI	Limited-Overs Internationals
Cap	Awarded 1st XI County Cap	Tests	Official Test Matches
Tours	Overseas tours involving first-class appearances		

Awards

BHC	Benson and Hedges Cup 'Gold' Award
NWT	NatWest Trophy or Gillette Cup 'Man of the Match' Award
Wisden 1985	One of *Wisden Cricketers' Almanack*'s Five Cricketers of 1985
YC 1985	Cricket Writers' Club Young Cricketer of 1985

Competitions

BHC	Benson and Hedges Cup
GC	Gillette Cup
JPL	John Player League
NWT	NatWest Trophy

Playing Categories

LB	Bowls right-arm leg-breaks
LF	Bowls left-arm fast
LFM	Bowls left-arm fast-medium
LHB	Bats left-handed
LM	Bowls left-arm medium pace
LMF	Bowls left-arm medium fast
OB	Bowls right-arm off-breaks
RHB	Bats right-handed
RM	Bowls right-arm medium pace
RMF	Bowls right-arm medium-fast
RF	Bowls right-arm fast
RFM	Bowls right-arm fast-medium
SLA	Bowls left-arm leg-breaks
WK	Wicket-keeper

Education

BHS	Boys' High School
BS	Boys' School
C	College
CE	College of Education
CFE	College of Further Education
CHE	College of Higher Education
CPE	College of Physical Education
CS	Comprehensive School
GS	Grammar School
HS	High School
LSE	London School of Economics
RGS	Royal Grammar School
S	School
SFC	Sixth Form College
SS	Secondary School
TC	Technical College
TGS	Technical Grammar School
THS	Technical High School
U	University

Abbreviations cont. p. 71

DERBYSHIRE

Formation of Present Club: 4 November 1870
Colours: Chocolate, Amber and Pale Blue
Badge: Rose and Crown
Championships: (1) 1936
NatWest Trophy/Gillette Cup Winners: (1) 1981
Benson and Hedges Cup Winners: (0) Finalists 1978
John Player League Champions: (0) Third 1970
Match Awards: GC 15; NWT 7; BHC 34

Chief Executive: R. Pearman, County Ground, Nottingham Road, Derby DE2 6DA
Captain: K.J. Barnett
Scorer: S.W. Tacey
Scores/Prospects: ☎ Derby (0332) 383211; Chesterfield (0246) 73090

ANDERSON, Iain Stuart (Dovecliff GS; Wulfric S). b Derby 24 Apr 1960. 6'0". RHB, OB. Debut 1978. Cap 1985. Boland 1983-84. 1000 runs (1): 1233 (1983). HS 112 v Kent (Chesterfield) 1983. BB 4-35 v Australians (Derby) 1981. **NWT:** HS 47 v Suffolk (Bury St. Edmunds) 1983. **BHC:** HS 32 v Notts (Nottingham) 1983. **JPL:** HS 64 v Somerset (Derby) 1985. BB 2-15 v Northants (Derby) 1983.

BARNETT, Kim John (Leek HS). b Stoke-on-Trent 17 Jul 1960. 6'1". RHB, LB. Debut 1979. Cap 1982. Captain 1983-. Staffordshire 1976. Boland 1982-85. Tours: NZ 1979-80 (DHR); SL 1985-86 (Eng B). 1000 runs (3); most – 1734 (1984). HS 144 v Middlesex (Derby) 1984. BB 6-115 v Yorks (Bradford) 1985. Awards: NWT 2; BHC 1. **NWT:** HS 88 v Middlesex (Derby) 1983. BB 6-24 v Cumberland (Kensal) 1984. **BHC:** HS 86 v Glos (Chesterfield) 1985. BB 1-10 v Worcs (Worcester) 1984. **JPL:** HS 131* v Essex (Derby) 1984. BB 3-39 v Yorks (Chesterfield) 1979.

BROWN, Andrew Mark (Aldercar CS; SE Derbyshire C). b Heanor 6 Nov 1964. 5'9". LHB, OB. Debut 1985. HS 74 v Warwicks (Chesterfield). **JPL:** HS 2*.

FINNEY, Roger John (Lady Manners S, Bakewell). b Darley Dale 2 Aug 1960. 6'1". RHB, LM. Debut 1982. Cap 1985. HS 82 v Glos (Derby) 1985. BB 7-61 v Lancs (Manchester) 1985. Awards: BHC 1. **NWT:** HS 14* v Suffolk (Bury St. Edmunds) 1983. BB 2-8 v Cumberland (Kensal) 1984. **BHC:** HS 46 v Lancs (Derby) 1984. BB 5-40 v Scotland (Aberdeen) 1985. **JPL:** HS 50* v Worcs (Worcester) 1984. BB 4-38 v Northants (Northampton) 1984.

HILL, Alan (New Mills GS; Chester CE). b Buxworth 29 Jun 1950. 6'0". RHB, OB. Debut 1972. Cap 1976. Orange Free State 1976-77. 1000 runs (4); most – 1352 (1984). HS 160* v Warwicks (Coventry) 1976. BB 3-5 OFS v Northern Transvaal (Pretoria) 1976-77. Awards: NWT 2; BHC 2. **NWT:** HS 72 v Middlesex (Derby) 1978. **BHC:** HS 107* v Scotland (Aberdeen) 1985. **JPL:** HS 120 v Northants (Buxton) 1976. BB 3-32 v Essex (Derby) 1984.

HOLDING, Michael Anthony (Kingston College HS). b Kingston, Jamaica 16 Feb 1954. 6'3". RHB, RF. Jamaica 1972-86. *Wisden* 1976. Lancashire 1981. Tasmania 1982-83. Derbyshire debut/cap 1983. Tests (WI): 55 (1975-76 to 1984-85); HS 69 v Eng (Birmingham) 1984; BB 8-92 v Eng (Oval) 1976. Tours (WI) Eng 1976, 1980, 1984; Aus 1975-76, 1979-80, 1981-82, 1984-85; NZ 1979-80; Ind 1983-84; Pak 1980-81, 1981-82 (Int XI). LOI (WI): 87. HS 80 v Yorks (Chesterfield) 1985. BB 8-92 (Tests). Derbyshire BB 6-65 v Notts (Derby) 1985. **NWT:** HS 27 v Durham (Derby) 1985. BB 3-35 Lancs v Hants (Southampton) 1981. **BHC:** HS 38 v Notts (Nottingham) 1985. BB 2-21 Lancs v Derbys (Manchester) 1981. **JPL:** HS 58 v Sussex (Hove) 1985. BB 3-19 v Hampshire (Derby) 1983.

MAHER, Bernard Joseph Michael (Abbotsfield CS; Bishopshalt GS; Loughborough U). b Hillingdon, Middlesex 11 Feb 1958. 5'10". RHB, WK. Debut 1981. HS 66 v Essex (Chesterfield) 1984. **BHC:** HS 2*. **JPL:** HS 14* v Worcs (Knypersley) 1985.

MALCOLM, Devon Eugene (Richmond C, Sheffield). b Kingston, Jamaica 22 Feb 1963. 6'2". RHB, RF. Debut 1984. HS 23 v Notts (Nottingham) 1984. BB 3-78 v Kent (Maidstone) 1984.

MARPLES, Christopher (Tupton Hall CS). b Chesterfield 3 Aug 1964. 5'11". RHB, WK. Debut 1985. HS 34 v Somerset (Derby). **JPL:** HS 20* v Kent.

MILLER, Geoffrey (Chesterfield GS). b Chesterfield 8 Sep 1952. 6'1". RHB, OB. Debut 1973. Cap 1976. YC 1976. Captain 1979-81. Natal 1983-84. Benefit 1985. Tests: 34 (1976 to 1984); HS 98* v Pak (Lahore) 1977-78; BB 5-44 v Aus (Sydney) 1978-79. LOI: 25. Tours: Aus 1976-77, 1978-79, 1979-80, 1982-83; WI 1980-81; NZ 1977-78; Ind and SL 1976-77; Pak 1977-78. HS 130 v Lancs (Manchester) 1984. BB 8-70 v Leics (Coalville) 1982. Awards: BHC 4. **NWT:** HS 59* v Worcs (Worcester) 1978. BB 3-28 v Suffolk (Bury St. Edmunds) 1983. **BHC:** HS 88* Minor C (Derby) 1982. BB 3-23 v Surrey (Derby) 1979. **JPL:** HS 84 v Somerset (Chesterfield) 1980. BB 4-22 v Yorks (Huddersfield) 1978.

MORRIS, John Edward (Shavington CS; Dane Bank CFE). b Crewe, Cheshire 1 Apr 1964. 5'10". RHB, RM. Debut 1982. HS 135 v Leics (Leicester) 1984. BB 1-35. **NWT:** HS 12 v Durham (Derby) 1985. **BHC:** HS 51 v Worcs (Worcester) 1984. **JPL:** HS 104 v Glos (Gloucester) 1984.

MORTENSEN, Ole Henrek (Brondbyoster S; Abedore C, Copenhagen). b Vejle, Denmark 29 Jan 1958. 6'3". RHB, RFM. Debut 1983. Denmark 1975-82. HS 40* v Glamorgan (Derby) 1984. BB 6-27 v Yorks (Sheffield) 1983. **NWT:** HS 4*. BB 3-16 v Suffolk (Bury St. Edmunds) 1983. **BHC:** HS 2. BB 3-30 v Lancs (Derby) 1984; 3-30 v Notts (Nottingham) 1985. **JPL:** HS 5. BB 4-10 v Leics (Chesterfield) 1985.

NEWMAN, Paul Geoffrey (Alderman Newton's GS, Leicester). b Evington, Leicester 10 Jan 1959. 6'2". RHB, RFM. Debut 1980. Tour: Zim 1984-85 (Eng Co). HS 115 v Leics (Chesterfield) 1985. BB 7-104 v Surrey (Oval) 1984. **NWT:** HS 35 v Leics (Leicester) 1984. BB 3-23 v Notts (Derby) 1981. **BHC:** HS 56* v Notts (Nottingham) 1985. BB 4-48 v Worcs (Worcester) 1982. **JPL:** HS 46 v Worcs (Knypersley) 1985. BB 4-21 v Hants (Derby) 1983.

ROBERTS, Bruce (Peterhouse; Prince Edward S, Salisbury), b Lusaka, N. Rhodesia 30 May 1962. 6'2". RHB, RM. Transvaal B 1982-86. Derbyshire debut 1984. 1000 runs (1): 1128 (1985). HS 100* v Glos (Derby). 1985 BB 4-32 Transvaal B v OFS (Johannesburg) 1982-83. Derbys BB 4-77 v Essex (Ilford) 1984. **NWT:** HS 13 v Durham (Derby) 1985. BB 2-73 v Leics (Leicester) 1984. **BHC:** HS 56 v Scotland (Aberdeen) 1985. BB 2-47 v Minor C (Shrewsbury) 1984. **JPL:** HS 77* v Notts (Heanor) 1985. BB 4-29 v Lancs (Derby) 1984.

SHARMA, Rajeshwar **('Reg')** (Parklands S, Sidcup; Bexley and Erith TS), b Nairobi, Kenya 27 Jun 1962. 6'3". RHB, RM/OB. Debut 1985. HS 41* v Yorkshire (Chesterfield) 1985. **NWT:** HS 11 v Durham (Derby). **JPL:** HS 8.

TAYLOR, Jonathan **Paul** (Pingle S, Swadlincote), b Ashby-de-la-Zouch 8 Aug 1964. 6'2". LHB, LFM. Debut 1984. HS 11 v Middx (Derby) 1984. BB 2-92 v Somerset (Taunton) 1984. **JPL:** HS 4. BB 2-38 v Sussex (Heanor) 1984.

WARNER, Alan Esmond (Tabernacle S, St. Kitts), b Birmingham 12 May 1957. 5'7". RHB, RFM. Worcestershire 1982-84. Derbyshire debut 1985. HS 67 Worcs v Warwicks (Birmingham) 1982. Derbys HS 60 v Surrey (Derby). BB 5-27 Worcs v Glamorgan (Worcester) 1984. Derbys BB 5-51 v Essex (Colchester). **NWT:** HS 17 v Durham (Derby) 1985. BB 1-38 Worcs v Notts (Worcester) 1983. **BHC:** HS 24* Worcs v Derbys (Worcester) 1982. BB 2-26 Worcs v Scotland (Aberdeen) 1983. **JPL:** HS 17 v Glos (Derby) 1985. BB 5-39 v Worcs (Knypersley) 1985.

WRIGHT, John Geoffrey (Christ's C, Christchurch; Otago U), b Darfield, NZ 5 July 1954. 6'1". LHB, RM. N. Districts 1975-85. Derbyshire debut/cap 1977. Tests (NZ): 41 (1977-78 to 1984-85). HS 141 v Aus (Christchurch) 1981-82. LOI: 71. Tours (NZ): Eng 1978, 1983; Aus 1980-81, 1985-86; WI 1982-83 (Int XI), 1984-85; Pak 1984-85; SL 1977-78 (DHR), 1983-84. 1000 runs (6+1); most – 1830 (1982). HS 190 v Yorks (Derby) 1982. BB 1-4. Awards: NWT 1; BHC 3. **NWT:** HS 87* v Sussex (Hove) 1977. **BHC:** 102 v Worcs (Chesterfield) 1977. **JPL:** 108 v Warwicks (Coventry) 1983.

VALETE

FELL, Mark Andrew (Grove CS), b Newark 17 Nov 1960. 5'11". RHB, SLA. Nottinghamshire 1982-83. Derbyshire debut 1985. Lincolnshire 1985. HS 108 Notts v Essex (Nottingham) 1982.

FOWLER, William Peter (Kamo HS; Otago U; Auckland U), b St. Helen's, Lancs 13 March 1959. 5'9". RHB, SLA. N. Districts 1979-85. Auckland 1981-82. Derbyshire debut 1983. HS 116 v Glam (Derby) 1984. BB 2-4. Awards: BHC 1.

MOIR, Dallas Gordon (Aberdeen GS), b Mtarfa, Malta, 13 Apr 1957. 6'8". RHB, SLA. Scotland 1980. Derbyshire debut 1981. Cap 1985. HS 107 v Warwicks (Chesterfield) 1984. BB 6-60 v Notts (Nottingham) 1984.

RUSSELL, Philip Edgar. County Coach. No appearances 1981-84 but played in 3 Championship and 3 JPL matches 1985. *See 1982 Annual (p. 70).*

DERBYSHIRE RECORDS

FIRST-CLASS CRICKET

Highest Total	For	645 v Hampshire; Derby	1898
	V	662 by Yorkshire; Chesterfield	1898
Lowest Total	For	16 v Notts; Nottingham	1879
	V	23 by Hampshire; Burton upon Trent	1958
Highest Innings	For	274 G. Davidson v Lancashire; Manchester	1896
	V	343* P.A. Perrin for Essex; Chesterfield	1904

Highest Partnerships

1st	322	H. Storer/J. Bowden v Essex; Derby	1929
2nd	349	C.S. Elliott/J.D. Eggar v Notts; Nottingham	1947
3rd	291	P.N. Kirsten/D.S. Steele v Somerset; Taunton	1981
4th	328	P. Vaulkhard/D. Smith v Notts; Nottingham	1946
5th	203	C.P. Wilkins/I.R. Buxton v Lancashire; Manchester	1971
6th	212	G.M. Lee/T.S. Worthington v Essex; Chesterfield	1932
7th	241*	G.H. Pope/A.E.G. Rhodes v Hampshire; Portsmouth	1948
8th	182	A.H.M. Jackson/W. Carter v Leics; Leicester	1922
9th	283	A. Warren/J. Chapman v Warwicks; Blackwell	1910
10th	93	J. Humphries/J. Horsley v Lancashire; Derby	1914

Best Bowling	For	10-40	W. Bestwick v Glamorgan; Cardiff	1921
(Innings)	V	10-47	T.F. Smailes for Yorkshire; Sheffield	1939
Best Bowling	For	16-84	C. Gladwin v Worcs; Stourbridge	1952
(Match)	V	16-101	G. Giffen for Australians; Derby	1886

Most Runs – Season	2165	D.B. Carr	(av 48.11)	1959
Most Runs – Career	20516	D. Smith	(av 31.4)	1927-1952
Most 100s – Season	8	P.N. Kirsten		1982
Most 100s – Career	30	D. Smith		1927-1952
Most Wkts – Season	168	T.B. Mitchell	(av 19.55)	1935
Most Wkts – Career	1670	H.L. Jackson	(av 17.11)	1947-1963

LIMITED-OVERS CRICKET

Highest Total	NWT	270-6 v Suffolk; Bury St. Edmunds	1981
	BHC	284-6 v Worcs; Worcester	1982
	JPL	292-9 v Worcs; Knypersley	1985
Lowest Total	NWT	79 v Surrey; The Oval	1967
	BHC	102 v Yorkshire; Bradford	1975
	JPL	70 v Surrey; Derby	1972
Highest Innings	NWT	110* P.N. Kirsten v Hampshire; Southampton	1982
	BHC	111* P.J. Sharpe v Glamorgan, Chesterfield	1976
	JPL	131* K.J. Barnett v Essex; Derby	1984
Best Bowling	NWT	6-18 T.J.P. Eyre v Sussex; Chesterfield	1969
	BHC	6-33 E.J. Barlow v Glos; Bristol	1978
	JPL	6-7 M. Hendrick v Notts; Nottingham	1972

DERBYSHIRE 1985

RESULTS SUMMARY

	Place	Won	Lost	Drew	Abandoned
Britannic Assurance Championship	13th	3	9	12	
All First-class Matches		3	9	13	
John Player League	4th	8	5		3
Natwest Bank Trophy	Lost to Durham (1st Round)				
Benson and Hedges Cup	Lost to Essex (Quarter-Final)				

BRITANNIC ASSURANCE CHAMPIONSHIP AVERAGES

BATTING AND FIELDING

Cap		*M*	*I*	*NO*	*HS*	*Runs*	*Avge*	*100*	*50*	*Ct/St*
1977	J.G. Wright	10	16	2	177*	797	56.92	2	4	5
1982	K.J. Barnett	24	41	1	134*	1568	40.20	4	7	13
1976	A. Hill	9	14	3	120	333	30.27	1	1	3
—	B. Roberts	24	42	4	100*	1128	29.68	2	2	21
1976	G. Miller	20	31	5	105	744	28.61	1	4	27
—	J.E. Morris	17	27	1	109*	722	27.76	1	3	5
1985	I.S. Anderson	19	35	3	95	876	27.37	—	7	16
—	P.G. Newman	19	29	3	115	604	23.23	1	3	2
1983	M.A. Holding	12	19	1	80	413	22.94	—	3	6
—	R. Sharma	7	12	2	41*	209	20.90	—	—	6
—	W.P. Fowler	9	14	1	79	266	20.46	—	2	3
1985	D.G. Moir	7	9	0	46	178	19.77	—	—	7
—	A.E. Warner	15	20	2	60	314	17.44	—	2	2
1985	R.J. Finney	24	37	10	82	381	14.11	—	1	3
—	B.J.M. Maher	13	18	6	46	150	12.50	—	—	17/2
—	M.A. Fell	5	8	0	27	98	12.25	—	—	—
—	C. Marples	11	15	5	34	114	11.40	—	—	23/1
—	O.H. Mortensen	13	15	7	16*	39	4.87	—	—	4

Also batted: A.M. Brown (2 matches) 3,16,74 (3 ct); D.E. Malcolm (1 match) 0; P.E. Russell (3 matches – cap 1975) 3*,2,0*.

BOWLING

	O	*M*	*R*	*W*	*Avge*	*Best*	*5 wI*	*10 wM*
M.A. Holding	354.5	67	1124	50	22.48	6-65	3	1
R.J. Finney	435.3	80	1401	53	26.43	7-61	4	—
K.J. Barnett	173.4	33	514	17	30.23	6-115	1	—
P.G. Newman	393.5	74	1288	42	30.66	4-29	—	—
O.H. Mortensen	340	75	1026	33	31.09	5-87	1	—
A.E. Warner	267.3	40	1013	24	42.20	5-51	1	—
G. Miller	346.2	72	1079	25	43.16	6-110	1	—
D.G. Moir	159	41	450	10	45.00	3-102	—	—

Also bowled: I.S. Anderson 3-1-9-0; D.E. Malcolm 17-2-82-3; J.E. Morris 5.1-0-55-0; B. Roberts 20-1-106-0; P.E. Russell 89.5-22-243-4; J.G. Wright 6-0-42-0.

The First-Class Averages (pp. 168–183) give the records of Derbyshire players in all first-class county matches, their other opponents being the Australians.

ESSEX

Formation of Present Club: 14 January 1876
Colours: Blue, Gold and Red
Badge: Three Seaxes above Scroll bearing 'Essex'
Championships: (3) 1979, 1983, 1984
NatWest Trophy/Gillette Cup Winners: (1) 1985
Benson and Hedges Cup Winners: (1) 1979
John Player League Champions: (3) 1981, 1984, 1985
Match Awards: GC 14; NWT 11; BHC 46

Secretary/Manager: P.J. Edwards, County Cricket Ground, New Writtle Street, Chelmsford CM2 0PG
Captain: G.A. Gooch
Scorer: C.F. Driver
Scores/Prospects: Chelmsford matches only ☎ (0245) 87921

ACFIELD, David Laurence (Brentwood S; Christ's, Cambridge), b Chelmsford 24 Jul 1947. 5'9½". RHB, OB. Cambridge U and Essex debuts 1966. Blue 1967-68. Cap 1970. Benefit 1981. HS 42 CU v Leics (Leicester) 1967. Essex HS 38 v Notts (Chelmsford) 1973. BB 8-55 v Kent (Canterbury) 1981. **NWT:** HS 2*. BB 3-9 v Scotland (Chelmsford) 1984. **BHC:** HS 8*. BB 2-14 v Combined Univs (Chelmsford) 1979. **JPL:** HS 9*. BB 5-14 v Northants (Northampton) 1970.

BORDER, Allan Robert (N. Sydney BHS) b Cremorne, Sydney, Aus 27 Jul 1955. 5'9". LHB, SLA. NSW 1976-80. Queensland 1980-86, captain since 1983-84. Glos 1977 (1 match). *Wisden* 1981. Joins Essex 1986. Tests (Aus): 72 (1978-79 to 1985, 9 as captain); HS 196 v Eng (Lord's) 1985. BB 3-20 v NZ (Christchurch) 1981-82. LOI: 114. Tours (Aus): Eng 1980, 1981, 1985 (capt); WI 1983-84; NZ 1981-82; Ind 1979-80; Pak 1979-80, 1982-83; SL 1982-83. 1000 runs (1+4); most – 1355 (1985). HS 200 NSW v Queensland (Brisbane) 1979-80. BB 4-61 Queensland v NSW (Sydney) 1980-81.

CHILDS, John Henry (Audley Park SS, Torquay), b Plymouth, Devon 15 Aug 1951. 6'0". LHB, SLA. Gloucestershire 1975-84 (cap 1977). Essex debut 1985. Devon 1973-74. HS 34* Glos v Notts (Cheltenham) 1982. BB 9-56 Glos v Somerset (Bristol) 1981. Awards: BHC 1. **NWT:** HS 14* Glos v Hants (Bristol) 1983. BB 2-15 Glos v Ire (Dublin) 1981. **BHC:** HS 10 Glos v Som (Bristol) 1979. BB 3-36 Glos v Glam (Bristol) 1982. **JPL:** HS 16* Glos v Warwicks (Bristol) 1981. BB 4-15 Glos v Northants (Northampton) 1976.

EAST, David Edward (Hackney Downs S; E. Anglia U), b Clapton 27 Jul 1959. 5'9". RHB, WK. Debut 1981. Cap 1982. HS 131 v Glos (Southend) 1985. Set world first-class record by catching the FIRST eight wickets to fall in an innings (v Somerset at Taunton 1985 on his 26th birthday). Awards: NWT 1. **NWT:** HS 25 v Scotland (Chelmsford) 1984. **BHC:** HS 33 v Glos (Chelmsford) 1984. **JPL:** HS 43 v Derbys (Derby) 1982.

FLETCHER, Keith William Robert (Comberton Village C, Cambs), b Worcester 20 May 1944. 5'9". RHB, LB. Debut 1962. Cap 1963. *Wisden* 1973. Benefit 1973 (£13,000). Captain 1974-85. Testimonial 1982 (£83,250). OBE 1985. Tests: 59 (1968 to 1981-82, 7 as captain); HS 216 v NZ (Auckland) 1974-75; BB 1-6. LOI: 24. Tours: Aus 1970-71, 1974-75, 1976-77; WI 1964-65 (Cav), 1973-74; NZ 1970-71, 1974-75; Ind/SL 1967-68 (Int XI), 1972-73, 1976-77, 1981-82 (captain); Pak 1966-67 (MCC

U-25), 1967-68 (Int XI), 1968-69, 1972-73; SL 1968-69, 1969-70. 1000 runs (20); most – 1890 (1968). HS 228* v Sussex (Hastings) 1968. BB 5-41 v Middx (Colchester) 1979. Awards: NWT 2; BHC 7. **NWT:** HS 97 v Kent (Chelmsford) 1982. BB 1-16. **BHC:** HS 101* v Sussex (Hove) 1982. BB 1-25. **JPL:** HS 99* v Notts (Ilford) 1974. BB 1-4.

FOSTER, Neil Alan (Philip Morant CS), b Colchester 6 May 1962. 6'3". RHB, RFM. Debut 1980. Cap 1983. YC 1983. Tests 9 (1983 to 1985); HS 18* v NZ (Auckland) 1983-84; BB 6-104 v Ind (Madras) 1984-85. LOI: 16. Tours: WI 1985-86; NZ/Pak 1983-84; Ind/SL 1984-85. HS 63 v Lancs (Ilford) 1985. BB 6-30 Eng XI v N. Districts (Hamilton) 1983-84. Essex BB 6-46 v Sussex (Ilford) 1983. Awards: BHC 1. **NWT:** HS 3. BB 3-19 v Dorset (Bournemouth) 1983. **BHC:** HS 23* v Middx (Chelmsford) 1985. BB 5-32 v Surrey (Oval) 1985. **JPL:** HS 10 (twice). BB 2-35 v Derbys (Colchester) 1985.

GLADWIN, Christopher (Langdon CS, Newham), b East Ham 10 May 1962. 5'11". LHB, RM. Debut 1981. Cap 1984. 1000 runs (1): 1396 (1984). HS 162 v CU (Cambridge) 1984. **NWT:** HS 15 v Middx (Chelmsford) 1985. **BHC:** HS 41 v Surrey (Chelmsford) 1984. **JPL:** HS 75 v Middx (Lord's) 1984.

GOOCH, Graham Alan (Norlington Jr HS), b Leytonstone 23 Jul 1953. 6'0". RHB, RM. Debut 1973. Cap 1975. *Wisden* 1979. Benefit 1985. Captain 1986. W. Province 1982-84. Tests: 48 (1975 to 1985); HS 196 v Aus (Oval) 1985; BB 2-12 v Ind (Delhi) 1981-82. LOI: 40. Tours: Aus 1978-79, 1979-80; SA 1981-82 (SAB); WI 1980-81, 1985-86; Ind 1979-80, 1981-82; SL 1981-82. 1000 runs (9+1); most – 2559 (1984). HS 227 v Derbys (Chesterfield) 1984. BB 7-14 v Worcs (Ilford) 1982. Awards: NWT 5; BHC 12 (record). **NWT:** HS 133 v Scotland (Chelmsford) 1984. BB 2-33 v Herts (Hitchin) 1981. **BHC:** HS 198* v Sussex (Hove) 1982. BB 3-24 v Sussex (Hove) 1982. **JPL:** HS 176 v Glam (Southend) 1983. BB 4-33 v Worcs (Chelmsford) 1984.

HARDIE, Brian Ross (Larbert HS), b Stenhousemuir 14 Jan 1950. 5'11". RHB, RM. Brother of K.M. (Scotland 1966-76). Scotland 1970-72. Essex debut 1973. Cap 1974. Benefit 1983. 1000 runs (10); most – 1522 (1975). HS 162 v Warwicks (Birmingham) 1975, and 162 v Somerset (Southend) 1985. BB 2-39 v Glamorgan (Ilford) 1979. Awards: NWT 1; BHC 1. **NWT:** HS 110 v Notts (Lord's) 1985. BB 1-16. **BHC:** HS 113 v Comb Us (Chelmsford) 1985. **JPL:** HS 108* v Yorks (Chelmsford) 1981. BB 1-4.

LEVER, John Kenneth (Dane SM), b Stepney 24 Feb 1949. 6'0½". RHB, LFM. Debut 1967. Cap 1970. *Wisden* 1978. Benefit 1980 (£66,110). Natal 1982-85. Tests: 20 (1976-77 to 1981-82); HS 53 and BB 7-46 (10-70 match) v India (Delhi) 1976-77 on debut. LOI: 22. Tours: Aus 1976-77, 1978-79, 1979-80; SA 1972-73 (DHR), 1973-74 (DHR), 1981-82 (SAB); NZ 1977-78; Ind/SL 1976-77, 1981-82; Ind 1979-80, 1980-81 (Overseas XI); Pak 1977-78; SL 1977-78 (DHR). 100 wickets (4); most – 116 (1984). HS 91 v Glamorgan (Cardiff) 1970. BB 8-37 v Glos (Bristol) 1984. Awards: NWT 4; BHC 2. **NWT:** HS 15* v Surrey (Chelmsford) 1984. BB 5-8 v Middx (Westcliff) 1972. **BHC:** HS 13 v Lancs (Chelmsford) 1984. BB 5-13 v Middx (Lord's) 1985. **JPL:** HS 23 v Worcs (Worcester) 1974. BB 5-13 v Glamorgan (Ebbw Vale) 1975.

LILLEY, Alan William (Caterham HS, Ilford), b Ilford 8 May 1959. 5'11". RHB, RM. Debut 1978 scoring 22 and 100* v Notts (Nottingham). HS 100* (on debut). BB 3-116 v Glamorgan (Swansea) 1985. Awards: BHC 1. **NWT:** HS 59* and BB 2-19 v Scotland (Chelmsford) 1984. **BHC:** HS 119 v Cambridge U (Chelmsford) 1979. BB 1-4. **JPL:** HS 23 v Northants (Chelmsford) 1980. BB 2-0 v Glos (Bristol) 1984.

PONT, Ian Leslie (Sir Anthony Browne's S), b Brentwood 28 Aug 1961. 6'2½". RHB, RFM. Brother of K.R. Notts 1982. Essex debut 1985. Natal 1985-86. HS 16 Notts v Middlesex (Lord's) 1982. BB 5-103 v Somerset (Taunton) 1985. **NWT:** HS 7*. BB 1-54. **BHC:** HS 13* Minor C v Essex (Slough) 1983. BB 1-42. **JPL:** BB 2-18 v Somerset (Taunton) 1985.

PONT, Keith Rupert (St. Martin's SM, Hutton), b Wanstead 16 Jan 1953. 6'2½". RHB, RFM. Brother of I.L. Debut 1970. Cap 1976. HS 125* v Glamorgan (Southend) 1983. BB 5-17 v Glamorgan (Cardiff) 1982. Awards: BHC 2. **NWT:** HS 39 v Som (Taunton) 1978. BB 2-18 v Durham (Chester le Street) 1973. **BHC:** HS 60* v Notts (Ilford) 1976. BB 4-60 v Northants (Lord's) 1980. **JPL:** HS 55* and BB 4-22 v Warwicks (Birmingham) 1981.

PRICHARD, Paul John (Brentwood HS), b Billericay 7 Jan 1965. 5'10". RHB. Debut 1984. HS 100 v Lancs (Manchester) 1984. **NWT:** HS 94 v Oxon (Chelmsford) 1985. **JPL:** HS 33 v Glos (Southend) 1985. **BHC:** HS 32 v Sussex (Chelmsford) 1984, and 32 v Leics (Lord's) 1985.

PRINGLE, Derek Raymond (Felsted S; Fitzwilliam C, Cambridge), b Nairobi, Kenya 18 Sep 1958. 6'4½". RHB, RMF. Son of D.J. (East Africa). Debut 1978. Cap 1982. Cambridge U 1979-82; blue 1979-80-81 (capt 1982). Tests: 10 (1982 to 1984); HS 47* v Aus (Perth) 1982-83; BB 5-108 v WI (Birmingham) 1984. LOI: 9. Tours: Aus 1982-83; SL 1985-86 (Eng B). HS 127* CU v Worcs (Cambridge) 1981. Essex HS 121* v Surrey (Oval) 1985. BB 7-32 v Middx (Chelmsford) 1983. Awards: NWT 1; BHC 2. **NWT:** HS 55 and BB 5-12 v Oxon (Chelmsford) 1985. **BHC:** HS 68 Comb Us v Som (Taunton) 1982. BB 5-35 v Lancs (Chelmsford) 1984. **JPL:** HS 81* v Warwicks (Birmingham) 1985. BB 5-41 v Glos (Southend) 1985.

STEPHENSON, John Patrick (Felsted S), b Stebbing 14 Mar 1965. 6'1". RHB, RM. Debut 1985. HS 10 v Glos (Bristol) 1985.

TOPLEY, Thomas **Donald** (Royal Hospital S, Holbrook, Suffolk), b Canterbury 25 Feb 1964. 6'3". RHB, RMF. Brother of P.A. (Kent 1972-75). Surrey (v CU) and Essex debuts 1985. Norfolk 1984-85. HS 9* and BB 4-57 v Middlesex (Lord's) 1985. **JPL:** BB 2-26 v Somerset (Taunton) 1985.

TURNER, Stuart (Epping SS), b Chester 18 Jul 1943. 6'0½". RHB, RMF. Debut 1965. Cap 1970. Benefit 1979. Natal 1976-78. Tour: SA 1974-75 (DHR). HS 121 v Som (Taunton) 1970. BB 6-26 v Northants (Northampton) 1977. Awards: BHC 4. **NWT:** HS 50* v Yorks (Leeds) 1982. BB 4-23 v Kent (Chelmsford) 1982. **BHC:** HS 55* v Hants (Chelmsford) 1982. BB 4-19 v Comb Us (Chelmsford) 1981. **JPL:** HS 87 v Worcs (Chelmsford) 1975. BB 5-35 v Hants (Chelmsford) 1978.

VALETE

McEWAN, Kenneth Scott (Queen's C, Queenstown), b Bedford, S. Africa 16 Jul 1952. 5'9". RHB, WK. E. Province 1972-78. Essex debut/cap 1974. *Wisden* 1977. W. Australia 1979-81. W. Province 1981-86. 1000 runs (12); most – 2176 (1983). HS 218 v Sussex (Chelmsford) 1977. BB 1-0. Awards: NWT 2; BHC 6.

PHILLIP, Norbert (Dominica GS), b Bioche, Dominica 12 Jun 1948. 6'2". RHB, RFM. Windward Is 1969-85 (capt 1982-85). Essex debut/cap 1978. Tests (WI): 9 (1977-78 to 1978-79); HS 47 (Calcutta) and BB 4-48 (Madras) v Ind 1978-79. LOI: 1. Tour (WI): Ind/SL 1978-79. HS 134 v Glos (Gloucester) 1978. BB 7-33 Windward Is v Leeward Is (Roseau) 1981-82. Essex BB 6-4 v Surrey (Chelmsford) 1983.

ESSEX RECORDS

FIRST-CLASS CRICKET

Highest Total	For	692 v Somerset; Taunton	1895
	V	803-4 by Kent; Brentwood	1934
Lowest Total	For	30 v Yorkshire; Leyton	1901
	V	14 by Surrey; Chelmsford	1983
Highest Innings	For	343* P.A. Perrin v Derbyshire; Chesterfield	1904
	V	332 W.H. Ashdown for Kent; Brentwood	1934

Highest Partnerships

1st	270	A.V. Avery/T.C. Dodds v Surrey; The Oval	1946
2nd	321	G.A. Gooch/K.S. McEwan v Northants; Ilford	1978
3rd	343	P.A. Gibb/R. Horsfall v Kent; Blackheath	1951
4th	298	A.V. Avery/R. Horsfall v Worcs; Clacton	1948
5th	287	C.T. Ashton/J. O'Connor v Surrey; Brentwood	1934
6th	206	J.W.H.T. Douglas/J. O'Connor v Glos; Cheltenham	1923
	206	B.R. Knight/R.A.G. Luckin v Middlesex; Brentwood	1962
7th	261	J.W.H.T. Douglas/J. Freeman v Lancashire; Leyton	1914
8th	263	D.R. Wilcox/R.M. Taylor v Warwicks; Southend	1946
9th	251	J.W.H.T. Douglas/S.N. Hare v Derbyshire; Leyton	1921
10th	218	F.H. Vigar/T.P.B. Smith v Derbyshire; Chesterfield	1947

Best Bowling (Innings)	For	10-32	H. Pickett v Leics; Leyton	1895
	V	10-40	E.G. Dennett for Glos; Bristol	1906
Best Bowling (Match)	For	17-119	W. Mead v Hampshire; Southampton	1985
	V	17-56	C.W.L. Parker for Glos; Gloucester	1925

Most Runs – Season	2559	G.A. Gooch	(av 67.34)	1984
Most Runs – Career	29162	P.A. Perrin	(av 36.18)	1896-1928
Most 100s – Season	9	J. O'Connor and D.J. Insole		1934 and 1955
Most 100s – Career	71	J. O'Connor		1921-1939
Most Wkts – Season	172	T.P.B. Smith	(av 27.13)	1947
Most Wkts – Career	1610	T.P.B. Smith	(av 26.68)	1929-1951

LIMITED-OVERS CRICKET

Highest Total	NWT	327-6 v Scotland; Chelmsford	1984
	BHC	350-3 v Comb Univs; Chelmsford	1979
	JPL	310-5 v Glamorgan; Southend	1983
Lowest Total	NWT	100 v Derbyshire; Brentwood	1965
	BHC	123 v Kent; Canterbury	1973
	JPL	69 v Derbyshire; Chesterfield	1974
Highest Innings	NWT	133 G.A. Gooch v Scotland; Chelmsford	1984
	BHC	198* G.A. Gooch v Sussex; Hove	1982
	JPL	176 G.A. Gooch v Glamorgan; Southend	1983
Best Bowling	NWT	5-8 J.K. Lever v Middlesex; Westcliff	1972
	BHC	5-13 J.K. Lever v Middlesex; Lord's	1985
	JPL	8-26 K.D. Boyce v Lancashire; Manchester	1971

ESSEX 1985

RESULTS SUMMARY

	Place	Won	Lost	Drew	Tied	Aban
Britannic Assurance Championship	4th	7	2	14		1
All First-class Matches		7	2	17		1
John Player League	1st	9	3		1	3
NatWest Bank Trophy	**Winners**					
Benson and Hedges Cup	Lost to Leicestershire (Final)					

BRITANNIC ASSURANCE CHAMPIONSHIP AVERAGES

BATTING AND FIELDING

Cap		M	I	NO	HS	Runs	Avge	100	50	Ct/St
1975	G.A. Gooch	11	17	2	202	1368	91.20	6	4	17
1982	D.E. East	23	26	3	131	754	32.78	2	4	63/4
1974	K.S. McEwan	23	36	4	121	1035	32.34	2	5	14
1974	B.R. Hardie	23	39	5	162	1074	31.58	2	4	22
1963	K.W.R. Fletcher	21	26	6	78*	631	31.55	—	6	11
—	P.J. Prichard	18	28	4	95	694	28.91	—	5	13
1984	C. Gladwin	12	20	2	92*	468	26.00	—	2	4
1982	D.R. Pringle	21	27	4	121*	573	24.91	1	1	15
—	A.W. Lilley	14	23	2	68*	474	22.57	—	4	6
1983	N.A. Foster	13	10	1	63	164	18.22	—	1	8
1976	K.R. Pont	8	12	2	38	177	17.70	—	—	3
—	I.L. Pont	6	5	2	12	48	16.00	—	—	—
1970	J.K. Lever	22	23	9	24*	193	13.78	—	—	8
1970	S. Turner	4	6	0	35	75	12.50	—	—	—
1978	N. Phillip	3	5	0	21	57	11.40	—	—	2
1970	D.L. Acfield	22	19	10	10*	65	7.22	—	—	5

Also batted: J.H. Childs (4 matches) 5,3,3* (1 ct); J.P. Stephenson (1 match) 10,4 (1 ct); T.D. Topley (4 matches) 0,0,9* (1 ct).

BOWLING

	O	M	R	W	Avge	Best	5 wI	10 wM
G.A. Gooch	155.3	35	432	18	24.00	5-46	1	—
N.A. Foster	366.5	77	1163	47	24.74	5-40	4	—
I.L. Pont	115.5	15	485	19	25.52	5-103	1	—
J.K. Lever	700.3	178	1963	75	26.17	6-47	6	—
T.D. Topley	134.1	31	400	15	26.66	4-57	—	—
D.R. Pringle	518.1	125	1374	45	30.53	6-42	1	—
D.L. Acfield	498.4	107	1462	38	38.47	6-81	1	—

Also bowled: J.H. Childs 130-38-377-3; K.W.R. Fletcher 4-0-35-1; C. Gladwin 3-0-12-0; B.R. Hardie 6-1-35-1; A.W. Lilley 28.4-0-179-3; N. Phillip 50-10-148-2; K.R. Pont 76-10-305-7; S. Turner 86.5-15-224-8.

The First-Class Averages (pp. 168–183) give the records of Essex players in all first-class county matches (their other opponents being MCC, the Australians and Cambridge U.), with the exception of: N.A. Foster 14-12-2-63-193-19.30-0-1-9 ct. 413.5-86-1351-51-26.49-5/40-4-0. G.A. Gooch 14-23-2-202-1706-81.23-6-7-20 ct. 227-54-625-26-24.03-5/46-1-0.

GLAMORGAN

Formation of Present Club: 6 July 1888
Colours: Blue and Gold
Badge: Gold Daffodil
Championships: (2) 1948, 1969
NatWest Trophy/Gillette Cup Winners: (0) Finalists 1977
Benson and Hedges Cup Winners: (0) Quarter-Finalists five times
John Player League Champions: (0) Eighth 1977
Match Awards: GC 13; NWT 3; BHC 28

Secretary: P.G. Carling, Sophia Gardens, Cardiff, CF1 9XR
Captain: R.C. Ontong
Scorer: B.T. Denning
Scores/Prospects: ☎ Cardiff (0222) 43478; Swansea (0792) 466321

BARWICK, Stephen Royston (Cwrt Sart CS; Dwr-y-Felin CS), b Neath 6 Sep 1960. 6'2". RHB, RMF. Debut 1981. HS 29 v Somerset (Cardiff) 1985. BB 8-42 v Worcs (Worcester) 1983. Awards: BHC 1. **NWT:** HS 6. BB 4-14 v Hants (Bournemouth) 1981. **BHC:** HS 18 v Kent (Canterbury) 1984. BB 4-11 v Minor C (Swansea) 1985. **JPL:** HS 12* v Sussex (Hastings) 1982. BB 3-35 v Lancs (Manchester) 1985.

DAVIES, Terry (Townsend SS, St. Albans), b St. Albans, Herts 25 Oct 1960. 5'6". RHB, WK. Debut 1979. Cap 1985. HS 75 v Middx (Cardiff) 1985. **NWT:** HS 12 v Sussex (Cardiff) 1985. **BHC:** HS 23 v Sussex (Hove) 1984. **JPL:** HS 46* v Kent (Cardiff) 1983.

DERRICK, John (Blaengwawr CS), b Cwmaman 15 Jan 1963. 6'1". RHB, RM. Debut 1983. HS 69* v Surrey (Swansea) 1984. BB 4-60 v Northants (Wellingborough) 1985. **NWT:** HS 4. BB 4-14 v Scot (Edinburgh) 1985. **BHC:** HS 42 v Kent (Cardiff) 1985. BB 1-26. **JPL:** HS 18* v Northants (Northampton) 1983. BB 2-32 v Somerset (Bath) 1983.

HOLMES, Geoffrey Clark (West Denton HS), b Newcastle-upon-Tyne 16 Sep 1958. 5'10". RHB, RM. Debut 1978. Cap 1985. 1000 runs (2); most – 1129 (1985). HS 112 v Leics (Leicester) 1985. BB 5-86 v Surrey (Oval) 1980. Awards: NWT 1. **NWT:** HS 20 and BB 5-24 v Scotland (Edinburgh) 1985. **BHC:** HS 70 v Somerset (Taunton) 1985. BB 3-26 v Minor C (Swansea) 1985. **JPL:** HS 73 v Warwicks (Birmingham) 1984. BB 5-2 v Derbys (Ebbw Vale) 1984.

HOPKINS, John Anthony (Ynysawdre CS; Trinity CE), b Maesteg 16 Jun 1953. 5'10". RHB, WK. Brother of J.D. (Middlesex 1969-72). Debut 1970. Cap 1977. E. Province 1981-82. 1000 runs (7); most – 1500 (1984). HS 230 v Worcs (Worcester) 1977. Awards: NWT 1; BHC 4. **NWT:** HS 63 v Leics (Swansea) 1977. **BHC:** HS 103* v Minor C (Swansea) 1980. **JPL:** HS 130* v Somerset (Bath) 1983.

JAMES, Stephen Peter, b Lydney, Gloucestershire 7 Sep 1967. RHB. Debut 1985.

JAVED MIANDAD Khan (Church Mission Soc SS, Karachi), b Karachi, Pakistan 12 Jun 1957. 5'9". RHB, LB. Brother of Anwar Miandad and Bashir Miandad (Karachi). Karachi (debut 1973-74 aged 16 years 5 months), Sind and Habib Bank. Sussex 1976-79 (cap 1977). Glamorgan debut/cap 1980. *Wisden* 1981. Captain 1982. Tests (Pakistan): 68 (1976-77 to 1984-85, 13 as captain, scoring 163 v NZ on debut); HS 280* v Ind (Hyderabad) 1982-83; BB 3-74 v NZ (Hyderabad) 1976-77. LOI: 75. Tours (Pak): Eng 1978, 1982; Aus 1976-77, 1978-79, 1981-82 (capt), 1982-83, 1983-84; WI 1976-77; NZ 1978-79, 1984-85 (capt); Ind 1979-80, 1983-84; SL 1975-76. 1000 runs (5+8); most – 2083 (1981) including 8 hundreds (both Glamorgan records). HS 311 Karachi Whites v National Bank (Karachi) 1974-75. Glamorgan HS 212* v Leics (Swansea) 1984. BB 7-39 Habib Bank v IDBP (Lahore) 1980-81. Glamorgan BB 3-52 v Warwicks (Birmingham) 1982. Awards: NWT 1; BHC 2. **NWT:** HS 75 Sussex v Lancashire (Hove) 1978. **BHC:** HS 95 v Comb Us (Camb) 1983. **JPL:** HS 107* v Leics (Leicester) 1981. BB 1-5.

JONES, Alan Lewis (Ystalyfera GS, Cwmtawe CS, Cardiff C of Ed), b Alltwen 1 Jun 1957. 5'8½. LHB. Debut 1973 aged 16 years 99 days. Cap 1983. 1000 runs (2); most – 1811 (1984). HS 132 v Hants (Cardiff) 1984. BB 1-60. **NWT:** HS 60* v Scot (Edinburgh) 1985. **BHC:** HS 36 v Worcs (Cardiff) 1979. **JPL:** HS 82 v Warwicks (Birmingham) 1982.

MAYNARD, Matthew Peter (Ysgol David Hughes, Anglesey), b Oldham, Lancs 21 March 1966. 5'10½. RHB, RM. Debut 1985 scoring 102 out of 117 in 87 minutes v Yorks (Swansea), and completing hundred with three sixes off successive balls. First Glamorgan hundred on debut since 1921 (F.B. Pinch). HS 102 (on debut). **JPL:** HS 18 v Yorkshire (Swansea) 1985.

MORRIS, Hugh (Blundell's S), b Cardiff 5 Oct 1963. 5'8". LHB, RM. Debut 1981. HS 114* v Yorks (Cardiff) 1984. BB 1-45. **NWT:** HS 75 v Worcs (Swansea) 1985. **BHC:** HS 10 v Kent (Canterbury) 1984. **JPL:** HS 91 v Lancs (Manchester) 1985.

NORTH, Philip David, b Newport 16 May 1965. RHB, RM. Debut 1985. BB 1-60.

ONTONG, Rodney Craig (Selbourne C, East London, SA), b Johannesburg, South Africa 9 Sep 1955. 5'11". RHB, OB. Border 1972-76 (debut aged 17 years 7 months), and 1982-85 (captain 1983-85). Transvaal 1976-78. Northern Transvaal 1978-82 and 1985-86. Glamorgan debut 1975. Cap 1979. Captain 1984-. 1000 runs (5); most – 1320 in 1984. HS 204* v Middx (Swansea) 1984. BB 8-67 (13-106 and 130 in match) v Notts (Nottingham) 1985. Awards: NWT 1; BHC 3. **NWT:** HS 64 v Somerset (Cardiff) 1978. BB 4-49 v Norfolk (Norwich) 1983. **BHC:** HS 81 v Somerset (Swansea) 1984. BB 5-30 v Somerset (Taunton) 1985. **JPL:** HS 100 v Northants (Abergavenny) 1982. BB 4-31 v Middlesex (Lord's) 1979.

PRICE, Mark Richard (Harper Green SS), b Liverpool, Lancs 20 Apr 1960. 6'1½". RHB, SLA. Debut 1984. HS 36 v Notts (Swansea) 1985. BB 4-97 v Leics (Swansea) 1985. **NWT:** HS 6. BB 3-22 v Worcs (Swansea) 1985. **JPL:** HS 22 v Surrey (Cardiff) 1985. BB 1-17.

ROBERTS, Martin Leonard (Helston CS), b Mullion, Cornwall 12 Apr 1966. 6'1". RHB, WK. Debut 1985. Cornwall 1983-84.

STEELE, John Frederick (Endon SS). b Stafford 23 Jul 1946. 5'10½". RHB, SLA. Brother of D.S. (Northants, Derbys and England 1963-84). Leics 1970-83 (cap 1971). Benefit 1983 (£33,470). Glamorgan debut/cap 1984. Natal 1973-78. Staffs 1965-69. Tour: SA 1974-75 (DHR). 1000 runs (6); most – 1347 (1972). HS 195 Leics v Derbys (Leicester) 1971. BB 7-29 Natal B v GW (Umzinto) 1973-74, and 7-29 Leics v Glos (Leicester) 1980. Awards: NWT 3; BHC 5. **NWT:** HS 108* Leics v Staffs (Longton) 1975. BB 5-19 Leics v Essex (Southend) 1977. **BHC:** HS 91 Leics v Somerset (Leicester) 1974. BB 5-11 Leics v Worcs (Worcester) 1983. **JPL:** HS 92 Leics v Essex (Leicester) 1973. BB 5-22 Leics v Glam (Leicester) 1979.

THOMAS, John **Gregory** (Cwmtawe HS; Cardiff CE). b Garnswllt 12 Aug 1960. 6'3". RHB, RF. Debut 1979. Border 1983-85. Tour: WI 1985-86. HS 84 v Surrey (Guildford) 1982. BB 5-56 v Somerset (Cardiff) 1984. Awards: NWT 1. **NWT:** HS 24 v Hants (Swansea) 1983. BB 5-17 v Sussex (Cardiff) 1985. **BHC:** HS 17 v Kent (Canterbury) 1984. BB 4-38 v Hants (Southampton) 1985. **JPL:** HS 37 v Notts (Nottingham) 1983. BB 5-38 v Yorks (Cardiff) 1983.

YOUNIS AHMED, Mohammad (Moslem HS, Lahore) b Jullundur, India 20 Oct 1947. 5'10½". LHB, LM/SLA. Half-brother of Saeed Ahmed (Lahore and Pakistan 1954-72). Debut 1961-62 for Pakistan Inter Board Schools XI at age of 14 years 4 months. Appeared for Lahore, Karachi and PIA 1961-70. Surrey 1965-78 (cap 1969). South Australia 1972-73. Worcestershire 1979-83 (cap 1979). Glamorgan debut 1984. Cap 1985. Tests (Pak): 2 (1969-70); HS 62 v NZ (Karachi). Tours: SA (Int Wanderers) 1974-75, 1975-76, 1973-74 (DHR), 1974-75; WI 1969-70 (Cavs); Pak 1970-71 (Cwlth). 1000 runs (13); most –1760 (1969). HS 221* Worcs v Notts (Nottingham) 1979. BB 4-10 Surrey v CU (Cambridge) 1975. Awards: BHC 3. **NWT:** HS 87 Surrey v Middx (Oval) 1970. BB 2-54 Worcs v Leics (Leicester) 1979. **BHC:** HS 115 Worcs v Yorks (Worcs) 1980. BB 4-37 Worcs v Northants (Northampton) 1980. **JPL:** HS 113 Surrey v Warwicks (Birmingham) 1976; 113 Worcs v Middx 1979. BB 3-20 v Northants (Wellingborough) 1985.

VALETE

HENDERSON, Stephen Peter (Downside S; Durham U, Magdalene C, Cambridge). b Oxford 24 Sep 1958. 6'2". LHB, RM. Son of Derek (Oxford U 1949-50). Worcestershire 1977-81. Blue 1982-83 (capt 1983). Glamorgan debut 1983. HS 209* CU v Middx (Cambridge) 1982. BB 2-48 v Surrey (Swansea) 1983.

McFARLANE, Leslie Leopold (Cherry Orchard SS; Nene C, Northampton). b Portland, Jamaica 19 Aug 1952. 5'10". RHB, RFM. Northamptonshire 1979. Lancashire 1982-84. Glamorgan debut 1985. HS 15* Lancs v Northants (Southport) 1984. BB 6-59 Lancs v Warwicks (Southport) 1982.

MALONE, Steven John (St. Edmund's, Ipswich; Kings S, Ely) b Chelmsford 19 Oct 1953. 6'2½". RHB, RMF. Essex 1975-78. Hampshire 1980-84. Glamorgan debut 1985. HS 23 Hants v Kent (Bournemouth) 1981. BB 7-55 Hants v Oxford U (Oxford) 1982.

GLAMORGAN RECORDS

FIRST-CLASS CRICKET

Highest Total	For	587-8d v Derbyshire; Cardiff	1951
	V	653-6d by Glos; Bristol	1928
Lowest Total	For	22 v Lancashire; Liverpool	1924
	V	33 by Leics; Ebbw Vale	1965
Highest Innings	For	287* D.E. Davies v Glos; Newport	1939
	V	302* W.R. Hammond for Glos; Bristol	1934
	V	302 W.R. Hammond for Glos; Newport	1939

Highest Partnerships

1st	330	A. Jones/R.C. Fredericks v Northants; Swansea	1972
2nd	338	A. Jones/A.R. Lewis v Sussex; Hastings	1962
3rd	313	D.E. Davies/W.E. Jones v Essex; Brentwood	1948
4th	306*	Javed Miandad/Younis Ahmed v Australians; Neath	1985
5th	264	M. Robinson/S.W. Montgomery v Hampshire; Bournemouth	1949
6th	230	W.E. Jones/B.L. Muncer v Worcs; Worcester	1953
7th	195*	W. Wooller/W.E. Jones v Lancashire; Liverpool	1947
8th	202	D. Davies/J.J. Hills v Sussex; Eastbourne	1928
9th	203*	J.J. Hills/J.C. Clay v Worcs; Swansea	1929
10th	143	T. Davies/S.A.B. Daniels v Glos; Swansea	1982

Best Bowling (Innings)	For	10-51	J. Mercer v Worcs; Worcester	1936
	V	10-18	G. Geary for Leics; Pontypridd	1929
Best Bowling (Match)	For	17-212	J.C. Clay v Worcs; Swansea	1937
	V	16-96	G. Geary for Leics; Pontypridd	1929

Most Runs – Season	2083	Javed Miandad	(av 69.43)	1981
Most Runs – Career	34056	A. Jones	(av 33.03)	1957-1983
Most 100s – Season	8	Javed Miandad		1981
Most 100s – Career	52	A. Jones		1957-1983
Most Wkts – Season	176	J. Clay	(av 17.34)	1937
Most Wkts – Career	2174	D.J. Shepherd	(av 20.87)	1950-1972

LIMITED-OVERS CRICKET

Highest Total	NWT	283-3 v Warwicks; Birmingham	1976
	BHC	245-7 v Hampshire; Swansea	1976
	JPL	277-6 v Derbyshire; Ebbw Vale	1984
Lowest Total	NWT	76 v Northants; Northampton	1968
	BHC	68 v Lancashire; Manchester	1973
	JPL	42 v Derbyshire; Swansea	1979
Highest Innings	NWT	124* A. Jones v Warwicks; Birmingham	1976
	BHC	103* M.A. Nash v Hampshire; Swansea	1976
	BHC	103* J.A. Hopkins v Minor C; Swansea	1980
	JPL	130* J.A. Hopkins v Somerset; Bath	1983
Best Bowling	NWT	5-17 J.G. Thomas v Sussex; Cardiff	1985
	BHC	5-17 A.H. Wilkins v Worcs; Worcester	1978
	JPL	6-29 M.A. Nash v Worcs; Worcester	1975

GLAMORGAN 1985

RESULTS SUMMARY

	Place	*Won*	*Lost*	*Drew*	*Tied*	*Aban*
Britannic Assurance Championship	12th	4	4	16		
All First-class Matches		4	4	19		
John Player League	14th	4	7		1	4
NatWest Bank Trophy	Lost to Worcestershire (Quarter-Final)					
Benson and Hedges Cup	Failed to qualify for Quarter-Final					

BRITANNIC ASSURANCE CHAMPIONSHIP AVERAGES

BATTING AND FIELDING

Cap		*M*	*I*	*NO*	*HS*	*Runs*	*Avge*	*100*	*50*	*Ct/St*
1985	Younis Ahmed	20	28	7	177	1190	56.66	3	4	3
1980	Javed Miandad	18	27	5	164*	1194	54.27	3	8	13
1979	R.C. Ontong	24	29	7	130	1105	50.22	2	8	10
1985	G.C. Holmes	24	36	3	112	1062	32.18	2	7	9
1985	T. Davies	24	24	7	75	457	26.88	—	2	42/5
—	S.P. Henderson	6	10	2	111	207	25.87	1	—	3
—	H. Morris	13	16	4	62	305	25.41	—	1	4
1983	A.L. Jones	16	23	2	75	521	24.80	—	3	8
1984	J.F. Steele	10	11	3	48	183	22.87	—	—	9
1977	J.A. Hopkins	20	30	2	114*	626	22.35	1	3	8
—	J.G. Thomas	14	15	2	60*	266	20.46	—	1	6
—	M.R. Price	12	9	3	36	98	16.33	—	—	2
—	J. Derrick	13	14	2	52	156	13.00	—	1	2
—	I. Smith	5	4	0	12	27	6.75	—	—	—
—	L.L. McFarlane	11	4	2	8	12	6.00	—	—	4
—	S.R. Barwick	21	15	5	29	57	5.70	—	—	4
—	S.J. Malone	7	4	1	0*	0	0.00	—	—	2

Also batted: M.P. Maynard (4 matches) 102,58,38 (1 ct); P.D. North (1 match) 0* S.P. James (1 match) did not bat.

BOWLING

	O	*M*	*R*	*W*	*Avge*	*Best*	*5 wI*	*10 wM*
R.C. Ontong	563.5	137	1726	62	27.83	8-67	4	1
J.G. Thomas	298.3	43	1104	34	32.47	4-61	—	—
S.R. Barwick	464	95	1345	36	37.36	7-43	1	—
M.R. Price	239.4	59	616	16	38.50	4-97	—	—
J. Derrick	211.1	37	650	14	46.42	4-60	—	—
G.C. Holmes	313.3	73	962	20	48.10	3-25	—	—
J.F. Steele	180.1	45	498	10	49.80	3-6	—	—
L.L. McFarlane	219	35	886	14	63.28	4-100	—	—

Also bowled: S.P. Henderson 8-2-31-0; J.A. Hopkins 6-1-22-0; Javed Miandad 27.3-2-120-3; A.L. Jones 1-0-24-0; S.J. Malone 129-12-517-9; M.P. Maynard 0.1-0-4-0; H. Morris 3-0-32-0; P.D. North 27-7-60-1; I. Smith 38.4-10-117-1; Younis Ahmed 67.4-19-158-2.

The First-Class Averages (pp. 168–183) give the records of Glamorgan players in all first-class county matches, their other opponents being the Australians, the Zimbabweans and Oxford U.

GLOUCESTERSHIRE

Formation of Present Club: 1871
Colours: Blue, Gold, Brown, Silver, Green and Red
Badge: Coat of Arms of the City and County of Bristol
Championships (since 1890): (0) Runners-up 1930, 1931, 1947, 1959, 1969
NatWest Trophy/Gillette Cup Winners: (1) 1973
Benson and Hedges Cup Winners: (1) 1977
John Player League Champions: (0) Sixth 1969, 1973, 1977, 1985
Match Awards: GC 17; NWT 8; BHC 29

Secretary: D.G. Collier, Phoenix County Ground, Nevil Road, Bristol BS7 9EJ
Captain: D.A. Graveney
Scorer: A.G. Avery
Scores/Prospects: ☎ Bristol (0272) 48461; Cheltenham College (0242) 522000, Gloucester (0452) 423011; Swindon (0793) 23088

ATHEY, Charles William Jeffrey (Stainsby SS; Acklam Hall HS), b Middlesbrough 27 Sep 1957. 5'9½". RHB, RM. Yorkshire 1976-83 (cap 1980). Glos debut 1984. Cap 1985. Tests: 3 (1980 and 1980-81); HS 9. LOI: 2. Tours: WI 1980-81; NZ 1979-80 (DHR); SL 1985-86 (Eng B). 1000 runs (4); most – 1812 (1984). HS 170 v Derbys (Derby) 1985. BB 3-3 v Hants (Bristol) 1985. Awards: NWT 3; BHC 3. **NWT:** 115 Yorks v Kent (Leeds) 1980. BB 1-18. **BHC:** HS 94* Yorks v Warwicks (Leeds) 1983. BB 4-48 v Comb Us (Bristol) 1984. **JPL:** HS 121* v Worcs (Moreton) 1985. BB 5-35 Yorks v Derbys (Chesterfield) 1981.

BAINBRIDGE, Philip (Hanley HS; Stoke-on-Trent SFC, Borough Road CE), b Sneyd Green, Stoke-on-Trent 16 Apr 1958. RHB, RM. 5'10". Debut 1977. Cap 1981. *Wisden* 1985. Tour: Zim 1984-85 (Eng Co). 1000 runs (5); most – 1644 (1985). HS 151* v Derbys (Derby) 1985. BB 6-59 v Glam (Swansea) 1982. Awards: NWT 1. **NWT:** HS 75 and BB 3-49 v Scotland (Bristol) 1983. **BHC:** HS 80 v Somerset (Taunton) 1982. BB 3-21 v Notts (Gloucester) 1981. **JPL:** HS 55 v Essex (Colchester) 1983. BB 4-27 v Middx (Cheltenham) 1980

BRASSINGTON, Andrew James (Endon SS), b Bagnall, Staffs 9 Aug 1954. 5'11". RHB, WK. Debut 1974. Cap 1978. HS 35 v Sussex (Hastings) 1982. **BHC:** HS 9. **NWT:** HS 20 v Hants (Bristol) 1979. **JPL:** HS 14* v Northants (Bristol) 1982.

BURROWS, Dean Andrew (Shotton Hall Co S), b Peterlee, Co. Durham 20 Jun 1966. RHB, RMF. Debut 1984. Durham 1984. No appearances 1985. **JPL:** BB 1-32.

CURRAN, Kevin Malcolm (Marandellas HS), b Rusape, S. Rhodesia 7 Sep 1959. 6'1". RHB, RFM. Son of K.P. (Rhodesia 1947-54). Irish-born grandparents. Zimbabwe 1980-85. Glos debut/cap 1985. Tour (Zim): Eng 1982; SL 1983-84. HS 96 Zimbabwe v Sri Lanka (Bulawayo) 1982-83. Glos HS 83 v Somerset (Bath) 1985. BB 5-35 v Australians (Bristol) 1985. Awards: NWT 1; BHC 1. **NWT:** HS 36 v Northants; 36 v Notts (Bristol) 1985. BB 4-34 v Northants (Bristol) 1985. **BHC:** HS 53* v Scotland (Bristol) 1985. BB 3-45 v Notts (Bristol) 1985. **JPL:** HS 50 v Sussex (Swindon) 1985. BB 4-11 v Leics (Cheltenham) 1985.

DAVISON, Brian Fettes (Gifford HS, Rhodesia), b Bulawayo, Rhodesia 21 Dec 1946. 6'1". RHB, RM. Rhodesia 1967-79. Leicestershire 1970-83 (cap 1971; captain 1980). Tasmania 1979-85. Benefit 1982. Gloucestershire debut/cap 1985. 1000 runs (13+1); most – 1818 (1976). HS 189 v Australians (Leicester) 1975. BB 5-52 Rhodesia v Griqualand West (Bulawayo) 1967-68. Awards: NWT 2; BHC 6. **NWT:** HS 99 Leics v Essex (Southend) 1977. BB 2-18 Leics v Derbys (Leicester) 1971. **BHC:** HS 158 Leics v Warwicks (Coventry) 1972. BB 1-16. **JPL:** HS 103 v Yorks (Gloucester) 1985. BB 4-29 Leics v Glam (Neath) 1971.

ELLIS, Richard Gary Peter (Haileybury C; St. Edmund Hall, Oxford), b Paddington, London 20 Dec 1960. 6'1". RHB, OB/RM. Oxford U 1981-83; blue 1981-82-83 (capt 1982). Middlesex 1982-84. Glos debut 1985. HS 105* and BB 2-40 Oxford U v Surrey (Oxford) 1982. **NWT:** HS 15* Middx v Northant (Northampton) 1983. **BHC:** HS 32 Comb Us v Essex (Chelmsford) 1981. **JPL:** HS 52 Middx v Northants (Milton Keynes) 1983.

GRAVENEY, David Anthony (Millfield S), b Bristol 2 Jan 1953. 6'4". RHB, SLA. Son of J.K. (Gloucestershire 1947-64). Debut 1972. Cap 1976. Captain 1981-. HS 119 v Oxford U (Oxford) 1980. BB 8-85 v Notts (Cheltenham) 1974. **NWT:** HS 44 v Surrey (Bristol) 1973. BB 5-11 v Ireland (Dublin) 1981. **BHC:** HS 49* v Somerset (Taunton) 1982. BB 3-13 v Scotland (Glasgow) 1983. **JPL:** HS 56* v Notts (Bristol) 1985. BB 4-22 v Hants (Lydney) 1974.

LAWRENCE, David Valentine (Linden S), b Gloucester 28 Jan 1964. 6'2". RHB, RF. Debut 1981. Cap 1985. YC 1985. Tour: SL 1985-86 (Eng B). HS 41 v Notts (Nottingham) 1985. BB 7-48 v Sussex (Hove) 1985. **NWT:** HS 1*. BB 2-51 v Leics (Leicester) 1983. **BHC:** HS 22* v Scot (Bristol) 1985. BB 5-48 v Hants (Bristol) 1984. **JPL:** HS 17 v Hants (Bristol) 1984. BB 4-32 v Lancs (Moreton) 1984.

LLOYDS, Jeremy William (Blundell's S), b Penang, Malaya 17 Nov 1954. 6'0". LHB, OB. Somerset 1979-84 (cap 1982). Orange Free State 1983-84. Gloucestershire debut/cap 1985. HS 132* Somerset v Northants (Northampton) 1982. BB 7-88 Somerset v Essex (Chelmsford) 1982. **NWT:** HS 40 v Northants (Bristol) 1985. **BHC:** HS 51 Somerset v Sussex (Taunton) 1983. **JPL:** HS 33 Somerset v Surrey (Oval) 1981. BB 2-1 Somerset v Hants (Taunton) 1981.

PAYNE, Ian Roger (Emanuel S), b Kennington, London 9 May 1958. 6'0". RHB, RM. Surrey 1977-84. Gloucestershire debut 1985. HS 43 Surrey v Essex (Oval) 1983. BB 5-13 Surrey v Glos (Oval) 1983. Awards: BHC 1. **NWT:** HS 56* and BB 5-36 Surrey v Lincs (Sleaford) 1983. **BHC:** HS 2. BB 3-20 Surrey v Leics (Oval) 1981. **JPL:** HS 37 v Hants (Bournemouth) 1985. BB 5-21 Surrey v Derbys (Derby) 1982.

ROLL, Lawson Macgregor (Colstons S), b Thornbury 8 Mar 1965. RHB, OB. Grandson of H.T. Roll (Warwickshire 1927). Debut 1984. No appearances 1985.

ROMAINES, Paul William (Leeholme S), b Bishop Auckland, Co Durham 25 Dec 1955. 6'0". RHB. Northants 1975-76. Gloucestershire debut 1982. Cap 1983. Griqualand West 1984-85. Durham 1977-81. 1000 runs (2); most – 1844 (1984). HS 186 v Warwicks (Nuneaton) 1982. BB 3-42 v Surrey (Oval) 1985. Awards: BHC 2. **NWT:** HS 82 v Hants (Bristol) 1983. **BHC:** HS 125 v Notts (Bristol) 1985. **JPL:** HS 105 v Northants (Northampton) 1985.

RUSSELL, Robert Charles (Jack) (Archway CS), b Stroud 15 Aug 1963. 5'8½". LHB, WK. Debut 1981. Cap 1985. HS 64* v Worcs (Bristol) 1983. Awards: BHC 1. **NWT:** HS 16 v Lancs (Bristol) 1984. **BHC:** HS 36* v Scotland (Glasgow) 1983. **JPL:** HS 43 v Glamorgan (Swansea) 1984.

SAINSBURY, Gary Edward (Beal GS, Bath U), b Wanstead 17 Jan 1958. 6'2". RHB, LMF. Essex 1979-80. Gloucestershire debut 1983. HS 13 v Glamorgan (Cheltenham) 1983. BB 7-38 v Northants (Northampton) 1985. **NWT:** HS 3. BB 3-58 v Lancs (Bristol) 1984. **BHC:** HS 1*. BB 4-28 v Northants (Northampton) 1983. **JPL:** HS 6*. BB 3-19 v Notts (Nottingham) 1984.

SHEPHERD, John Neil (Alleyn's S, Barbados), b St. Andrew, Barbados 9 Nov 1943. 5'9". RHB, RM. Barbados 1964-71. Kent 1966-81 (cap 1967). Rhodesia 1975-76. *Wisden* 1978. Benefit 1979 (£58,537). Glos debut 1982. Cap 1983. Tests (WI): 5 (1969 and 1970-71); HS 32 v Eng (Lord's) 1969; BB 5-104 v Eng (Manchester) 1969 – on debut. Tours: Eng 1969 (WI); SA 1973-74 (DHR), 1974-75 (DHR and IW). 1000 runs (2); most – 1157 (1968). HS 170 Kent v Northants (Folkestone) 1968. BB 8-40 West Indians v Glos (Bristol) 1969. Awards: NWT 2; BHC 3. **NWT:** HS 101 Kent v Middlesex (Canterbury) 1977. BB 4-20 v Staffs (Stone) 1984. **BHC:** HS 96 Kent v Middx (Lord's) 1975. BB 4-25 Kent v Derbys (Lord's) 1978. **JPL:** HS 94 Kent v Hants (Southampton) 1978. BB 6-52 v Kent (Bristol) 1983.

STOVOLD, Andrew Willis (Filton HS; Loughborough C), b Bristol 19 Mar 1953. 5'8". RHB, WK. Brother of Martin (Glos 1979-82). Debut 1973. Cap 1976. Orange Free State 1974-76. 1000 runs (6); most – 1671 (1983). HS 212* v Northants (Northampton) 1982. BB 1-0. Awards: NWT 2; BHC 6. **NWT:** HS 82 v Scotland (Bristol) 1983. **BHC:** HS 123 v Comb Us (Oxford) 1982. **JPL:** HS 98* v Kent (Cheltenham) 1977.

TWIZELL, Peter Henry (Ponteland HS), b Rothbury, Northumb 18 Jun 1959. 6'2". RHB, RFM. Debut 1985. Northumberland 1978-84. BB 2-65 v Zim. **JPL:** BB 1-23.

WALSH, Courtney Andrew (Excelsior HS), b Kingston, Jamaica 30 Oct 1962. 6'5½". RHB, RF. Jamaica 1981-86. Gloucestershire debut 1984. Cap 1985. Tests (WI): 6 (1984-85); HS 18* v Aus (Melbourne); BB 3-55 v Aus (Brisbane). LOI: 4. Tours (WI): Eng 1984; Aus 1984-85; Zim 1983-84 (Young WI). HS 37 v Hants (Bristol) 1985. BB 7-51 (13-128 match) v Warwicks (Cheltenham) 1985. **NWT:** HS 6*. BB 2-7 v Beds (Luton) 1985. **BHC:** BB 2-19 v Scotland 1985. **JPL:** HS 14 v Worcs (Worcester) 1984. BB 3-28 v Northants (Northampton) 1985.

WRIGHT, Anthony John (Alleyn's GS) b Stevenage, Herts 27 Jun 1962. 6'0". RHB, RM. Gloucestershire debut 1982. HS 139 v Surrey (Cheltenham) 1984. **NWT:** HS 14 v Middx 1982. **BHC:** HS 7. **JPL:** HS 52 v Essex (Cheltenham) 1982.

VALETE

ZAHEER ABBAS, Syed, b Sialkot, India 24 Jul 1947. 5'11½". RHB, OB. Karachi, PWD, Dawood Industries, Sind, PIA since 1965-66. *Wisden* 1971. Glos debut 1972. Cap 1975. Benefit 1983. Tests (Pak): 76 (1969-70 to 1984-85, 14 as captain); HS 274 v Eng (Birmingham) 1971; BB 2-21. LOI: 58. Tours (Pak): Eng 1971, 1974, 1982; Aus 1971-72 (RW), 1972-73, 1976-77, 1978-79, 1981-82, 1983-84; WI 1976-77; NZ 1972-73, 1978-79, 1984-85; Ind 1979-80, 1983-84; SL 1975-76. 1000 runs (11+6); most -2554 (1976). HS 274 (Tests). BB 5-15 Dawood Club v Railways (Lahore) 1975-76. Awards: NWT 5; BHC 1.

GLOUCESTERSHIRE RECORDS

FIRST-CLASS CRICKET

Highest Total	For	653-6d v Glamorgan; Bristol	1928
	V	774-7d by Australians; Bristol	1948
Lowest Total	For	17 v Australians; Cheltenham	1896
	V	12 by Northants; Gloucester	1907
Highest Innings	For	318* W.G. Grace v Yorkshire; Cheltenham	1876
	V	296 A.O. Jones for Notts; Nottingham	1903

Highest Partnerships

1st	395	D.M. Young/R.B. Nicholls v Oxford U; Oxford	1962
2nd	256	C.T.M. Pugh/T.W. Graveney v Derbyshire; Chesterfield	1960
3rd	336	W.R. Hammond/B.H. Lyon v Leics; Leicester	1933
4th	321	W.R. Hammond/W.L. Neale v Leics; Gloucester	1937
5th	261	W.G. Grace/W.O. Moberley v Yorkshire; Cheltenham	1876
6th	320	G.L. Jessop/J.H. Board v Sussex; Hove	1903
7th	248	W.G. Grace/E.L. Thomas v Sussex; Hove	1896
8th	239	W.R. Hammond/A.E. Wilson v Lancashire; Bristol	1938
9th	193	W.G. Grace/S.A.P. Kitcat v Sussex; Bristol	1896
10th	131	W.R. Gouldsworthy/J.G. Bessant v Somerset; Bristol	1923

Best Bowling (Innings)	For	10-40 E.G. Dennett v Essex; Bristol	1906
	V	10-66 A.A. Mailey for Australians; Cheltenham	1921
		10-66 K. Smales for Notts; Stroud	1956
Best Bowling (Match)	For	17-56 C.W.L. Parker v Essex; Gloucester	1925
	V	15-87 A.J. Conway for Worcs; Moreton-in-Marsh	1914

Most Runs – Season	2860	W.R. Hammond	(av 69.75)	1933
Most Runs – Career	33664	W.R. Hammond	(av 57.05)	1920-1951
Most 100s – Season	13	W.R. Hammond		1938
Most 100s – Career	113	W.R. Hammond		1920-1951
Most Wkts – Season	222	T.W.J. Goddard	(av 16.80) (av 16.37)	1937 and 1947
Most Wkts – Career	3170	C.W.L. Parker	(av 19.43)	1903-1935

LIMITED-OVERS CRICKET

Highest Total	NWT	327-7 v Berkshire; Reading	1966
	BHC	300-4 v Comb Univs; Oxford	1982
	JPL	272-4 v Middlesex; Lord's	1983
Lowest Total	NWT	85 v Essex; Bristol	1981
	BHC	62 v Hampshire; Bristol	1975
	JPL	49 v Middlesex; Bristol	1978
Highest Innings	NWT	158 Zaheer Abbas v Leics; Leicester	1983
	BHC	154* M.J. Procter v Somerset; Taunton	1972
	JPL	131 Sadiq Mohammad v Som; Bristol (Imp)	1975
Best Bowling	NWT	5-11 D.A. Graveney v Ireland; Dublin	1981
	BHC	6-13 M.J. Procter v Hampshire; Southampton	1977
	JPL	6-52 D.J. Shepherd v Kent; Bristol	1983

GLOUCESTERSHIRE 1985

RESULTS SUMMARY

	Place	Won	Lost	Drew	Abandoned
Britannic Assurance Championship	3rd	7	3	13	1
All First-class Matches		8	4	14	1
John Player League	6th	8	8		
NatWest Bank Trophy	Lost to Nottinghamshire (Quarter-Final)				
Benson and Hedges Cup	Failed to qualify for Quarter-Final				

BRITANNIC ASSURANCE CHAMPIONSHIP AVERAGES

BATTING AND FIELDING

Cap		M	I	NO	HS	Runs	Avge	100	50	Ct/St
1981	P. Bainbridge	21	33	8	151*	1456	58.24	4	10	9
1985	C.W.J. Athey	21	35	6	170	1247	43.00	4	6	24
1985	B.F. Davison	22	33	6	111	902	33.40	1	4	8
1985	J.W. Lloyds	22	30	5	101	734	29.36	1	4	23
1985	K.M. Curran	23	31	3	83	677	24.17	—	4	7
—	I.R. Payne	6	6	1	37	106	21.20	—	—	2
1976	A.W. Stovold	20	33	2	112	656	21.16	2	2	18
1976	D.A. Graveney	22	23	10	53*	239	18.38	—	1	17
—	A.J. Wright	7	12	2	47*	173	17.30	—	—	2
1985	C.A. Walsh	20	16	5	37	183	16.63	—	—	4
1983	P.W. Romaines	17	28	2	64	423	16.26	—	2	9
1985	D.V. Lawrence	23	24	5	41	258	13.57	—	—	10
1985	R.C. Russell	21	23	4	34	253	13.31	—	—	55/5
—	G.E. Sainsbury	4	5	3	8*	11	5.50	—	—	2

Also batted: A.J. Brassington (2 matches – cap 1975) 3* (4 ct); R.G.P. Ellis (1 match) 3,20 (2 ct). J.N. Shepherd (1 match – cap 1983) did not bat.

BOWLING

	O	M	R	W	Avge	Best	5 wI	10 wM
G.E. Sainsbury	138	45	380	21	18.09	7-38	2	—
C.A. Walsh	540.3	122	1636	82	19.95	7-51	4	1
D.A. Graveney	360.5	116	887	38	23.34	4-91	—	—
D.V. Lawrence	500.5	59	1923	79	24.34	7-48	5	—
K.M. Curran	414.2	87	1288	52	24.76	5-42	1	—
P. Bainbridge	182	45	492	18	27.33	5-60	1	—
J.W. Lloyds	131.1	25	450	15	30.00	5-37	1	—

Also bowled: C.W.J. Athey 41.1-6-189-8; R.G.P. Ellis 3-1-7-1; I.R. Payne 39-9-112-3; P.W. Romaines 10-0-42-3; J.N. Shepherd 14-3-41-0.

The First-Class Averages (pp. 168–183) give the records of Gloucestershire players in all first-class county matches (their other opponents being the Australians, the Zimbabweans and Cambridge U.), with the exception of: C.W.J. Athey 23-38-7-170-1442-46.51-5-7-26 ct. 41.1-6-189-8-23.62-3/3.

HAMPSHIRE

Formation of Present Club: 12 August 1863
Substantial Reorganisation: July 1879
Colours: Blue, Gold and White
Badge: Tudor Rose and Crown
Championships: (2) 1961, 1973
NatWest Trophy/Gillette Cup Semi-Finalists: (4) 1966, 1976, 1983, 1985
Benson and Hedges Cup Semi-Finalists: (2) 1975, 1977
John Player League Champions: (2) 1975, 1978
Match Awards: GC 25; NWT 8; BHC 33

Chief Executive: A.K. James (*retires 30 Apr 1986*)/A.F. Baker (*w.e.f. 1 May*). County Cricket Ground, Northlands Road, Southampton SO9 2TY.
Captain: M.C.J. Nicholas
Scorer: V.H. Isaacs
Scores/Prospects: ☎ Southampton (0703) 333788/9; Basingstoke (0256) 3646; Bournemouth (0202) 25872

ANDREW, Stephen Jon Walter (Milton Abbey S; Portchester SS), b London 27 Jan 1966. 6'3". RHB, RMF. Debut 1984. HS 6*. BB 6-43 v Glos (Bournemouth) 1985. Awards: BHC 1. **NWT:** BB 1-28. **BHC:** HS 1*. BB 3-12 v Surrey (Oval) 1984. **JPL:** BB 3-38 v Northants (Southampton) 1984.

CHIVERS, Ian James (Richard Taunton SFC, Southampton), b Southampton 5 Nov 1964. 5'9". RHB, OB. Debut 1985. BB 1-5.

CONNOR, Cardigan Adolphus (The Valley SS, Anguilla; Langley C, Berkshire), b The Valley, Anguilla 24 Mar 1961. 5'9". RHB, RFM. Debut 1984. Buckhinghamshire 1979-83. HS 36 v Northants (Northampton) 1985. BB 7-37 v Kent (Bournemouth) 1984. **NWT:** HS 3*. BB 3-52 v Essex (Southampton) 1985. **BHC:** HS 0. BB 4-27 v Kent (Canterbury) 1985. **JPL:** HS 2*. BB 4-16 v Yorks (Bournemouth) 1984.

COWLEY, Nigel Geoffrey (Dutchy Manor SS, Mere), b Shaftesbury, Dorset 1 Mar 1953. 5'7". RHB, OB. Debut 1974. Cap 1978. Dorset 1972. 1000 runs (1): 1042 (1984). HS 109* v Somerset (Taunton) 1977. BB 6-48 v Leics (Southampton) 1982. Awards: NWT 1. **NWT:** HS 63* v Glos (Bristol) 1979. BB 5-24 v Norfolk (Norwich) 1984. **BHC:** HS 59 v Glos (Southampton) 1977. BB 3-39 v Sussex (Bournemouth) 1982. **JPL:** HS 74 v Warwicks (Birmingham) 1981. BB 4-42 v Surrey (Portsmouth) 1983.

GOLDIE, Christopher Frederick Evelyn (St. Paul's S; Pembroke C, Cambridge) b Johannesburg, South Africa, 2 Nov 1960. 5'6". RHB, WK. Cambridge U 1981-82; blue 1981-82. Hampshire debut 1983. HS 77 v OU (Lord's) 1981. **BHC:** HS 3*

GREENIDGE, Cuthbert Gordon (St. Peter's BS, Barbados; Sutton SS, Reading), b St. Peter, Barbados 1 May 1951. 5'9½". RHB, RM. Debut 1970. Cap 1972. Barbados 1972-86. *Wisden* 1976. Benefit 1983. MBE 1985. Tests (WI): 66 (1974-75 to 1984-85); HS 223 v Eng (Manchester) 1984. LOI: 68. Tours: Eng 1976, 1980, 1984; Aus 1975-76, 1979-80, 1981-82, 1984-85; NZ 1979-80; Ind 1974-75, 1983-84; Pak 1974-75; 1980-81; SL 1974-75. 1000 (14+1); most – 1952 (1976). HS 273* D.H. Robins' XI v Pakistanis (Eastbourne) 1974. Hants HS 259 v Sussex (Southampton) 1975. BB 5-49 v Surrey (Southampton) 1971. Awards: NWT 4. BHC 7. **NWT:** HS 177 v Glamorgan (Southampton) 1975. **BHC:** HS 173* v Minor C (S) (Amersham) 1973. **JPL:** HS 163* v Warwicks (Birmingham) 1979. BB 1-36.

JAMES, Kevan David (Edmonton County HS), b Lambeth 18 Mar 1961. 6'0". LHB, LMF. Middlesex 1980-84. Wellington 1982-83. Hampshire debut 1985. HS 124 v Somerset (Taunton) 1985. BB 6-22 v Australians (Southampton) 1985. **BHC:** HS 27 v Leics (Southampton) 1985. BB 2-31 Middx v Kent (Canterbury) 1983. **JPL:** HS 34 v Warwicks (Birmingham) 1985. BB 2-25 Middx v Notts (Cleethorpes) 1983.

MARSHALL, Malcolm Denzil (Parkinson CS, Barbados), b St. Michael, Barbados 18 Apr 1958. 5'11". RHB, RF. Barbados 1977-86. Hampshire debut 1979. Cap 1981. *Wisden* 1982. Tests (WI): 40 (1978-79 to 1984-85); HS 92 v Ind (Kanpur) 1983-84; BB 7-53 v Eng (Leeds) 1984. LOI 60. Tours: Eng 1980, 1984; Aus 1979-80, 1981-82, 1984-85; NZ 1979-80; Ind 1978-79, 1983-84; Pak 1980-81; SL 1978-79; Zim 1981-82 (Young WI). 100 wickets (1): 134 (1982). HS 116* v Lancs (Southampton) 1982. BB 8-71 v Worcs (Southampton) 1982. **NWT:** HS 29 v Essex (Southampton) 1985. BB 4-15 v Kent (Canterbury) 1983. **BHC:** HS 25 v Leics (Southampton) 1985. BB 4-26 v Kent (Canterbury) 1983. **JPL:** HS 46 v Leics (Leicester) 1982. BB 5-13 v Glamorgan (Portsmouth) 1979.

MARU, Rajesh Jaman (Rook's Heath HS, Harrow; Pinner SFC), b Nairobi, Kenya 28 Oct 1962. 5'6". RHB, SLA. Middlesex 1980-82. Hampshire debut 1984. Tour: Zim 1980-81 (Middx). HS 62 v Sussex (Portsmouth) 1985. BB 7-79 v Middx (Bournemouth) 1984. **JPL:** HS 3*. BB 2-41 Middx v Kent (Lord's) 1980.

MIDDLETON, Tony Charles (Montgomery of Alamein S, and Peter Symonds SFC, Winchester), b Winchester 1 Feb 1964. 5'10½". RHB, SLA. Debut 1984. HS 10 v Kent (Bournemouth) 1984. No appearance 1985.

NICHOLAS, Mark Charles Jefford (Bradfield C), b London 29 Sep 1957. 5'11" RHB, RM. Grandson of F.W.H. (Essex 1912-29). Debut 1978. Cap 1982. Captain 1985-. Tours: SL 1985-86 (Eng B; captain); Zim 1984-85 (Eng Co; captain). 1000 runs (4); most – 1559 (1984). HS 206* v OU (Oxford) 1982. BB 5-45 v Worcs (Southampton) 1983. Awards: BHC 1. **NWT:** HS 63 v Norfolk (Norwich) 1984. BB 2-39 v Berks (Southampton) 1985. **BHC:** HS 74 v Glamorgan (Southampton) 1985. BB 4-34 v Minor C (Reading) 1985. **JPL:** HS 108 v Glos (Bristol) 1984. BB 4-50 v Notts (Nottingham) 1985.

PARKS, Robert James (Eastbourne GS; Southampton Inst of Technology), b Cuckfield, Sussex 15 Jun 1959. 5'8". RHB, WK. Son of J.M. (Sussex, Somerset and England 1949-76) and grandson of J.H. (Sussex and England 1924-52). Debut 1980. Cap 1982. Tour: Zim 1984-85 (Eng Co). Held 10 catches in match v Derbys (Portsmouth) 1981. HS 89 v CU (Cambridge) 1984. Awards: BHC 1. **NWT:** HS 25 v Kent (Southampton) 1984. **JPL:** HS 36* v Leics (Leicester) 1982. **BHC:** HS 11* v Essex (Southampton) 1984, 11* v Kent (Canterbury) 1985.

SMITH, Christopher Lyall ('Kippy') (Northlands HS, Durban), b Durban, South Africa 15 Oct 1958. 5'10". RHB, OB. Brother of R.A. and grandson of Dr. V.L. Shearer (Natal). Natal 1977-83. Glamorgan 1979. Hampshire debut 1980. Cap 1981. *Wisden* 1983. Tests: 7 (1983 to 1983-84); HS 91 v NZ (Auckland) 1983-84; 2-31 v NZ (Nottingham) 1983. LOI: 4. Tours: NZ 1983-84; Pak 1983-84; SL 1985-86 (Eng B). 1000 runs (4); most – 2000 (1985). HS 193 v Derbys (Derby) 1983. BB 3-35 v Glamorgan (Southampton) 1983. Awards: NWT 1; BHC 2. **NWT:** HS 101* v Glos (Bristol) 1983. BB 3-32 v Berks (Southampton) 1985. **BHC:** HS 82* v Comb Us (Southampton) 1984. **JPL:** HS 95 v Leics (Basingstoke) 1984. BB 2-3 v Glos (Bristol) 1984.

SMITH, Robin Arnold (Northlands HS), b Durban, South Africa, 13 Sep 1963. 5'11". RHB, LB. Brother of C.L. and grandson of Dr. V.L. Shearer (Natal). Natal 1980-85. Hampshire debut 1982. Cap 1985. 1000 (1): 1533 (1985). HS 140* v Derbys (Basingstoke) 1985. BB 2-11 v Surrey (Southampton) 1985. Awards: NWT 1. **NWT:** HS 110 v Somerset (Taunton) 1985. BB 2-13 v Berks (Southampton) 1985. **BHC:** HS 81 v Leics (Southampton) 1985. **JPL:** HS 104 v Glamorgan (Cardiff) 1984, 104 v Surrey (Southampton) 1985.

TERRY, Vivian **Paul** (Millfield S), b Osnabruck, West Germany 14 Jan 1959. 6'0". RHB, RM. Debut 1978. Cap 1983. Tests: 2 (1984); HS 8. Tour: Zim 1984-85 (Eng Co). 1000 runs (3); most – 1284 (1985). HS 175* v Glos (Bristol) 1985. Awards: NWT 2. **NWT:** HS 165* v Berkshire (Southampton) 1985. **BHC:** HS 72 v Kent (Canterbury) 1983, 72 v Essex (Southampton) 1984. **JPL:** HS 110 v Notts (Southampton) 1984.

TREMLETT, Timothy Maurice (Bellemoor SS; Richard Taunton SFC, Southampton), b Wellington, Somerset 26 Jul 1956. 6'2". RHB, RMF. Son of M.F. (Somerset, Central Districts and England 1947-60). Debut 1976. Cap 1983. Tours: SL 1985-86 (Eng B); Zim 1984-85 (Eng Co). HS 102* v Somerset (Taunton) 1985. BB 6-82 v Derbys (Portsmouth) 1983. **NWT:** HS 17 v Kent (Southampton) 1984. BB 4-38 v Kent (Canterbury) 1983. **BHC:** HS 29 v Surrey (Bournemouth) 1981. BB 4-54 v Glamorgan (Southampton) 1985. **JPL:** HS 35 v Worcs (Worcester) 1984. BB 5-28 v Kent (Canterbury) 1985.

TURNER, David Roy (Chippenham BHS), b Chippenham, Wiltshire 5 Feb 1949. 5'6". LHB, RM. Debut 1966. Cap 1970. Western Province 1977-78. Benefit 1981. Tour: SA 1972-73 (DHR). 1000 runs (7); most – 1365 (1984). HS 181* v Surrey (Oval) 1969. BB 2-7 v Glamorgan (Bournemouth) 1981. Awards: NWT 1; BHC 4. **NWT:** HS 86 v Northants (Southampton) 1976. **BHC:** HS 123* v Minor C (S) (Amersham) 1973. **JPL:** HS 114 v Essex (Colchester) 1984.

HAMPSHIRE RECORDS

FIRST-CLASS CRICKET

Highest Total	For	672-7d v Somerset; Taunton	1899
	V	742 by Surrey; The Oval	1909
Lowest Total	For	15 v Warwicks; Birmingham	1922
	V	23 by Yorkshire; Middlesbrough	1965
Highest Innings	For	316 R.H. Moore v Warwicks; Bournemouth	1937
	V	302* P. Holmes for Yorkshire; Portsmouth	1920

Highest Partnerships

1st	249	R.E. Marshall/J.R. Gray v Middlesex; Portsmouth	1960
2nd	321	G. Brown/E.I.M. Barrett v Glos; Southampton	1920
3rd	344	C.P. Mead/G. Brown v Yorks; Portsmouth	1927
4th	263	R.E. Marshall/D.A. Livingstone v Middlesex; Lord's	1970
5th	235	G. Hill/D.F. Walker v Sussex; Portsmouth	1937
6th	411	R.M. Poore/E.G. Wynyard v Somerset; Taunton	1899
7th	325	G. Brown/C.H. Abercrombie v Essex; Leyton	1913
8th	227	K.D. James/T.M. Tremlett v Somerset; Taunton	1985
9th	230	D.A. Livingstone/A.T. Castell v Surrey; Southampton	1962
10th	192	H.A.W. Bowell/W.H. Livsey v Worcs; Bournemouth	1921

Best Bowling (Innings)	For	9-25	R.M.H. Cottam v Lancashire; Manchester	1965
	V	10-46	W. Hickton for Lancashire; Manchester	1870
Best Bowling (Match)	For	16-88	J.A. Newman v Somerset; W-s-M	1927
	V	17-119	W. Mead for Essex; Southampton	1895

Most Runs – Season	2854	C.P. Mead	(av 79.27)	1928
Most Runs – Career	48892	C.P. Mead	(av 48.84)	1905-1936
Most 100s – Season	12	C.P. Mead		1928
Most 100s – Career	138	C.P. Mead		1905-1936
Most Wkts – Season	190	A.S. Kennedy	(av 15.61)	1922
Most Wkts – Career	2669	D. Shackleton	(av 18.23)	1948-1969

LIMITED-OVERS CRICKET

Highest Total	NWT	371-4 Glamorgan; Southampton	1975
	BHC	321-1 v Minor C (S); Amersham	1973
	JPL	292-1 v Surrey; Portsmouth	1983
Lowest Total	NWT	98 v Lancashire; Manchester	1975
	BHC	94 v Glamorgan; Swansea	1973
	JPL	43 v Essex; Basingstoke	1972
Highest Innings	NWT	177 C.G. Greenidge v Glam; Southampton	1975
	BHC	173* C.G. Greenidge v Minor C (S); Amersham	1973
	JPL	166* T.E. Jesty v Surrey; Portsmouth	1983
Best Bowling	NWT	7-30 P.J. Sainsbury v Norfolk; Southampton	1965
	BHC	5-24 R.S. Herman v Glos; Bristol	1975
		5-24 K.St.J.D. Emery v Essex; Chelmsford	1982
	JPL	6-20 T.E. Jesty v Glamorgan; Cardiff	1975

HAMPSHIRE 1985

RESULTS SUMMARY

	Place	*Won*	*Lost*	*Drew*	*Abandoned*
Britannic Assurance Championship	2nd	7	2	15	
All First-class Matches		7	2	17	
John Player League	3rd	8	4		4
NatWest Bank Trophy	Lost to Essex (Semi-Final)				
Benson and Hedges Cup	Lost to Leicestershire (Quarter-Final)				

BRITANNIC ASSURANCE CHAMPIONSHIP AVERAGES

BATTING AND FIELDING

Cap		*M*	*I*	*NO*	*HS*	*Runs*	*Avge*	*100*	*50*	*Ct/St*
1981	C.L. Smith	21	35	3	143*	1720	53.75	5	11	10
1972	C.G. Greenidge	19	32	2	204	1236	41.20	2	8	16
1985	R.A. Smith	24	40	6	140*	1351	39.73	2	7	13
—	K.D. James	6	9	3	124	217	36.16	1	—	5
—	J.J.E. Hardy	14	22	4	107*	624	34.66	1	3	4
1982	M.C.J. Nicholas	22	35	3	146	1109	34.65	1	7	18
1983	V.P. Terry	24	40	2	148*	1224	32.21	2	9	34
1983	T.M. Tremlett	24	29	15	102*	450	32.14	1	—	5
1981	M.D. Marshall	22	33	2	66*	768	24.77	—	5	10
1982	R.J. Parks	24	23	9	53*	344	24.57	—	2	54/4
1978	N.G. Cowley	12	13	4	51	202	22.44	—	1	3
—	R.J. Maru	21	18	8	62	223	22.30	—	1	15
1970	D.R. Turner	6	8	1	44	153	21.85	—	—	2
—	C.A. Connor	15	8	3	36	61	12.20	—	—	6
—	S.J.W. Andrew	10	4	3	6*	8	8.00	—	—	5

BOWLING

	O	*M*	*R*	*W*	*Avge*	*Best*	*5 wI*	*10 wM*
M.D. Marshall	688.1	193	1680	95	17.68	7-59	5	—
T.M. Tremlett	665.5	181	1620	75	21.60	5-42	2	—
N.G. Cowley	234.5	56	650	24	27.08	3-17	—	—
R.J. Maru	652	178	1809	64	28.26	5-16	3	—
S.J.W. Andrew	258	46	915	28	32.67	6-43	1	—
C.A. Connor	417.5	83	1310	29	45.17	4-62	—	—

Also bowled: C.G. Greenidge 4-1-16-0; K.D. James 126-17-549-7; M.C.J. Nicholas 119-21-436-6; C.L. Smith 61-6-269-4; R.A. Smith 26.4-8-72-4.

The First-Class Averages (pp. 168–183) give the records of Hampshire players in all first-class county matches (their other opponents being the Australians and Oxford U.), with the exception of: M.C.J. Nicholas 24-39-4-146-1183-33.80-1-8-19 ct. 119-21-436-6-72.66-2/22.

KENT

Formation of Present Club: 1 March 1859
Substantial Reorganisation: 6 December 1870
Colours: Red and White
Badge: White Horse
Championships: (6) 1906, 1909, 1910, 1913, 1970, 1978. **Joint:** (1) 1977
NatWest Trophy/Gillette Cup Winners: (2) 1967, 1974
Benson and Hedges Cup Winners: (3) 1973, 1976, 1978
John Player League Champions: (3) 1972, 1973, 1976
Match Awards: GC 23; NWT 12; BHC 46

Secretary: D.B. Dalby, St. Lawrence Ground, Canterbury, CT1 3NZ
Captain: C.S. Cowdrey
Scorer: C. Lewis
Scores/Prospects: ☎ Canterbury (0227) 457323/4

ALDERMAN, Terence Michael (Aquinas C and Churchlands C, Perth), b Subiaco, Perth, Australia 12 Jun 1956. 6'2½". RHB, RFM. Western Australia 1974-85. *Wisden* 1981. Kent debut 1984. Tests (Aus): 22 (1981-84-85); HS 23* and BB 6-128 v WI (Perth) 1984-85. LOI: 23. Tours (Aus): Eng 1981; SA 1985-86 (Aus XI); WI 1983-84; NZ 1981-82; Pak 1982-83. HS 52* v Sussex (Hastings) 1984. BB 7-28 Western Australia v New South Wales (Perth) 1981-82. **NWT:** BB 4-21 v Hampshire (Southampton) 1984. **BHC:** HS 4*. BB 2-9 v Middlesex (Lord's) 1984. **JPL:** HS 11 and BB 5-36 v Lancashire (Maidstone) 1984.

ASLETT, Derek George (Dover GS; Leicester U), b Dover 12 Feb 1958. 5'11". RHB, LB. Debut 1981 scoring 146* and 20* v Hampshire at Bournemouth. Cap 1983. 1000 runs (2); most – 1491 (1984). HS 221* v Sri Lankans (Canterbury) 1984. BB 4-119 v Sussex (Hove) 1982. **NWT:** HS 67 v Hants (Southampton) 1984. BB 1-0 **BHC:** HS 49 v Hants (Canterbury) 1985. **JPL:** HS 100 v Somerset (Taunton) 1983.

BAPTISTE, Eldine Ashworth Elderfield (All Saints SS, Liberta), b Liberta, Antigua 12 Mar 1960. 6'0". RHB, RFM. Debut 1981. Cap 1983. Leeward Islands 1981-86. Tests (WI): 9 (1983-84 to 1984); HS 87* v Eng (Birmingham) 1984; BB 3-31 v Eng (Manchester) 1984. LOI: 29. Tours (WI): Eng 1984; Aus 1984-85; Ind 1983-84. HS 136* v Yorkshire (Sheffield) 1983. BB 6-42 v Northants (Northampton) 1985. Awards: NWT 1; BHC 1. **NWT:** HS 22 v Warwicks (Canterbury) 1985. BB 5-20 v Hants (Canterbury) 1983. **BHC:** HS 43* v Somerset (Taunton) 1985. BB 5-30 v Glamorgan (Cardiff) 1985. **JPL:** HS 60 v Warwicks (Canterbury) 1985. BB 4-29 v Worcs (Canterbury) 1983.

BENSON, Richard Mark (Sutton Valence S), b Shoreham, Sussex 6 Jul 1958. 5'10". LHB, OB. Debut 1980. Cap 1981. 1000 runs (4); most – 1515 (1983). HS 162 v Hampshire (Southampton) 1985. BB 1-4. Awards: NWT 2. **NWT:** HS 113* v Warwicks (Birmingham) 1984. **BHC:** HS 65 v Surrey (Canterbury) 1982. **JPL:** HS 97 v Surrey (Oval) 1982.

COWDREY, Christopher Stuart (Tonbridge S), b Farnborough, Kent 20 Oct 1957. 6'1". RHB, RM. Brother of G.R., son of M.C. (Kent and England 1950-76) and grandson of E.A. (Europeans). Kent 2nd XI debut when aged 15. Debut 1977. Cap 1979. Captain 1985-. Tests: 5 (1984-85); HS 38 v Ind (Delhi) 1984-85; BB 2-65 v Ind (Madras) 1984-85. LOI: 3. Tours: NZ 1979-80 (DHR); Ind/SL 1984-85; SL 1977-78 (DHR). 1000 runs (3); most – 1364 (1983). HS 159 v Surrey (Canterbury) 1985. BB 3-5 v Northants (Maidstone) 1985. Awards: NWT 3; BHC 2. **NWT:** HS 122* v Essex (Chelmsford) 1983. BB 4-36 v Hants (Canterbury) 1983. **BHC:** HS 114 v Sussex (Canterbury) 1977. BB 3-38 v Hants (Canterbury) 1985. **JPL:** HS 95 v Worcs (Canterbury) 1983. BB 5-28 v Leics (Canterbury) 1984.

COWDREY, Graham Robert (Tonbridge S; Durham U), b Farnborough, Kent 27 Jun 1964. 5'11". RHB, RM. Brother of C.S., son of M.C. (Kent and England 1950-76) and grandson of E.A. (Europeans). Debut 1984. HS 53 v Worcs (Worcester) 1985. BB 1-22. **JPL:** HS 21 v Derbys (Folkestone) 1985.

DILLEY, Graham Roy (Dartford West SS), b Dartford 18 May 1959. 6'3". LHB, RF. Debut 1977. Cap 1980. YC 1980. No appearances 1984. Natal 1985-86. Tests: 18 (1979-80 to 1983-84); HS 56 v Aus (Leeds) 1981; BB 4-24 v Aus (Nottingham) 1981. LOI: 18. Tours: Aus 1979-80; WI 1980-81; NZ 1983-84; Ind 1979-80, 1981-82; Pak 1983-84; SL 1981-82. HS 81 v Northants (Northampton) 1979. BB 6-66 v Middlesex (Lord's) 1979. Awards: BHC 1. **NWT:** HS 19 v Som 1983, 19 v Essex 1985. BB 4-29 v Somerset (Lord's) 1983. **BHC:** HS 37* v Hants (Canterbury) 1983. BB 4-14 v Comb Us (Canterbury) 1981. **JPL:** HS 33 v Northants (Northampton) 1982. BB 4-20 v Glos (Canterbury) 1980.

ELLISON, Richard Mark (Tonbridge S; Exeter U), b Ashford, Kent 21 Sep 1959. 6'2". LHB, RMF. Brother of C.C. Ellison (Cambridge U). Debut 1981. Cap 1983. *Wisden* 1985. Tests: 7 (1984 to 1985); HS 41 v Sri Lanka (Lord's) 1984; BB 6-77 v Aus (Birmingham) 1985. LOI: 9. Tours: WI 1985-86; Ind/SL 1984-85. HS 108 v OU (Oxford) 1984. BB 7-87 v Northants (Maidstone) 1985. Awards: NWT 1; BHC 3. **NWT:** HS 49* v Warwicks (Birmingham) 1984. BB 4-19 v Cheshire (Canterbury) 1983. **BHC:** HS 72 v Middlesex (Lord's) 1984. BB 4-28 v Glam (Canterbury) 1984. **JPL:** HS 84 v Glos (Canterbury) 1984. BB 4-25 v Hants (Canterbury) 1983.

HINKS, Simon Graham (St. George's S, Gravesend), b Northfleet, Kent 12 Oct 1960. 6'2". LHB, RM. Debut 1982. Cap 1985. 1000 (1): 1536 (1985). HS 117 v Surrey (Oval) 1985. BB 1-18. Awards: NWT 1. **NWT:** HS 95 v Surrey (Canterbury) 1985. **BHC:** HS 49 v Glamorgan (Cardiff) 1985. **JPL:** HS 52* v Hants (Bournemouth) 1984. BB 1-3.

JARVIS, Kevin Bertram Sidney (Springhead S, Northfleet; Thames Polytechnic) b Dartford 23 Apr 1953. 6'3". RHB, RFM. Debut 1975. Cap 1977. Tours: WI 1982-83 (Int XI); SL 1977-78 (DHR). HS 19 v Derbys (Maidstone) 1984. BB 8-97 v Worcs (Worcester) 1978. Awards: NWT 1; BHC 1. **NWT:** HS 5*. BB 4-19 v Warwicks (Canterbury) 1983. **BHC:** HS 4. BB 4-34 v Worcs (Lord's) 1976. **JPL:** HS 8*. BB 5-24 v Notts (Nottingham) 1985.

MARSH, Steven Andrew (Walderslade SS; Mid-Kent CFE), b Westminster 27 Jan 1961. 5'10". RHB, WK. Debut 1982. HS 48 v Notts (Folkestone) 1984. **JPL:** HS 2.

PENN, Christopher (Dover GS). b Dover 19 Jun 1963. 6'1". LHB. RFM. Debut 1982. HS 115 v Lancs (Manchester) 1984. BB 4-63 v Middlesex (Lord's) 1985. **NWT:** HS 5. BB 1-34. **BHC:** HS 17 v Somerset (Canterbury) 1984. BB 4-34 v Surrey (Canterbury) 1982. **JPL:** HS 40 v Sussex (Maidstone) 1982. BB 3-35 v Yorks (Canterbury) 1982.

TAVARÉ, Christopher James (Sevenoaks S; St. John's, Oxford). b Orpington. Kent 27 Oct 1954. 6'1½". RHB. RM. Debut 1974. Oxford U 1975-77; blue 1975-76-77. Cap 1978. Captain 1983-84. Tests: 30 (1980 to 1984); HS 149 v Ind (Delhi) 1981-82. LOI: 29. Tours: Aus 1982-83; NZ 1983-84; Ind/SL 1981-82; Pak 1983-84. 1000 runs (9); most – 1770 (1981). HS 168* v Essex (Chelmsford) 1982. BB 1-20. Awards: NWT 3; BHC 6. **NWT:** HS 118* v Yorks (Canterbury) 1981. **BHC:** HS 143 v Som (Taunton) 1985. **JPL:** HS 136* v Glos (Canterbury) 1978.

TAYLOR, Neil Royston (Cray Valley THS). b Orpington. Kent 21 Jul 1959. 6'1". RHB. OB. Debut 1979 scoring 110 and 11 v Sri Lankans at Canterbury. Cap 1982. 1000 runs (3); most – 1340 (1982). HS 155* v Glam (Cardiff) 1983. BB 2-20 v Somerset (Canterbury) 1985. Awards: BHC 4. **NWT:** HS 51 v Essex (Chelmsford) 1985. **BHC:** HS 121 v Sussex (Hove) 1982. 121 v Somerset (Canterbury) 1982. **JPL:** HS 74 v Glos (Folkestone) 1982.

UNDERWOOD, Derek Leslie (Beckenham and Penge GS). b Bromley 8 Jun 1945. 5'11". RHB. LM. Debut 1963 – youngest to take 100 wickets in first season. Cap 1964. YC 1966. *Wisden* 1968. Benefit 1975. Testimonial 1986. MBE 1981. Tests: 86 (1966 to 1981-82); HS 45* v Aus (Leeds) 1968; BB 8-51 (13-71 match) v Pak (Lord's) 1974. LOI: 26. Tours: Aus 1970-71. 1974-75. 1976-77. 1979-80; SA 1975-76 (Int Wan). 1981-82 (SAB); WI 1969-70 (Cav/DN). 1973-74; NZ 1970-71. 1974-75; Ind 1979-80; Ind/SL 1967-68. 1972-73. 1976-77. 1981-82; Pak 1966-67 (MCC U-25). 1968-69. 1972-73; SL 1968-69. 100 wickets (10); most – 157 (1966). HS 111 v Sussex (Hastings) 1984. BB 9-28 v Sussex (Hastings) 1964. Awards: BHC 2. **NWT:** HS 28 v Sussex (Tunbridge Wells) 1963. BB 4-57 v Leics (Canterbury) 1974. **BHC:** HS 27 v Surrey (Canterbury) 1983. BB 5-35 v Surrey (Oval) 1976. **JPL:** HS 22 v Worcs (Dudley) 1969. BB 6-12 v Sussex (Hastings) 1984.

VALETE

JOHNSON, Graham William (Beckenham and Penge GS; Shooter's Hill GS; LSE). b Beckenham 8 Nov 1946. 6'1". RHB. OB. Debut 1965. Cap 1970. Benefit 1983. Transvaal 1981-82. Transvaal B 1984-85 (captain). Tour: SA 1973-74 (DHR). 1000 runs (3); most – 1438 runs (1973. 1975). HS 168 v Surrey (Oval) 1976. BB 7-76 v Northants (Canterbury) 1983. Awards: NWT 1; BHC 3.

KNOTT, Alan Philip Eric (Northumberland Heath SS. Erith). b Belvedere 9 Apr 1946. 5'8". RHB. WK. OB. Debut 1964. Cap 1965. YC 1965. *Wisden* 1969. Tasmania 1969-70. Benefit 1976 (£27,037). Tests: 95 (1967 to 1981); HS 135 v Aus (Nottingham) 1977. LOI: 20. Tours: Aus 1970-71. 1974-75. 1976-77; SA 1981-82 (SAB); WI 1964-65 (Cav). 1967-68. 1973-74; NZ 1970-71. 1974-75; Ind 1972-73. 1976-77; Pak 1966-67 (MCC U-25). 1968-69. 1972-73; SL 1968-69. 1972-73. 1976-77. 1000 runs (2); most – 1209 (1971). HS 156 MCC v South Zone (Bangalore) 1972-73. Kent HS 144 v Sussex (Canterbury) 1976. BB 1-5. Awards: NWT 2; BHC 1.

LUCKHURST, Brian William. County Manager. No appearances 1977-84 but played v Australians at Canterbury. *See 1976 Annual (p. 91).*

KENT RECORDS

FIRST-CLASS CRICKET

Highest Total	For	803-4d v Essex; Brentwood	1934
	V	676 by Australians; Canterbury	1921
Lowest Total	For	18 v Sussex; Gravesend	1867
	V	16 by Warwicks; Tonbridge	1913
Highest Innings	For	332 W.H. Ashdown v Essex; Brentwood	1934
	V	344 W.G. Grace for MCC; Canterbury	1876

Highest Partnerships

1st	283	A.E. Fagg/P.R. Sunnucks v Essex; Colchester	1938
2nd	352	W.H. Ashdown/F.E. Woolley v Essex; Brentwood	1934
3rd	321*	A. Hearne/J.R. Mason v Notts; Nottingham	1899
4th	297	H.T.W. Hardinge/A.P.F. Chapman v Hampshire; Southampton	1926
5th	277	F.E. Woolley/L.E.G. Ames v N. Zealand; Canterbury	1931
6th	284	A.P.F. Chapman/G.B. Legge v Lancashire; Maidstone	1927
7th	248	A.P. Day/E. Humphreys v Somerset; Taunton	1908
8th	157	A.L. Hilder/A.C. Wright v Essex; Gravesend	1924
9th	161	B.R. Edrich/F. Ridgway v Sussex; Tunbridge Wells	1949
10th	235	F.E. Woolley/A. Fielder v Worcs; Stourbridge	1909

Best Bowling (Innings)	For	10-30	C. Blythe v Northants; Northampton	1907
	V	10-48	C.H.G. Bland for Sussex; Tonbridge	1899
Best Bowling (Match)	For	17-48	C. Blythe v Northants; Northampton	1907
	V	17-106	T.W.J. Goddard for Glos; Bristol	1939

Most Runs – Season	2894	F.E. Woolley	(av 59.06)	1928
Most Runs – Career	47868	F.E. Woolley	(av 41.77)	1906-1938
Most 100s – Season	10	F.E. Woolley		1928 and 1934
Most 100s – Career	122	F.E. Woolley		1906-1938
Most Wkts – Season	262	A.P. Freeman	(av 14.74)	1933
Most Wkts – Career	3340	A.P. Freeman	(av 17.64)	1914-1936

LIMITED-OVERS CRICKET

Highest Total	NWT	297-3 v Worcs; Canterbury	1970
	BHC	293-6 v Somerset; Taunton	1985
	JPL	281-5 v Warwicks; Folkestone	1983
Lowest Total	NWT	60 v Somerset; Taunton	1979
	BHC	73 v Middlesex; Canterbury	1979
	JPL	83 v Middlesex; Lord's	1984
Highest Innings	NWT	129* B.W. Luckhurst v Durham; Canterbury	1974
	BHC	143 C.J. Tavaré v Somerset; Taunton	1985
	JPL	142 B.W. Luckhurst v Somerset; W-s-M	1970
Best Bowling	NWT	7-15 A.L. Dixon v Surrey; The Oval	1967
	BHC	5-21 B.D. Julien v Surrey; The Oval	1973
	JPL	6-9 R.A. Woolmer v Derbyshire; Chesterfield	1979

KENT 1985

RESULTS SUMMARY

	Place	*Won*	*Lost*	*Drew*	*Abandoned*
Britannic Assurance Championship	9th	4	5	15	
All First-class Matches		4	6	16	
John Player League	10th	6	7		3
NatWest Bank Trophy	Lost to Essex (Quarter-Final)				
Benson and Hedges Cup	Lost to Leicestershire (Semi-Final)				

BRITANNIC ASSURANCE CHAMPIONSHIP AVERAGES

BATTING AND FIELDING

Cap		*M*	*I*	*NO*	*HS*	*Runs*	*Avge*	*100*	*50*	*Ct/St*
1982	N.R. Taylor	14	22	6	102*	715	44.68	2	3	6
—	G.R. Cowdrey	5	7	2	53	187	37.40	—	1	5
1981	M.R. Benson	23	42	3	162	1446	37.07	3	10	14
1978	C.J. Tavaré	23	40	6	150*	1225	36.02	3	4	20
1985	S.G. Hinks	24	44	3	117	1423	34.70	1	9	20
1979	C.S. Cowdrey	19	34	3	159	1035	33.38	2	4	19
1983	E.A.E. Baptiste	21	33	4	82	897	30.93	—	6	12
1983	D.G. Aslett	11	20	1	111	521	27.42	1	1	4
1983	R.M. Ellison	14	22	5	98	457	26.88	—	3	3
—	C. Penn	8	7	2	50	102	20.40	—	1	9
1965	A.P.E. Knott	19	24	5	87*	379	19.94	—	2	53/1
1970	G.W. Johnson	10	14	3	30*	198	18.00	—	—	5
—	L. Potter	11	13	2	55	159	14.45	—	1	6
1980	G.R. Dilley	16	19	5	31	153	10.92	—	—	1
1964	D.L. Underwood	23	23	9	16*	121	8.64	—	—	7
1977	K.B.S. Jarvis	18	18	5	7	41	3.15	—	—	5

Also batted: S.A. Marsh (2 matches) 25,3 (3 ct, 3 st); S.N.V. Waterton 16*,6* (5 ct, 2 st).

BOWLING

	O	*M*	*R*	*W*	*Avge*	*Best*	*5 wI*	*10 wM*
R.M. Ellison	318.2	78	863	44	19.61	7-87	3	1
D.L. Underwood	745	277	1635	64	25.54	6-56	1	1
E.A.E. Baptiste	518	106	1521	52	29.25	6-42	2	—
L. Potter	203.3	57	554	18	30.77	4-87	—	—
K.B.S. Jarvis	513.4	111	1636	51	32.07	5-43	2	—
C. Penn	124.4	17	466	14	33.28	4-63	—	—
G.R. Dilley	323.1	62	1031	27	38.18	5-53	2	—
C.S. Cowdrey	200.1	27	721	14	51.50	3-5	—	—

Also bowled: D.G. Aslett 6-0-25-0; M.R. Benson 20.2-0-138-1; S.G. Hinks 21-0-72-1; G.W. Johnson 115.3-16-409-9; N.R. Taylor 52-8-168-5.

The First-Class Averages (pp. 168–183) give the records of Kent players in all first-class county matches (their other opponents being the Australians and Oxford U.), with the exception of R.M. Ellison 16-25-6-98-536-28.21-0-3-3 ct. 356.2-93-933-48-19.43-7/87-3-1. D.L. Underwood 24-25-9-16*-124-7.75-0-0-7 ct. 776-283-1706-66-25.84-6/56-1-1.

LANCASHIRE

Formation of Present Club: 12 January 1864
Colours: Red, Green and Blue
Badge: Red Rose
Championships (since 1890): (7) 1897, 1904, 1926, 1927, 1928, 1930, 1934
Joint Championships: (1) 1950
NatWest Trophy/Gillette Cup Winners: (4) 1970, 1971, 1972, 1975
Benson and Hedges Cup Winners: (1) 1984
John Player League Champions: (2) 1969, 1970
Match Awards: GC 35; NWT 7; BHC 38

Secretary: C.D. Hassell, Old Trafford, Manchester M16 0PX
Captain: C.H. Lloyd
Scorer: A. Lowe
Scores/Prospects: ☎ Manchester (061) 872 0261

ABRAHAMS, John (Heywood GS), b Cape Town, S. Africa 21 Jul 1952. 5'8". LHB, OB. Debut 1973. Cap 1982. Captain 1984-85. 1000 runs (3); most – 1261 (1983). HS 201* v Warwicks (Nuneaton) 1984. BB 3-27 v Worcs (Manchester) 1981. Awards: BHC 2. **NWT:** HS 51* v Durham (Chester le Street) 1983. BB 2-36 v Suffolk (Bury St. Edmunds) 1985. **BHC:** HS 66* v Minor C (Bowdon) 1984. **JPL:** HS 79* v Sussex (Horsham) 1983. BB 1-23.

ALLOTT, Paul John Walter (Altrincham GS; Durham U), b Altrincham, Cheshire 14 Sep 1956. 6'4". RHB, RFM. Debut 1978. Cap 1981. Cheshire 1976. Tests: 13 (1981 to 1985); HS 52* v Aus (Manchester) 1981 – on debut. BB 6-61 v WI (Leeds) 1984. LOI: 13. Tours: WI 1982-83 (Int XI); Ind/SL 1981-82, 1984-85. HS 78 v Glos (Bristol) 1985. BB 8-48 v Northants (Northampton) 1981. **NWT:** HS 19* v Worcs (Worcester) 1980. BB 4-34 v Bucks (Manchester) 1984. **BHC:** HS 15* v Derbys (Derby) 1984. BB 3-15 v Warwicks (Lord's) 1984. **JPL:** HS 32* v Yorkshire (Leeds) 1983. BB 4-28 v Kent (Manchester) 1985.

CHADWICK, Mark Robert (Roch Valley HS, Milnrow), b Rochdale 9 Feb 1963. 6'1". RHB, RM. Debut 1983. HS 132 v Somerset (Manchester) 1985. Awards: BHC 1. **NWT:** HS 87 v Glos (Bristol) 1983. **BHC:** HS 43 v Worcs (Manchester) 1985. **JPL:** HS 10 v Notts (Nottingham) 1984.

DAVIDSON, Ian Charles (Ellesmere Park HS; Eccles SFC), b Roe Green, Worsley 21 Dec 1964. 5'8". RHB, OB. Debut 1985. HS 13 and BB 2-24 v Warwicks (Birmingham).

FAIRBROTHER, Neil Harvey (Lymm GS), b Warrington 9 Sep 1963. 5'8". LHB, LM. Debut 1982. Cap 1985. 1000 runs (2); most – 1395 (1985). HS 164* v Hants (Liverpool) 1985. BB 1-3. Awards: NWT 1. **NWT:** HS 52* v Suffolk (Bury St Edmunds) 1985. **BHC:** HS 45* v Minor C (Bowdon) 1984. **JPL:** HS 54* v Hants (Portsmouth) 1984.

FOLLEY, Ian (Mansfield HS; Colne C), b Burnley 9 Jan 1963. 5'9½". RHB, SLA. Debut 1982. HS 69 v Yorks (Manchester) 1985. BB 6-8 v OU (Oxford) 1985. **NWT:** HS 3*. BB 2-10 v Lancs (Chester le Street) 1983. **BHC:** HS 11* v Notts (Nottingham) 1982. BB 4-18 v Middx (Lord's) 1982. **JPL:** HS 11* v Somerset (Manchester) 1983. BB 2-25 v Notts (Manchester) 1983.

FOWLER, Graeme (Accrington GS; Durham U), b Accrington 20 Apr 1957. 5'9½". LHB, RM. Debut 1979. Cap 1981. Tests: 21 (1982 to 1984-85); HS 201 v Ind (Madras) 1984-85. LOI: 24. Tours: Aus 1982-83; WI 1982-83 (Int XI); NZ 1983-84; Ind/SL 1984-85; Pak 1983-84. 1000 runs (4) most – 1560 (1981). HS 226 v Kent (Maidstone) 1984. BB 2-43 Eng XI v Tas (Hobart) 1982-83. Awards: NWT 2; BHC 2. **NWT:** HS 122 v Glos (Bristol) 1984. **BHC:** HS 97 v Northants (Manchester) 1983. **JPL:** HS 98* v Derbys (Manchester) 1985.

HAYES, Kevin Anthony (Queen Elizabeth's GS, Blackburn; Merton C, Oxford), b Thurnscoe, Yorks 26 Sep 1962. 5'7". RHB, RM. Debut 1980. Oxford U 1981-84; blue 1981-82-83-84 (captain 1984). HS 152 OU v Warwicks (Oxford) 1982. Lancs HS 117 v Somerset (Manchester) 1985. BB 6-58 OU v Warwicks (Birmingham) 1983. **BHC:** HS 67 Comb Us v Hants (Southampton) 1984. BB 3-40 Comb Us v Glos (Bristol) 1984. **JPL:** HS 53 v Glos (Moreton) 1984.

HAYHURST, Andrew Neil (Worsley Wardley HS; Eccles SFC; Leeds Polytechnic), b Davyhulme, Manchester 23 Nov 1962. 5'11". RHB, RM. Debut 1985. HS 17 and BB 3-37 v Leics (Manchester) 1985. **NWT:** HS 7. **JPL:** HS 12* v Surrey (Oval) 1985.

HENRIKSEN, Soren, b Rodoure, Copenhagen, Denmark 1 Dec 1964. 6'3". RHB, RFM. Debut 1985. HS 10* and BB 1-44 v Surrey (Oval) 1985. **NWT:** HS 1*. BB 2-51 v Worcs (Manchester) 1985. **JPL:** HS 1. BB 1-35.

HUGHES, David Paul (Newton-le-Willows GS), b Newton-le-Willows 13 May 1947. 5'11". RHB, SLA. Debut 1967. Cap 1970. Tasmania 1975-77. Benefit of £76,500 in 1981. Tour: SA 1972-73 (DHR). 1000 runs (2); most – 1303 (1982). HS 153 v Glam (Manchester) 1983. BB 7-24 v OU (Oxford) 1970. Awards: NWT 1; BHC 1. **NWT:** HS 71 v Durham (Chester le Street) 1983. BB 4-61 v Somerset (Manchester) 1972. **BHC:** HS 52 v Derbys (Manchester) 1981. BB 5-23 v Minor C (W) (Watford) 1978. **JPL:** HS 92 v Kent (Maidstone) 1984. BB 6-29 v Somerset (Manchester) 1977.

LLOYD, Clive Hubert (Chatham HS, Georgetown), b Georgetown, British Guiana 31 Aug 1944. 6'4½". LHB, RM. British Guiana/Guyana 1963-83. Lancashire debut 1968. Cap 1969. *Wisden* 1970. Benefit 1977 (£27,118). Captain 1981-83, 1986. Tests (WI): 110 (1966-67 to 1984-85); HS 242* v Ind (Bombay) 1974-75; BB 2-13. Most matches (74) and most wins (36) as captain. LOI: 87. Tours (C = captain): Eng 1969, 1973, 1976C, 1980C, 1984C; Aus 1968-69, 1971-72 (RW), 1975-76C, 1979-80C, 1981-82C, 1984-85C; NZ 1968-69, 1979-80C; Ind/SL 1966-67, 1974-75C, 1983-84C; Pak 1970-71 (RW), 1973-74 (RW), 1974-75C, 1980-81C. 1000 runs (10+4); most – 1603 (1970). HS 242* (Tests). Lancs HS 217* v Warwicks (Manchester) 1971. BB 4-48 v Leics (Manchester) 1970. Awards: NWT 8; BHC 1. **NWT:** HS 126 v Warwicks (Lord's) 1972. BB 3-39 v Somerset (Taunton) 1970. **BHC:** HS 124 v Warwicks (Manchester) 1981. BB 3-23 v Derbys (Manchester) 1974. **JPL:** HS 134* v Somerset (Manchester) 1970. BB 4-33 v Middx (Lord's) 1971.

MAKINSON, David John (St. Mary's HS, Leyland) b Eccleston 12 Jan 1961. 6'3". RHB, LFM. Debut 1984. HS 58* v Northants (Lytham) 1985. BB 5-60 v Derbys (Manchester) 1985. **NWT:** HS 17 v Worcs (Manchester) 1985. BB 1-69. **BHC:** HS 5. BB 2-45 v Worcs (Worcester) 1985. **JPL:** HS 13 v Hants (Manchester) 1985. BB 4-28 v Derbys (Manchester) 1985.

MAYNARD, Christopher (Bishop Vesey's GS, Sutton Coldfield), b Haslemere, Surrey 8 Apr 1958. 5'11". RHB, WK. Warwickshire 1978-1982. Registered for Lancashire in mid-season 1982. Tour: NZ 1979-80 (DHR). HS 85 Warwicks v Kent (Birmingham) 1979. **NWT:** HS 16 v Somerset (Manchester) 1983. **BHC:** HS 60 v Notts (Nottingham) 1982. **JPL:** HS 46 v Notts (Manchester) 1983.

MENDIS, Gehan Dixon (St. Thomas C, Colombo; Brighton, Hove & Sussex GS; Durham U), b Colombo, Ceylon 24 Apr 1955. 5'9". RHB, RM. Sussex 1974-85 (cap 1980). Joins Lancashire 1986. Tours: WI 1982-83 (Int XI); Pak 1981-82 (Int XI). 1000 runs (6); most – 1756 (1985). HS 209* Sussex v Somerset (Hove) 1984. BB 1-65. Awards: NWT 2; BHC 3. **NWT:** HS 141* Sussex v Warwicks (Hove) 1980. **BHC:** HS 109 Sussex v Glos (Hove) 1980. **JPL:** HS 125* Sussex v Glos (Hove) 1981.

MURPHY, Anthony John (Xaverian C, Swansea U), b Manchester 6 Aug 1962. 6'0". RHB, RMF. Debut 1985. Cheshire 1984-85. HS 2*. BB 3-84 v Worcs (Worcester).

O'SHAUGHNESSY, Steven Joseph (Harper Green SS, Farnworth), b Bury 9 Sep 1961. 5'10½". RHB, RM. Debut 1980. Cap 1985. Scored 100 in 35 minutes to equal world record v Leics (Manchester) 1983. 1000 runs (1): 1167 (1984). HS 159* v Somerset (Bath) 1984. BB 4-66 v Notts (Nottingham) 1982. Awards: BHC 2. **NWT:** HS 49* v Somerset (Manchester) 1983. BB 3-28 v Suffolk (Bury St. Edmunds) 1985. **BHC:** HS 90 v Worcs (Worcester) 1985. BB 4-17 v Leics (Manchester) 1985. **JPL:** HS 101* v Leics (Leicester) 1984. BB 3-18 v Middx (Manchester) 1984.

PATTERSON, Balfour **Patrick** (Happy Grove HS; Wolmer's HS), b Portland, Jamaica 15 Sep 1961. 6'2½". RHB, RFM. Jamaica 1982-86. Lancashire debut 1984. HS 22 v Northants (Lytham) 1985. BB 7-49 v OU (Oxford) 1985. **NWT:** HS 4. BB 1-69. **BHC:** HS 15* v Leics (Manchester) 1985. BB 1-34. **JPL:** HS 3*.

SIMMONS, Jack (Accrington TS; Blackburn TC), b Clayton-le-Moors 28 Mar 1941. 6'1½". RHB, OB. Debut 1968. Cap 1971. Tasmania 1972-79. Benefit of £128,300 in 1980. *Wisden* 1984. Tour: Ind 1980-81 (Overseas XI). HS 112 v Sussex (Hove) 1970. BB 7-59 Tasmania v Queensland (Brisbane) 1978-79. Lancs BB 7-64 v Hants (Southport) 1973. Awards: NWT 1; BHC 2. **NWT:** HS 54* v Essex (Manchester) 1979. BB 5-37 v Glos (Bristol) 1984. **BHC:** HS 64 v Derbys (Manchester) 1978. BB 4-31 v Yorks (Manchester) 1975. **JPL:** HS 65 v Essex (Manchester) 1980. BB 5-17 v Worcs (Worcester) 1982.

STANWORTH, John (Chadderton GS; N. Cheshire C), b Oldham 30 Sep 1960. 5'10". RHB, WK. Debut 1983. HS 50* v Glos (Bristol) 1985. **BHC:** HS 8*. **JPL:** HS 2.

VAREY, David William (Birkenhead S; Pembroke C, Cambridge), b Darlington, Co Durham 15 Oct 1961. 6'2". RHB. Twin of J.G. (Oxford 1982-83). Cambridge U 1981-83; blue 1982-83. Lancs debut 1984. Cheshire 1982-83. HS 156* CU v Northants (Cambridge) 1982. Lancs HS 112 v OU (Oxford) 1985. **BHC:** HS 27 v Worcs (Manchester) 1984.

WATKINSON, Michael (Rivington and Blackrod HS, Horwich), b Westhoughton 1 Aug 1961. 6'1". RHB, RMF. Debut 1982. Cheshire 1982. 106 v Surrey (Southport) 1985. BB 6-39 v Leics (Leicester) 1984. **NWT:** HS 56 v Worcs (Manchester) 1985. BB 3-63 v Middx (Lord's) 1984. **BHC:** HS 34 v Leics (Manchester) 1985. BB 4-39 v Notts (Manchester) 1983. **JPL:** HS 34* v Kent (Manchester) 1985. BB 3-25 v Essex (Manchester) 1984.

VALETE

See p. 158

LANCASHIRE RECORDS

FIRST-CLASS CRICKET

Highest Total	For	801 v Somerset; Taunton	1895
	V	634 by Surrey; The Oval	1898
Lowest Total	For	25 v Derbyshire; Manchester	1871
	V	22 by Glamorgan; Liverpool	1924
Highest Innings	For	424 A.C. MacLaren v Somerset; Taunton	1895
	V	315* T.W. Hayward for Surrey; The Oval	1898

Highest Partnerships

1st	368	A.C. MacLaren/R.H. Spooner v Glos; Liverpool	1903
2nd	371	F. Watson/E. Tyldesley v Surrey; Manchester	1928
3rd	306	E. Paynter/N. Oldfield v Hampshire; Southampton	1938
4th	324	A.C. MacLaren/J.T. Tyldesley v Notts; Nottingham	1904
5th	249	B. Wood/A. Kennedy v Warwicks; Birmingham	1975
6th	278	J. Iddon/H.R.W. Butterworth v Sussex; Manchester	1932
7th	245	A.H. Hornby/J. Sharp v Leics; Manchester	1912
8th	158	J. Lyon/R.M. Ratcliffe v Warwicks; Manchester	1979
9th	142	L.O.S. Poidevin/A. Kermode v Sussex; Eastbourne	1907
10th	173	J. Briggs/R. Pilling v Surrey; Liverpool	1885

Best Bowling (Innings)	For	10-46	W. Hickton v Hampshire; Manchester	1870
	V	10-40	G.O.B. Allen for Middlesex; Lord's	1929
Best Bowling (Match)	For	17-91	H. Dean v Yorkshire; Liverpool	1913
	V	16-65	G. Giffen for Australians; Manchester	1886

Most Runs – Season	2633	J.T. Tyldesley	(av 56.02)	1901
Most Runs – Career	34222	E. Tyldesley	(av 45.20)	1909-1936
Most 100s – Season	11	C. Hallows		1928
Most 100s – Career	90	E. Tyldesley		1909-1936
Most Wkts – Season	198	E.A. McDonald	(av 18.55)	1925
Most Wkts – Career	1816	J.B. Statham	(av 15.12)	1950-1968

LIMITED-OVERS CRICKET

Highest Total	NWT	349-6 v Glos; Bristol	1984
	BHC	290-5 v Northants; Manchester	1983
	JPL	255-5 v Somerset; Manchester	1970
Lowest Total	NWT	59 v Worcs; Worcester	1963
	BHC	82 v Yorkshire; Bradford	1972
	JPL	76 v Somerset; Manchester	1972
Highest Innings	NWT	131 A. Kennedy v Middlesex; Manchester	1978
	BHC	124 C.H. Lloyd v Warwicks; Manchester	1981
	JPL	134* C.H. Lloyd v Somerset; Manchester	1970
Best Bowling	NWT	5-28 J.B. Statham v Leics; Manchester	1963
	BHC	6-10 C.E.H. Croft v Scotland; Manchester	1982
	JPL	6-29 D.P. Hughes v Somerset; Manchester	1977

LANCASHIRE 1985

RESULTS SUMMARY

	Place	Won	Lost	Drew	Tied	Aban
Britannic Assurance Championship	14th	3	7	14		
All First-class Matches		4	7	14		
John Player League	14th	3	6		2	5
NatWest Trophy	Lost to Worcestershire (2nd Round)					
Benson and Hedges Cup	Failed to qualify for Quarter-Final					

BRITANNIC ASSURANCE CHAMPIONSHIP AVERAGES

BATTING AND FIELDING

Cap		*M*	*I*	*NO*	*HS*	*Runs*	*Avge*	*100*	*50*	*Ct/St*
1969	C.H. Lloyd	4	7	1	131	288	48.00	1	1	3
—	K.A. Hayes	5	7	0	117	310	44.28	1	2	3
—	S.T. Jefferies	4	7	0	93	274	39.14	—	3	—
1985	N.H. Fairbrother	24	38	3	164*	1327	37.91	3	6	10
—	D.J. Makinson	14	21	9	58*	372	31.00	—	1	2
—	D.W. Varey	21	33	3	87	848	28.26	—	2	5
1981	P.J.W. Allott	14	15	5	78	242	24.20	—	1	5
1970	D.P. Hughes	9	15	1	68	336	24.00	—	2	9
1982	J. Abrahams	24	38	3	77*	831	23.74	—	4	14
—	M. Watkinson	18	28	1	106	633	23.44	1	3	6
—	M.R. Chadwick	11	16	1	132	347	23.13	1	—	4
1971	J. Simmons	21	30	4	101	485	18.65	1	2	18
1981	G. Fowler	15	24	0	88	404	16.83	—	1	4
—	I. Folley	20	27	8	69	262	13.78	—	1	8
1985	S.J. O'Shaughnessy	13	23	2	63	275	13.09	—	1	10
—	C. Maynard	18	26	4	43	240	10.90	—	—	36/7
—	J. Stanworth	6	10	2	50*	70	8.75	—	1	6/3
1984	J.A. Ormrod	4	7	0	23	54	7.71	—	—	3
—	B.P. Patterson	15	15	5	22	38	3.80	—	—	4

Also batted: I.C. Davidson (1 match) 13,0 (2 ct); A.N. Hayhurst (1 match) 17; S. Henriksen (1 match) 10*,0* (1 ct); A.J. Murphy (2 matches) 2*,1,0.

BOWLING

	O	*M*	*R*	*W*	*Avge*	*Best*	*5 wI*	*10 wM*
P.J.W. Allott	403.2	128	927	49	18.91	6-71	3	—
S.T. Jefferies	116.1	13	379	12	31.58	4-64	—	—
B.P. Patterson	341.5	54	1085	34	31.91	6-45	2	1
D.J. Makinson	346	62	1029	31	33.19	5-60	1	—
S.J. O'Shaughnessy	142	21	521	15	34.73	4-68	—	—
M. Watkinson	391.5	83	1182	34	34.76	5-109	1	—
I. Folley	436.3	100	1271	35	36.31	4-39	—	—
J. Simmons	543.1	155	1427	37	38.56	4-55	—	—

Also bowled: J. Abrahams 25.2-7-93-3; M.R. Chadwick 5-0-20-0; I.C. Davidson 10-3-24-2; N.H. Fairbrother 26-7-75-1; A.N. Hayhurst 13-4-37-3; S. Henriksen 12-1-44-1; D.P. Hughes 21-12-26-1; A.J. Murphy 56.2-15-207-6.

The First-Class Averages (pp. 168–183) give the records of Lancashire players in all first-class county matches (their other opponents being Oxford U.), with the exception of P.J.W. Allott and G. Fowler whose full county figures are as above.

LEICESTERSHIRE

Formation of Present Club: 25 March 1879
Colours: Scarlet and Dark Green
Badge: Gold Running Fox on Green Background
Championships: (1) 1975
NatWest Trophy/Gillette Cup Winners: (0) Semi-Finalists 1977
Benson and Hedges Cup Winners: (3) 1972, 1975, 1985
John Player League Champions: (2) 1974, 1977
Match Awards: GC 15; NWT 6; BHC 43

Secretary/Manager: F.M. Turner, County Ground, Grace Road, Leicester LE2 8AD
Captain: D.I. Gower
Scorer: G.R. Blackburn
Scores/Prospects: ☎ Leicester (0533) 836236

AGNEW, Jonathan Philip (Uppingham S), b Macclesfield, Cheshire 4 Apr 1960. 6'3½". RHB, RF. Debut 1978. Cap 1984. Tests 3 (1984-85); HS 5; BB 2-51 v WI (Oval) 1984. LOI: 3. Tours: Ind 1984-85; SL 1985-86 (Eng B); Zim 1980-81 (Leicester). HS 56 v Worcs (Worcester) 1982. BB 9-70 v Kent (Leicester) 1985. **NWT:** HS 5. BB 2-36 v Derbys (Leics) 1984. **BHC:** 23* and BB 5-43 v Warwicks (Leicester) 1984. **JPL:** HS 13* v Sussex (Hove) 1985. BB 3-36 v Glamorgan (Leicester) 1985.

BALDERSTONE, John **Christopher** (Paddock Council S, Huddersfield), b Longwood, Huddersfield, Yorks 16 Nov 1940. 6'0". RHB, SLA. Yorkshire 1961-69. Leicestershire debut 1971. Cap 1973. Testimonial 1984. Tests: 2 (1976); HS 35 v WI (Leeds); BB 1-80. Tour: Zim 1980-81 (Leics). 1000 runs (11); most – 1482 (1982). HS 181* v Glos (Leicester) 1984. BB 6-25 v Hants (Southampton) 1978. Awards: NWT 2; BHC 10. Soccer for Huddersfield Town, Carlisle United, Doncaster Rovers and Queen of the South. **NWT:** HS 119* v Somerset (Taunton) 1973. BB 4-33 v Herts (Leicester) 1977. **BHC:** HS 113* v Glos (Leicester) 1977. BB 2-13 v Warwicks (Leicester) 1972. **JPL:** HS 96 v Northants (Leicester) 1976. BB 3-29 v Worcs (Leicester) 1971.

BENJAMIN, Winston Keith Roy, b All Saints, Antigua 31 Dec 1964. RHB, RF. Debut Rest of the World XI v D.B. Close's XI at Scarborough 1985 (HS 15, BB 2-31). Leeward Islands 1985-86. Joins Leicestershire 1986.

BILLINGTON, David James (Kendal GS; Leeds U; Loughborough U), b Leyland, Lancs 6 Dec 1965. 5'7". RHB. Debut 1985. HS 19 v Warwicks (Hinckley) 1985.

BLACKETT, Mark (Edmonton County S), b Edmonton, London 3 Feb 1964. 5'8". RHB. Debut 1985. HS 28* v Worcs (Leicester) 1985. **JPL:** HS 21* v Worcs (Leicester) 1985.

BOON, Timothy James (Edlington CS, Doncaster), b Doncaster, Yorks 1 Nov 1961. 6'0". RHB, RM. Debut 1980. Tour: Zim 1980-81 (Leics). 1000 runs (1): 1233 (1984). No appearances 1985. HS 144 v Glos (Leicester) 1984. **NWT:** HS 22* v Derbys (Leics) 1984. **BHC:** HS 36* v Northants (Leics) 1984. **JPL:** HS 48 v Notts (Leicester) 1984.

BRIERS, Nigel Edwin (Lutterworth GS; Borough Road CE), b Leicester 15 Jan 1955. 6'0". RHB, RM. Debut 1971 – youngest player at 16 years 103 days to represent Leicestershire. Cap 1981. Tour: Zim 1980-81 (Leics). 1000 runs (3); most – 1289 (1983). HS 201* v Warwicks (Birmingham) 1983. BB 4-29 v Derbys (Leicester) 1985. Awards: BHC 1. **NWT:** HS 59 v Wilts (Swindon) 1984. BB 2-6 v Worcs (Leicester) 1979. **BHC:** HS 71* v Hants (Southampton) 1979. BB 1-27. **JPL:** HS 119* v Hants (Bournemouth) 1981. BB 3-29 v Middx (Leicester) 1984.

BUTCHER, Ian Paul (John Ruskin HS), b Farnborough, Kent 1 Jul 1962. 6'0". RHB, RM. Brother of A.R. and M.S. (Surrey). Debut 1980. Cap 1984. 1000 runs (2); most – 1349 (1984). HS 139 v Notts (Leicester) 1983. BB 1-2. **NWT:** HS 81 v Northants (Northampton) 1984. BB 1-6. **BHC:** HS 101 v Yorks (Leicester) 1985. **JPL:** HS 71 v Northants (Leics) 1982.

CLIFT, Patrick Bernard (**'Paddy'**) (St. George's C, Salisbury), b Salisbury, Rhodesia 14 Jul 1953. 6'1". RHB, RM. Rhodesia 1971-80. Leicestershire debut 1975. Cap 1976. Natal 1980-85; captain 1984-85. HS 106 v Essex (Chelmsford) 1985. BB 8-17 v MCC (Lord's) 1976. Awards: BHC 1. **NWT:** HS 48* and BB 3-36 v Worcs (Leicester) 1979. **BHC:** HS 91 v Notts (Leicester) 1980. BB 4-13 v Minor C (E) (Chesham) 1978. **JPL:** HS 51* v Somerset (Leicester) 1979. BB 4-12 v Lancs (Leicester) 1978.

COBB, Russell Alan (Trent C), b Leicester 18 May 1961. 5'11". RHB, SLA. Debut 1980. Tours: NZ 1979-80 (DHR); Zim 1980-81 (Leics). HS 78 v Surrey (Leicester) 1985. **JPL:** HS 24 v Worcs (Leicester) 1981.

DE FREITAS, Phillip Anthony Jason (Willesden HS, London), b Scotts Head, Dominica 18 Feb 1966. 6'0". RHB, RFM. UK resident since 1976. Debut 1985. HS 30* and BB 5-39 v Lancs (Leicester) 1985. **JPL:** HS 27 v Worcs (Leicester) 1985. BB 3-27 v Lancs and 3-27 v Essex 1985.

FERRIS, George John Fitzgerald (Jennings SS, Antigua), b Urlings Village, Antigua 18 Oct 1964. 6'3". RHB, RF. Leeward Islands 1982-86. Leicestershire debut 1983. Tour: Zim 1983-84 (Young WI). HS 26 Leeward Is v Guyana (Nevis) 1982-83. BB 7-42 v Glamorgan (Hinckley) 1983. **BHC:** HS 0*. BB 4-31 v Lancs (Manchester) 1985. **JPL:** HS 9*. BB 3-40 v Worcs (Leicester) 1985.

GOWER, David Ivon (Kings S, Canterbury; London U), b Tunbridge Wells, Kent 1 Apr 1957. 6'0". LHB, OB. Debut 1975. Cap 1977. *Wisden* 1978. YC 1978. Captain 1984-. Tests: 76 (1978-85, 20 as captain); HS 215 v Aus (Birmingham) 1985; BB 1-1. LOI: 77. Tours (C = captain): Aus 1978-79, 1979-80, 1982-83; WI 1980-81, 1985-86C; NZ 1983-84; Ind 1979-80, 1981-82, 1984-85C; Pak 1983-84; SL 1977-78 (DHR), 1981-82, 1984-85C. 1000 runs (6); most – 1530 (1982). HS 215 (Tests). BB 3-47 v Essex (Leicester) 1977. Awards: NWT 3; BHC 1. **NWT:** HS 156 v Derbys (Leicester) 1984. **BHC:** HS 114* v Derbys (Derby) 1980. **JPL:** HS 135* v Warwicks (Leicester) 1977.

POTTER, Laurie (Kelmscott HS, Perth, Aus), b Bexleyheath, Kent 7 Nov 1962. 6'1". RHB, SLA. Kent 1981-85. Griqualand West 1984-86 (captain 1985-86). Joins Leicestershire 1986. HS 165* GW v Border (East London) 1984-85. BB 4-63 GW v Boland (Stellenbosch) 1984-85. **NWT:** HS 45 Kent v Essex (Chelmsford) 1982. **BHC:** HS 49 Kent v Sussex (Hove) 1982. **JPL:** HS 52 Kent v Essex (Chelmsford) 1985. BB 4-9 Kent v Derbys (Folkestone) 1985.

TAYLOR, Leslie Brian (Heathfield HS), b Earl Shilton 25 Oct 1953. 6'3½". RHB, RFM. Debut 1977. Cap 1981. Natal 1981-84. Tests: 2 (1985); HS 1* and BB 2-34 v Aus (Oval). Tours: SA 1981-82 (SAB); WI 1985-86; Zim 1980-81 (Leics). HS 47 v Derbys (Derby) 1983. BB 7-28 v Derbys (Leics) 1981. Awards: NWT 1. **NWT:** HS 5*. BB 4-14 v Norfolk (Norwich) 1985. **BHC:** HS 5. BB 6-35 v Worcs (Worcester) 1982. **JPL:** HS 15* v Somerset (Taunton) 1980. BB 5-23 v Notts (Nottingham) 1978.

WHITAKER, John James (Uppingham S), b Skipton, Yorks 5 May 1962. 5'10". RHB, OB. Debut 1983. 1000 runs (2); most – 1103 (1985). HS 160 v Somerset (Leicester) 1984. Awards: NWT 1; BHC 1. **NWT:** HS 155 v Wilts (Swindon) 1984. **BHC:** HS 73* v Warwicks (Birmingham) 1985. **JPL:** HS 132 v Glamorgan (Swansea) 1984.

WHITTICASE, Philip (Crestwood CS, Kingswinford), b Marston Green, Solihull 15 Mar 1965. 5'11". RHB, WK. Debut 1984. HS 55* v Sussex (Hove) 1985. **JPL:** HS 5*.

WILLEY, Peter (Seaham SS) b Sedgefield, Co Durham 6 Dec 1949. 6'1". RHB, OB. Northamptonshire 1966-83. Cap 1971. Benefit of £31,400 in 1981. Leicestershire debut/cap 1984. Eastern Province 1982-85. Tests: 21 (1976-85); HS 102* v WI (St. John's) 1980-81; BB 2-73 v WI (Lord's) 1980. LOI: 22. Tours: Aus 1979-80; SA 1972-73 (DHR), 1981-82 (SAB); WI 1981-81, 1985-86; Ind 1979-80; SL 1977-78 (DHR). 1000 runs (6); most – 1783 (1982). HS 227 Northants v Somerset (Northampton) 1976. BB 7-37 Northants v OU (Oxford) 1975. Awards: NWT 5; BHC 5. **NWT:** HS 89 Northants v Sussex (Hove) 1979. BB 3-33 v Derbys (Leicester) 1984. **BHC:** HS 88* v Northants (Leicester) 1984. BB 3-12 Northants v Minor C (E) (Horton) 1977. **JPL:** HS 107 Northants v Warwicks 1975, 107 Northants v Hants 1976. BB 4-38 Northants v Leics (Leicester) 1980.

VALETE

ADDISON, James Paul (Blythe Bridge HS), b Leek, Staffs 14 Nov 1965. 6'0". RHB, SLA. Debut 1983 (only match) scoring 51 and 16 v New Zealanders at Leicester. 2nd XI debut 1981 when aged 15.

GARNHAM, Michael Anthony (Camberwell GS, Melbourne; Scotch C, Perth; Barnstaple GS; N. Devon SFC; East Anglia U), b Johannesburg, SA 20 Aug 1960. 5'10". RHB, WK. Gloucestershire 1979. Leicestershire 1980-85. HS 100 v OU (Oxford) 1985. Awards: BHC 1.

LEICESTERSHIRE RECORDS

FIRST-CLASS CRICKET

Highest Total	For	701-4d v Worcs; Worcester	1906
	V	739-7d by Notts; Nottingham	1903
Lowest Total	For	25 v Kent; Leicester	1912
	V	24 by Glamorgan; Leicester	1971
		24 by Oxford U; Oxford	1985
Highest Innings	For	252* S. Coe v Northants; Leicester	1914
	V	341 G.H. Hirst for Yorks; Leicester	1905

Highest Partnerships

1st	390	B. Dudleston/J.F. Steele v Derbyshire; Leicester	1979
2nd	289*	J.C. Balderstone/D.I. Gower v Essex; Leicester	1981
3rd	316*	W. Watson/A. Wharton v Somerset; Taunton	1961
4th	290*	P. Willey/T.J. Boon v Warwicks; Leicester	1984
5th	233	N.E. Briers/R.W. Tolchard v Somerset; Leicester	1979
6th	262	A.T. Sharpe/G.H.S. Fowke v Derbyshire; Chesterfield	1911
7th	206	B. Dudleston/J. Birkenshaw v Kent; Canterbury	1969
8th	164	M.R. Hallam/C.T. Spencer v Essex; Leicester	1964
9th	160	W.W. Odell/R.T. Crawford v Worcs; Leicester	1902
10th	228	R. Illingworth/K. Higgs v Northants; Leicester	1977

Best Bowling (Innings)	For	10-18	G. Geary v Glamorgan; Pontypridd	1929
	V	10-32	H. Pickett for Essex; Leyton	1895
Best Bowling (Match)	For	16-96	G. Geary v Glamorgan; Pontypridd	1929
	V	16-102	C. Blythe for Kent; Leicester	1909

Most Runs – Season	2446	L.G. Berry	(av 52.04)	1937
Most Runs – Career	30143	L.G. Berry	(av 30.32)	1924-1951
Most 100s – Season	7	L.G. Berry		1937
		W. Watson		1959
		B.F. Davison		1982
Most 100s – Career	45	L.G. Berry		1924-1951
Most Wkts – Season	170	J.E. Walsh	(av 18.96)	1948
Most Wkts – Career	2130	W.E. Astill	(av 23.19)	1906-1939

LIMITED-OVERS CRICKET

Highest Total	NWT	354-7 v Wiltshire; Swindon	1984
	BHC	327-4 v Warwicks; Coventry	1972
	JPL	291-5 v Glamorgan; Swansea	1984
Lowest Total	NWT	56 v Northants; Leicester	1964
	BHC	56 v Minor Counties; Wellington	1982
	JPL	36 v Sussex; Leicester	1973
Highest Innings	NWT	156 D.I. Gower v Derbys; Leicester	1984
	BHC	158* B.F. Davison v Warwicks; Coventry	1972
	JPL	152 B. Dudleston v Lancashire; Manchester	1975
Best Bowling	NWT	6-20 K. Higgs v Staffs; Longton	1975
	BHC	6-35 L.B. Taylor v Worcs; Worcester	1982
	JPL	6-17 K. Higgs v Glamorgan; Leicester	1973

LEICESTERSHIRE 1985

RESULTS SUMMARY

	Place	Won	Lost	Drew	Tied	Aban
Britannic Assurance Championship	16th	2	3	19		
All First-class Matches		3	3	20		
John Player League	6th	5	5		1	5
NatWest Bank Trophy	Lost to Hampshire (2nd Round)					
Benson and Hedges Cup	**Winners**					

BRITANNIC ASSURANCE CHAMPIONSHIP AVERAGES

BATTING AND FIELDING

Cap		M	I	NO	HS	Runs	Avge	100	50	Ct/St
1984	P. Willey	19	28	3	147	1194	47.76	3	5	10
1977	D.I. Gower	12	17	2	128	575	38.33	2	2	1
—	J.J. Whitaker	23	32	3	109	1089	37.41	3	5	4
—	P. Whitticase	3	5	1	55*	149	37.25	—	1	9
1973	J.C. Balderstone	23	37	4	101	1130	34.24	1	6	9
—	R.A. Cobb	16	23	4	78	601	31.63	—	4	11
1984	I.P. Butcher	23	36	2	120	1043	30.67	1	7	18
1981	N.E. Briers	21	27	4	129	561	24.39	1	1	7
1976	P.B. Clift	21	25	5	106	472	23.60	1	1	9
—	M. Blackett	2	4	2	28*	41	20.50	—	—	—
—	M.A. Garnham	21	24	3	51	415	19.76	—	1	46/7
—	P.A.J. De Freitas	8	11	3	30*	117	14.62	—	—	2
1984	G.J. Parsons	14	14	4	32	139	13.90	—	—	—
1982	N.G.B. Cook	17	15	4	45	151	13.72	—	—	7
—	G.J.F. Ferris	10	9	6	22*	29	9.66	—	—	—
1981	L.B. Taylor	16	15	7	20*	77	9.62	—	—	5
1984	J.P. Agnew	14	13	2	36	100	9.09	—	—	3

Also batted: D.J. Billington (1 match) 19 (1 ct).

BOWLING

	O	M	R	W	Avge	Best	5 wI	10 wM
L.B. Taylor	472.2	120	1102	52	21.19	5-45	3	—
J.P. Agnew	396.4	85	1269	52	24.40	9-70	3	1
P. Willey	343.5	102	834	31	26.90	6-43	3	—
P.A.J. De Freitas	208.4	34	619	21	29.47	5-39	1	—
P.B. Clift	577.3	165	1407	45	31.26	5-38	1	—
N.G.B. Cook	529.1	177	1245	29	42.93	4-59	—	—
G.J.F. Ferris	231.3	32	826	15	55.06	3-84	—	—
G.J. Parsons	306.2	61	869	14	62.07	3-31	—	—

Also bowled: J.C. Balderstone 15-3-68-1; N.E. Briers 88-18-303-8; I.P. Butcher 2-1-5-0; D.I. Gower 2.1-0-16-0.

The First-Class Averages (pp. 168–183) give the records of Leicestershire players in all first-class county matches (their other opponents being the Australians and Oxford U.), with the exception of: J.P. Agnew 15-14-2-36-119-9.91-0-0-3 ct. 422.4-87-1413-55-25.69-9/70-3-1. D.I. Gower 14-19-2-135-719-42.29-3-2-3 ct. 2.1-0-16-0. L.B. Taylor 18-17-8-20*-88-9.77-0-0-5 ct. 503.2-130-1198-56-21.39-5/45-3-0. P. Willey 21-30-3-147-1253-46.40-3-6-10 ct. 379.3-111-950-35-27.14-6/43-3-0.

MIDDLESEX

Formation of Present Club: 15 December 1863
Colours: Blue
Badge: Three Seaxes
Championships (since 1890): (8) 1903, 1920, 1921, 1947, 1976 1980, 1982, 1985
Joint Championships: (2) 1949, 1977
NatWest Trophy/Gillette Cup Winners: (3) 1977, 1980, 1984
Benson and Hedges Cup Winners: (1) 1983
John Player League Champions: (0) Second 1982
Match Awards: GC 27; NWT 8; BHC 33

Secretary/General Manager: T.M. Lamb, Lord's Cricket Ground, London NW8 8QN
Captain: M.W. Gatting
Scorer: H.P.H. Sharp
Scores/Prospects: ☎ London (01) 286 8011

BARLOW, Graham Derek (Ealing GS; Loughborough CE), b Folkestone 26 Mar 1950. 5'9½". LHB, RM. Debut 1969. Cap 1976. Benefit 1984. Tests: 3 (1976-77 and 1977); HS 7*. LOI: 6. Tour: Aus 1976-77; Ind/SL 1976-77. 1000 runs (7); most – 1545 (1983). HS 177 v Lancs (Southport) 1981. BB 1-6. Awards: NWT 3; BHC 2. **NWT:** HS 158 v Lancs (Lord's) 1984. **BHC:** HS 129 v Northants (Northampton) 1977. BB 1-18. **JPL:** HS 114 v Warwicks (Lord's) 1979. BB 2-13 v Surrey (Lord's) 1976.

BROWN, Keith Robert (Chace S, Enfield), b Edmonton 18 Mar 1963. 5'11". RHB, WK. Debut 1984. HS 102 v Aus (Lord's) 1985. **JPL:** HS 33 v Warwicks (Birmingham) 1985.

BUTCHER, Roland Orlando (Shephalbury SS, Stevenage), b East Point, St. Philip, Barbados 14 Oct 1953. 5'8". UK resident since 1967. RHB, RM. Debut 1974. Barbados 1974-75, Tasmania 1982-83. Cap 1979. Tests (Eng): 3 (1980-81); HS 32 v WI (Kingston). LOI: 3. Tours: WI 1980-81, 1982-83 (Int XI); Pak 1981-82 (Int XI); Zim 1980-81 (Middx). 1000 runs (3); most – 1326 (1984). HS 197 v Yorks (Lord's) 1982. BB 1-13. Awards: BHC 1. **NWT:** HS 59 v Cumberland (Uxbridge) 1985. BB 1-18. **BHC:** HS 85 v Surrey (Oval) 1983. **JPL:** HS 100 v Glos (Lord's) 1983.

CARR, John Donald – *see OXFORD UNIVERSITY (page 165)*. **JPL:** HS 4. **BHC:** HS 66 Comb Us v Essex (Chelmsford) 1985. BB 3-22 Comb Us v Glos (Bristol) 1984.

COWANS, Norman George (Park High SS, Stanmore), b Enfield St. Mary, Jamaica 17 Apr 1961. 6'3". RHB, RF. Debut 1980. YC 1982. Cap 1984. Tests: 19 (1982-83 to 1985); HS 36 v Aus (Perth) 1982-83; BB 6-77 v Aus (Melbourne) 1982-83. LOI: 23. Tours: Aus 1982-83; NZ 1983-84; Ind 1984-85; Pak 1983-84; SL 1984-85, 1985-86 (Eng B); Zim 1980-81 (Middx). HS 66 v Surrey (Lord's) 1984. BB 6-31 v Leics (Leicester) 1985. Awards: NWT 1; BHC 1. **NWT:** HS 12* v Lancs (Lord's) 1984. BB 4-26 v Lancs (Lord's) 1982. **BHC:** HS 6. BB 4-33 v Lancs (Lord's) 1983. **JPL:** HS 20 v Notts (Nottingham) 1985. BB 4-44 v Sussex (Hove) 1982.

DANIEL, Wayne Wendell (Princess Margaret S), b St. Philip, Barbados 16 Jan 1956. 6'1". RHB, RF. Barbados 1975-85. Middlesex debut/cap 1977. W. Australia 1981-82. Tests (WI): 10 (1975-76 to 1983-84); HS 11 v Ind (Kingston) 1975-76; BB 5-39 v Ind (Ahmedabad) 1983-84. LOI: 18. Tours: Eng 1976; Ind 1983-84; Zim 1981-82 (Young WI). HS 53* Barbados v Jamaica (Bridgetown) 1979-80, 53* v Yorks (Lord's) 1981. BB 9-61 v Glam (Swansea) 1982. Awards: NWT 2; BHC 2. **NWT:** HS 14 v Lancs (Manchester) 1978. BB 6-15 v Sussex (Hove) 1980. **BHC:** HS 20* v Derbys (Derby) 1978. BB 7-12 v Minor C (E) (Ipswich) 1978. **JPL:** HS 14 v Kent (Lord's) 1980. BB 5-27 v Lancs (Lord's) 1982.

DOWNTON, Paul Rupert (Sevenoaks S; Exeter U), b Farnborough, Kent 4 Apr 1957. 5'10". RHB, WK, OB. Son of G.C. (Kent 1948). Kent 1977-79 (cap 1979). Middlesex debut 1980. Cap 1981. Tests: 21 (1980-81 to 1985); HS 74 v Ind (Delhi) 1984-85. LOI: 11. Tours: WI 1980-81, 1985-86; NZ 1977-78; Ind/SL 1984-85; Pak 1977-78; Zim 1980-81 (Middx). HS 104 v Northants (Uxbridge) 1985. **NWT:** HS 62 v Notts (Nottingham) 1984. **BHC:** HS 28 v Somerset (Taunton) 1984. **JPL:** HS 70 v Notts (Nottingham) 1985.

EDMONDS, Philippe Henri (Gilbert Rennie HS, Lusaka; Skinners S, Tunbridge Wells; Cranbrook S; Fitzwilliam C, Cambridge), b Lusaka, N. Rhodesia 8 Mar 1951. 6'1½". RHB, SLA. Cambridge U and Middlesex debuts 1971. CU 1971-73; blue 1971-72-73 (capt 1973). Cap 1974. YC 1974. Eastern Province 1975-76. Benefit 1983. Tests: 33 (1975 to 1985); HS 64 v Ind (Lord's) 1982; BB 7-66 v Pak (Karachi) 1977-78. LOI: 23. Tours: Aus 1978-79; SA 1975-76 (Int Wand); WI 1985-86; NZ 1977-78; Ind/SL 1984-85; Pak 1977-78. HS 142 v Glam (Swansea) 1984. BB 8-53 v Hants (Bournemouth) 1984. Awards: NWT 1; BHC 3. **NWT:** HS 63* v Somerset (Lord's) 1979. BB 5-12 v Cheshire (Enfield) 1982. **BHC:** HS 44* v Notts (Newark) 1976. BB 5-43 v Comb Us (Cambridge) 1985. **JPL:** HS 52 v Somerset (Taunton) 1980. BB 3-19 v Leics (Lord's) 1973.

EMBUREY, John Ernest (Peckham Manor SS), b Peckham, London 20 Aug 1952. 6'2". RHB, OB. Debut 1973. Cap 1977. *Wisden* 1983. Western Province 1982-84. Benefit 1986. Tests: 28 (1978 to 1985); HS 57 v Aus (Manchester) 1981; BB 6-33 v SL (Colombo) 1981-82. LOI: 8. Tours: Aus 1978-79, 1979-80; SA 1981-82 (SAB); WI 1980-81, 1985-86; Ind 1979-80, 1981-82; SL 1977-78 (DHR), 1981-82; Zim 1980-81 (Middx). 100 wickets (1): 103 (1983). HS 133 v Essex (Chelmsford) 1983. BB 7-36 v CU (Cambridge) 1977. Awards: NWT 1; BHC 3. **NWT:** HS 36* v Lancs (Manchester) 1978. BB 3-20 v Northumb (Jesmond) 1984. **BHC:** HS 50 v Kent (Lord's) 1984. BB 4-36 v Essex (Chelmsford) 1985. **JPL:** HS 40* v Leics (Lord's) 1983. BB 5-36 v Warwicks (Lord's) 1983.

FRASER, Angus Robert Charles (Gayton HS, Harrow), b Billinge, Lancs 8 Aug 1965. 6'5". RHB, RFM. Debut 1984. HS 1. BB 4-48 v CU (Cambridge) 1985. **BHC:** HS 2. BB 1-31. **JPL:** HS 7. BB 3-46 v Yorks (Bradford) 1985.

GATTING, Michael William (John Kelly HS), b Kingsbury 6 Jun 1957. 5'10". RHB, RM. Debut 1975. Cap 1977. Captain 1983-. *Wisden* 1983. YC 1981. Tests 41 (1977-78 to 1985); HS 207 v Ind (Madras) 1984-85; BB 1-14. LOI: 42. Tours: WI 1980-81, 1985-86; NZ 1977-78, 1983-84; Ind/SL 1981-82, 1984-85; Pak 1977-78, 1983-84; Zim 1980-81 (Middx). 1000 runs (7+1); most – 2257 (1984). HS 258 v Somerset (Bath) 1984. BB 5-34 v Glam (Swansea) 1982. Awards: NWT 1; BHC 4. **NWT:** HS 95* v Notts (Nottingham) 1980. BB 2-14 v Ire 1980, 2-14 v Lancs 1984. **BHC:** HS 143* v Sussex (Hove) 1985. BB 4-49 v Sussex (Lord's) 1984. **JPL:** HS 109 v Leics (Leicester) 1984. BB 4-32 v Kent (Lord's) 1978.

HUGHES, Simon Peter (Latymer Upper S, Hammersmith; Durham U), b Kingston upon Thames 20 Dec 1959. 5'10". RHB, RFM. Debut 1980. Cap 1981. N. Transvaal 1982-83. Tours: Ind 1981-81 (Overseas XI); Zim 1980-81 (Middx). HS 41* v Glos (Uxbridge) 1984. BB 6-32 v Glos (Bristol) 1983. Awards: NWT 1. **NWT:** HS 1*. BB 3-23 v Worcs (Worcester) 1980. **BHC:** HS 8*. BB 2-43 v Somerset (Taunton) 1984. **JPL:** HS 22* v Surrey (Lord's) 1985. BB 3-31 v Kent (Canterbury) 1985.

METSON, Colin Peter (Enfield GS; Stanborough S, Welwyn Garden City), b Goffs Oak, Herts 2 Jul 1963. 5'5½". RHB, WK. Debut 1981. HS 96 v Glos (Uxbridge) 1984. **JPL:** HS 15* v Sussex (Hove) 1984.

MILLER, Andrew John Trevor – *see OXFORD UNIVERSITY (page 165)*. **NWT:** HS 0. **BHC:** HS 101 Comb Us v Glos (Bristol) 1984. BB 1-30.

RADLEY, Clive Thornton (King Edward VI GS, Norwich), b Hertford 13 May 1944. 5'8". RHB, LB. Debut 1964. Cap 1967. Benefit 1977 (£26,000). *Wisden* 1978. Norfolk 1961. Tests: 8 (1977-78 and 1978); HS 158 v NZ (Auckland) 1977-78. LOI: 4. Tours: Aus 1978-79; SA 1972-73 (DHR), 1974-75 (DHR); NZ 1977-78; Zim 1980-81 (Middx). 1000 runs (16); most – 1491 (1980). HS 200 v Northants (Uxbridge) 1985. BB 2-38 v Glam (Cardiff) 1985. Awards: NWT 3; BHC 4. **NWT:** HS 105* v Worcs (Worcester) 1975. **BHC:** HS 121* v Minor C (E) (Lord's) 1976. **JPL:** HS 133* v Glamorgan (Lord's) 1969. BB 1-2.

ROSE, Graham David (Northumberland Park S, Tottenham), b Tottenham 12 Apr 1964. 6'4". RHB, RM. Debut 1985. Limited-overs appearances 1983 and 1984. HS 15 v Somerset (Lord's) 1985. BB 6-41 v Worcs (Worcester) 1985 – on debut. **BHC:** HS 3. **JPL:** HS 33 v Notts (Cleethorpes) 1983. BB 1-38.

ROSEBERRY, Michael Anthony (Durham S), b Houghton-le-Spring, Co Durham 28 Nov 1966. 6'0". RHB, RM. Played in one JPL match 1985. Awaiting f-c debut. **JPL:** HS 15 v Warwicks (Birmingham) 1985.

SLACK, Wilfred Norris (Troumaca Govt S; Wellesbourne SS, High Wycombe), b Troumaca, St. Vincent 12 Dec 1954. 5'11". LHB, RM. Debut 1977. Cap 1981. Windward Is 1981-83. Buckinghamshire 1976. Tours: Pak 1981-82 (Int XI); SL 1985-86 (Eng B); Zim 1980-81 (Middx); WI 1985-86. 1000 runs (5); most – 1900 (1985). HS 248* v Worcs (Lord's) 1981. BB 3-17 v Leics (Uxbridge) 1982. Awards: NWT 2. **NWT:** HS 98 v Cumberland (Uxbridge) 1985. BB 3-37 v Northants (Northampton) 1983. **BHC:** HS 60* v Comb Us (Cambridge) 1982. **JPL:** HS 77 v Somerset (Weston) 1982. BB 5-32 v Leics (Lord's) 1983.

SYKES, James Frederick (**'Jamie'**) (Bow CS), b Shoreditch, London 30 Dec 1965. 6'1". RHB, OB. Debut 1983. HS 126 v CU (Cambridge) 1985. BB 3-58 v Notts (Lord's) 1985. **JPL:** HS 25 v Kent (Canterbury) 1985. BB 1-22.

WILLIAMS, Neil FitzGerald (Acland Burghley CS), b Hope Well, St. Vincent 2 Jul 1962. 5'11". RHB, RFM. Debut 1982. Windward Is 1982-83. Tasmania 1983-84. Cap 1984. Tour: Zim 1984-85 (Eng Co). HS 67 v CU (Cambridge) 1985. BB 7-55 Eng Co XI v Zimbabwe (Harare) 1984-85. Middx BB 5-15 v Essex (Lord's) 1985. **NWT:** HS 10 v Northumb (Jesmond) 1984. BB 4-36 v Derbys (Derby) 1983. **BHC:** HS 29* v Surrey (Lord's) 1985. BB 3-16 v Comb Us (Cambridge) 1982. **JPL:** HS 31* v Notts (Cleethorpes) 1983. BB 4-40 v Derbys (Chesterfield) 1983.

VALETE

See p. 158.

MIDDLESEX RECORDS

FIRST-CLASS CRICKET

Highest Total	For	642-3d v Hampshire; Southampton	1923
	V	665 by West Indians; Lord's	1939
Lowest Total	For	20 v MCC; Lord's	1864
	V	31 by Glos; Bristol	1924
Highest Innings	For	331* J.D. Robertson v Worcester; Worcester	1949
	V	316* J.B. Hobbs for Surrey; Lord's	1926

Highest Partnerships

1st	367*	G.D. Barlow/W.N. Slack v Kent; Lord's	1981
2nd	380	F.A. Tarrant/J.W. Hearne v Lancashire; Lord's	1914
3rd	424*	W.J. Edrich/D.C.S. Compton v Somerset; Lord's	1948
4th	325	J.W. Hearne/E.H. Hendren v Hampshire; Lord's	1919
5th	338	R.S. Lucas/T.C. O'Brien v Sussex; Hove	1895
6th	227	C.T. Radley/F.J. Titmus v S. Africans; Lord's	1965
7th	271*	E.H. Hendren/F.T. Mann v Notts; Nottingham	1925
8th	182*	M.H.C. Doll/H.R. Murrell v Notts; Lord's	1913
9th	160*	E.H. Hendren/T.J. Durston v Essex; Leyton	1927
10th	230	R.W. Nicholls/W. Roche v Kent; Lord's	1899

Best Bowling (Innings)	For	10-40	G.O.B. Allen v Lancashire; Lord's		1929
	V	9-38	R.C. Robertson-Glasgow for Somerset; Lord's		1924
Best Bowling (Match)	For	16-114	G. Burton v Yorkshire; Sheffield		1888
	For	16-114	J.T. Hearne v Lancashire; Manchester		1898
	V	16-109	C.W.L. Parker for Glos; Cheltenham		1930
Most Runs – Season		2650	W.J. Edrich	(av 85.48)	1947
Most Runs – Career		40302	E.H. Hendren	(av 48.82)	1907-1937
Most 100s – Season		13	D.C.S. Compton		1947
Most 100s – Career		119	E.H. Hendren		1907-1937
Most Wkts – Season		158	F.J. Titmus	(av 14.63)	1955
Most Wkts – Career		2361	F.J. Titmus	(av 21.27)	1949-1982

LIMITED-OVERS CRICKET

Highest Total	NWT	283-9 v Cumberland; Uxbridge	1985
	BHC	303-7 v Northants; Northampton	1977
	JPL	270-5 v Glos; Lord's	1983
Lowest Total	NWT	41 v Essex; Westcliff	1972
	BHC	73 v Essex; Lord's	1985
	JPL	23 v Yorkshire; Leeds	1974
Highest Innings	NWT	158 G.D. Barlow v Lancashire; Lord's	1984
	BHC	143* M.W. Gatting v Sussex; Hove	1985
	JPL	133* C.T. Radley v Glamorgan; Lord's	1969
Best Bowling	NWT	6-15 W.W. Daniel v Sussex; Hove	1980
	BHC	7-12 W.W. Daniel v Minor C (E); Ipswich	1978
	JPL	6-6 R.W. Hooker v Surrey; Lord's	1969

1985 RESULTS SUMMARY

	Place	*Won*	*Lost*	*Drew*	*Abandoned*
Britannic Assurance Championship	1st	8	4	12	
All First-class Matches		8	4	14	
John Player League	12th	5	7		4
NatWest Bank Trophy	Lost to Essex (2nd Round)				
Benson and Hedges Cup	Lost to Essex (Semi-Final)				

MIDDLESEX 1985

BRITANNIC ASSURANCE CHAMPIONSHIP AVERAGES

BATTING AND FIELDING

Cap		M	I	NO	HS	Runs	Avge	100	50	Ct/St
1967	C.T. Radley	24	33	9	200	1260	52.50	3	7	10
1977	M.W. Gatting	14	21	2	114	929	48.89	1	8	18
1976	G.D. Barlow	20	32	4	141	1343	47.96	6	2	6
1981	W.N. Slack	24	41	7	112	1618	47.58	3	10	27
1981	P.R. Downton	14	20	5	104	663	44.20	1	5	34/4
1979	R.O. Butcher	24	36	6	120	1154	38.46	1	8	24
1977	J.E. Emburey	15	16	2	68	432	30.85	—	4	14
—	K.R. Brown	7	10	2	67	196	24.50	—	1	8
1983	K.P. Tomlins	8	13	0	58	306	23.53	—	1	6
1984	N.F. Williams	19	20	4	46	311	19.43	—	—	3
1981	S.P. Hughes	11	11	6	30*	94	18.80	—	—	6
—	J.F. Sykes	10	12	3	52*	149	16.55	—	1	9
1974	P.H. Edmonds	15	16	5	29*	155	14.09	—	—	11
—	C.P. Metson	8	9	3	14*	59	9.83	—	—	18
—	J.D. Carr	5	7	0	29	59	8.42	—	—	3
1984	N.G. Cowans	19	14	2	15*	99	8.25	—	—	5
1977	W.W. Daniel	22	15	5	19*	48	4.80	—	—	7

Also batted: A.J.T. Miller (2 matches) 16,15,13*; G.D. Rose (2 matches) 4,15. A.R.C. Fraser (1 match) did not bat.

BOWLING

	O	M	R	W	Avge	Best	5 wI	10 wM
N.G. Cowans	362.4	65	1268	60	21.13	6-31	4	—
P.H. Edmonds	542	158	1206	51	23.64	6-87	2	
W.W. Daniel	575.1	89	2111	79	26.72	7-62	2	—
N.F. Williams	434.2	65	1542	54	28.55	5-15	2	—
J.E. Emburey	451	124	976	30	32.53	6-35	1	—
S.P. Hughes	246.2	42	871	23	37.86	5-64	1	—
J.F. Sykes	175.5	41	540	13	41.53	3-58	—	—

Also bowled: G.D. Barlow 3-0-14-0; R.O. Butcher 18-5-39-2; J.D. Carr 65.1-17-154-9; P.R. Downton 8-6-0-5; A.R.C. Fraser 19.5-3-71-4; M.W. Gatting 73.5-15-222-8; C.T. Radley 13-3-43-2; G.D. Rose 45.1-8-142-9; W.N. Slack 9-1-29-0; K.P. Tomlins 2-0-9-0.

The First-Class Averages (pp. 168–183) give the records of Middlesex players in all first-class county matches (their other opponents being the Australians and Cambridge U.), with the exception of J.D. Carr and A.J.T. Miller, whose full county figures are as above, and: N.G. Cowans 21-15-2-15*-105-8.07-0-0-5 ct. 392.2-70-1377-65-21.18-6/31-5-0. P.R. Downton 6-22-6-104-742-46.37-1-6-38 ct/4 st. 8-6-5-0. P.H. Edmonds 16-16-5-29*-155-14.09-0-0-13ct. 561-162-1252-53-23.62-6/87-2-0. J.E. Emburey 17-17-2-68-439-29.26-0-4-16ct. 501-141-1086-30-36.20-6/35-1-0. M.W. Gatting 16-23-2-114-1016-48.38-1-9-19ct. 87.5-17-277-11-25.18-3/55-0-0. C.T. Radley 26-36-11-200-1348-53.92-3-8-11ct. 13-3-43-2-21.50-2/38-0-0. N.F. Williams 21-21-4-67-378-22.23-0-1-3 ct. 462.2-67-1669-55-30.34-5/15-2-0.

NORTHAMPTONSHIRE

Formation of Present Club: 1820
Substantial reorganisation: 31 July 1878
Colours: Maroon
Badge: Tudor Rose
Championships: (0) Runners-up 1912, 1957, 1965, 1976
NatWest Trophy/Gillette Cup Winners: (1) 1976
Benson and Hedges Cup Winners: (1) 1980
John Player League Champions: (0) Fourth 1974
Match Awards: GC 17; NWT 10; BHC 25

Secretary: S.P. Coverdale, County Ground, Wantage Road, Northampton, NN1 4TJ
Captain: G. Cook
Scorer: B.H. Clarke
Scores/Prospects: ☎ Northampton (0604) 37040

BAILEY, Robert John (Biddulph HS), b Biddulph, Staffs 28 Oct 1963. 6'3". RHB, OB. Debut 1982. YC 1984. Cap 1985. Staffs 1980. 1000 runs (2); most – 1405 (1984). HS 114 v Somerset (Northampton) 1984. BB 3-33 v CU (Cambridge) 1983. **NWT:** HS 56* v Middx (Lord's) 1984. BB 1-2. **BHC:** HS 77 v Scot (Northampton) 1984. BB 1-22. **JPL:** HS 103 v Middx (Tring) 1985.

BOYD-MOSS, Robin James (Bedford S; Magdalene C, Cambridge), b Hatton, Ceylon 16 Dec 1959. 5'10½". RHB, SLA. Cambridge U and Northamptonshire debuts 1980. CU 1980-83; blue 1980-81-82-83. Cap 1984. Bedfordshire 1977-79. 1000 runs (2); most – 1602 (1982). HS 139 and BB 5-27 CU v OU (Lord's) 1983. Awards: NWT 1. **NWT:** HS 88* v Leics (Northampton) 1984. BB 3-47 v Shropshire (Telford) 1985. **BHC:** HS 58 Comb Us v Northants (Northampton) 1980. **JPL:** HS 99 v Glos (Bristol) 1984.

CAPEL, David John (Roade CS), b Northampton 6 Feb 1963. 5'11". RHB, RM. Debut 1981. Eastern Province 1985-86. HS 109* v Somerset (Northampton) 1983. BB 7-62 v Lancs (Lytham) 1985. **NWT:** HS 27 v Middx (Northampton) 1983. BB 2-74 v Glos (Bristol) 1985. **BHC:** HS 28 v Lancs (Manchester) 1983. BB 3-24 v Leics (Leicester) 1983. **JPL:** HS 79 v Kent (Northampton) 1982. BB 4-30 v Yorks (Middlesbrough) 1982.

COOK, Geoffrey (Middlesbrough HS), b Middlesbrough 9 Oct 1951. 6'0". RHB, SLA. Debut 1971. Cap 1975. E. Province 1978-81. Captain 1981-. Benefit 1985. Tests: 7 (1981-82 to 1982-83); HS 66 v Ind (Manchester) 1982. LOI: 6. Tours: Aus 1982-83; Ind/SL 1981-82. 1000 runs (10); most – 1759 (1981). HS 172 E. Province v N. Transvaal (Port Elizabeth) 1979-80. Northants HS 155 v Derbys (Northampton) 1978. BB 3-47 England XI v S. Australia (Adelaide) 1982-83. Awards: NWT 5; BHC 3. **NWT:** HS 130 v Shropshire (Telford) 1985. **BHC:** HS 96 v Minor C (E) (Northampton) 1978. **JPL:** HS 98 v Lancs (Northampton) 1985.

COOK, Nicholas Grant Billson (Lutterworth GS), b Broughton Astley, Leicester 17 June 1956. 6'0". RHB, SLA. Leicestershire 1978-85. Cap 1982. Joins Northamptonshire 1986. Tests: 9 (1983-84); HS 26 v NZ (Nottingham) 1983; BB 6-65 (11-83 match) v Pak (Karachi) 1983-84. LOI: 1. Tours: NZ 1979-80 (DHR), 1983-84; Pak 1983-84; SL 1985-86 (Eng B); Zim 1980-81 (Leics), 1984-85 (Eng Co). HS 75 Leics v Somerset (Taunton) 1980. BB 7-63 Leics v Somerset (Taunton) 1982. **NWT:** BB 2-33 Leics v Wilts (Swindon) 1984. **BHC:** HS 23 Leics v Warwicks (Leicester) 1984. BB 1-25. **JPL:** HS 13* Leics v Kent 1979, 13* Leics v Middx 1981. BB 3-26 Leics v Middx (Lord's) 1985.

GRIFFITHS, Brian **James** (Irthlingborough & Finedon SS), b Wellingborough 13 Jun 1949. 6'3". RHB, RFM. Debut 1974. Cap 1978. HS 16 v Glos (Bristol) 1982. BB 8-50 v Glam (Northampton) 1981. Awards: NWT 1. **NWT:** HS 1*. BB 5-33 v Yorks (Leeds) 1983. **BHC:** HS 6. BB 5-43 v Sussex (Eastbourne) 1979. **JPL:** HS 11* v Surrey (Tring) 1982. BB 4-22 v Somerset (Weston) 1977.

HARPER, Roger Andrew (Queen's College HS, Georgetown), b Georgetown, British Guiana 17 Mar 1963. 6'5". RHB, OB. Brother of M.A. (Guyana). Demerara 1979-83. Guyana 1979-86. Northants debut 1985. Tests (WI): 14 (1983-84 to 1984-85); HS 39* and BB 6-57 v Eng (Manchester) 1984. LOI: 18. Tours (WI): Eng 1984; Aus 1984-85; Ind 1983-84. HS 127 v Kent (Maidstone) 1985. BB 6-57 (Tests). Northants BB 5-94 v Leics (Northampton) 1985. **NWT:** HS 0. **BHC:** BB 3-48 v Notts (Nottingham) 1985. **JPL:** HS 18 v Worcs (Worcester) 1985. BB 2-29 v Warwicks (Birmingham) 1985.

LAMB, Allan Joseph (Wynberg HS; Abbots C) b Langebaanweg, Cape Province, SA 20 Jun 1954. 5'8". RHB, RM. W. Province 1972-82. Northants debut/cap 1978. *Wisden* 1980. Tests: 38 (1982-85); HS 137* v NZ (Nottingham) 1983; BB 1-6. LOI: 43. Tours: Aus 1982-83; WI 1985-86; NZ 1983-84; Ind/SL 1984-85; Pak 1983-84. 1000 runs (6); most – 2049 (1981). HS 178 v Leics (Leicester) 1979. BB 1-1. Awards: NWT 1: BHC 5. **NWT:** HS 101 v Sussex (Hove) 1979. BB 1-4. **BHC:** HS 106* v Leics (Leics) 1983. **JPL:** HS 132* v Surrey (Guildford) 1985.

LARKINS, Wayne (Bushmead SS, Eaton Secon), b Roxton, Beds 22 Nov 1953. 5'11". RHB, RM. Debut 1972. Cap 1976. E. Province 1982-84. Benefit 1986. Tests: 6 (1979-80 to 1981); HS 34 v Aus (Oval) 1981. LOI: 6. Tours: Aus 1979-80; SA 1981-82 (SAB); Ind 1979-80, 1980-81 (Overseas XI). 1000 runs (8); most – 1863 (1982). HS 252 v Glam (Cardiff) 1983. BB 5-59 v Worcs (Worcester) 1984. Awards: NWT 1; BHC 5. **NWT:** HS 92* v Leics (Northampton) 1979. BB 2-38 v Glos (Bristol) 1985. **BHC:** HS 132 v Warwicks (Birmingham) 1982. BB 4-37 v Comb Us (Northampton) 1980. **JPL:** HS 172* v Warwicks (Luton) 1983. BB 5-32 v Essex (Ilford) 1978.

MALLENDER, Neil Alan (Beverley GS), b Kirk Sandall, Yorks 13 Aug 1961. 6'0". RHB, RFM. Debut 1980. Cap 1984. Otago 1983-86. HS 88 Otago v Central Districts (Oamaru) 1984-85. Northants HS 71* v OU (Oxford) 1983. BB 7-27 Otago v Auckland (Auckland) 1984-85. Northants BB 7-41 v Derbys (Northampton) 1982. Awards: NWT 1. **NWT:** HS 11* v Yorks (Leeds) 1983. BB 7-37 v Worcs (Northampton) 1984. **BHC:** HS 7. BB 3-12 v Worcs (Worcester) 1983. **JPL:** HS 22 v Warwicks 1981, 22 v Somerset 1983. BB 5-34 v Middx (Tring) 1981.

RIPLEY, David (Royds SS, Leeds), b Leeds, Yorkshire 13 Sep 1966. 5'9". RHB, WK. Debut 1984. HS 61 v Surrey (Northampton) 1984. **NWT:** HS 27* v Durham (Darlington) 1984. **JPL:** HS 24 v Derbys (Northampton) 1984.

STORIE, Alastair Caleb (St. Stithians C, Johannesburg), b Bishopbriggs, Glasgow 25 Jul 1965. 5'9". RHB, RM. Debut 1985 scoring 10 and 106 v Hampshire at Northampton. HS 106 (*above*).

WALKER, Alan (Shelley HS), b Emley, Yorks 7 Jul 1962. 5'11". LHB, RFM. Debut 1983. HS 19 v Sussex (Horsham) 1984. BB 4-38 v Kent (Northampton) 1985. **NWT:** BB 2-43 v Durham (Darlington) 1984. **BHC:** BB 4-46 v Glos (Northampton) 1985. **JPL:** HS 13 v Yorks (Tring) 1983. BB 4-21 v Worcs (Worcester) 1985.

WATERTON, Stuart Nicholas Varney (Gravesend S; LSE), b Dartford 6 Dec 1960. 5'11½". RHB, WK. Kent 1980-85. HS 50 Kent v Lancs (Manchester) 1984. **NWT:** HS 4*. **JPL:** HS 15 Kent v Glam (Canterbury) 1984.

WILD, Duncan James (Northampton GS), b Northampton 28 Nov 1962. 5'11½". LHB, RM. Son of John (Northamptonshire 1953-61). Debut 1980. HS 144 v Lancs (Southport) 1984. BB 3-15 v Hants (Southampton) 1984. **NWT:** HS 11 v Middx (Lord's) 1984. BB 3-47 v Leics (Northampton) 1984. **BHC:** HS 48 v Warwicks (Northampton) 1984. **JPL:** HS 63* v Glos (Northampton) 1985. BB 4-33 v Yorks (Leeds) 1985.

WILLIAMS, Richard Grenville (Ellesmere Port GS), b Bangor, Caernarvonshire 10 Aug 1957. 5'6½". RHB, OB. Debut 1974. Cap 1979. Tours: NZ 1979-80 (DHR); Zim 1984-85 (Eng Co). 1000 runs (6); most – 1262 (1980). HS 175* v Leics (Leicester) 1980. BB 7-73 v CU (Cambridge) 1980. Awards: NWT 1; BHC 3. **NWT:** HS 94 v Worcs (Northampton) 1984. BB 3-15 v Leics (Northampton) 1979. **BHC:** HS 83 v Yorks (Bradford) 1980. BB 2-11 v Worcs (Worcester) 1981. **JPL:** HS 82 v Glos (Bristol) 1982. BB 5-30 v Warwicks (Luton) 1983.

VALETE

JOSEPH, Ray Fitzpatrick (Belladrum SS), b Belladrum, Guyana 12 Feb 1961. 6'1". RHB, RFM. Berbice 1979-85. Guyana 1979-86. Northamptonshire 1985 (2 matches). HS 26* v Hants (Northampton) 1985. BB 6-114 Guyana v Jamaica (Kingston) 1983-84.

SHARP, George (Elwick Road SS), b West Hartlepool, Co Durham 12 Mar 1950. 5'11". RHB, WK, SLA. Northamptonshire 1968-85 (cap 1973). Benefit 1982. HS 98 v Yorks (Northampton) 1983. BB 1-47.

WHEELER, Matthew Benjamin Harold (Winchester C; Exeter U), b Windlesham, Surrey 14 Aug 1962. 6'2". RHB, RMF. Debut 1985. Did not bat. BB 1-87.

NORTHAMPTONSHIRE RECORDS

FIRST-CLASS CRICKET

Highest Total	For	557-6d v Sussex; Hove	1914
	V	670-9d by Sussex; Hove	1921
Lowest Total	For	12 v Glos; Gloucester	1907
	V	33 by Lancashire; Northampton	1977
Highest Innings	For	300 R. Subba Row v Surrey; The Oval	1958
	V	333 K.S. Duleepsinhji for Sussex; Hove	1930

Highest Partnerships

1st	361	N. Oldfield/V. Broderick v Scotland; Peterborough	1953
2nd	342	W. Larkins/P. Willey v Lancashire; Northampton	1983
3rd	320	L. Livingston/F. Jakeman v S. Africans; Northampton	1951
4th	370	R.T. Virgin/P. Willey v Somerset; Northampton	1976
5th	347	D. Brookes/D.W. Barrick v Essex; Northampton	1952
6th	376	R. Subba Row/A. Lightfoot v Surrey; The Oval	1958
7th	229	W.W. Timms/F.A. Walden v Warwicks; Northampton	1926
8th	155	F.R. Brown/A.E. Nutter v Glamorgan; Northampton	1952
9th	156	R. Subba Row/S. Starkie v Lancashire; Northampton	1955
10th	148	B.W. Bellamy/J.V. Murdin v Glamorgan; Northampton	1925

Best Bowling	For	10-127	V.W.C. Jupp v Kent; Tunbridge Wells	1932
(Innings)	V	10-30	C. Blythe for Kent; Northampton	1907
Best Bowling	For	15-31	G.E. Tribe v Yorkshire; Northampton	1958
(Match)	V	17-48	C. Blythe for Kent; Northampton	1907

Most Runs – Season	2198	D. Brookes	(av 51.06)	1952
Most Runs – Career	28980	D. Brookes	(av 36.13)	1934-1959
Most 100s – Season	8	R.A. Haywood		1921
Most 100s – Career	67	D. Brookes		1934-1959
Most Wkts – Season	175	G.E. Tribe	(av 18.70)	1955
Most Wkts – Career	1097	E.W. Clark	(av 21.32)	1922-1947

LIMITED-OVERS CRICKET

Highest Total	NWT	285-6 v Wiltshire; Swindon	1983
	BHC	259-5 v Scotland; Glasgow	1982
	JPL	306-2 v Surrey; Guildford	1985
Lowest Total	NWT	62 v Leics; Leicester	1974
	BHC	85 v Sussex; Northampton	1978
	JPL	41 v Middlesex; Northampton	1972
Highest Innings	NWT	130 G. Cook v Shropshire; Telford	1985
	BHC	132 W. Larkins v Warwicks; Birmingham	1982
	JPL	172* W. Larkins v Warwicks; Luton	1983
Best Bowling	NWT	7-37 N.A. Mallender v Worcs; Northampton	1984
	BHC	5-21 Sarfraz Nawaz v Middlesex; Lord's	1980
	JPL	7-39 A. Hodgson v Somerset; Northampton	1976

NORTHAMPTONSHIRE 1985

RESULTS SUMMARY

	Place	Won	Lost	Drew	Tied	Aban
Britannic Assurance Championship	10th	5	4	15		
All First-class Matches		5	4	16		
John Player League	5th	7	4		1	4
NatWest Bank Trophy	Lost to Gloucestershire (2nd Round)					
Benson and Hedges Cup	Lost to Kent (Quarter-Final)					

BRITANNIC ASSURANCE CHAMPIONSHIP AVERAGES

BATTING AND FIELDING

Cap		*M*	*I*	*NO*	*HS*	*Runs*	*Avge*	*100*	*50*	*Ct/St*
—	A.C. Storie	7	12	2	106	407	40.70	1	3	3
—	R.A. Harper	22	26	7	127	734	38.63	1	3	20
1975	G. Cook	23	37	4	126	1271	38.51	1	9	19
1976	W. Larkins	24	39	0	163	1490	38.20	3	4	18
1985	R.J. Bailey	24	36	6	101	1054	35.13	1	7	5
1978	A.J. Lamb	11	17	2	111	525	35.00	1	4	6
1979	R.G. Williams	20	30	2	118	845	30.17	2	4	2
—	D.J. Wild	18	22	4	80	525	29.16	—	2	4
1984	R.J. Boyd-Moss	19	30	3	121	748	27.70	2	2	6
—	D.J. Capel	22	30	6	81	599	24.95	—	5	5
1984	N.A. Mallender	23	25	8	52*	267	15.70	—	1	5
—	A. Walker	12	14	8	18*	83	13.83	—	—	6
1973	G. Sharp	11	13	1	25	111	9.25	—	—	16/3
—	D. Ripley	13	14	4	27	83	8.30	—	—	21/4
1978	B.J. Griffiths	12	9	4	12	17	3.40	—	—	2

Also batted: R.F. Joseph (2 matches) 26*. M.B.H. Wheeler (1 match) did not bat.

BOWLING

	O	*M*	*R*	*W*	*Avge*	*Best*	*5 wI*	*10 wM*
B.J. Griffiths	288.4	71	846	31	27.29	6-76	1	—
D.J. Capel	362.3	63	1192	40	29.80	7-62	1	—
N.A. Mallender	506.4	97	1479	48	30.81	5-83	1	—
A. Walker	251.4	51	786	23	34.17	4-38	—	—
R.A. Harper	737.4	185	1996	56	35.64	5-94	1	—
R.J. Boyd-Moss	125.4	30	380	10	38.00	3-48	—	—
R.G. Williams	291.2	70	913	23	39.69	5-34	1	—

Also bowled: R.J. Bailey 3-0-16-0; G. Cook 1-0-6-0; R.F. Joseph 38-5-143-4; A.J. Lamb 1-1-0-0; W. Larkins 77-16-258-1; G. Sharp 1-0-2-0; A.C. Storie 18-6-51-0; M.B.H. Wheeler 14-3-30-0; D.J. Wild 82.5-7-368-2.

The First-Class Averages (pp. 168–183) give the records of Northamptonshire players in all first-class county matches (their other opponents being the Australians), with the exception of N.A. Mallender, whose full county figures are as above, and: R.J. Bailey 25-37-7-107*-1161-38.70-2-7-5 ct. 3-0-16-0. R.A. Harper 23-26-7-127-734-38.63-1-3-20 ct. 748.4-188-2023-56-36.12-5/94-1-0. A.J. Lamb 12-17-2-111-525-35.00-1-4-7 ct. 3-1-7-0. W. Larkins 25-40-0-163-1534-38.35-3-4-18 ct. 83-16-284-1-284.00-1/34-0-0.

NOTTINGHAMSHIRE

Formation of Present Club: March/April 1841
Substantial Reorganisation: 11 December 1866
Colours: Green and Gold
Badge: County Badge of Nottinghamshire
Championships (since 1890): (3) 1907, 1929, 1981
NatWest Trophy/Gillette Cup Winners: (0) Finalists 1985
Benson and Hedges Cup Winners: (0) Finalists 1982
John Player League Champions: (0) Second 1984
Match Awards: GC 13; NWT 8; BHC 36

Secretary: B. Robson, Trent Bridge, Nottingham NG2 6AG
Captain: C.E.B. Rice
Scorer: L. Tomlinson
Scores/Prospects: ☎ Nottingham (0602) 822753

AFFORD, John Andrew (Spalding GS; Stamford CFE), b Crowland, Lincs 12 May 1964. 6'1½". RHB, SLA. Debut 1984. HS 2. BB 2-49 v Lancs (Blackpool) 1984.

BIRCH, John Dennis (William Crane Bilateral S), b Nottingham 18 Jun 1955. 5'11". RHB, RM. Debut 1973. Cap 1981. 1000 runs (2); most – 1086 (1983). HS 125 v Leics (Nottingham) 1982. BB 6-64 v Hants (Bournemouth) 1975. Awards: BHC 1. **NWT:** HS 32 v Yorks (Bradford) 1978. BB 1-58. **BHC:** HS 85 v Minor C (N) (Nottingham) 1979. BB 2-14 v Minor C (N) (Newark) 1975. **JPL:** HS 92 v Sussex (Nottingham) 1983. BB 3-29 v Glam (Swansea) 1976.

BROAD, Brian **Christopher** (Colston's S, Bristol; St. Paul's C, Cheltenham), b Bristol 29 Sep 1957. 6'4". LHB, RM. Gloucestershire 1979-83 (cap 1981). Nottinghamshire debut/cap 1984. Orange Free State 1985-86 (captain). Tests: 5 (1984); HS 86 v SL (Lord's). Tour: Zim 1984-85 (Eng Co). 1000 runs (5); most – 1786 (1985). HS 171 v Derbys (Derby) 1985. BB 2-14 Glos v West Indians (Bristol) 1980. Awards: NWT 1; BHC 1. **NWT:** HS 98 Glos v Middx (Bristol) 1982. **BHC:** HS 122 v Derbys (Derby) 1984. BB 2-73 v Lancs (Nottingham) 1984. **JPL:** HS 96 Glos v Yorks (Cheltenham) 1983. BB 3-46 Glos v Worcs (Bristol) 1982.

COOPER, Kevin Edwin (Hucknall National SS), b Hucknall, Notts, 27 Dec 1957. 6'1". LHB, RFM. Debut 1976. Cap 1980. HS 46 v Middx (Nottingham) 1985. BB 8-44 v Middx (Lord's) 1984. **NWT:** HS 11 v Glos (Nottingham) 1982. BB 4-49 v Warwicks (Nottingham) 1985. **BHC:** HS 25* v Lancs (Manchester) 1983. BB 4-23 v Kent (Canterbury) 1979. **JPL:** HS 31 v Glos (Nottingham) 1984. BB 4-25 v Hants (Nottingham) 1976.

EVANS, Kevin Paul (Colonel Frank Seely S) b Calverton 10 Sep 1963. 6'2". RHB, RMF. Brother of R.J. Debut 1984. HS 42 and BB 2-31 v CU (Nottingham) 1984. **NWT:** HS 8. BB 1-24. **BHC:** HS 20 v Glos (Bristol) 1985. BB 1-47. **JPL:** HS 28 v Glos 1985, 28 v Kent 1985. BB 3-36 v Middx (Nottingham) 1985.

EVANS, Russell John (Colonel Frank Seely S), b Calverton 1 Oct 1965. 6'0". RHB, RM. Brother of K.P. Played in one JPL match 1985. Awaiting f-c debut. **JPL:** HS 20 v Hants (Nottingham) 1985.

FRASER-DARLING, Callum **David** (The Edinburgh Academy). b Sheffield. Yorkshire 30 Sep 1963. 6'5". RHB. RFM. Debut 1984. HS 23* v Warwicks (Nuneaton) 1985. BB 2-14 v CU (Nottingham) 1984. **JPL:** HS 7. BB 1-24.

FRENCH, Bruce Nicholas (The Meden CS). b Warsop 13 Aug 1959. 5'6". RHB. WK. Debut 1976 aged 16 years 287 days. Cap 1980. LOI: 3. Tours: WI 1985-86; Ind/SL 1984-85. HS 98 v Lancs (Nottingham) 1984. Awards: BHC 1. **NWT:** HS 49 v Staffs (Nottingham) 1985. **BHC:** HS 48* v Worcs (Nottingham) 1984. **JPL:** HS 37 v Glos (Bristol) 1985.

HADLEE, Richard John (Christchurch BHS). b Christchurch, NZ 3 Jul 1951. 6'1". LHB. RFM. Fourth son of W.A. (Canterbury, Otago and NZ); brother of D.R. (Canterbury and NZ), and B.G. (Canterbury); wife Karen (NZ). Canterbury 1971-85. Nottinghamshire debut/cap 1978. Tasmania 1979-80. MBE 1980. *Wisden* 1981. Tests (NZ): 57 (1972-73 to 1984-85); HS 103 v WI (Christchurch) 1979-80; BB 7-23 v Ind (Wellington) 1975-76. LOI: 75. Tours: Eng 1973, 1978, 1983; Aus 1972-73, 1973-74, 1980-81, 1985-86; WI 1984-85; Ind/Pak 1976-77; SL 1983-84. 1000 runs (1): 1179 (1984). 100 wickets (2); most – 117 (1984). Double 1984 (first since 1967). HS 210* v Middx (Lord's) 1984. BB 8-41 v Lancs (Nottingham) 1985. Awards: NWT 1; BHC 6. **NWT:** HS 56 v Warwicks (Nottingham) 1985. BB 2-14 v Kent (Canterbury) 1981. **BHC:** HS 70 v Warwicks (Nottingham) 1982. BB 4-13 v Derbys (Nottingham) 1980. **JPL:** HS 100* v Glos (Cheltenham) 1982. BB 6-12 v Lancs (Nottingham) 1980.

HEMMINGS, Edward Ernest (Campion S). b Leamington Spa, Warwickshire 20 Feb 1949. 5'10". RHB. OB. Warwickshire 1966-1978 (cap 1974). Nottinghamshire debut 1979. Cap 1980. Tests: 5 (1982 and 1982-83); HS 95 and BB 3-68 v Aus (Sydney) 1982-83. LOI: 5. Tours: Aus 1972-73; SA 1974-75 (DHR); WI 1982-83 (Int XI); Pak 1981-82 (Int XI). HS 127* v Yorks (Worksop) 1982. BB 10-175 Int XI v West Indies XI (Kingston) 1982-83. Notts BB 7-23 v Lancs (Nottingham) 1983. **NWT:** HS 31* v Staffs (Nottingham) 1985. BB 3-27 v Warwicks (Nottingham) 1985. **BHC:** HS 61* Warwicks v Leics (Birmingham) 1974. BB 3-12 v Surrey (Nottingham) 1984. **JPL:** HS 44* Warwicks v Kent (Birmingham) 1971. BB 5-22 Warwicks v Notts (Birmingham) 1974.

JOHNSON, Paul (Grove CS, Balderton). b Newark 24 Apr 1965. 5'7". RHB. RM. Debut 1982. HS 133 v Kent (Folkestone) 1984. BB 1-0. Awards: NWT 1. **NWT:** HS 101* v Staffs (Nottingham) 1985. **BHC:** HS 16 v Glos (Bristol) 1985. **JPL:** HS 63 v Warwicks (Birmingham) 1985.

MARTINDALE, Duncan John Richardson (Lymm GS; Trent Polytechnic). b Harrogate, Yorkshire 13 Dec 1963. 5'11". RHB. OB. Debut 1985. HS 104* v Lancs (Manchester). **NWT:** HS 20* v Essex (Lord's) 1985. **JPL:** HS 33 v Essex (Nottingham) 1985.

NEWELL, Michael (West Bridgford CS). b Blackburn, Lancs 25 Feb 1965. 5'8". RHB, LB. Debut 1984. HS 76 v CU (Nottingham) 1984. BB 1-38.

PICK, Robert **Andrew** (Alderman Derbyshire CS; High Pavement SFC). b Nottingham 19 Nov 1963. 5'10". LHB. RMF. Debut 1983. HS 63 v Warwicks (Nuneaton) 1985. BB 5-25 v OU (Oxford) 1984. **NWT:** HS 34* v Sussex (Hove) 1983. BB 2-46 v Worcs (Worcester) 1985. **BHC:** HS 3*. **JPL:** HS 11 v Essex (Nottingham) 1985. BB 4-36 v Leics (Leicester) 1984.

RANDALL, Derek William (Sir Frederick Milner SS). b Retford 24 Feb 1951. 5'9". RHB. RM. Debut 1972. Cap 1973. *Wisden* 1979. Benefit 1983. Tests: 47 (1976-77 to 1984); HS 174 v Aus (Melbourne) 1976-77. LOI: 49. Tours: Aus 1976-77. 1978-79. 1979-80. 1982-83; SA 1975-76 (DHR); NZ 1977-78. 1983-84; Ind/SL 1976-77; Pak 1977-78. 1983-84; Zim 1985-86 (Eng B). 1000 runs (10); most – 2151 (1985). HS 209 v Middx (Nottingham) 1979. BB 3-15 v MCC (Lord's) 1982. Awards: NWT 2; BHC 3. **NWT:** HS 75 v Sussex (Hove) 1979. **BHC:** HS 103* v Minor C (N) (Nottingham) 1979. **JPL:** HS 107* v Middx (Lord's) 1976.

RICE, Clive Edward Butler (Sandringham S; St. John's C; Damelin C; Natal U). b Johannesburg. SA 23 Jul 1949. 6'0". RHB. RMF. Grandson of P.S.S. Bower (Oxford U 1919). Transvaal 1969-86 (capt 1981-86). Nottinghamshire debut/cap 1975. Captain 1979-. *Wisden* 1980. Benefit 1985. 1000 runs (11); most – 1871 (1978). HS 246 v Sussex (Hove) 1976. BB 7-62 Transvaal v W. Province (Johannesburg) 1975-76. Notts BB 6-16 v Worcs (Worcester) 1977. Awards: NWT 1; BHC 8. **NWT:** HS 71 v Yorks (Bradford) 1978. BB 6-18 v Sussex (Hove) 1982. **BHC:** HS 130* v Scotland (Glasgow) 1982. BB 6-22 v Northants (Northampton) 1981. **JPL:** HS 120* v Glamorgan (Swansea) 1978. BB 4-15 v Hants (Nottingham) 1980.

ROBINSON, Robert **Timothy** (Dunstable GS; High Pavement SFC; Sheffield U). b Sutton-in-Ashfield 21 Nov 1958. 6'0". RHB. RM. Debut 1978. Cap 1983. *Wisden* 1985. Tests: 11 (1984-85 and 1985); HS 175 v Aus (Leeds) 1985. LOI: 7. Tours: WI 1985-86; Ind/SL 1984-85. 1000 runs (3); most – 2032 (1984). HS 207 v Warwicks (Nottingham) 1983. BB 1-22. Awards: NWT 3; BHC 2. **NWT:** HS 139 v Worcs (Worcester) 1985. **BHC:** HS 120 v Scotland (Glasgow) 1985. **JPL:** HS 97* v Worcs (Worcester) 1984.

SAXELBY, Kevin (Magnus GS). b Worksop 23 Feb 1959. 6'2". RHB. RMF. Debut 1978. Cap 1984. HS 59* v Derbys (Chesterfield) 1982. BB 6-64 v Kent (Tunbridge Wells) 1985. **NWT:** HS 12 v Worcs (Worcester) 1983. BB 4-28 v Middx (Nottingham) 1984. **BHC:** HS 13* v Lancs (Nottingham) 1982. BB 3-12 v Surrey (Nottingham) 1984. **JPL:** HS 23* v Middx (Cleethorpes) 1983. BB 4-29 v Warwicks (Birmingham) 1983.

SCOTT, Christopher Wilmot (Robert Pattinson CS). b Thorpe-on-the-Hill. Lincolnshire 23 Jan 1964. 5'8". RHB. WK. Debut 1981. HS 78 v CU (Cambridge) 1973. **JPL:** HS 9.

SUCH, Peter Mark (Harry Carlton CS. E. Leake. Notts). b Helensburgh. Dunbartonshire 12 Jun 1964. 5'11". RHB. OB. Debut 1982. HS 16 v Middx (Lord's) 1984. BB 6-123 v Kent (Nottingham) 1983. **BHC:** BB 3-50 v Scotland (Glasgow) 1985. **JPL:** HS 0*. BB 2-50 v Glos (Bristol) 1985.

VALETE

HASSAN, Basharat (City HS. Nairobi). b Nairobi. Kenya 24 March 1944. 5'10½". RHB. RM. WK. Debut 1963-64 (East African XI). Nottinghamshire 1966-85 (cap 1970; benefit of £20,000 in 1978). 1000 runs (5); most – 1395 (1970). HS 182* v Glos (Nottingham) 1977. BB 3-33 v Lancs (Manchester) 1976. Awards: BHC 1.

NOTTINGHAMSHIRE RECORDS

FIRST-CLASS CRICKET

Highest Total	For	739-7d v Leics; Nottingham	1903
	V	706-4d by Surrey; Nottingham	1947
Lowest Total	For	13 v Yorkshire; Nottingham	1901
	V	16 by Derbyshire; Nottingham	1879
		16 by Surrey; The Oval	1880
Highest Innings	For	312* W.W. Keeton v Middx; The Oval	1939
	V	345 C.G. Macartney for Australians; Nottingham	1921

Highest Partnerships

1st	391	A.O. Jones/A. Shrewsbury v Glos; Bristol	1899
2nd	398	W. Gunn/A. Shrewsbury v Sussex; Nottingham	1890
3rd	369	W. Gunn/J.R. Gunn v Leics; Nottingham	1903
4th	361	A.O. Jones/J.R. Gunn v Essex; Leyton	1905
5th	266	A. Shrewsbury/W. Gunn v Sussex; Hove	1884
6th	303*	F. H. Winrow/P.F. Harvey v Derbyshire; Nottingham	1947
7th	204	M.J. Smedley/R.A. White v Surrey; The Oval	1967
8th	220	G.F.H. Heane/R. Winrow v Somerset; Nottingham	1935
9th	165	W. McIntyre/G. Wootton v Kent; Nottingham	1869
10th	152	E.B. Alletson/W. Riley v Sussex; Hove	1911

Best Bowling (Innings)	For	10-66 K. Smales v Glos; Stroud	1956
	V	10-10 H. Verity for Yorkshire; Leeds	1932
Best Bowling (Match)	For	17-89 F.C. Matthews v Northants; Nottingham	1923
	V	17-89 W.G. Grace for Glos; Cheltenham	1877

Most Runs – Season	2620	W.W. Whysall	(av 53.46)	1929
Most Runs – Career	31592	G. Gunn	(av 35.70)	1902-1932
Most 100s – Season	9	W.W. Whysall and M.J. Harris		1928 and 1971
Most 100s – Career	65	J. Hardstaff, jr		1930-1955
Most Wkts – Season	181	B. Dooland	(av 14.96)	1954
Most Wkts – Career	1653	T.G. Wass	(av 20.34)	1896-1920

LIMITED-OVERS CRICKET

Highest Total	NWT	287-8 v Glos; Bristol	1985
	BHC	282-4 v Derbyshire; Derby	1984
	JPL	260-5 v Warwicks; Birmingham	1976
Lowest Total	NWT	123 v Yorkshire; Scarborough	1969
	BHC	94 v Lancashire; Nottingham	1975
	JPL	66 v Yorkshire; Bradford	1969
Highest Innings	NWT	139 R.T. Robinson v Worcs; Worcester	1985
	BHC	130* C.E.B. Rice v Scotland; Glasgow	1982
	JPL	120* C.E.B. Rice v Glamorgan; Swansea	1978
		120* B. Hassan v Warwicks; Birmingham	1981
Best Bowling	NWT	6-18 C.E.B. Rice v Sussex; Hove	1982
	BHC	6-22 M.K. Bore v Leics; Leicester	1980
		6-22 C.E.B. Rice v Northants; Northampton	1981
	JPL	6-12 R.J. Hadlee v Lancashire; Nottingham	1980

NOTTINGHAMSHIRE 1985

RESULTS SUMMARY

	Place	*Won*	*Lost*	*Drew*	*Abandoned*
Britannic Assurance Championship	8th	4	2	18	
All First-class Matches		4	2	19	
John Player League	12th	6	8		2
NatWest Bank Trophy	Lost to Essex (Final)				
Benson and Hedges Cup	Failed to qualify for Quarter-Final				

BRITANNIC ASSURANCE CHAMPIONSHIP AVERAGES

BATTING AND FIELDING

Cap		*M*	*I*	*NO*	*HS*	*Runs*	*Avge*	*100*	*50*	*Ct/St*
1983	R.T. Robinson	11	21	3	130*	1107	61.50	4	8	8
1975	C.E.B. Rice	20	33	8	171*	1394	55.76	4	6	21
1973	D.W. Randall	24	45	6	117	1977	50.69	4	13	24
1984	B.C. Broad	24	45	3	171	1706	40.61	2	13	15
1978	R.J. Hadlee	19	29	11	73*	592	32.88	—	5	17
—	P. Johnson	20	32	4	118	890	31.78	1	6	13
—	D.J.R. Martindale	9	14	3	104*	317	28.81	1	1	6
1970	B. Hassan	3	5	1	34	109	27.25	—	—	4
1981	J.D. Birch	13	21	6	68*	392	26.13	—	2	4
—	R.A. Pick	12	14	4	63	240	24.00	—	1	3
1980	E.E. Hemmings	21	22	5	56*	297	17.47	—	1	7
1980	B.N. French	23	33	8	52*	432	17.28	—	1	61/7
—	M. Newell	6	11	0	59	177	16.09	—	1	2
1980	K.E. Cooper	21	16	4	46	139	11.58	—	—	4
—	C.D. Fraser-Darling	2	4	1	23*	33	11.00	—	—	4
1984	K. Saxelby	17	13	4	29*	78	8.66	—	—	1
—	P.M. Such	14	12	5	8	18	2.57	—	—	7

Also batted: J.A. Afford (2 matches) 2 (2 ct); K.P. Evans (2 matches) 11,0. C.W. Scott (1 match) did not bat.

BOWLING

	O	*M*	*R*	*W*	*Avge*	*Best*	*5 wI*	*10 wM*
R.J. Hadlee	473.5	136	1026	59	17.38	8-41	2	—
K.E. Cooper	576.3	168	1552	53	29.28	6-53	1	—
C.E.B. Rice	284	82	779	25	31.16	4-24	—	—
P.M. Such	405.1	105	1152	32	36.00	5-73	1	—
K. Saxelby	404	95	1333	35	38.08	6-64	2	1
E.E. Hemmings	716.3	171	2103	55	38.23	6-51	2	—
R.A. Pick	267	44	1021	25	40.84	4-51	—	—

Also bowled: J.A. Afford 22-3-76-2; J.D. Birch 5-0-14-0; B.C. Broad 9.3-2-40-2; K.P. Evans 9-1-38-0; C.D. Fraser-Darling 19-3-88-0; P. Johnson 23-3-129-1; D.J.R. Martindale 2-0-8-0; M. Newell 9-2-38-1; D.W. Randall 28-2-174-5.

The First-Class Averages (pp. 168–183) give the records of Nottinghamshire players in all first-class county matches (their other opponents being Cambridge U.), with the exception of B.N. French and R.T. Robinson whose full county figures are as above.

SOMERSET

Formation of Present Club: 18 August 1875
Colours: Black, White and Maroon
Badge: Wessex Wyvern
Championships: (0) Third in 1892, 1958, 1963, 1966, 1981
NatWest Trophy/Gillette Cup Winners: (2) 1979, 1983
Benson and Hedges Cup Winners: (2) 1981, 1982
John Player League Champions: (1) 1979
Match Awards: GC 26; NWT 8; BHC 37

Secretary: A.S. Brown, The County Ground, St. James Street, Taunton TA1 1JT
Captain: P.M. Roebuck
Scorer: D.A. Oldam
Scores/Prospects: ☎ Taunton (0823) 70007

ATKINSON, Jonathon Colin Mark (Millfield S), b Butleigh 10 July 1968. 6'3". RHB, RMF. Debut 1985. HS 79 v Northants (Weston) 1985 – on debut. BB 1-36.

BAIL, Paul Andrew Clayton (Millfield S), b Burnham-on-Sea 23 Jun 1965. 5'10". RHB, OB. Debut 1985. HS 78* v Kent (Canterbury) 1985.

BOOTH, Stephen Charles (Boston Spa CS), b Leeds 30 Oct 1963. 5'8½". RHB, SLA. Debut 1983. HS 42 v Derbys (Taunton) 1984. BB 4-26 v Middx (Lord's) 1983.

BOTHAM, Ian Terence (Buckler's Mead SS, Yeovil), b Heswall, Cheshire 24 Nov 1955. 6'1". RHB, RFM. Debut 1974. Cap 1976. *Wisden* 1977. YC 1977. Captain 1984-85. Benefit 1984. Tests: 79 (1977 to 1985, 12 as captain); HS 208 v India (Oval) 1982; BB 8-34 v Pak (Lord's) 1978. Unique Test double of 4000 runs and 300 wickets. First to score a hundred and take 10 wickets in same Test. LOI: 75. Tours: Aus 1978-79, 1979-80, 1982-83; WI 1980-81 (capt), 1985-86; NZ 1977-78, 1983-84; Ind 1979-80, 1981-82; Pak 1977-78, 1983-84; SL 1981-82. 1000 runs (4); most – 1530 (1985). 100 wickets (1): 100 (1978). Set world first-class record by hitting 80 sixes in 1985. HS 228 v Glos (Taunton) 1980. BB 8-34 (*Tests*). Awards: NWT 2; BHC 5. Soccer for Scunthorpe United. **NWT:** HS 96* v Middx (Lord's) 1983. BB 4-20 v Sussex (Hove) 1983. **BHC:** HS 57* v Kent (Taunton) 1981. BB 4-16 v Comb Us (Taunton) 1978. **JPL:** HS 106 v Hants (Taunton) 1981. BB 4-10 v Yorks (Scarborough) 1979.

COOMBS, Robert Vincent Jerome (King's C, Taunton; St. Luke's C, Exeter), b Barnet, Herts 20 July 1959. 6'4". RHB, SLA. Debut 1985. Dorset 1979-85. HS 1. BB 5-58 v Middx (Weston) 1985 – on debut. Took 16 wickets in first 4 innings.

DAVIS, Mark Richard (West Somerset S; Bridgwater C), b Kilve, Somerset 26 Feb 1962. 6'1". LHB, LFM. Debut 1982. HS 60* v Glam (Taunton) 1984. BB 7-55 v Northants (Northampton) 1984. Awards: BHC 1. **NWT:** HS 6. BB 1-31. **BHC:** HS 28 v Glam (Taunton) 1985. BB 3-21 v Minor C (Shrewsbury) 1985. **JPL:** HS 11 v Middx 1982, 11 v Glam 1985. BB 3-30 v Essex (Chelmsford) 1984.

DREDGE, Colin Herbert (Oakfield SS, Frome) b Frome 4 Aug 1954. 6'5". LHB. RMF. Debut 1976, Cap 1978. HS: 56* v Yorks (Harrogate) 1977. BB 6-37 v Glos (Bristol) 1981. Awards: NWT 1. **NWT:** HS 9. BB 4-23 v Kent (Canterbury) 1978. **BHC:** HS 17* v Warwicks (Birmingham) 1984. BB 4-10 v Hants (Bournemouth) 1980. **JPL:** HS 25* v Middx 1982, 25* v Glam 1983. BB 5-35 v Middx (Lord's) 1981.

FELTON, Nigel Alfred (Millfield S; Loughborough U). b Guildford, Surrey 24 Oct 1960. 5'8". LHB. Debut 1982. HS 173* v Kent (Taunton) 1983. **NWT:** HS 87 v Kent (Taunton) 1984. **JPL:** HS 84* v Glam (Cardiff) 1984.

GARD, Trevor (Huish Episcopi CS). b West Lambrook 2 Jun 1957. 5'7". RHB, WK. Debut 1976. Cap 1983. HS 51* v Indians (Taunton) 1979. Awards: NWT 1; BHC 1. **NWT:** HS 17 v Shropshire (Weston) 1983. **BHC:** HS 19 v Warwicks (Birmingham) 1984. **JPL:** HS 14* v Derbys (Heanor) 1983.

GARNER, Joel (Boys' Foundation S, Christ Church). b Christ Church, Barbados 16 Dec 1952. 6'8". RHB, RF. Barbados 1975-86. Somerset debut 1977. Cap 1979. *Wisden* 1979. S. Australia 1982-83. MBE 1985. Tests (WI): 51 (1976-77 to 1984-85); HS 60 v Aus (Brisbane) 1979-80; BB 6-56 v NZ (Auckland) 1979-80. LOI: 76. Tours (WI): Eng 1980, 1984; Aus 1979-80, 1981-82, 1984-85; NZ 1979-80; Pak 1980-81. HS 104 West Indians v Glos (Bristol) 1980. Som HS 90 v Glos (Bath) 1981. BB 8-31 v Glam (Cardiff) 1977. Awards: NWT 2; BHC 2. **NWT:** HS 38* v Glam (Cardiff) 1978. BB 6-29 v Northants (Lord's) 1979. **BHC:** HS 17 v Sussex (Hove) 1978. BB 5-14 v Surrey (Lord's) 1981. **JPL:** HS 59* v Surrey (Bath) 1982. BB 5-27 v Yorks (Bath) 1985.

HARDEN, Richard John (King's C, Taunton). b Bridgwater 16 Aug 1965. 5'11". RHB, LM. Debut 1985. HS 107 v CU (Taunton) 1985. BB 1-4. **BHC:** HS 13 v Hants (Southampton) 1985. **JPL:** HS 20 v Kent (Canterbury) 1985.

HARDY, Jonathan James Ean (Canford S). b Nakaru, Kenya 2 Oct 1960. 6'3½". LHB. Hampshire 1984-85. Joins Somerset 1986. HS 107* Hants v Essex (Southampton) 1985. **NWT:** HS 1*. **BHC:** HS 4. **JPL:** HS 58 Hants v Northants (Southampton) 1984.

JONES, Andrew Paul (Toynbee SS; and Barton Peveril C, Eastleigh). b Southampton 22 Sep 1964. 6'2". RHB, RMF. Debut 1985. HS 1*. BB 1-9.

MARKS, Victor James (Blundell's S; St. John's C, Oxford). b Middle Chinnock 25 Jun 1955. 5'9". RHB, OB. Oxford U and Somerset debuts 1975. Blue 1975-76-77-78; captain 1976-77. Cap 1979. Tests: 6 (1982 to 1983-84); HS 83 v Pak (Faisalabad) 1983-84; BB 3-78 v NZ (Oval) 1983. LOI: 33. Tours: Aus 1982-83; NZ 1983-84; Ind/SL 1984-85; Pak 1983-84. 1000 runs (1): 1262 (1984). HS 134 v Worcs (Weston) 1984. BB 8-17 v Lancs (Bath) 1985. Awards: NWT 2; BHC 3. **NWT:** HS 55 v Warwicks (Taunton) 1982. BB 3-15 v Herts (St. Albans) 1984. **BHC:** HS 81* v Hants (Bournemouth) 1980. BB 3-25 v Sussex (Taunton) 1982. **JPL:** HS 72 v Worcs (Taunton) 1982. BB 4-11 v Surrey (Weston) 1984.

PALMER, Gary Vincent (Queen's C). b Taunton 1 Nov 1965. 6'1". RHB, RMF. Son of K.E. (Somerset and England 1955-69). Debut 1982. HS 78 v Glos (Bristol) 1983. BB 5-38 v Warwicks (Taunton) 1983. **NWT:** BB 1-47. **BHC:** HS 15* v Hants (Southampton) 1985. BB 2-56 v Kent (Taunton) 1985. **JPL:** HS 32* v Leics (Leicester) 1984. BB 5-34 v Kent (Canterbury) 1985.

RICHARDS, Isaac **Vivian** Alexander (Antigua GS). b St. John's, Antigua 7 Mar 1952. 5'11". RHB, OB. Leeward Islands 1971-86. Combined Islands 1971-81. Somerset debut/cap 1974. *Wisden* 1976. Queensland 1976-77. Benefit 1982 (£56,440). Tests (WI): 77 (1974-75 to 1984-85, 6 as captain); HS 291 v Eng (Oval) 1976; BB 2-20 v Pak (Lahore) 1980-81. LOI: 98. Tours (WI): Eng 1976, 1980, 1984; Aus 1975-76, 1979-80, 1981-82, 1984-85; Ind 1974-75, 1983-84; Pak 1974-75, 1980-81; SL 1974-75. 1000 runs (11+3); most – 2161 (1977). HS 322 v Warwicks (Taunton)

1985. BB 5-88 West Indians v Queensland (Brisbane) 1981-82. Som BB 4-55 v Glam (Taunton) 1981. Awards: NWT 4; BHC 6. **NWT:** HS 139* v Warwicks (Taunton) 1978. BB 3-15 v Beds (Bedford) 1982. **BHC:** HS 132* v Surrey (Lord's) 1981. BB 1-9. **JPL:** HS 126* v Glos (Bristol Imp) 1975. BB 6-24 v Lancs (Manchester) 1983.

ROEBUCK, Peter Michael (Millfield S; Emmanuel C, Cambridge), b Oxford 6 Mar 1956. 6'0". RHB, LB. Brother of P.G.P. (CU and Glos 1983-85). Debut 1974. Cambridge U 1975-77; blue 1975-76-77. Cap 1978. Captain 1986. 2nd XI debut 1969 when aged 13. 1000 runs (5); most – 1702 (1984). HS 159 v Northants (Northampton) 1984. BB 6-50 CU v Kent (Canterbury) 1977. Awards: BHC 1. **NWT:** HS 98 v Sussex (Hove) 1984. **BHC:** HS 53* v Notts (Lord's) 1982. BB 2-13 v Comb Us (Taunton) 1982. **JPL:** HS 105 v Glos (Bath) 1983. BB 2-4 v Warwicks (Birmingham) 1982.

ROSE, Brian Charles (Weston-super-Mare GS; Borough Road CE, Isleworth), b Dartford, Kent 4 Jun 1950. 6'1½". LHB. LM. Debut 1969. Cap 1975. Captain 1978-83. *Wisden* 1979. Benefit 1983. Tests: 9 (1977-78 to 1980-81); HS 70 v WI (Manchester) 1980. LOI: 2. Tours: WI 1980-81; NZ 1977-78; Pak 1977-78. 1000 runs (8); most – 1624 (1976). HS 205 v Northants (Weston) 1977. BB 3-9 v Glos (Taunton) 1975. Awards: NWT 2; BHC 2. **NWT:** HS 128 v Derbys (Ilkeston) 1977. **BHC:** HS 137* v Kent (Canterbury) 1980. **JPL:** HS 112* v Essex (Ilford) 1980. BB 3-25 v Lancs (Manchester) 1975.

TURNER, Simon Jonathan (Broadoak S), b Cuckfield, Sussex 28 Apr 1960. 6'1½". LHB, WK. Debut 1984. HS 278 v Glam (Taunton) 1984. **NWT:** HS 7. **JPL:** HS 8*.

WYATT, Julian George (Wells Cathedral S), b Paulton 19 Jun 1963. 5'10". RHB, RM. Debut 1983. HS 145 v OU (Oxford) 1985. BB 1-0. **NWT:** HS 3. **BHC:** HS 22 v Kent (Taunton) 1985. **JPL:** HS 21 v Worcs (Taunton) 1984.

VALETE

FERGUSON, Simon Alexander Ross (Framlingham C; Lancaster U), b Lagos, Nigeria 13 May 1961. 6'3". RHB, RM. Debut 1985. HS 8.

HAYWARD, Richard Edward (Latymer Upper S, Hammersmith), b Hillingdon, Middx 15 Feb 1954. 6'0". LHB, LM. Minor Counties 1979. Hampshire 1981-82. Central Districts 1982-85 (captain 1984-85). Somerset 1985. Bucks 1978-84. HS 102 Central Districts v Wellington (Palmerston North) 1983-84. Awards: BHC 1.

OLLIS, Richard Leslie (Wellsway CS, Keynsham), b Clifton, Bristol 14 Jan 1961. 6'0". LHB, RM. Debut 1981. HS 99* v Glos (Bristol) 1983.

POPPLEWELL, Nigel Francis Mark (Radley C; Selwyn C, Cambridge), b Chislehurst, Kent 8 Aug 1957. 5'10". RHB, RM. Son of O.B. (QC; Cambridge U 1949-51). Cambridge U 1977-79; blue 1977-78-79. Somerset 1979-85. Cap 1983. 1000 runs (2); most – 1116 (1984). HS 172 v Essex (Southend) 1985. BB 5-33 v Northants (Weston) 1981. Awards: NWT 1; BHC 2.

SULLY, Royston Cyril John, b Taunton 10 Apr 1951. RHB, RM. One JPL match '85.

TURNER, Murray Stewart (Richard Huish GS), b Shaftesbury 27 Jan 1964. 6'2". RHB, RFM. Somerset 1984-85. HS 24* and BB 4-74 v Warwicks (Taunton) 1985.

SOMERSET RECORDS

FIRST-CLASS CRICKET

Highest Total	For	675-9d v Hampshire; Bath	1924
	V	811 by Surrey; The Oval	1899
Lowest Total	For	25 v Glos; Bristol	1947
	V	22 by Glos; Bristol	1920
Highest Innings	For	322 I.V.A. Richards v Warwicks; Taunton	1985
	V	424 A.C. MacLaren for Lancashire; Taunton	1895

Highest Partnerships

1st	346	H.T. Hewett/L.C.H. Parlairet v Yorkshire; Taunton	1892
2nd	290	J.C.W. MacBryan/M.D. Lyon v Derbyshire; Buxton	1924
3rd	319	P.M. Roebuck/M.D. Crowe v Leics; Taunton	1984
4th	310	P.W. Denning/I.T. Botham v Glos; Taunton	1980
5th	235	J.C. White/C.C.C. Case v Glos; Taunton	1927
6th	265	W.E. Alley/K.E. Palmer v Northants; Northampton	1961
7th	240	S.M.J. Woods/V.T. Hill v Kent; Taunton	1898
8th	172	I.V.A. Richards/I.T. Botham v Leics; Leicester	1983
9th	183	C.H.M. Greetham/H.W. Stephenson v Leics; Weston-super-Mare	1963
10th	143	J.J. Bridges/A.H.D. Gibbs v Essex; Weston-super-Mare	1919

Best Bowling	For	10-49	E.J. Tyler v Surrey; Taunton	1895
(Innings)	V	10-35	A. Drake for Yorkshire; Weston-super-Mare	1914
Best Bowling	For	16-83	J.C. White v Worcs; Bath	1919
(Match)	V	17-137	W. Brearley for Lancashire; Manchester	1905

Most Runs – Season	2761	W.E. Alley	(av 58.74)	1961
Most Runs – Career	21142	H. Gimblett	(av 36.96)	1935-1954
Most 100s – Season	10	W.E. Alley		1961
Most 100s – Career	49	H. Gimblett		1935-1954
Most Wkts – Season	169	A.W. Wellard	(av 19.24)	1938
Most Wkts – Career	2166	J.C. White	(av 18.02)	1909-1937

LIMITED-OVERS CRICKET

Highest Total	NWT	330-4 v Glamorgan; Cardiff	1978
	BHC	307-6 v Glos; Taunton	1982
	JPL	286-7 v Hampshire; Taunton	1981
Lowest Total	NWT	59 v Middlesex; Lord's	1977
	BHC	98 v Middlesex; Lord's	1982
	JPL	58 v Essex; Chelmsford	1977
Highest Innings	NWT	145 P.W. Denning v Glamorgan; Cardiff	1978
	BHC	137* B.C. Rose v Kent; Canterbury	1980
	JPL	131 D.B. Close v Yorkshire; Bath	1974
Best Bowling	NWT	6-29 J. Garner v Northants; Lord's	1979
	BHC	5-14 J. Garner v Surrey; Lord's	1981
	JPL	6-24 I.V.A. Richards v Lancashire; Manchester	1983

SOMERSET 1985

RESULTS SUMMARY

	Place	Won	Lost	Drew	Abandoned
Britannic Assurance Championship	17th	1	7	16	
All First-class Matches		1	8	18	
John Player League	10th	5	6		5
NatWest Bank Trophy	Lost to Hampshire (Quarter-Final)				
Benson and Hedges Cup	Failed to qualify for Quarter-Final				

BRITANNIC ASSURANCE CHAMPIONSHIP AVERAGES

BATTING AND FIELDING

Cap		*M*	*I*	*NO*	*HS*	*Runs*	*Avge*	*100*	*50*	*Ct/St*
1976	I.T. Botham	11	17	5	152	1211	100.91	5	6	5
1974	I.V.A. Richards	19	24	0	322	1836	76.50	9	6	9
—	J.C.M. Atkinson	6	5	1	79	167	41.75	—	1	—
1978	P.M. Roebuck	19	29	3	132*	1058	40.69	1	7	9
1983	N.F.M. Popplewell	16	27	1	172	972	37.38	1	6	9
—	M.S. Turner	7	10	6	24*	134	33.50	—	—	1
—	N.A. Felton	17	25	0	112	794	31.76	1	5	3
1979	V.J. Marks	24	32	5	82	787	29.14	—	6	8
—	J.G. Wyatt	15	23	0	100	620	26.95	1	2	6
—	R.J. Harden	10	13	4	52	240	26.66	—	1	7
—	M.R. Davis	15	17	6	40*	274	24.90	—	—	4
—	G.V. Palmer	7	11	3	45*	164	20.50	—	—	2
1978	C.H. Dredge	14	12	6	31	119	19.83	—	—	6
—	R.E. Hayward	8	11	2	57*	178	19.77	—	1	3
—	P.A.C. Bail	5	9	2	78*	127	18.14	—	1	—
—	R.L. Ollis	12	16	1	55	271	18.06	—	1	4
—	S.C. Booth	8	6	2	28	69	17.25	—	—	10
1975	B.C. Rose	4	8	0	43	115	14.37	—	—	2
1979	J. Garner	15	11	3	22	92	11.50	—	—	4
1983	T. Gard	23	23	3	47	230	11.50	—	—	30/7
—	A.P. Jones	3	4	2	1*	3	1.50	—	—	1

Also batted: R.V.J. Coombs (4 matches) 0,0,1; S.A.R. Ferguson (1 match) 8; S.J. Turner (1 match) 9* (2 ct, 2 st).

BOWLING

	O	*M*	*R*	*W*	*Avge*	*Best*	*5 wI*	*10 wM*
R.V.J. Coombs	93	27	268	16	16.75	5-58	1	—
J. Garner	295.4	75	739	31	23.83	5-46	1	—
V.J. Marks	745.4	180	2208	67	32.95	8-17	4	2
C.H. Dredge	286	61	863	21	41.09	5-95	1	—
I.T. Botham	130.4	25	464	11	42.18	4-63	—	—
S.C. Booth	275.2	73	819	19	43.10	4-88	—	—
M.R. Davis	298	45	1029	19	54.15	4-83	—	—

Also bowled: J.C.M. Atkinson 65-9-250-2; P.A.C. Bail 4-2-4-0; R.J. Harden 8.3-2-29-1; A.P. Jones 37-4-142-3; G.V. Palmer 147-13-627-7; N.F.M. Popplewell 18-1-95-0; I.V.A. Richards 183-48-494-7; P.M. Roebuck 7-0-28-0; B.C. Rose 1-0-8-0; M.S. Turner 121.4-22-403-8.

The First-Class Averages (pp. 168–183) give the records of Somerset players in all first-class county matches (their other opponents being the Australians, Cambridge U. and Oxford U.), with the exception of: I.T. Botham 13-19-5-152-1280-91.42-5-7-9 ct. 154.4-31-521-13-40.07-4/63-0-0.

SURREY

Formation of Present Club: 22 August 1845
Colours: Chocolate
Badge: Prince of Wales's Feathers
Championships (since 1890): (15) 1890, 1891, 1892, 1894, 1895, 1899, 1914, 1952, 1953, 1954, 1955, 1956, 1957, 1958, 1971. **Joint:** (1) 1950
NatWest Trophy/Gillette Cup Winners: (1) 1982
Benson and Hedges Cup Winners: (1) 1974
John Player League Champions: (0) Fifth 1969, 1980
Match Awards: GC 18; NWT 6; BHC 35

Secretary: I.F.B. Scott-Browne, Kennington Oval, London SE11 5SS
Captain: P.I. Pocock
Scorer: T. Billson
Scores/Prospects: ☎ London (01) 735 4911

BULLEN, Christopher Keith (Rutlish S, Merton) b Clapham 5 Nov 1962. 6'4½". RHB, OB. Debut 1982. No appearances 1983-84. HS 19 v Glos (Oval) 1985. BB 2-36 v CU (Cambridge) 1985. **JPL:** HS 10 v Kent (Oval) 1985.

BUTCHER, Alan Raymond (Heath Clark GS), b Croydon 7 Jan 1954. 5'8½". LHB, SLA/LM. Brother of I.P. (Leics 1980-) and M.S. (Surrey 1982). Debut 1972. Cap 1975. Benefit 1985. Tests: 1 (1979); HS 20 v India (Oval). LOI: 1. Tours: WI 1983-84 (Int XI); Ind 1980-81 (Overseas XI). 1000 runs (7); most – 1713 (1980). HS 216* v CU (Cambridge) 1980. BB 6-48 v Hants (Guildford) 1972. Awards: BHC 5. **NWT:** HS 86* v Warwicks (Lord's) 1982. BB 1-43. **BHC:** HS 80 v Sussex (Oval) 1982. BB 4-36 v Middx (Lord's) 1985. **JPL:** HS 113* v Warwicks (Birmingham) 1978. BB 5-19 v Glos (Bristol) 1975.

CLARKE, Sylvester Theophilus (St. Bartholomew's BS), b Christ Church, Barbados 11 Dec 1954. 6'1". RHB, RF. Barbados 1977-1982. Surrey debut 1979. Cap 1980 Transvaal 1983-86. Tests (WI): 11 (1977-78 to 1981-82); HS 35* v Pak (Faisalabad) 1980-81; BB 5-126 v Ind (Bangalore) 1978-79. LOI: 10. Tours (WI): Aus 1981-82; SA (WI XI) 1982-83, 1983-84; Ind/SL 1978-79; Pak 1980-81. HS 100* v Glam (Swansea) 1981. BB 7-34 WI XI v SA XI (Johannesburg) 1982-83. Surrey BB 7-53 v Warwicks (Oval) 1983. Awards: NWT 1; BHC 2. Missed 1985 season (spine injury). **NWT:** HS 45* v Leics (Oval) 1981. BB 4-38 v Yorks (Oval) 1980. **BHC:** HS 39 v Hants (Southampton) 1982. BB 5-23 v Kent (Oval) 1980. **JPL:** HS 34* v Hants (Oval) 1980. BB 3-18 v Somerset (Weston) 1984.

CLINTON, Grahame Selvey (Chislehurst and Sidcup GS), b Sidcup 5 May 1953. 5'10". LHB, RM. Kent 1974-78. Surrey debut 1979. Cap 1980. Rhodesia 1979-80. 1000 runs (4); most – 1240 (1980). HS 192 v Yorks (Oval) 1984. BB 2-8 Kent v Pak (Canterbury) 1978. Awards: BHC 3. **NWT:** HS 146 v Kent (Canterbury) 1985. **BHC:** HS 106 v Middx (Lord's) 1985. **JPL:** HS 105* v Yorks (Scarborough) 1981.

DAVIES, Alec George (Monmouth S; Bulmershe C, Reading), b Rawalpindi, Pakistan 14 Aug 1962. 6'1". RHB, WK. Debut 1985. HS 26* v Zimbabweans (Oval).

DOUGHTY, Richard James (Scarborough C), b Bridlington, Yorks 17 Nov 1960. 6'0". RHB, RFM. Gloucestershire 1981-84. Surrey debut 1985. HS 65 v Derbys (Derby) 1985. BB 6-33 v Warwicks (Oval) 1985. **NWT:** HS 5*. BB 1-28. **BHC:** HS 31 and 2-32 Glos v Essex (Chelmsford) 1984. **JPL:** HS 50* Glos v Kent (Bristol) 1983. BB 3-34 Glos v Som (Bristol) 1982.

FALKNER, Nicholas James (Reigate GS). b Redhill 30 Sep 1962. 5'10". RHB. RM. Debut 1984 scoring 101* (HS) v CU (Banstead) – his only first-class innings to date. **BHC:** HS 2. **JPL:** HS 44 v Glos (Oval) 1985.

FELTHAM, Mark Andrew (Tiffin S). b St. John's Wood, London 26 Jun 1963. 6'2½". RHB. RM. Debut 1983. HS 44 v Derbys (Oval) 1984. BB 5-62 v Warwicks (Birmingham) 1984. **NWT:** HS 4. BB 1-5. **BHC:** HS 22* v Hants (Oval) 1984. BB 3-25 v Glos (Oval) 1984. **JPL:** HS 31 v Northants (Guildford) 1985. BB 3-41 v Warwicks (Birmingham) 1984.

GRAY, Anthony Hollis (Malick SS). b Port-of-Spain, Trinidad 23 May 1963. 6'7". RHB. RF. Debut (N/E Trinidad in Beaumont Cup) 1983-84. Trinidad 1984-86 Surrey debut/cap 1985. HS 41* Trinidad v Australians (Pointe-à-Pierre) 1983-84. Surrey HS 20 v Yorks (Oval) 1985. BB 8-40 v Yorks (Sheffield) 1985. **NWT:** BB 2-62 v Kent (Canterbury) 1985. **JPL:** HS 2* BB 3-22 v Middx (Lord's) 1985.

JESTY, Trevor Edward (Privet County SS, Gosport). b Gosport 2 Jun 1948. 5'8½". RHB. RM. Hampshire 1966-84 (Cap 1971; benefit 1982). Border 1973-74. Griqualand West 1974-76, 1980-81. Canterbury 1979-80. *Wisden* 1982. Surrey debut/cap 1985. Captain 1985. Tours: WI 1982-83 (Int XI); Aus/NZ 1982-83 (no f-c matches). LOI: 10. 1000 runs (8); most – 1645 (1982). HS 248 Hants v CU (Cambridge) 1984. Surrey HS 141* v Yorks (Oval) 1985. BB 7-75 Hants v Worcs (Southampton) 1976. Surrey BB 2-32 v Kent (Canterbury) 1985. Awards: NWT 5; BHC 8. **NWT:** HS 118 Hants v Derbys (Derby) 1980. BB 6-46 Hants v Glos (Bristol) 1979. **BHC:** HS 105 Hants v Glam (Swansea) 1977. BB 4-22 Hants v Minor C (Southampton) 1981. **JPL:** HS 166* Hants v Surrey (Portsmouth) 1983. BB 6-20 Hants v Glam (Cardiff) 1976.

LYNCH, Monte Alan (Ryden's S, Walton-on-Thames). b Georgetown, British Guiana 21 May 1958. 5'8". RHB, RM/OB. Debut 1977. Cap 1982. Guyana 1982-83. Tours: SA 1983-84 (WI XI); Pak 1981-82 (Int XI). 1000 runs (4); most – 1714 (1985). HS 145 v Warwicks (Oval) 1985. BB 3-6 v Glam (Swansea) 1981. Awards: NWT 1; BHC 1. **NWT:** HS 129 v Durham (Oval) 1982. BB 1-25. **BHC:** HS 85 v Comb Us (Oxford) 1984. **JPL:** HS 136 v Yorks (Bradford) 1985.

MEDLYCOTT, Keith Thomas (Parmiters GS, Wandsworth). b Whitechapel, London 12 May 1965. 5'11". RHB, SLA. Debut 1984 scoring 117* v CU (Banstead). BB 2-15 v Kent (Canterbury) 1984.

MONKHOUSE, Graham (Penrith Queen Elizabeth GS; Notts C of Agriculture). b Langwathby, Cumberland 26 Apr 1955. 6'1". RHB, RMF. Debut 1981. Cap 1984. Cumberland 1973-79. Tour: Zim 1984-85 (Eng Co). HS 100* v Kent (Oval) 1984. BB 7-51 v Notts (Oval) 1983. Soccer: Carlisle United and Workington Town. **NWT:** HS 8. BB 3-26 v Lincs (Sleaford) 1983. **BHC:** HS 24* v Sussex (Hove) 1985. BB 3-43 v Comb Us (Oxford) 1984. **JPL:** HS 27 v Sussex (Hove) 1983. BB 3-22 v Hants (Oval) 1982.

NEEDHAM, Andrew (Ecclesbourne GS; Paisley GS; Watford GS). b Calow, Derbyshire 23 Mar 1957. 5'9". RHB, OB. Debut 1977. Cap 1985. 1000 runs (1): 1223 (1985). HS 138 v Warwicks (Oval) 1985. BB 6-30 v OU (Oval) 1983. **NWT:** HS 26 and BB 2-55 v Kent (Canterbury) 1985. **BHC:** HS 30 v Glos (Oval) 1984. **JPL:** HS 55 v Essex (Southend) 1982. BB 3-41 v Lancs (Manchester) 1982.

PAULINE, Duncan Brian (Bishop Fox S, East Molesey). b Aberdeen 15 Dec 1960. 5'10". RHB, RM. Debut 1979. HS 115 v Sussex (Oval) 1983. BB 5-52 v Derbys (Derby) 1985. **NWT:** HS 5. **BHC:** HS 69* and BB 2-28 v Comb Us (Oval) 1985. **JPL:** HS 92 v Worcs (Oval) 1981. BB 3-34 v Lancs (Oval) 1985.

POCOCK, Patrick Ian ('Percy') (Merton SS; Wimbledon TC), b Bangor, Caernarvonshire 24 Sep 1946. 6'1". RHB, OB. Debut 1964. Cap 1967. Benefit 1977 (£18,500). Testimonial 1986. Captain 1986. Northern Transvaal 1971-72. Tests: 25 (1967-68 to 1984-85); HS 33 v Pak (Hyderabad) 1972-73; BB 6-79 v Aus (Manchester) 1968. LOI: 1. Tours: WI 1967-68, 1973-74; Ind 1972-73, 1984-85; Pak 1966-67 (MCC U-25), 1968-69, 1970-71 (RW), 1972-73; SL 1968-69, 1969-70, 1972-73, 1984-85. 100 wickets (1): 112 (1967). Set world records v Sussex (Eastbourne) 1972 by taking 6 wickets in 9 balls and 7 in 11 (including 4 in 4 and 5 in 6). HS 75* v Notts (Oval) 1968. BB 9-57 v Glam (Cardiff) 1979. Awards: BHC 2. **NWT:** HS 14 v Essex (Colchester) 1978. BB 3-34 v Somerset (Oval) 1975. **BHC:** HS 19 v Middx (Oval) 1972. BB 4-11 v Yorks (Barnsley) 1978. **JPL:** HS 22 v Notts (Nottingham) 1971. BB 4-27 v Essex (Chelmsford) 1974.

RICHARDS, Clifton James (**'Jack'**) (Humphrey Davy GS, Penzance) b Penzance 10 Aug 1958. 5'11". RHB, WK, OB. Debut 1976. Cap 1978. Orange Free State 1983-84. LOI: 3. Tours: WI 1982-83 (Int XI); NZ 1979-80 (DHR); Ind/SL 1981-82. HS 117* v Notts (Oval) 1982. BB 2-42 v Somerset (Oval) 1985. Awards: NWT 1. **NWT:** HS 105* v Lincs (Sleaford) 1983. **BHC:** HS 32 v Leics (Oval) 1981. **JPL:** HS 52 v Lancs (Manchester) 1982.

STEWART, Alec James (Tiffin S) b Merton 8 Apr 1963. 5'11". RHB, WK. Son of M.J. (Surrey and England 1954-72). Debut 1981. Cap 1985. 1000 runs (1): 1009 (1985). HS 158 v Kent (Canterbury) 1985. **NWT:** HS 37 v Kent (Canterbury) 1985. **BHC:** HS 16 v Essex (Oval) 1985. **JPL:** HS 86 v Warwicks (Oval) 1985.

THOMAS, David James (Licensed Victuallers' S, Slough), b Solihull 30 Jun 1959. 6'0". LHB, LFM. Debut 1977. Cap 1982. N. Transvaal 1980-81. Natal 1983-84. HS 119 v Notts (Oval) 1983. BB 6-36 v Somerset (Oval) 1984. Awards: NWT 1. **NWT:** HS 53 v Warwicks (Birmingham) 1984. BB 3-16 v Durham (Oval) 1982. **BHC:** HS 19 v Notts (Nottingham) 1984. BB 3-30 v Leics (Oval) 1981. **JPL:** HS 72 v Glam (Swansea) 1983. BB 4-13 v Sussex (Oval) 1978.

WARD, David Mark (Haling Manor HS), b Croydon 10 Feb 1961. 6'1". RHB, OB. Debut 1985. Limited-overs appearances 1984. HS 143 v Derbys (Derby) 1985. **JPL:** HS 59* v Worcs (Oval) 1984.

VALETE

HOWARTH, Geoffrey Philip (Auckland GS), b Auckland 29 Mar 1951. 5'11". RHB, OB. Brother of H.J. (Auckland and New Zealand 1972-79). Debut (NZ U-23) 1968-69. Auckland 1972-74. Northern Districts 1974-86. Surrey 1971-85 (Cap 1974; benefit 1983; Captain 1984). MBE 1981. OBE 1984. Tests (NZ): 47 (1974-75 to 1984-85, 30 as captain); HS 147 v WI (Christchurch) 1979-80; BB 1-13. LOI: 69. Tours (C = captain): Eng 1978, 1983C; Aus 1980-81C, 1982-83C; WI 1984-85C; SA 1975-76 (DHR); Ind/Pak 1976-77; SL 1977-78 (DHR), 1983-84C. 1000 runs: (4); most – 1554 (1976). HS 183 v Hants (Oval) 1979. BB 5-32 Auckland v Central Districts (Auckland) 1973-74. Surrey BB 3-20 v Northants (Northampton) 1976. Awards: BHC 1.

TAYLOR, Nicholas Simon (Gresham's S, Holt), b Holmfirth, Yorks 2 Jun 1963. 6'3". RHB, RFM. Son of K. (Yorkshire and England). Yorkshire 1982-83. Surrey 1984-85. HS 21* v Kent (Canterbury) 1985. BB 7-44 v CU (Cambridge) 1985.

WATERMAN, Peter Andrew (Rooks Heath HS; Pinner SFC), b Hendon, Middx 26 Mar 1961. 6'1½". RHB, RFM. Surrey 1983-85. HS 7. BB 3-22 v CU (Cambridge) 1985.

SURREY RECORDS

FIRST-CLASS CRICKET

Highest Total	For	811 v Somerset; The Oval	1899
	V	705-8d by Sussex; Hastings	1902
Lowest Total	For	14 v Essex; Chelmsford	1983
	V	16 by MCC; Lord's	1872
Highest Innings	For	357* R. Abel v Somerset; The Oval	1899
	V	300* F. Watson for Lancashire; Manchester	1928
		300 R. Subba Row for Northants; The Oval	1958

Highest Partnerships

1st	428	J.B. Hobbs/A. Sandham v Oxford U; The Oval	1926
2nd	371	J.B. Hobbs/E.G. Hayes v Hampshire; The Oval	1909
3rd	353	A. Ducat/E.G. Hayes v Hampshire; Southampton	1919
4th	448	R. Abel/T.W. Hayward v Yorkshire; The Oval	1899
5th	308	J.N. Crawford/F.C. Holland v Somerset; The Oval	1908
6th	298	A. Sandham/H.S. Harrison v Sussex; The Oval	1913
7th	200	T.F. Shepherd/J.W. Hitch v Kent; Blackheath	1921
8th	204	T.W. Hayward/L.C. Braund v Lancashire; The Oval	1898
9th	168	E.R.T. Holmes/E.W.J. Brooks v Hampshire; The Oval	1936
10th	173	A. Ducat/A. Sandham v Essex; Leyton	1921

Best Bowling	For	10-43 T. Rushby v Somerset; Taunton	1921
(Innings)	V	10-28 W.P. Howell for Australians; The Oval	1899
Best Bowling	For	16-83 G.A.R. Lock v Kent; Blackheath	1956
(Match)	V	15-57 W.P. Howell for Australians; The Oval	1899

Most Runs – Season	3246	T.W. Hayward	(av 72.13)	1906
Most Runs – Career	43554	J.B. Hobbs	(av 49.72)	1905-1934
Most 100s – Season	13	T.W. Hayward and J.B. Hobbs		1906 and 1925
Most 100s – Career	144	J.B. Hobbs		1905-1934
Most Wkts – Season	252	T. Richardson	(av 17.87)	1895
Most Wkts – Career	1775	T. Richardson	(av 17.88)	1892-1904

LIMITED-OVERS CRICKET

Highest Total	NWT	297-6 v Lincs; Sleaford	1983
	BHC	276-6 v Essex; The Oval	1982
	JPL	304-6 v Warwicks: The Oval	1985
Lowest Total	NWT	74 v Kent; The Oval	1967
	BHC	89 v Notts; Nottingham	1984
	JPL	64 v Worcs; Worcester	1978
Highest Innings	NWT	146 G.S. Clinton v Kent; Canterbury	1985
	BHC	115 G.R.J. Roope v Essex; Chelmsford	1973
	JPL	136 M.A. Lynch v Yorkshire; Bradford	1985
Best Bowling	NWT	7-33 R.D. Jackman v Yorkshire; Harrogate	1970
	BHC	5-21 P.H.L. Wilson v Comb Univs; The Oval	1979
	JPL	6-25 Intikhab Alam v Derbys; The Oval	1974

SURREY 1985

RESULTS SUMMARY

	Place	Won	Lost	Drew	Abandoned
Britannic Assurance Championship	6th	5	5	14	
All First-class Matches		5	5	16	
John Player League	17th	4	9		3
NatWest Bank Trophy	Lost to Kent (1st Round)				
Benson and Hedges Cup	Failed to qualify for Quarter-Final				

BRITANNIC ASSURANCE CHAMPIONSHIP AVERAGES

BATTING AND FIELDING

Cap		*M*	*I*	*NO*	*HS*	*Runs*	*Avge*	*100*	*50*	*Ct/St*
1982	M.A. Lynch	24	37	7	145	1672	55.73	7	6	36
—	D.M. Ward	5	8	3	143	256	51.20	1	—	2
1980	G.S. Clinton	18	32	6	123	1225	47.11	3	7	13
1978	C.J. Richards	22	27	12	75*	665	44.33	—	3	41/7
1985	T.E. Jesty	23	34	7	141*	1062	39.33	3	4	19
1985	A. Needham	23	33	4	138	1032	35.58	2	5	10
1975	A.R. Butcher	24	42	3	126	1335	34.23	2	5	10
1984	G. Monkhouse	15	14	8	47	203	33.83	—	—	8
1985	A.J. Stewart	21	32	3	158	886	30.55	1	4	27/1
—	D.B. Pauline	12	16	2	77	374	26.71	—	3	4
—	R.J. Doughty	10	12	2	65	239	23.90	—	2	8
1967	P.I. Pocock	23	18	6	41	183	15.25	—	—	2
—	C.K. Bullen	2	4	0	19	53	13.25	—	—	2
1982	D.J. Thomas	11	12	3	25*	116	12.88	—	—	2
—	N.S. Taylor	6	7	3	21*	51	12.75	—	—	—
1985	A.H. Gray	19	10	1	20	48	5.33	—	—	3

Also batted: M.A. Feltham (1 match) 8,27; K.T. Medlycott (1 match) 5; P.A. Waterman (4 matches) 0,1* (2 ct).

BOWLING

	O	*M*	*R*	*W*	*Avge*	*Best*	*5 wI*	*10 wM*
A.H. Gray	524	99	1816	79	22.98	8-40	6	1
R.J. Doughty	207.5	35	806	31	26.00	6-33	1	—
G. Monkhouse	370.5	76	1020	37	27.56	5-61	1	—
D.J. Thomas	328.2	54	1055	32	32.96	5-51	1	—
P.I. Pocock	564.2	127	1608	47	34.21	7-42	1	—
T.E. Jesty	144.2	28	517	14	36.92	2-32	—	—
D.B. Pauline	158.4	31	560	15	37.33	5-52	1	—
A.R. Butcher	150	32	439	10	43.90	3-43	—	—
A. Needham	326.4	67	978	22	44.45	5-42	1	—

Also bowled: C.K. Bullen 7-1-39-0; G.S. Clinton 6-0-46-0; M.A. Feltham 11-1-74-0; M.A. Lynch 6-1-46-0; C.J. Richards 27-2-120-4; A.J. Stewart 6-0-43-0; N.S. Taylor 120.2-16-516-9; P.A. Waterman 69-11-284-5.

The First-Class Averages (pp. 168–183) give the records of Surrey players in all first-class county matches (their other opponents being the Zimbabweans and Cambridge U.), with the exception of D.J. Thomas, whose full county figures are as above, and: T.D. Topley (1 match) 6* (1 ct). 27-6-64-2-32.00-2/42.

SUSSEX

Formation of Present Club: 1 March 1839
Substantial Reorganisation: August 1857
Colours: Dark Blue, Light Blue and Gold
Badge: County Arms of Six Martlets
Championships: (0) Runners up 1902, 1903, 1932, 1933, 1934, 1953, 1981
NatWest Trophy/Gillette Cup Winners: (3) 1963, 1964, 1978
Benson and Hedges Cup Winners: (0) Semi-Finalists 1982
John Player League Champions: (1) 1982
Match Awards: GC 30; NWT 4; BHC 34

Secretary: R.H. Renold, County Ground, Eaton Road, Hove BN3 3AN
Captain: J.R.T. Barclay
Scorer: L.V. Chandler
Scores/Prospects: ☎ Brighton (0273) 772766

BARCLAY, John Robert Troutbeck (Eton C), b Bonn, West Germany 22 Jan 1954. 5'11". RHB, OB. Debut 1970 aged 16 years 205 days. Cap 1976. Captain 1981-. Orange Free State 1978-79. 1000 runs (4); most – 1093 (1979). HS 119 v Leics (Hove) 1980. BB 6-61 v Sri Lankans (Hove) 1979. Awards: NWT 1; BHC 3. **NWT:** HS 48 v Ireland (Dublin) 1983. BB 5-53 v Devon (Hove) 1984. **BHC:** HS 93* v Surrey (Oval) 1976. BB 5-43 v Comb Us (Oxford) 1979. **JPL:** HS 48 v Derbys (Derby) 1974. BB 3-11 v Worcs (Eastbourne) 1978.

GOULD, Ian James (Westgate SS, Cippenham), b Slough, Bucks 19 Aug 1957. 5'8". LHB, WK. Middlesex 1975-80 (Cap 1977). Auckland 1979-80. Sussex debut/cap 1981. LOI: 18. Tours: Aus 1982-83; Pak 1980-81 (Int XI); Zim 1980-81 (Middx). HS 128 Middx v Worcs (Worcester) 1978. Sussex HS 101 v Leics (Hove) 1985. Awards: BHC 1. **NWT:** HS 58 Middx v Derbys (Derby) 1978. **BHC:** HS 72 v Kent (Hove) 1982. **JPL:** HS 69* v Hants (Basingstoke) 1981.

GREEN, Allan Michael (Knoll S, Hove; Brighton SFC), b Pulborough 28 May 1960. 5'11". RHB, RM. Debut 1980. Cap 1985. Orange Free State 1984-86. 1000 runs (1): 1646 (1985). HS 133 v Surrey (Oval) 1985. BB 2-20 v Glam (Hove) 1985. Awards: NWT 1. **NWT:** HS 74 v Devon (Hove) 1984. **BHC:** HS 38 v Essex (Chelmsford) 1985. BB 1-4. **JPL:** HS 83 v Derbys (Heanor) 1984.

IMRAN KHAN NIAZI (Aitchison C, and Cathedral S, Lahore; Worcester RGS; Keble C, Oxford), b Lahore, Pakistan 25 Nov 1952. 6'0". RHB, RF. Lahore, Dawood Industries, and PIA since 1969-70. Worcestershire 1971-76 (Cap 1976). Oxford U 1973-75 (blue 1973-74-75; captain 1974). Sussex debut 1977. Cap 1978. *Wisden* 1982. Tests (Pak): 51 (1971 to 1983-84, 14 as captain); HS 123 v WI (Lahore) 1980-81; BB 8-58 (14-116 match) v SL (Faisalabad) 1981-82. LOI: 48. Tours (C = captain): Eng 1971, 1974, 1982C; Aus 1976-77, 1978-79, 1981-82, 1983-84C; WI 1976-77; NZ 1978-79; Ind 1979-80; SL 1975-76; 1985-86C. 1000 runs (3); most – 1339 (1978). HS 170 OU v Northants (Oxford) 1974. Sussex HS 167 v Glos (Hove) 1978. BB 8-58 (*Tests*). Sussex BB 7-52 v Glos (Bristol) 1978. Awards: NWT 5; BHC 7. **NWT:** HS 114* v Notts (Hove) 1983. BB 4-27 v Staffs (Stone) 1978. **BHC:** HS 82* v Comb Us (Oxford) 1985. BB 5-8 v Northants (Northampton) 1978. **JPL:** HS 104* v Hants (Hove) 1985. BB 5-29 Worcs v Leics (Leicester) 1973.

JONES, Adrian Nicholas (Seaford C). b Woking, Surrey 22 Jul 1961. 6'2". LHB, RFM. Border 1981-82. HS 35 v Middx (Hove) 1984. BB 5-29 v Glos (Hove) 1984. **NWT:** HS 3*. BB 1-49. **BHC:** HS 4. **JPL:** HS 1*. BB 5-28 v Essex (Eastbourne) 1984.

LENHAM, Neil John (Brighton C). b Worthing 17 Dec 1965. 5'11". RHB, RMF. Son of L.J. (Sussex 1956-70). Debut 1984. HS 89 v Kent (Canterbury) 1985. **JPL:** HS 1*.

LE ROUX, Garth Stirling (Wynberg BHS; Stellenbosch U). b Kenilworth, Cape Town 4 Sep 1955. 6'3". RHB, RFM. W. Province 1975-86. Sussex debut 1978. Cap 1981. HS 83 v Surrey (Hove) 1982. BB 8-107 v Somerset (Taunton) 1981. Awards: BHC 1. **NWT:** HS 22 v Ire 1983, 22 v Devon 1984. BB 5-7 v Ireland (Hove) 1985. **BHC:** HS 50 v Yorks (Hove) 1984. BB 4-22 v Hants (Hove) 1983. **JPL:** HS 88 v Glam (Hastings) 1982. BB 4-18 v Notts (Hove) 1982.

MOORES, Peter (King Edward VI S, Macclesfield). b Macclesfield, Cheshire 18 Dec 1962. 6'0". RHB, WK. Worcestershire 1983-84. Sussex debut 1985. HS 45 Worcs v Somerset (Weston) 1984. **JPL:** HS 14* Worcs v Northants (Wellingborough) 1984.

PARKER, Paul William Giles (Collyer's GS; St. Catharine's C, Cambridge). b Bulawayo, Rhodesia 15 Jan 1956. 5'10". RHB, RM. CU and Sussex debuts 1976. Blue 1976-77-78. Cap 1979. YC 1979. Tests: 1 (1981); HS 13 v Aus (Oval). 1000 runs (6); most – 1692 (1984). BB 2-21 v Surrey (Guildford) 1984. Awards: NWT 3; BHC 3. **NWT:** HS 109 v Ire (Hove) 1985. BB 1-10. **BHC:** HS 77 v Hants (Bournemouth) 1982. **JPL:** HS 121* v Northants (Hastings) 1983. BB 1-2.

PHILLIPSON, Christopher **Paul** (Ardingly C; Loughborough C). b Brindaban, India 10 Feb 1952. 6'1". RHB, RM. Debut 1970. Cap 1980. Benefit 1985. HS 87 v Hants (Hove) 1980. BB 6-56 v Notts (Hove) 1972. Awards: BHC 2. **NWT:** HS 70* v Suffolk (Hove) 1980. BB 2-14 v Lancs (Hove) 1978. **BHC:** HS 66* v Surrey (Oval) 1982. BB 5-32 v Comb Us (Oxford) 1977. **JPL:** HS 71 v Lancs (Hastings) 1979. BB 4-25 v Middx (Eastbourne) 1972.

PIGOTT, Anthony Charles Shackleton (Harrow S). b London 4 Jun 1958. 6'1". RHB, RFM. Debut 1978. Cap 1982. Tour: NZ 1979-80 (DHR). Wellington 1982-84. Tests: 1 (1983-84); HS 8* and BB 2-75 v NZ (Christchurch). HS 63 v Hants (Eastbourne) 1983. BB 7-74 v Northants (Eastbourne) 1982. **NWT:** HS 30 v Northants (Hove) 1979. BB 3-4 v Ire (Hove) 1985. **BHC:** HS 6*. BB 3-33 v Hants (Bournemouth) 1982. **JPL:** HS 49 v Warwicks (Hove) 1979. BB 5-28 v Surrey (Guildford) 1982.

REEVE, Dermot Alexander (King George V S, Kowloon). b Kowloon, Hong Kong 2 Apr 1963. 6'0". RHB, RMF. Debut 1983. Hong Kong 1982 (ICC Trophy). HS 119 v Surrey (Guildford) 1984. BB 5-22 v CU (Cambridge) 1984. **NWT:** HS 16* and BB 3-26 v Ire (Dublin) 1983. **BHC:** HS 16 v Middx (Lord's) 1984. BB 3-34 v Glamorgan (Hove) 1984. **JPL:** HS 19 v Leics (Hove) 1985. BB 4-31 v Somerset (Hove) 1984.

STANDING, David Kevin (Tideway CS, Newhaven; Brighton and Hove GS). b Brighton 21 Oct 1963. 5'7". RHB, OB. Debut 1983. HS 60 v Worcs (Worcester) 1983.

WALLER, Christopher Edward (St. Bede's S, Send), b Guildford 3 Oct 1948. 5'11". RHB, SLA. Surrey 1967-73 (Cap 1972). Sussex debut 1974. Cap 1976. Benefit 1984. HS 51* v CU (Cambridge) 1981. BB 7-61 v Derbys (Derby) 1985. **NWT:** HS 14* v Notts (Nottingham) 1975. BB 3-28 v Warwicks (Birmingham) 1981. **BHC:** HS 11* v Essex (Chelmsford) 1975. BB 4-25 v Minor C (S) (Hove) 1975. **JPL:** HS 18* v Glamorgan (Hove) 1975. BB 4-28 v Essex (Hove) 1976.

WARING, Ian Charles (Tupton Hall S), b Chesterfield, Derbys 6 Dec 1963. 6'1". LHB, RFM. Debut 1985 (only appearance and without batting or bowling).

WELLS, Alan Peter (Tideway CS, Newhaven), b Newhaven 2 Oct 1961. 6'0". RHB, RM. Brother of C.M. Debut 1981. Border 1981-82. 1000 runs (1): 1045 (1984). HS 127 v Northants (Northampton) 1984. **NWT:** HS 24 v Somerset (Hove) 1984. **BHC:** HS 62 v Surrey (Hove) 1985. BB 1-17. **JPL:** HS 71* v Hants (Southampton) 1984.

WELLS, Colin Mark (Tideway CS, Newhaven), b Newhaven 3 Mar 1960. 5'11". RHB, RM. Brother of A.P. Debut 1979. Cap 1982. Border 1980-81. Western Province 1984-85. 1000 runs (3); most – 1389 (1984). HS 203 v Hants (Hove) 1984. BB 5-25 v Kent (Hastings) 1984. Awards: BHC 1. **NWT:** HS 76 v Ire (Hove) 1985. BB 2-20 v Suffolk (Hove) 1979. **BHC:** HS 80 v Kent (Hove) 1982. BB 4-21 v Middx (Lord's) 1980. **JPL:** HS 104* v Warwicks (Hove) 1983. BB 4-15 v Worcs (Worcester) 1983.

VALETE

GREIG, Ian Alexander (Queen's S, Queenstown; Downing C, Cambridge), b Queenstown, S. Africa 8 Dec 1955. 5'11½". RHB, RMF. Brother of A.W. (Border, Sussex, E. Province and England 1965-78). Border 1974-75, 1979-80. Griqualand West 1975-76. Cambridge U 1977-79 (blue 1977-78-79; Captain 1979). Sussex 1980-85 (Cap 1981). Tests: 2 (1982); HS 14 and BB 4-53 v Pak (Birmingham). HS 147* v OU (Oxford) 1983. BB 7-43 v CU (Cambridge) 1981. Awards: NWT 1; BHC 1.

SMITH, David James (Hove GS), b Brighton 28 Apr 1962. 5'7½". LHB, WK. Sussex 1981-84. HS 13 v Somerset (Hove) 1983.

SUSSEX RECORDS

FIRST-CLASS CRICKET

Highest Total	For	705-8d v Surrey; Hastings	1902
	V	726 by Notts; Nottingham	1895
Lowest Total	For	19 v Surrey; Godalming	1830
	For	19 v Notts; Hove	1873
	V	18 by Kent; Gravesend	1867
Highest Innings	For	333 K.S. Duleepsinhji v Northants; Hove	1930
	V	322 E. Paynter for Lancashire; Hove	1937

Highest Partnerships

1st	490	E.H. Bowley/J.G. Langridge v Middlesex; Hove	1933
2nd	385	E.H. Bowley/M.W. Tate v Northants; Hove	1921
3rd	298	K.S. Ranjitsinhji/E.H. Killick v Lancashire; Hove	1901
4th	326*	J. Langridge/G. Cox v Yorkshire; Leeds	1949
5th	297	J.H. Parks/H.W. Parks v Hampshire; Portsmouth	1937
6th	255	K.S. Duleepsinhji/M.W. Tate v Northants; Hove	1930
7th	344	K.S. Ranjitsinhji/W. Newham v Essex; Leyton	1902
8th	229*	C.L.A. Smith/G. Brann v Kent; Hove	1902
9th	178	H.W. Parks/A.F. Wensley v Derbyshire; Horsham	1930
10th	156	G.R. Cox/H.R. Butt v Cambridge U; Cambridge	1908

Best Bowling (Innings)	For	10-48	C.H.G. Bland v Kent; Tonbridge	1899
	V	9-11	A.P. Freeman for Kent; Hove	1922
Best Bowling (Match)	For	17-106	G.R. Cox v Warwicks; Horsham	1926
	V	17-67	A.P. Freeman for Kent; Hove	1922

Most Runs – Season	2850	J.G. Langridge	(av 64.77)	1949
Most Runs – Career	34152	J.G. Langridge	(av 37.69)	1928-1955
Most 100s – Season	12	J.G. Langridge		1949
Most 100s – Career	76	J.G. Langridge		1928-1955
Most Wkts – Season	198	M.W. Tate	(av 13.47)	1925
Most Wkts – Career	2223	M.W. Tate	(av 16.34)	1912-1937

LIMITED-OVERS CRICKET

Highest Total	NWT	314-7 v Kent; Tunbridge Wells	1963
	BHC	305-6 v Kent; Hove	1982
	JPL	293-4 v Worcs; Horsham	1980
Lowest Total	NWT	49 v Derbyshire; Chesterfield	1969
	BHC	61 v Middlesex; Hove	1978
	JPL	61 v Derbyshire; Derby	1978
Highest Innings	NWT	141* G.D. Mendis v Warwicks; Hove	1980
	BHC	117 R.D.V. Knight v Surrey; The Oval	1977
	JPL	129 A.W. Greig v Yorkshire; Scarborough	1976
Best Bowling	NWT	6-30 D.L. Bates v Glos; Hove	1968
	BHC	5-8 Imran Khan v Northants; Northampton	1978
	JPL	6-14 M.A. Buss v Lancashire; Hove	1973

SUSSEX 1985

RESULTS SUMMARY

	Place	Won	Lost	Drew	Abandoned
Britannic Assurance Championship	7th	6	1	16	1
All First-class Matches		7	1	17	1
John Player League	2nd	10	5		1
NatWest Bank Trophy	Lost to Glamorgan (2nd Round)				
Benson and Hedges Cup	Failed to qualify for Quarter-Final				

BRITANNIC ASSURANCE CHAMPIONSHIP AVERAGES

BATTING AND FIELDING

Cap		*M*	*I*	*NO*	*HS*	*Runs*	*Avge*	*100*	*50*	*Ct/St*
1978	Imran Khan	13	19	7	117*	846	70.50	1	6	0
1980	G.D. Mendis	23	39	5	143*	1604	47.17	6	5	8
1985	A.M. Green	23	39	4	133	1547	44.20	3	10	14
1981	I.J. Gould	22	23	8	101	614	40.93	1	4	33/4
1981	G.S. Le Roux	17	14	3	61	401	36.45	0	2	1
1979	P.W.G. Parker	14	24	4	105	680	34.00	1	4	12
—	N.J. Lenham	11	16	2	89	473	33.78	0	3	4
1982	C.M. Wells	23	33	5	100*	840	30.00	1	4	6
1981	I.A. Greig	13	14	4	43	241	24.10	0	0	11
—	A.P. Wells	21	29	6	102	532	23.13	1	1	11
—	A.N. Jones	11	9	5	26	83	20.75	0	0	1
1976	J.R.T. Barclay	20	14	4	37*	192	19.20	0	0	10
—	D.A. Reeve	16	15	5	56	170	17.00	0	1	6
1976	C.E. Waller	15	7	2	8	27	5.40	0	0	1

Also batted: A.C.S. Pigott (8 matches – cap 1982) 10*,0*,0 (6 ct); D.K. Standing (1 match) 7,3. P. Moores (1 match) (1 ct) and I.C. Waring (1 match) did not bat.

BOWLING

	O	*M*	*R*	*W*	*Avge*	*Best*	*5 wI*	*10 wM*
Imran Khan	388.5	99	952	48	19.83	5-49	2	—
G.S. Le Roux	392.2	70	1113	39	28.53	6-46	2	—
D.A. Reeve	451.1	101	1377	45	30.60	5-24	2	—
J.R.T. Barclay	252.4	39	804	24	33.50	6-78	2	—
A.C.S. Pigott	166.4	31	612	17	36.00	3-22	—	—
C.M. Wells	470.4	126	1275	34	37.50	4-76	—	—
I.A. Greig	233	44	794	20	39.70	5-80	1	—
A.N. Jones	231	33	814	20	40.70	5-39	1	—
C.E. Waller	318.5	99	755	17	44.71	7-61	1	—

Also bowled: I.J. Gould 4-0-75-0; A.M. Green 32-6-77-2; G.D. Mendis 4-0-65-1.

The First-Class Averages (pp. 168–183) give the records of Sussex players in all first-class county matches (their other opponents being the Australians and Cambridge U.), with the exception of: C.M. Wells 25-36-6-100*-923-30.76-1-4-7 ct. 520.4-142-1416-38-37.26-4/76-0-0.

WARWICKSHIRE

Formation of Present Club: March 1882
Colours: Blue, Gold and Silver
Badge: Bear and Ragged Staff
Championships: (3) 1911, 1951, 1972
NatWest Trophy/Gillette Cup Winners: (2) 1966, 1968
Benson and Hedges Cup Winners: (0) Finalists 1984
John Player League Champions: (1) 1980
Match Awards: GC 21; NWT 8; BHC 33

Secretary: A.C. Smith, County Ground, Edgbaston, Birmingham B5 7QU
Captain: N. Gifford, MBE
Scorer: S.P. Austin
Scores/Prospects: ☎ Birmingham (021) 440 3624

AMISS, Dennis Leslie (Oldknow S), b Harborne, Birmingham 7 Apr 1943. 5'11". RHB, SLA. Debut 1960. Cap 1965. *Wisden* 1974. Benefit 1975 (£34,947). Testimonial 1985. Tests: 50 (1966 to 1977); HS 262* v WI (Kingston) 1973-74. LOI: 18. Tours: Aus 1974-75, 1976-77; SA 1981-82 (SAB); WI 1973-74; NZ 1974-75; Ind/SL 1967-68 (Int XI), 1972-73, 1976-77; Pak 1966-67 (MCC U-25), 1967-68 (Int XI), 1970-71 (RW), 1972-73. 1000 runs (21+1); most – 2239 (1984). HS 262* (*Tests*). Wa HS 232* v Glos (Bristol) 1979. BB 3-21 v Middx (Lord's) 1970. Awards: NWT 4; BHC 4. **JPL:** HS 117* v Sussex (Horsham) 1981. BB 1-15. **NWT:** HS 135 v CU (Birmingham) 1982. **BHC:** HS 115 v Leics (Leicester) 1984.

ASIF DIN, Mohamed (Ladywood CS, Birmingham), b Kampala, Uganda 21 Sep 1960. 5'9½". RHB, LB. Debut 1981. HS 102 v Middx (Coventry) 1982. BB 5-100 v Glam (Birmingham) 1982. **NWT:** HS 45 v Surrey (Lord's) 1982. **BHC:** HS 61 v Notts (Nottingham) 1982. **JPL:** HS 56* v Hants (Bournemouth) 1982. BB 1-18.

DYER, Robin Ian Henry Benbow (Wellington C; Durham U), b Hertford 22 Dec 1958. 6'4". RHB, RM. Debut 1981. 1000 runs (2); most – 1242 (1985). HS 109* v Zimbabweans (Birmingham) 1985. Awards: NWT 1. **NWT:** HS 119 v Salop (Birmingham) 1984. **BHC:** HS 54 v Yorks (Leeds) 1984. **JPL:** HS 50 v Somerset (Taunton) 1985.

FERREIRA, Anthonie Michal (**'Anton'**) (Hillview HS; Pretoria U), b Pretoria, S. Africa 13 Apr 1955. 6'3". RHB, RMF. Northern Transvaal 1974-86. Warwickshire debut 1979. Cap 1983. HS 112* v Indians (Birmingham) 1982. BB 8-38 N. Transvaal v Traansvaal B (Pretoria) 1977-78. Wa BB 6-70 v Leics (Birmingham) 1984. **NWT:** HS 21 v Shropshire (Birmingham) 1984. BB 4-50 v Notts (Birmingham) 1979. **BHC:** HS 71 v Yorks (Birmingham) 1984. BB 4-42 v Scotland (Birmingham) 1982. **JPL:** HS 52 v Hants (Birmingham) 1983. BB 4-26 v Sussex (Horsham) 1981.

GIFFORD, Norman (Ulverston SS), b Ulverston, Lancs 30 Mar 1940. 5'10½". LHB, SLA. Worcestershire 1960-82 (Cap 1961; Captain 1971-80; benefit of £11,047 in 1974; testimonial 1981). *Wisden* 1974. MBE 1978. England selector 1982. Warwickshire debut/cap 1983. Captain 1985-86. Tests: 15 (1964 to 1973); HS 25* v NZ (Nottingham) 1973; BB 5-55 v Pak (Karachi) 1972-73. Tours: Aus 1971-72 (RW); Rhod/Zim 1961-62 (Int XI), 1964-65 (Worcs), 1972-73 (IW), 1985–86 (Eng B); Ind 1972-73; Pak 1961-62 (Int XI), 1970-71 (RW), 1972-73. 100 wkts (4); most – 133 (1961). HS 89 Worcs v OU (Oxford) 1963. BB 8-28 Worcs v Yorks (Sheffield) 1968. Awards: NWT 1; BHC 2. **NWT:** HS 38 Worcs v Warwicks (Lord's) 1966. BB 4-7 Worcs v Surrey (Worcester) 1972. **BHC:** HS 33 Worcs v Kent (Lord's) 1973. BB 6-8 Worcs v Minor C (S) (High Wycombe) 1979. **JPL:** HS 32* v Northants (Luton) 1983. BB 6-20 v Northants (Birmingham) 1985.

HOFFMAN, Dean Stuart (Moor End CS), b Erdington, Birmingham 13 Jun 1966. 6'2". RHB, RMF. Debut 1985. HS 13* v Worcs (Worcester) 1985. BB 4-100 v Notts (Nuneaton) 1985. **NWT:** HS 3. BB 2-56 v Notts (Nottingham) 1985. **JPL:** HS 2*. BB 2-18 v Somerset (Taunton) 1985.

HUMPAGE, Geoffrey William (Golden Hillock CS), b Sparkhill, Birmingham 24 Apr 1954. 5'9". RHB, WK, RM. Debut 1974. Cap 1976. Orange Free State 1981-82. *Wisden* 1984. LOI: 3. Tour: SA 1981-82 (SAB). 1000 runs (8); most – 1891 (1984). HS 254 v Lancs (Southport) 1982, adding 470 with A.I. Kallicharran (English 4th wicket record). BB 2-13 v Glos (Birmingham) 1980. Awards: BHC 2. **NWT:** HS 77 v Shropshire (Birmingham) 1984. **BHC:** HS 100* v Scotland (Birmingham) 1984. BB 2-43 v Worcs (Worcester) 1980. **JPL:** HS 109* v Glos (Birmingham) 1984. BB 4-53 v Glos (Moreton) 1979.

KALLICHARRAN, Alvin Isaac (Port Mourant CS), b Paidama, British Guiana 21 Mar 1949. 5'4". LHB, OB. Brother of D.I. (Trinidad). Guyana 1966-81. Warwickshire debut 1971. Cap 1972. Queensland 1977-78. Transvaal 1981-84. Orange Free State 1984-85 (captain). *Wisden* 1982. Benefit 1983. Tests (WI): 66 (1971-72 to 1980-81, 9 as captain); scored 100* and 101 in first two innings (v NZ); HS 187 v Ind (Bombay) 1979-80; BB 2-16 v NZ (Christchurch) 1979-80. LOI: 31. Tours: Eng 1973, 1976, 1980; Aus 1975-76, 1979-80; SA (WI XI) 1982-83, 1983-84; NZ 1979-80; Ind/SL 1974-75, 1978-79 (capt); Pak 1973-74 (RW), 1974-75, 1980-81. 1000 runs (11+1); most – 2301 (1984). HS 243* v Glam (Birmingham) 1983. BB 5-45 Transvaal v W. Province (Cape Town) 1982-83. Wa BB 4-48 v Derbys (Birmingham) 1978. Awards: NWT 3; BHC 3. **NWT:** HS 206 and BB 6-32 v Oxfordshire (Birmingham) 1984. **BHC:** HS 122* v Northants (Northampton) 1984. **JPL:** HS 102* v Notts (Birmingham) 1981. BB 3-32 v Lancs (Birmingham) 1985.

LLOYD, Timothy **Andrew** (Oswestry HS; Dorset CHE), b Oswestry, Shropshire 5 Nov 1956. 5'10". LHB, RM. Debut 1977. Cap 1980. Orange Free State 1978-80. Shropshire 1975. Tests: 1 (1984); HS 10* (rtd hurt) v WI (Birmingham). LOI: 3. Tour: Zim 1984-85 (Eng Co). 1000 runs (5); most – 1673 (1983). HS 208* v Glos (Birmingham) 1983. BB 3-62 v Surrey (Birmingham) 1985. Awards: NWT 2; BHC 2. **NWT:** HS 81 v Devon (Birmingham) 1980. BB 1-4. **BHC:** HS 137* v Lancs (Birmingham) 1985. **JPL:** HS 90 v Kent (Birmingham) 1980. BB 1-42.

LORD, Gordon John (Warwick S; Durham U), b Edgbaston, Birmingham 25 Apr 1961. 5'10". LHB, SLA. Debut 1983. HS 199 v Yorks (Birmingham) 1985. **JPL:** HS 103 v Derbyshire (Birmingham) 1985.

MONKHOUSE, Steven (Derby TGS; Peel C, Bury), b Bury, Lancs 24 Nov 1962. 6'3". RHB, LFM. Debut 1985. HS 5. BB 1-61.

MORTON, William (Wallace HS), b Stirling, Scot 21 Apr 1961. 6'2". LHB, SLA. Scotland 1982-83. Warwickshire debut 1984. HS 13* v Surrey (Birmingham) 1984. BB 4-40 Scotland v Ireland (Downpatrick) 1983. Wa BB 4-85 v Glam (Birmingham) 1984. **NWT:** HS 11* and BB 4-47 Scotland v Glos (Bristol) 1983. **BHC:** HS 11* and BB 3-17 Scotland v Glos (Glasgow) 1983. **JPL:** HS 10 v Kent (Birmingham) 1984.

MUNTON, Timothy Alan (Sarson HS; King Edward HS), b Melton Mowbray, Leics 30 Jul 1965. 6'5". RHB, RFM. Debut 1985 (did not bat).

OLD, Christopher Middleton (Acklam Hall GS), b Middlesbrough 22 Dec 1948. 6'3". LHB, RFM. Brother of A.G.B. (Warwickshire 1969). Yorkshire 1966-82 (Cap 1969; benefit of £32,916 in 1979; Captain 1981-82). YC 1970. *Wisden* 1978.

Warwickshire debut 1983. Cap 1984. N. Transvaal 1981-83. Tests: 46 (1972-73 to 1981); HS 65 v Pak (Oval) 1974; BB 7-50 (inc 4 wkts in 5 balls) v Pak (Birmingham) 1978. LOI: 32. Tours: Aus 1974-75, 1978-79; SA 1975-76 (IW); 1981-82 (SAB); WI 1969-70 (DN), 1973-74, 1980-81; NZ 1974-75, 1977-78; Ind 1972-73, 1976-77; Pak 1972-73, 1977-78. HS 116 Yorks v Indians (Bradford) 1974. BB 7-20 Yorks v Glos (Middlesbrough) 1969. Awards: BHC 4. **NWT:** HS 55* Yorks v Worcs (Leeds) 1982. BB 4-9 Yorks v Durham (Middlesbrough) 1978. **BHC:** HS 78* Yorks v Scot (Bradford) 1981. BB 5-19 v Scot (Birmingham) 1984. **JPL:** HS 82* v Somerset (Glastonbury) 1976. BB 5-33 Yorks v Sussex (Hove) 1971.

PARSONS, Gordon James (Woodside County SS, Slough), b Slough, Bucks 17 Oct 1959. 6'1". LHB, RMF. Leicestershire 1978-85; Cap 1984. Boland 1983-85. Griqualand West 1985-86. Joins Warwickshire 1986. Buckinghamshire 1977. Tours: NZ 1979-80 (DHR); Zim 1980-81 (Leics). HS 76 Boland v W. Province B (Cape Town) 1984-85. BB 9-72 Boland v Transvaal B (Johannesburg) 1984-85. Awards: BHC 1. **NWT:** HS 23 Leics v Northants (Northampton) 1984. BB 2-11 Leics v Wilts (Swindon) 1984. **BHC:** HS 29* Leics v Northants (Leicester) 1983. BB 4-33 Leics v Worcs (Leicester) 1981. **JPL:** HS 24* Leics v Som (Taunton) 1985. BB 4-19 Leics v Essex (Harlow) 1982.

PIERSON, Adrian Roger Kirshaw (Kent C, Canterbury; Hatfield Polytechnic), b Enfield, Middx 21 Jul 1963. 6'4". RHB, OB. Debut 1985. HS 17* v Kent (Canterbury) 1985. BB 3-92 v OU (Oxford) 1985. **NWT:** HS 1*. **JPL:** HS 4. BB 1-29.

SMALL, Gladstone Cleophas (Moseley S; Hall Green TC), b St. George, Barbados 18 Oct 1961. 5'11". RHB, RFM. Debut 1979-80 (DHR XI in NZ). Warwickshire debut 1980. Cap 1982. South Australia 1985-86. Tours: NZ 1979-80 (DHR); Pak 1981-82 (Int XI). HS 57* v OU (Oxford) 1982. BB 7-68 v Yorks (Birmingham) 1982. **NWT:** HS 33 v Surrey (Lord's) 1982. BB 3-22 v Glam (Cardiff) 1982. **BHC:** HS 19* v Yorks (Birmingham) 1981. BB 3-41 v Leics (Leicester) 1984. **JPL:** HS 40* v Essex (Ilford) 1984. BB 5-29 v Surrey (Birmingham) 1980.

SMITH, Paul Andrew (Heaton GS), b Jesmond, Newcastle upon Tyne 15 Apr 1964. 6'2". RHB, RFM. Son of K.D. sr (Leics 1950-51) and brother of K.D. jr (Warwicks 1973-85). Debut 1982. 1000 runs (1): 1040 (1984). HS 114 v OU (Birmingham) 1983. BB 4-25 v Lancs (Birmingham) 1985. **NWT:** HS 51* v Devon (Birmingham) 1985. BB 3-10 v Shropshire (Birmingham) 1984. **BHC:** HS 37 v Somerset (Birmingham) 1984. BB 2-30 v Lancs (Birmingham) 1985. **JPL:** HS 50* v Sussex (Hove) 1985. BB 4-23 v Notts (Birmingham) 1983.

TEDSTONE, Geoffrey Alan (Warwick S; St. Paul's C, Cheltenham), b Southport, Lancs 19 Jan 1961. 5'7". RHB, WK. Debut 1982. HS 67* v CU (Cambridge) 1983. **JPL:** HS 23 v Middx (Birmingham) 1982.

THORNE, David Anthony – *see OXFORD UNIVERSITY (page 165)* **NWT:** HS 8. **BHC:** HS 28* Comb Us v Glos (Bristol) 1984. **JPL:** HS 42 v Glos (Moreton) 1983. BB 3-48 v Kent (Canterbury) 1985.

WALL, Stephen (Dondales S), b Ulverston, Lancs 10 Dec 1959. 6'0". RHB, RMF. Debut 1984. Cumberland 1983. HS 28 v Lancs (Manchester) 1985, and 28 v Notts (Birmingham) 1985. BB 4-59 v Glam (Birmingham) 1985. **BHC:** HS 6. BB 1-30. **JPL:** HS 6*. BB 2-31 v Worcs (Worcester) 1985.

VALETE see p. 158.

WARWICKSHIRE RECORDS

FIRST-CLASS CRICKET

Highest Total	For	657-6d v Hampshire; Birmingham	1899
	V	887 by Yorkshire; Birmingham	1896
Lowest Total	For	16 v Kent; Tonbridge	1913
	V	15 by Hampshire; Birmingham	1922
Highest Innings	For	305* F.R. Foster v Worcs; Dudley	1914
	V	322 I.V.A. Richards for Somerset; Taunton	1985

Highest Partnerships

1st	377*	N.F. Horner/K. Ibadulla v Surrey; The Oval	1960
2nd	465*	J.A. Jameson/R.B. Kanhai v Glos; Birmingham	1974
3rd	327	S.P. Kinneir/W.G. Quaife v Lancashire; Birmingham	1901
4th	470	A.I. Kallicharran/G.W. Humpage v Lancashire; Southport	1982
5th	268	W. Quaife/W.G. Quaife v Essex; Leyton	1900
6th	220	H.E. Dollery/J. Buckingham v Derbyshire; Derby	1938
7th	250	H.E. Dollery/J.S. Ord v Kent; Maidstone	1953
8th	228	A.J.W. Croom/R.E.S. Wyatt v Worcs; Dudley	1925
9th	154	G.W. Stephens/A.J.W. Croom v Derbyshire; Birmingham	1925
10th	128	F.R. Santall/W. Sanders v Yorkshire; Birmingham	1930

Best Bowling	For	10-41 J.D. Bannister v Comb Servs; Birmingham	1959
(Innings)	V	10-36 H. Verity for Yorkshire; Leeds	1931
Best Bowling	For	15-76 S. Hargreave v Surrey; The Oval	1903
(Match)	V	17-92 A.P. Freeman for Kent; Folkestone	1932

Most Runs – Season	2417	M.J.K. Smith	(av 60.42)	1959
Most Runs – Career	33862	W.G. Quaife	(av 36.18)	1894-1928
Most 100s – Season	9	A.I. Kallicharran		1984
Most 100s – Career	72	D.L. Amiss		1960-1985
Most Wkts – Season	180	W.E. Hollies	(av 15.13)	1946
Most Wkts – Career	2201	W.E. Hollies	(av 20.45)	1932-1957

LIMITED-OVERS CRICKET

Highest Total	NWT	392-5 v Oxfordshire; Birmingham	1984
	BHC	291-5 v Lancashire; Manchester	1981
	JPL	301-6 v Essex; Colchester	1982
Lowest Total	NWT	109 v Kent; Canterbury	1971
	BHC	96 v Leics; Leicester	1972
	JPL	65 v Kent; Maidstone	1979
Highest Innings	NWT	206 A.I., Kallicharran v Oxfordshire; Birmingham	1984
	BHC	137* T.A. Lloyd v Lancashire; Birmingham	1985
	JPL	123* J.A. Jameson v Notts; Nottingham	1973
Best Bowling	NWT	6-32 K. Ibadulla v Hampshire; Birmingham	1965
		6-32 A.I. Kallicharran v Oxfordshire; Birmingham	1984
	BHC	7-32 R.G.D. Willis v Yorkshire; Birmingham	1981
	JPL	6-20 N. Gifford v Northants; Birmingham	1985

WARWICKSHIRE 1985

RESULTS SUMMARY

	Place	*Won*	*Lost*	*Drew*	*Abandoned*
Britannic Assurance Championship	15th	2	8	14	
All First-class Matches		3	8	15	
John Player League	6th	7	7		2
NatWest Bank Trophy	Lost to Nottinghamshire (2nd Round)				
Benson and Hedges Cup	Failed to qualify for Quarter-Final				

BRITANNIC ASSURANCE CHAMPIONSHIP AVERAGES

BATTING AND FIELDING

Cap		*M*	*I*	*NO*	*HS*	*Runs*	*Avge*	*100*	*50*	*Ct/St*
1965	D.L. Amiss	24	40	4	140	1326	36.83	4	6	23
1976	G.W. Humpage	23	38	5	159	1197	36.27	2	5	70/3
—	Asif Din	6	11	2	89	325	36.11	—	2	2
1980	T.A. Lloyd	16	30	2	160	989	35.32	1	6	4
1972	A.I. Kallicharran	21	35	2	152*	1052	31.87	2	6	6
—	G.J. Lord	7	10	1	199	263	29.22	1	—	—
—	R.I.H.B. Dyer	24	42	2	106	1112	27.80	1	8	17
1983	A.M. Ferreira	23	35	8	101*	693	25.66	1	1	12
—	P.A. Smith	23	35	3	93	783	24.46	—	5	9
1984	C.M. Old	7	7	2	41	122	24.40	—	—	1
1982	G.C. Small	21	27	8	31*	285	15.00	—	—	7
1978	K.D. Smith	4	7	0	42	99	14.14	—	—	1
—	S. Wall	10	15	5	28	125	12.50	—	—	4
—	A.R.K. Pierson	10	12	5	17*	85	12.14	—	—	2
1983	N. Gifford	24	25	8	26	132	7.76	—	—	9
—	D.S. Hoffman	15	15	4	13*	39	3.54	—	—	3

Also batted: C. Lethbridge (3 matches) 15,22*,47; S. Monkhouse (1 match) 2*,5; G.A. Tedstone (1 match) 22 (1 ct, 1 st); D.A. Thorne (1 match) 0,0

BOWLING

	O	*M*	*R*	*W*	*Avge*	*Best*	*5 wI*	*10 wM*
G.C. Small	592.3	114	1850	69	26.81	5-24	5	—
A.M Ferreira	624.3	118	2039	71	28.71	5-41	2	1
N. Gifford	611.5	188	1541	46	33.50	5-128	1	—
C.M. Old	153.2	38	466	13	35.84	6-68	1	—
D.S. Hoffman	287.1	41	1081	26	41.57	4-100	0	—
P.A. Smith	234.2	24	1130	26	43.46	4-25	0	—
S. Wall	243.1	36	790	18	43.88	4-59	0	—

Also bowled: Asif Din 5.2-2-7-1; A.I. Kallicharran 11.4-0-56-0; C. Lethbridge 65-7-263-5; T.A. Lloyd 31-1-127-4; S. Monkhouse 17-2-61-1; A.R K. Pierson 89-19-340-1.

The First-Class Averages (pp. 168–183) give the records of Warwickshire players in all first-class county matches (their other opponents being the Zimbabweans and Oxford U.), with the exception of D.A. Thorne whose full county figures are as above.

WORCESTERSHIRE

Formation of Present Club: 5 March 1865
Colours: Dark Green and Black
Badge: Shield Argent bearing Fess between Three Pears Sable
Championships: (3) 1964, 1965, 1974
NatWest Trophy/Gillette Cup Winners: (0) Finalists 1963, 1966
Benson and Hedges Cup Winners: (0) Finalists 1973, 1976
John Player League Champions: (1) 1971
Match Awards: GC 18; NWT 3; BHC 31

Secretary: M.D. Vockins, County Ground, New Road, Worcester WR2 4QQ
Captain: P.A. Neale
Scorer: J.W. Sewter
Scores/Prospects: ☎ Worcester (0905) 422011

BARRETT, Brian Joseph, b Auckland, New Zealand 16 Nov 1966. 6'2". RHB, RFM. Debut 1985. Did not bat. BB 1-40. **JPL:** HS 5*.

BENT, Paul (Worcester RGS), b Worcester 1 May 1965. 6'0". RHB, OB. Debut 1985. HS 14 v CU (Cambridge) 1985.

CURTIS, Timothy Stephen (Worcester RGS; Durham U; Magdalene C, Cambridge), b Chislehurst, Kent 15 Jan 1960. 5'11". RHB, LB. Debut 1979. Cambridge U 1983 (blue 1983). Cap 1984. 1000 runs (2); most – 1405 (1984). HS 129 v CU (Worcester) 1984. BB 2-58 CU v Notts (Cambridge) 1983. Awards: NWT 1. **NWT:** HS 92 v Notts (Worcester) 1985. **BHC:** HS 75 v Warwicks (Worcs) 1985. **JPL:** HS 76 v Derbys (Knypersley) 1985.

D'OLIVEIRA, Damian Basil (Blessed Edward Oldcorne SS), b Cape Town 19 Oct 1960. 5'9". RHB, OB. Son of B.L. (Worcs and England 1964-80). Debut 1982. Cap 1985. Tour: Zim 1984-85 (Eng Co). 1000 runs (1): 1244 (1985). HS 139 v Sussex (Eastbourne) 1985. BB 2-50 v Lancs (Manchester) 1984. Awards: NWT 1; BHC 1. **NWT:** HS 48 and 2-28 v Notts (Worcester) 1983. **BHC:** HS 57 v Derbys (Worcester) 1984. BB 2-13 v Scot (Aberdeen) 1983. **JPL:** HS 103 v Surrey (Worcester) 1985. BB 3-23 v Derbys (Derby) 1983.

ELLCOCK, Ricardo McDonald (Combermere S, Barbados; Malvern C), b Bridgetown, Barbados 17 Jun 1965. 5'11". RHB, RF. Debut 1982. Barbados 1983-84. HS 45* v Essex (Worcester) 1984. BB 4-34 v Glamorgan (Worcester) 1984. **NWT:** HS 6. BB 3-49 v Notts (Worcester) 1983. **BHC:** HS 12 and BB 2-45 v Notts (Nottingham) 1984. **JPL:** HS 5*. BB 4-43 v Kent (Canterbury) 1983.

HICK, Graeme Ashley (Prince Edward HS, Salisbury), b Salisbury, Rhodesia 23 May 1966. 6'3". RHB, OB. Debut (Zimbabwe) 1983-84. Worcestershire debut 1984. Tours (Zim): Eng 1985; SL 1983-84. 1000 runs (1): 1265 (1985). HS 230 Zimbabweans v OU (Oxford) 1985. Worcs HS 174* v Somerset (Worcester) 1985. BB 3-39 Zimbabweans v Sri Lanka Board President's XI (Moratuwa) 1983-84 **JPL:** HS 90 v Glos (Moreton) 1985. BB 2-36 v Warwicks (Worcester) 1985.

HUSSAIN, Mehriyar (**'Mel'**), b South Shields, Co. Durham 17 Oct 1963. 6'1". RHB, OB. Debut 1985. HS 4.

ILLINGWORTH, Richard Keith (Salts GS), b Bradford 23 Aug 1963. 5'11". RHB, SLA. Debut 1982. HS 55 v Leics (Hereford) 1983. BB 7-50 v OU (Oxford) 1985. **NWT:** HS 22 v Northants (Northampton) 1984. BB 2-14 v Notts (Worcester) 1983. **BHC:** HS 11* v Leics (Worcester) 1983. BB 4-36 v Yorks (Bradford) 1985. **JPL:** HS 21 v Middx (Worcester) 1982. BB 5-24 v Somerset (Worcester) 1983.

INCHMORE, John Darling (Ashington GS: St. Peter's CE, Birmingham), b Ashington, Northumberland 22 Feb 1949. 6'2½". RHB, RFM. Debut 1973. Cap 1976. Northumberland 1970. N. Transvaal 1976-77. Benefit 1985. HS 113 v Essex (Worcester) 1974. BB 8-58 v Yorks (Worcester) 1977. Awards: NWT 1; BHC 3. **NWT:** HS 32* v Yorks (Leeds) 1982. BB 5-25 v Glam (Swansea) 1985. **BHC:** HS 49* v Somerset (Taunton) 1976. BB 6-29 v Lancs (Manchester) 1984. **JPL:** HS 45 v Northants 1981, 45 v Derbys 1981. BB 4-9 v Northants (Dudley) 1975.

KAPIL DEV NIKHANJ (Punjab U), b Chandigarh, India 6 Jan 1959. 6'0". RHB, RFM. Debut 1975-76 (Haryana) aged 16 years 10 months, taking 6-39 v Punjab. Northamptonshire 1981-83. Worcestershire debut 1984. *Wisden* 1982. Tests (Ind): 68 (1978-79 to 1984-85, 14 as captain); HS 126* v WI (Delhi) 1978-79; BB 9-83 v WI (Ahmedabad) 1983-84. LOI: 61. Tours (Ind): Eng 1979, 1982; Aus 1980-81, 1985-86; WI 1982-83 (capt); NZ 1980-81; Pak 1978-79, 1982-83; SL 1985-86. HS 193 Haryana v Punjab (Chandigarh) 1979-80. Worcs HS 100 v Middx (Lord's) 1985. BB 9-83 (*Tests*). Worcs BB 5-30 v Somerset (Worcester) 1984. **NWT:** HS 38* and BB 5-52 v Lancs (Manchester) 1985. **BHC:** HS 49 Northants v Lancs (Manchester) 1983. BB 2-10 Northants v Worcs (Worcester) 1983. **JPL:** HS 75 Northants v Derbys (Milton Keynes) 1982. BB 3-20 v Middx (Lord's) 1984.

LAMPITT, Stuart Richard (Kingswinford S; Dudley TC), b Wolverhampton 29 Jul 1966. 5'11". RHB, RM. Debut 1985.

McEWAN, Steven Michael (Worcester RGS), b Worcester 5 May 1962. 6'1". RHB, RFM. Debut 1985. HS 13* v OU (Oxford) 1985. BB 3-47 v Leics (Leicester) 1985. **JPL:** HS 0. BB 3-36 v Leics (Leicester) 1985.

NEALE, Phillip Anthony (Frederick Gough CS; John Leggott SFC; Leeds U), b Scunthorpe, Lincolnshire 5 Jun 1954. 5'11". RHB, RM. Debut 1975. Cap 1978. Captain 1982. Lincolnshire 1972. 1000 runs (7); most – 1706 (1984). HS 163* v Notts (Worcester) 1979. BB 1-15. Awards: BHC 1. Soccer: Lincoln City. **NWT:** HS 81 v Lancs (Manchester) 1985. **BHC:** HS 128 v Lancs (Manchester) 1980. **JPL:** HS 102 v Northants (Luton) 1982. BB 2-46 v Warwicks (Worcester) 1976.

NEWPORT, Philip John (High Wycombe RGS; Portsmouth Polytechnic), b High Wycombe, Bucks 11 Oct 1962. 6'3". RHB, RFM. Debut 1982. Buckinghamshire 1981-82. HS 41* v Warwicks (Birmingham) 1983. BB 5-18 v Glos (Gloucester) 1985. **NWT:** HS 25 v Northants (Northampton) 1984. BB 1-32. **JPL:** HS 24 v Northants (Wellingborough) 1984. BB 3-20 v Somerset (Taunton) 1984.

PATEL, Dipak Narshibhai (George Salter CS, West Bromwich), b Nairobi, Kenya 25 Oct 1958. 5'11". RHB, OB. Debut 1976. Cap 1979. Tour: NZ 1979-80 (DHR). 1000 runs (5); most – 1615 (1983). HS 197 v CU (Worcester) 1984. BB 7-46 v Lancs (Worcester) 1982. Awards: BHC 2. **NWT:** HS 54 v Glam (Swansea) 1985. BB 4-22 v Suffolk (Worcester) 1984. **BHC:** HS 90* v Lancs (Manchester) 1984. BB 3-42 v Yorks (Worcester) 1980. **JPL:** HS 125 v Hants (Southampton) 1982. BB 5-27 v Northants (Worcester) 1983.

PRIDGEON, Alan Paul (Summerhill SS, Kingswinford), b Wall Heath, Staffs 22 Feb 1954. 6'3". RHB, RM. Debut 1972. Cap 1980. HS 67 v Warwicks (Worcester) 1984. BB 7-35 v OU (Oxford) 1976. **NWT:** HS 13* and BB 3-25 v Somerset (Taunton) 1980. **BHC:** HS 13* v Leics (Worcester) 1982. BB 3-57 v Warwicks (Birmingham) 1976. **JPL:** HS 17 v Kent (Worcester) 1982. BB 6-26 v Surrey (Worcester) 1978.

RADFORD Neal Victor (Athlone BHS, Johannesburg), b Luanshya, Northern Rhodesia 7 Jun 1957. 5'11". RHB, RFM. Brother of W.R. (Orange Free State). Transvaal 1978-86. Lancashire 1980-84. Worcestershire debut/cap 1985. *Wisden* 1985. 100 wickets (1); 101 (1985). HS 76* Lancs v Derbys (Blackpool) 1981. BB 6-41 Transvaal B v Griqualand West (Kimberley) 1980-81. **NWT:** HS 16 v Notts (Worcester) 1985. BB 3-20 Lancs v Middx (Manchester) 1981. **BHC:** HS 14 and BB 2-27 Lancs v Middx (Lord's) 1983. **JPL:** HS 48* Lancs v Glam (Cardiff) 1981. BB 4-24 v Warwicks (Worcester) 1985.

RHODES, Steven John (Lapage Middle S; Carlton-Bolling S, Bradford), b Bradford 17 Jun 1964. 5'7". RHB, WK. Son of W.E. (Nottinghamshire 1961-64). Yorkshire 1981-84. Worcestershire debut 1985. Tour: SL 1985-86 (Eng B). HS 58* v Yorks (Worcester) 1985. **NWT:** HS 9. **BHC:** HS 27* v Leics (Leicester) 1985. **JPL:** HS 45* v Middx (Worcester) 1985.

SCOTHERN, Mark, b Skipton 9 Mar 1961. 5'9½". RHB, RFM. Debut 1985. BB 1-42.

SMITH, David Mark (Battersea GS), b Balham, London 9 Jan 1956. 6'4". LHB, RM. Surrey 1973-83 (Cap 1980). Worcestershire debut/cap 1984. Tour: WI 1985-86. 1000 runs (3); most – 1113 (1985). HS 189* v Kent (Worcester) 1984. BB 3-40 Surrey v Sussex (Oval) 1976. Awards: NWT 1; BHC 2. **NWT:** HS 109 v Lancs (Manchester) 1985. BB 3-39 Surrey v Derbys (Ilkeston) 1976. **BHC:** HS 126 v Warwicks (Worcester) 1985. BB 4-29 Surrey v Kent (Oval) 1980. **JPL:** HS 87* Surrey v Hants (Oval) 1980. BB 2-21 Surrey v Worcs (Byfleet) 1973.

SMITH, Lawrence Kilner, b Mirfield, Yorkshire 6 Jan 1964. 5'10". RHB. Son of D.H.K. (Derbyshire 1965-70 and Orange Free State 1976-78). Debut 1985. HS 28 v CU (Cambridge) 1985. **JPL:** HS 3.

WESTON, Martin John (Samuel Southall SS), b Worcester 8 Apr 1959. 6'1". RHB, RM. Debut 1979. 1000 runs (1): 1061 (1984). HS 145* v Northants (Worcester) 1984. BB 4-44 v Northants (Wellingborough) 1984. **NWT:** HS 35 v Herts (Hitchin) 1985. BB 4-30 v Suffolk (Worcester) 1984. **BHC:** HS 56 v Scot (Aberdeen) 1983. **JPL:** HS 109 v Somerset (Taunton) 1982. BB 4-24 v Kent (Worcester) 1984.

VALETE

BANKS, David Andrew (Pensnett SS; Dudley TC), b Pensnett, Staffs 11 Jan 1961. 6'3". RHB, RM. Debut 1983 scoring 100 (HS) v OU (Oxford).

HUMPHRIES, David John (Bridgnorth SS; Wulfrun C), b Alveley, Shropshire 6 Aug 1953. 5'8". LHB, WK. Leicestershire 1974-76. Worcestershire 1977-85. Cap 1978. Shropshire 1971-73. HS 133* v Derbys (Worcester) 1984. Awards: NWT 1.

KIMBER, Simon Julian Spencer, b Ormskirk, Lancs 6 Oct 1963. 6'2". RHB, RMF. Debut 1985. HS 14* v OU (Oxford) 1985. BB 3-40 v CU (Cambridge) 1985.

PATEL, Harshad Vallabh (George Salter HS), b Nairobi, Kenya 29 Jan 1964. 5'8". RHB. Cousin of D.N. Debut 1985 (only match) scoring 39 v CU (Fenner's).

WORCESTERSHIRE RECORDS

FIRST-CLASS CRICKET

Highest Total	For	633 v Warwicks; Worcester	1906
	V	701-4d by Leics; Worcester	1906
Lowest Total	For	24 v Yorkshire; Huddersfield	1903
	V	30 by Hampshire; Worcester	1903
Highest Innings	For	311* G.M. Turner v Warwicks; Worcester	1982
	V	311* J.D. Robertson for Middlesex; Worcester	1949

Highest Partnerships

1st	309	F.L. Bowley/H.K. Foster v Derbyshire; Derby	1901
2nd	274	H.H.I. Gibbons/Pataudi, sr v Kent; Worcester	1933
	274	H.H.I. Gibbons/Pataudi, sr v Glamorgan; Worcester	1934
3rd	314	M.J. Horton/T.W. Graveney v Somerset; Worcester	1962
4th	281	J.A. Ormrod/Younis Ahmed v Notts; Nottingham	1979
5th	393	E.G. Arnold/W.B. Burns v Warwicks; Birmingham	1909
6th	227	E.J.O. Hemsley/D.N. Patel v Oxford U; Oxford	1976
7th	197	H.H.I. Gibbons/R. Howorth v Surrey; The Oval	1938
8th	145*	F. Chester/W.H. Taylor v Essex; Worcester	1914
9th	181	J.A. Cuffe/R.D. Burrows v Glos; Worcester	1907
10th	119	W.B. Burns/G.A. Wilson v Somerset; Worcester	1906

Best Bowling	For	9-23	C.F. Root v Lancashire; Worcester	1931
(Innings)	V	10-51	J. Mercer for Glamorgan; Worcester	1936
Best Bowling	For	15-87	A.J. Conway v Glos; Moreton-in-Marsh	1914
(Match)	V	17-212	J.C. Clay for Glamorgan; Swansea	1937

Most Runs – season	2654	H.H.I. Gibbons	(av 52.03)	1934
Most Runs – Career	34490	D. Kenyon	(av 34.04)	1946-1967
Most 100s – Season	10	G.M. Turner		1970
Most 100s – Career	72	G.M. Turner		1967-1982
Most Wkts – Season	207	C.F. Root	(av 17.52)	1925
Most Wkts – Career	2143	R.T.D. Perks	(av 23.73)	1930-1955

LIMITED-OVERS CRICKET

Highest Total	NWT	312-5 v Lancashire; Manchester	1985
	BHC	314-5 v Lancashire; Manchester	1980
	JPL	307-4 v Derbyshire; Worcester	1975
Lowest Total	NWT	98 v Durham; Chester-le-Street	1968
	BHC	81 v Leicestershire; Worcester	1983
	JPL	86 v Yorkshire; Leeds	1969
Highest Innings	NWT	117* G.M. Turner v Lancashire; Worcester	1971
	BHC	143* G.M. Turner v Warwicks; Birmingham	1976
	JPL	147 G.M. Turner v Sussex; Horsham	1980
Best Bowling	NWT	6-14 J.A. Flavell v Lancashire; Worcester	1963
	BHC	6-8 N. Gifford v Minor C (S); High Wycombe	1979
	JPL	6-26 A.P. Pridgeon v Surrey; Worcester	1978

WORCESTERSHIRE 1985

RESULTS SUMMARY

	Place	Won	Lost	Drew	Abandoned
Britannic Assurance Championship	5th	5	6	13	
All First-class Matches		6	6	15	
John Player League	16th	5	9		2
NatWest Bank Trophy	Lost to Nottinghamshire (Semi-Final)				
Benson and Hedges Cup	Lost to Middlesex (Quarter-Final)				

BRITANNIC ASSURANCE CHAMPIONSHIP AVERAGES

BATTING AND FIELDING

Cap		*M*	*I*	*NO*	*HS*	*Runs*	*Avge*	*100*	*50*	*Ct/St*
1984	D.M. Smith	18	27	4	112	1113	48.39	3	7	11
—	G.A. Hick	10	15	1	174*	664	47.42	2	2	5
—	Kapil Dev	12	21	2	100	816	42.94	1	5	11
1978	P.A. Neale	24	40	9	152*	1290	41.61	2	7	5
1984	T.S. Curtis	24	42	2	126*	1279	31.97	1	11	9
1985	D.B. D'Oliveira	24	41	2	139	1200	30.76	2	7	17
1979	D.N. Patel	24	39	3	88	1006	27.94	—	5	15
—	M.J. Weston	17	27	1	132	706	27.15	1	2	4
—	S.J. Rhodes	24	32	12	58*	518	25.90	—	1	53/2
—	P.J. Newport	16	23	8	36	277	18.46	—	—	2
—	D.A. Banks	4	5	1	30	70	17.50	—	—	1
1985	N.V. Radford	23	25	7	57*	306	17.00	—	1	3
1976	J.D. Inchmore	16	9	2	24	100	14.28	—	—	6
—	R.K. Illingworth	18	19	8	39*	129	11.72	—	—	6
—	S.M. McEwan	9	7	4	7*	12	4.00	—	—	1

Also batted: R.M. Ellcock (1 match) 3.

BOWLING

	O	*M*	*R*	*W*	*Avge*	*Best*	*5 wI*	*10 wM*
Kapil Dev	304.5	83	805	37	21.75	4-56	—	—
P.J. Newport	334.2	57	1089	46	23.67	5-18	3	—
N.V. Radford	764.4	130	2416	100	24.16	6-45	4	—
J.D. Inchmore	320.5	66	806	30	26.86	4-42	—	—
S.M. McEwan	169	28	611	16	38.18	3-47	—	—
D.N. Patel	381	101	1084	28	38.71	3-33	—	—
R.K. Illingworth	344.4	92	940	24	39.16	4-76	—	—
M.J. Weston	259.5	66	746	17	43.88	3-37	—	—

Also bowled: D.B. D'Oliveira 9-0-30-1; R.M. Ellcock 28-0-91-0; G.A. Hick 74-17-265-5.

The First-Class Averages (pp. 168–183) give the records of Worcestershire players in all first-class county matches (their other opponents being the Australians, Cambridge U. and Oxford U.), with the exception of: G.A. Hick 11-16-1-174*-667-44.46-2-2-6 ct. 75-18-265-5-53.00-2/34.

YORKSHIRE

Formation of Present Club: 8 January 1863
Substantial Reorganisation: 10 December 1891
Colours: Oxford Blue, Cambridge Blue and Gold
Badge: White Rose
Championships (since 1890): (29) 1893, 1896, 1898, 1900, 1901, 1902, 1905, 1908, 1912, 1919, 1922, 1923, 1924, 1925, 1931, 1932, 1933, 1935, 1937, 1938, 1939, 1946, 1959, 1960, 1962, 1963, 1966, 1967, 1968. **Joint:** (1) 1949
NatWest Trophy/Gillette Cup Winners: (2) 1965, 1969
Benson and Hedges Cup Winners: (0) Finalists 1972
John Player League Champions: (1) 1983
Match Awards: GC 14; NWT 4; BHC 36

Secretary: J. Lister, Headingley Cricket Ground, Leeds LS6 3BU
Captain: D.L. Bairstow
Scorer: E.I. Lester
Scores/Prospects: ☎ Leeds (0532) 787394

BAIRSTOW, David Leslie (Hanson GS, Bradford), b Bradford 1 Sep 1951. 5'9½". RHB, WK, RM. Debut 1970. Cap 1973. Captain 1984-. Griqualand West 1976-78 (Captain 1977-78). Benefit 1982 (£56,913). Tests: 4 (1979 to 1980-81); HS 59 v Ind (Oval) on debut. LOI: 21. Tours: Aus 1978-79, 1979-80; WI 1980-81. 1000 runs (3); most – 1181 (1985). HS 145 v Middx (Scarborough) 1980. BB 3-82 GW v Transvaal B (Johannesburg) 1976-77. Held 11 catches v Derbys (Scarborough) 1982 to equal world record for a first-class match. Awards: NWT 1; BHC 6. Soccer: Bradford City. **NWT:** HS 92 v Worcs (Leeds) 1982. **BHC:** HS 103* v Derbys (Derby) 1981. **JPL:** HS 78 v Surrey (Scarborough) 1981.

BLAKEY, Richard John (Rastrick GS), b Huddersfield 15 Jan 1967. 5'9". RHB, WK. Debut 1985. HS 90 v Somerset (Leeds) 1985.

BOOTH, Paul Antony (Hanley HS), b Huddersfield 5 Sep 1965. 5'10". LHB, SLA. Debut 1982. HS 26 v Worcs (Scarborough) 1984. BB 3-22 v Northants (Northampton) 1984. **NWT:** HS 6*. **BHC:** HS 1. BB 2-28 v Worcs (Bradford) 1985. **JPL:** BB 1-57.

BOYCOTT, Geoffrey (Hemsworth GS), b Fitzwilliam 21 Oct 1940. 5'10". RHB, RM. Yorkshire debut 1962. Cap 1963. *Wisden* 1964. YC 1964. Captain 1971-78. Northern Transvaal 1971-72. Benefit 1974 (£20,639). OBE 1980. Testimonial 1984. Yorkshire Committee 1984-. Tests: 108 (1964 to 1981-82, 4 as captain); HS 246* v Ind (Leeds) 1967; BB 3-47 v SA (Cape Town) 1964-65. LOI: 36. Tours: Aus 1965-66, 1970-71, 1978-79, 1979-80; SA 1964-65, 1981-82 (SAB); WI 1967-68, 1973-74, 1980-81; NZ 1965-66, 1977-78 (capt); Ind 1979-80, 1981-82; Pak 1977-78; SL 1969-70. 1000 runs (23+3); most – 2503 (1971). HS 261* MCC v WIBC President's XI (Bridgetown) 1973-74. Yorks HS 260* v Essex (Colchester) 1970. BB 4-14 v Lancs (Leeds) 1979. Awards: NWT 2; BHC 9. **NWT:** HS 146 v Surrey (Lord's) 1965. BB 2-12 v Essex (Leeds) 1982. **BHC:** HS 142 v Worcs (Worcester) 1980. BB 1-16. **JPL:** HS 108* v Northants (Huddersfield) 1974. BB 3-15 v Middx (Hull) 1983.

BYAS, David (Scarborough C), b Kilham 26 Aug 1963. 6'4". LHB, RM. Awaiting f-c debut. **BHC:** HS 2. **JPL:** HS 15 v Leics (Leicester) 1985.

CARRICK, Phillip (Bramley SS; Intake SS; Park Lane CPE), b Armley 16 Jul 1952. 5'11½". RHB, SLA. Debut 1970. Cap 1976. E. Province 1976-77. N. Transvaal 1982-83. Benefit 1985. Tours: SA 1975-76 (DHR); SL 1977-78 (DHR). HS 131* v Northants (Northampton) 1980. BB 8-33 v CU (Cambridge) 1973. Awards: BHC 1. **NWT:** HS 37 v Salop (Telford) 1984. BB 3-27 v Northants (Leeds) 1983. **BHC:** HS 53 v Warwicks (Leeds) 1985. BB 3-40 v Warwicks (Birmingham) 1984. **JPL:** HS 43* v Surrey (Oval) 1984. BB 4-13 v Derbys (Bradford) 1983.

DENNIS, Simon John (Scarborough C), b Scarborough 18 Oct 1960. 6'1". RHB, LFM. Nephew of F. Dennis (Yorkshire 1928-33) and Sir Leonard Hutton (Yorkshire and England 1934-55). Debut 1980. Cap 1983. Orange Free State 1982-83. HS 53* v Notts (Nottingham) 1984. BB 5-35 v Somerset (Sheffield) 1981. **NWT:** HS 14 v Salop (Telford) 1984. BB 2-45 v Northants (Leeds) 1983. **BHC:** HS 10 v Warwicks (Birmingham) 1984. BB 3-41 v Northants (Bradford) 1984. **JPL:** HS 16* v Glam, 16* v Derbys 1983. BB 3-19 v Hants (Middlesbrough) 1981.

FLETCHER, Stuart David (Reins Wood SS), b Keighley 8 Jun 1964. 5'10". RHB, RMF. Debut 1983. HS 28* v Kent (Tunbridge Wells) 1984. BB 4-24 v Somerset (Middlesbrough) 1984. **NWT:** BB 3-34 v Somerset (Leeds) 1985. **BHC:** BB 2-42 v Sussex (Hove) 1984. **JPL:** HS 8. BB 2-31 v Derbys (Chesterfield) 1984.

HARTLEY, Peter John (Greenhead GS; Bradford C), b Keighley 18 Apr 1960. 6'0". RHB, RMF. Warwickshire 1982. Yorkshire debut 1985. HS 35 v Warwicks (Birmingham) 1985. BB 5-75 v Notts (Scarborough) 1985. **JPL:** HS 2. BB 1-20.

HARTLEY, Stuart **Neil** (Beckfoot GS, Bingley; Cannington HS, Perth, WA), b Shipley 18 Mar 1956. 6'0". RHB, RM. Debut 1978, Cap 1981. OFS 1981-83. HS 114 v Glos (Bradford) 1982. BB 4-51 v Surrey (Oval) 1985. Awards: BHC 1. **NWT:** HS 69 v Somerset (Leeds) 1985. BB 2-16 v Warwicks (Birmingham) 1981. **BHC:** HS 65* v Warwicks (Birmingham) 1984. BB 4-39 v Scotland (Perth) 1984. **JPL:** HS 73 v Warwicks (Scarborough) 1984. BB 3-31 v Notts (Scarborough) 1980.

JARVIS, Paul William (Bydales CS, Marske), b Redcar 29 Jun 1965. 5'10". RHB, RFM. Debut 1981 aged 16 years 75 days (youngest Yorkshire player). HS 37 v Surrey (Oval) 1984. BB 7-105 v Kent (Maidstone) 1985. **NWT:** HS 16 v Somerset (Leeds) 1985. BB 2-36 v Cheshire (Birkenhead) 1985. **BHC:** HS 20 v Worcs (Bradford) 1985. BB 3-31 v Warwicks (Leeds) 1985. **JPL:** HS 9*. BB 4-28 v Glamorgan (Leeds) 1984.

LOVE, James Derek (Brudenell SS), b Leeds 22 Apr 1955. 6'2½". RHB, RM. Debut 1975. Cap 1980. LOI: 3. 1000 runs (2); most – 1203 (1981). HS 170* v Worcs (Worcester) 1979. BB 1-8. Awards: BHC 2. **NWT:** HS 61* v Hants (Southampton) 1980. **BHC:** HS 118* v Scot (Bradford) 1981. **JPL:** HS 100* v Glos (Gloucester) 1985.

METCALFE, Ashley Anthony (Bradford GS; University C, London), b Horsforth 25 Dec 1963. 5'8". RHB, OB. Debut 1983 scoring 122 (HS) v Notts (Bradford). **NWT:** HS 33 v Somerset (Leeds) 1985. **JPL:** HS 115* v Glos (Scarborough) 1984.

MOXON, Martyn Douglas (Holgate GS, Barnsley), b Barnsley 4 May 1960. 6'0". RHB, RM. Debut v Essex (Leeds) 1981 scoring 5 and 116. Cap 1984. Griqualand West 1982-84. LOI: 5. Tours: Ind 1984-85; SL 1984-85, 1985-86 (Eng B). 1000 runs (2); most – 1447 (1985). HS 168 v Worcs (Worcester) 1985. BB 3-26 D.B. Close's XI v Sri Lankans (Scarborough) 1984. Awards: NWT 2; BHC 1. **NWT:** HS 82* v Cheshire (Birkenhead) 1985. **BHC:** HS 79 v Sussex (Hove) 1984. BB 1-23. **JPL:** HS 86 v Somerset (Bath) 1985. BB 1-16.

OLDHAM, Stephen (Crossfield High Green S), b High Green, Sheffield 27 Jul 1948. 6'1". RHB, RFM. Yorkshire 1974-79 and 1984-. Derbyshire 1980-83 (Cap 1980). HS 50 v Sussex (Hove) 1979. BB 7-78 Derbys v Warwicks (Birmingham) 1982. Awards: BHC 1. **NWT:** HS 19 v Salop (Telford) 1984. BB 3-29 Derbys v Notts (Derby) 1981. **BHC:** HS 4*. BB 5-32 v Minor C (N) (Scunthorpe) 1975. **JPL:** HS 38* v Glam (Cardiff) 1977. BB 5-37 Derbys v Lancs (Derby) 1982.

PICKLES, Christopher Stephen (Whitcliffe Mount CS), b Mirfield 30 Jan 1966. 6'1". RHB, RM. Debut 1985. HS 31* v Leics (Bradford) 1985. BB 2-31 v Kent (Scarborough) 1985. **JPL:** HS 13* v Kent (Scarborough) 1985. BB 3-15 v Glam (Swansea) 1985.

ROBINSON, Phillip Edward (Greenhead GS, Keighley), b Keighley 3 Aug 1963. 5'9". RHB, LM. Debut 1984. HS 92 v Glam (Bradford) 1984. **NWT:** HS 0. **BHC:** HS 42 v Leics (Leicester) 1985. **JPL:** HS 78* v Leics (Leicester) 1985.

SHARP, Kevin (Abbey Grange HS, Leeds), b Leeds 6 Apr 1959. 5'9". LHB, OB. Debut 1976. Cap 1982. Griqualand West 1981-84. Tour: NZ 1979-80 (DHR). 1000 runs (1): 1445 (1984). HS 173 v Derbys (Chesterfield) 1984. BB 2-13 v Glam (Bradford) 1984. **NWT:** HS 25 v Middx (Lord's) 1979. **BHC:** HS 87* v Northants (Bradford) 1984. **JPL:** HS 114 v Essex (Chelmsford) 1985.

SHAW, Christopher (Crofton HS), b Hemsworth 17 Feb 1964. 6'1". RHB, RFM. Debut 1984. HS 17 v Worcs (Scarborough) 1984. BB 5-76 v Kent (Scarborough) 1985. **NWT:** HS 6*. BB 1-14. **JPL:** HS 26 v Glam (Leeds) 1984. BB 5-41 v Hants (Bournemouth) 1984.

SIDEBOTTOM, Arnold (Broadway GS, Barnsley), b Barnsley 1 Apr 1954. 6'1". RHB, RMF. Debut 1973. Cap 1980. Orange Free State 1981-84. Tests: 1 (1985); HS 2 and BB 1-65 v Aus (Nottingham). Tours: SA 1981-82 (SAB). HS 124 v Glam (Cardiff) 1977. BB 7-18 v OU (Oxford) 1980. Awards: BHC 1. Soccer: Manchester United, Huddersfield Town and Halifax Town. **NWT:** HS 45 v Hants (Bournemouth) 1977. BB 4-35 v Kent (Leeds) 1980. **BHC:** HS 32 v Notts (Leeds) 1983. BB 5-27 v Worcs (Bradford) 1985. **JPL:** HS 52* v Northants (Middlesbrough) 1982. BB 4-24 v Surrey (Scarborough) 1975.

STEVENSON, Graham Barry (Minsthorpe HS), b Ackworth 16 Dec 1955. 5'11". RHB, RMF. Debut 1973. Cap 1978. Tests: 2 (1979-80 and 1980-81); HS 27* v Ind (Bombay) 1979-80; BB 3-111 v WI (St. John's) 1980-81. LOI: 4. Tours: Aus 1979-80; WI 1980-81; Ind 1979-80. HS 115* (batting number 11) v Warwicks (Birmingham) 1982. BB 8-57 v Northants (Leeds) 1980. Awards: NWT 1; BHC 1. **NWT:** HS 34 v Northants (Leeds) 1983. BB 5-27 v Berks (Reading) 1983. **BHC:** HS 36 v Warwicks (Leeds) 1984. BB 5-28 v Kent (Canterbury) 1978. **JPL:** HS 81* v Somerset (Middlesbrough) 1984. BB 5-41 v Leics (Leicester) 1976.

SWALLOW, Ian Geoffrey (Hoyland Kirk CS, Balk), b Barnsley 18 Dec 1962. 5'7½". RHB, OB. Debut 1983. HS 34* v Somerset (Middlesbrough) 1984. BB 4-52 v Kent (Tunbridge Wells) 1984. **BHC:** HS 10* v Worcs (Bradford) 1985. BB 1-40. **JPL:** HS 2.

YORKSHIRE RECORDS

FIRST-CLASS CRICKET

Highest Total	For	887 v Warwicks; Birmingham	1896
	V	630 by Somerset; Leeds	1901
Lowest Total	For	23 v Hampshire; Middlesbrough	1965
	V	13 by Notts; Nottingham	1901
Highest Innings	For	341 G.H. Hirst v Leics; Leicester	1905
	V	318* W.G. Grace for Glos; Cheltenham	1876

Highest Partnerships

1st	555	P. Holmes/H. Sutcliffe v Essex; Leyton	1932
2nd	346	W. Barber/M. Leyland v Middlesex; Sheffield	1932
3rd	323*	H. Sutcliffe/M. Leyland v Glamorgan; Huddersfield	1928
4th	312	D. Denton/G.H. Hirst v Hampshire; Southampton	1914
5th	340	E. Wainwright/G.H. Hirst v Surrey; The Oval	1899
6th	276	M. Leyland/E. Robinson v Glamorgan; Swansea	1926
7th	254	W. Rhodes/D.C.F. Burton v Hampshire; Dewsbury	1919
8th	292	R. Peel/Lord Hawke v Warwicks; Birmingham	1896
9th	192	G.H. Hirst/S. Haigh v Surrey; Bradford	1898
10th	149	G. Boycott/G.B. Stevenson v Warwicks; Birmingham	1982

Best Bowling (Innings)	For	10-10 H. Verity v Notts; Leeds	1932
	V	10-37 C.V. Grimmett for Australians; Sheffield	1930
Best Bowling (Match)	For	17-91 H. Verity v Essex; Leyton	1933
	V	17-91 H. Dean for Lancashire; Liverpool	1913

Most Runs – Season	2883	H. Sutcliffe	(av 80.08)	1932
Most Runs – Career	38561	H. Sutcliffe	(av 50.20)	1919-1945
Most 100s – Season	12	H. Sutcliffe		1932
Most 100s – Career	112	H. Sutcliffe		1919-1945
Most Wkts – Season	240	W. Rhodes	(av 12.72)	1900
Most Wkts – Career	3608	W. Rhodes	(av 16.00)	1895-1930

LIMITED-OVERS CRICKET

Highest Total	NWT	317-4 v Surrey; Lord's	1965
	BHC	273-8 v Warwicks; Leeds	1984
	JPL	263-8 v Surrey; Bradford	1985
Lowest Total	NWT	76 v Surrey; Harrogate	1970
	BHC	114 v Kent; Canterbury	1978
	JPL	74 v Warwicks; Birmingham	1972
Highest Innings	NWT	146 G. Boycott v Surrey; Lord's	1965
	BHC	142 G. Boycott v Worcs; Worcester	1980
	JPL	119 J.H. Hampshire v Leics; Hull	1971
Best Bowling	NWT	6-15 F.S. Trueman v Somerset; Taunton	1965
	BHC	6-27 A.G. Nicholson v Minor C (N); Middlesbrough	1972
	JPL	7-15 R.A. Hutton v Worcs; Leeds	1969

YORKSHIRE 1985

BRITANNIC ASSURANCE CHAMPIONSHIP AVERAGES

RESULTS SUMMARY

	Place	*Won*	*Lost*	*Drew*	*Abandoned*
Britannic Assurance Championship	11th	3	4	16	1
All First-class Matches		3	4	18	1
John Player League	6th	6	6		4
NatWest Bank Trophy	Lost to Somerset (2nd Round)				
Benson and Hedges Cup	Failed to qualify for Quarter-Final				

BATTING AND FIELDING

Cap		*M*	*I*	*NO*	*HS*	*Runs*	*Avge*	*100*	*50*	*Ct/St*
1963	G. Boycott	19	31	11	184	1545	77.25	6	8	9
1973	D.L. Bairstow	23	31	9	122*	1148	52.18	3	3	44/12
1984	M.D. Moxon	20	31	1	168	1224	40.80	3	5	8
1980	J.D. Love	19	26	4	93	830	37.72	—	6	7
—	P.E. Robinson	13	16	1	79	450	30.00	—	3	2
1980	A. Sidebottom	8	9	2	55	191	27.28	—	1	1
—	R.J. Blakey	13	21	2	90	487	25.63	—	2	11
1981	S.N. Hartley	15	19	1	60	446	24.77	—	3	7
1978	G.B. Stevenson	4	6	2	35*	99	24.75	—	—	1
1982	K. Sharp	17	29	3	96	613	23.57	—	2	14
1976	P. Carrick	23	25	2	92	540	23.47	—	3	15
—	P.J. Hartley	12	11	3	35	159	19.87	—	—	1
—	A.A. Metcalfe	5	10	0	77	125	12.50	—	1	—
—	S.D. Fletcher	12	10	7	15*	36	12.00	—	—	2
—	I.G. Swallow	10	11	2	25*	101	11.22	—	—	4
—	P.W. Jarvis	14	16	2	28	151	10.78	—	—	6
—	C. Shaw	16	13	5	12	57	7.12	—	—	5

Also batted: P.A. Booth (2 matches) 0 (1 ct); S. Oldham (2 matches) 6,2* (1 ct); C.S. Pickles (5 matches) 31*,12,9 (3 ct). S.J. Dennis (1 match – cap 1983) (1 ct) did not bat.

BOWLING

	O	*M*	*R*	*W*	*Avge*	*Best*	*5 wI*	*10 wM*
P. Carrick	709.3	183	1914	65	29.44	7-99	2	1
P.W. Jarvis	371.5	53	1330	44	30.22	7-105	3	—
A. Sidebottom	203.2	28	667	22	30.31	4-70	—	—
P.J. Hartley	315.5	40	1175	31	37.90	5-75	2	—
C. Shaw	398	90	1230	32	38.43	5-76	1	—
S.D. Fletcher	323.5	45	1185	24	49.37	4-91	—	—
I.G. Swallow	225	46	670	12	55.83	4-53	—	—

Also bowled: P.A. Booth 80.1-29-189-3; G. Boycott 10-2-29-0; S.J. Dennis 20.2-2-50-2; S.N. Hartley 74.4-10-272-9; J.D. Love 1-0-8-1; M.D. Moxon 27-1-131-4; S. Oldham 39-10-102-4; C.S. Pickles 112.3-24-345-5; K. Sharp 26-8-60-1; G.B. Stevenson 72.4-10-252-6.

The First-Class Averages (pp. 168–183) give the records of Yorkshire players in all first-class county matches (their other opponents being the Australians and Oxford U.), with the exception of: D.L. Bairstow 25-33-10-122*-1163-50.56-3-3-44 ct/12 st. M.D. Moxon 21-33-1-168-1256-39.25-3-5-9 ct. 36-4-153-4-38.25-1/16. K. Sharp 19-32-4-96-723-25.82-0-3-14 ct. 35-11-89-1-89.00-1/15. A. Sidebottom 9-10-3-55-194-27.71-0-1-1 ct. 223-32-740-23-32.17-4/70-0-0.

LANCASHIRE (contd from p. 105)

VALETE

JEFFERIES, Stephen Thomas (Plumstead HS), b Cape Town, S. Africa 8 Dec 1959. 6'0". LHB, LFM. W. Province 1978-86. Derbyshire 1982. Lancashire 1983-85. HS 93 v Sussex (Manchester) 1985. BB 8-46 v Notts (Nottingham) 1983. Awards: BHC 1.

ORMROD, Joseph **Alan** (Kirkcaldy HS, Fife), b Ramsbottom 22 Dec 1942. 5'11". RHB, OB. Worcestershire 1962-83 (cap 1966). Benefit 1977 (£19,000). Lancashire 1984-85 (cap 1984). Tours: WI 1965-66 (Worcs); Pak 1966-67 (MCC U-25). 1000 runs (13); most – 1535 (1978). HS 204* Worcs v Kent (Dartford) 1973. BB 5-27 Worcs v Glos (Bristol) 1972. Awards: BHC 4.

WATSON, Roger Graeme (Fearns County SS), b Rawtenstall 14 Jan 1964. 5'8". LHB, OB. Lancashire 1982-85. No appearances 1983-84. HS 18 v OU (Oxford) 1985.

MIDDLESEX (contd from p. 115)

VALETE

TOMLINS, Keith Patrick (St. Benedict's, Ealing; Durham U), b Kingston upon Thames 23 Oct 1957. 5'9". RHB, RM. Middlesex 1977-85. Cap 1983. Tour: Zim 1980-81 (Middx). HS 146 v OU (Oxford) 1982. BB 2-28 v Kent (Lord's) 1982. **NWT:** HS 80 v Cambs (Wisbech) 1983. **BHC:** HS 40 v Somerset (Taunton) 1984. **JPL:** HS 59 v Somerset (Bath) 1984. BB 4-24 v Notts (Lord's) 1978.

WARWICKSHIRE (contd from p. 145)

VALETE

LETHBRIDGE, Christopher (Normanton County SS), b Castleford, Yorks 23 Jun 1961. 5'10". RHB, RMF. Debut 1981 taking wicket of G. Boycott with his first ball. HS 87* v Somerset (Taunton) 1982. BB 5-68 v Glam (Cardiff) 1982.

SMITH, Kenneth **David** (Heaton GS), b Jesmond, Newcastle upon Tyne 9 Jul 1956. 6'0". RHB. Son of K.D. (Leics 1950-51) and brother of P.A. Warwickshire 1973-85. Cap 1978. 1000 runs (4); most – 1582 (1980). HS 140 v Worcs (Worcester) 1980. Awards: NWT 1; BHC 1.

The fastest century in NatWest.

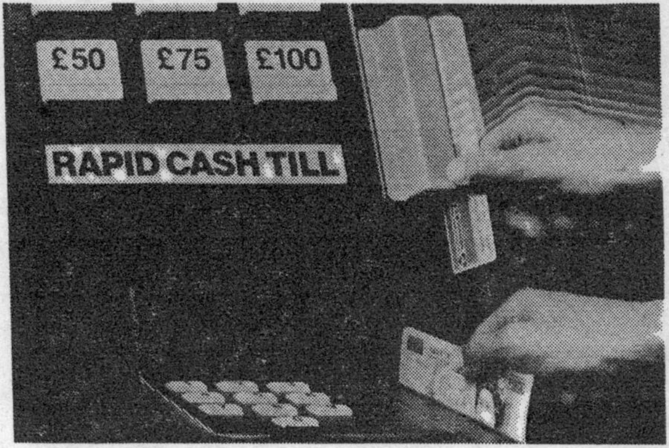

NatWest have installed 650 Rapid Cash Tills inside branches nationwide for those who want a quick century.

The Rapid Cash Till certainly lives up to its name.

You can draw up £100 in just 15 seconds.

You can make as many withdrawals a day as you like up to a limit agreed with your branch.

You can keep a check on your money because each withdrawal is accompanied by a slip showing how much you've taken out.

All you need to use a Rapid Cash Till is a Servicecard.

The same card that you can use at over 2,400 of our Servicetills and Midland AutoBanks. So if you want a fast century, track down your nearest Rapid Cash Till. Nothing beats it.

NatWest
The Action Bank

1985 UNIVERSITY MATCH

Played at Lord's, London, on 3, 4, 5 July Toss: Oxford. Result: match drawn

CAMBRIDGE UNIVERSITY

A.E. Lea c Carr b Toogood	41		not out	47
*C.R. Andrew b Toogood	12		c Franks b Toogood	12
D.J. Fell b Lawrence	8		lbw b Toogood	0
P.G.P. Roebuck c Thorne b Toogood	2	(5)	not out	34
D.G. Price lbw b Toogood	12			
†A.G. Davies lbw b Toogood	11			
T.A. Cotterell lbw b Toogood	24			
S.R. Gorman b Toogood	6	(4)	c Toogood b Rutnagur	43
C.C. Ellison c Franks b Toogood	4			
A.M.G. Scott c Franks b Thorne	5			
J.E. Davidson not out	1			
Extras (B3, LB1, W3, NB1)	8		(B2, LB3)	5
Total	134		(3 wickets)	141

OXFORD UNIVERSITY

*A.J.T. Miller b Andrew	78
W.R. Bristowe c Lea b Ellison	16
G.J. Toogood c Andrew b Ellison	149
J.D. Carr not out	84
D.A. Thorne c Davies b Ellison	17
†J.G. Franks c Gorman b Andrew	0
P.C. MacLarnon b Andrew	2
C.D.M. Tooley	
R.S. Ratnagur } did not bat	
J.D. Quinlan }	
M.P. Lawrence	
Extras (B3, LB8, W5, NB2)	18
Total (6 wickets declared)	364

OXFORD	*O*	*M*	*R*	*W*	*O*	*M*	*R*	*W*	FALL OF WICKETS			
										C	*O*	*C*
									Wkt	*1st*	*1st*	*2nd*
Thorne	9.3	1	23	1	9	3	14	0	1st	41	22	20
Quinlan	13	5	18	0	7	3	21	0	2nd	62	172	24
MacLarnon	4	1	13	0	—	—	—	—	3rd	65	318	96
Toogood	24	7	52	8	13	3	41	2	4th	74	351	—
Lawrence	13	8	8	1	—	—	—	—	5th	87	352	—
Carr	11	4	16	0	11	5	25	0	6th	92	364	—
Rutnagar	—	—	—	—	13	2	35	1	7th	100	—	—
CAMBRIDGE									8th	104	—	—
Davidson	10	1	40	0	—	—	—	—	9th	132	—	—
Ellison	27	6	76	3	—	—	—	—	10th	134	—	—
Scott	11	1	43	0	—	—	—	—				
Cotterell	25	8	78	0	—	—	—	—				
Gorman	4	0	14	0	—	—	—	—				
Lea	1	0	1	0	—	—	—	—				
Andrew	25.4	5	101	3	—	—	—	—				

Umpires: B. Leadbeater and K.E. Palmer

UNIVERSITY MATCH RESULTS

Played: 141 Wins: Cambridge 53; Oxford 46 Draws: 42

This, the oldest surviving first-class fixture, dates from 1827 and, wartime interruptions apart, it has been played annually since 1838. With the exception of five matches played in the area of Oxford (1829, 1843, 1846, 1848 and 1850), all the fixtures have been played at Lord's.

1827	Drawn	1882	Cambridge	1933	Drawn
1829	Oxford	1883	Cambridge	1934	Drawn
1836	Oxford	1884	Oxford	1935	Cambridge
1838	Oxford	1885	Cambridge	1936	Cambridge
1839	Cambridge	1886	Oxford	1937	Oxford
1840	Cambridge	1887	Oxford	1938	Drawn
1841	Cambridge	1888	Drawn	1939	Oxford
1842	Cambridge	1889	Cambridge	1946	Oxford
1843	Cambridge	1890	Cambridge	1947	Drawn
1844	Drawn	1891	Cambridge	1948	Oxford
1845	Cambridge	1892	Oxford	1949	Cambridge
1846	Oxford	1893	Cambridge	1950	Drawn
1847	Cambridge	1894	Oxford	1951	Oxford
1848	Oxford	1895	Cambridge	1953	Cambridge
1849	Cambridge	1896	Oxford	1954	Drawn
1850	Oxford	1897	Cambridge	1955	Drawn
1851	Cambridge	1898	Oxford	1956	Drawn
1852	Oxford	1899	Drawn	1957	Cambridge
1853	Oxford	1900	Drawn	1958	Cambridge
1854	Oxford	1901	Drawn	1959	Oxford
1855	Oxford	1902	Cambridge	1960	Drawn
1856	Cambridge	1903	Oxford	1961	Drawn
1857	Oxford	1904	Drawn	1962	Drawn
1858	Oxford	1905	Cambridge	1963	Drawn
1859	Cambridge	1906	Cambridge	1964	Drawn
1860	Cambridge	1907	Cambridge	1965	Drawn
1861	Cambridge	1908	Oxford	1966	Oxford
1862	Cambridge	1909	Drawn	1967	Drawn
1863	Oxford	1910	Oxford	1968	Drawn
1864	Oxford	1911	Oxford	1969	Drawn
1865	Oxford	1912	Cambridge	1970	Drawn
1866	Oxford	1913	Cambridge	1971	Drawn
1867	Cambridge	1914	Oxford	1972	Cambridge
1868	Cambridge	1919	Oxford	1973	Drawn
1869	Cambridge	1920	Drawn	1974	Drawn
1870	Cambridge	1921	Cambridge	1975	Drawn
1871	Oxford	1922	Cambridge	1976	Oxford
1872	Cambridge	1923	Oxford	1977	Drawn
1873	Oxford	1924	Cambridge	1978	Drawn
1874	Oxford	1925	Drawn	1979	Cambridge
1875	Oxford	1926	Cambridge	1980	Drawn
1876	Cambridge	1927	Cambridge	1981	Drawn
1877	Oxford	1928	Drawn	1982	Drawn
1878	Cambridge	1929	Drawn	1982	Cambridge
1879	Cambridge	1930	Cambridge	1983	Drawn
1880	Cambridge	1931	Oxford	1984	Oxford
1881	Oxford	1932	Drawn	1985	Drawn

CAMBRIDGE UNIVERSITY

AHLUWALIA, Manraj Singh (**'Manny'**) (Latymer Upper S; Emmanuel). b Isleworth Middx 27 Dec 1965. 5'4½". RHB. OB. Debut 1985. HS 31 v Surrey (Cambridge) 1985.

ANDREW, Christopher **Robert** (Barnard Castle S; St. John's). b Richmond. Yorks 18 Feb 1963. 5'10". LHB. OB. Debut 1984. Blue 1984-85. Captain 1985. HS 101* v Notts (Nottingham) 1984. BB 3-77 v Leics (Cambridge) 1984. Rugby for CU and England (fly half); kicked all 21 points in defeat of Wales 1985-86.

BROWNE, David William (Stamford S; St. Catharine's). b Stamford. Lincs 4 Apr 1964. 6'6". RHB. Debut 1985. HS 10 v Middlesex (Cambridge) 1985.

COTTERELL, Thomas Archbold (**'Archie'**) (Downside S; Peterhouse). b London 12 May 1963. 6'1". RHB. SLA. Debut 1983. Blue 1983-84-85. Secretary 1984. HS 69* v Essex (Cambridge) 1985. BB 5-89 v Essex (Cambridge) 1983.

DAVIDSON, John Edward (Penglais CS; Trinity). b Aberystwyth. Cardiganshire 23 Oct 1964. 6'3". RHB. RFM. Debut/blue 1985. HS 22 v Somerset (Taunton) 1985. BB 3-22 v Surrey (Cambridge) 1985.

DAVIES, Andrew George (Birkenhead S; Robinson). b Altrincham. Cheshire 15 May 1962. 6'2". RHB. WK. Unrelated to Alec G. Davies (Surrey). Debut 1982. Blue 1984-85. Secretary 1985. HS 69 v Surrey (Banstead) 1984.

ELLISON, Charles Christopher (Tonbridge S; Homerton). b Pembury. Kent 11 Feb 1962. 6'2". RHB. RM. Brother of R.M. (Kent and England). Debut 1982. Blue 1982-83-85. Wiltshire 1984-86. HS 51 v Surrey (Cambridge) 1985. BB 4-36 v Notts (Cambridge) 1983.

FELL, David John (The John Lyon S, Harrow; Trinity). b Stafford 27 Oct 1964. 5'9". RHB. LB. Debut/blue 1985. HS 109* v Notts (Cambridge) 1985.

GORMAN, Shaun Rodney (St. Peter's S. York; Emmanuel). b Middlesbrough 28 Apr 1965. 6'2". RHB. OB. Debut/blue 1985. HS 43 v OU (Lord's) 1985. BB 1-27.

GRIMES, Alexander David Hugh (Tonbridge S; Pembroke). b Beirut. Lebanon 8 Jan 1965. 6'0". RHB. RM. Debut/blue 1984. HS 22* v Middlesex (Cambridge) 1985. BB 3-99 v Essex (Cambridge) 1985.

LEA, Antony Edward (High Arcal S; Churchill). b Wolverhampton 29 Sep 1962. 6'0½". RHB. LB. Debut 1984. Blue 1984-85. HS 119 v Essex (Cambridge) 1984. BB 2-27 v Notts (Nottingham) 1984.

PRICE, David Gregory (Haberdashers' Aske's S; Homerton). b Luton 7 Feb 1965. 5'11". RHB. OB. Debut 1984. Blue 1984-85. **Captain 1986**. HS 49 v Warwicks (Cambridge) 1984.

ROEBUCK, Paul Gerrard Peter (Millfield S; Emmanuel). b Bath 13 Oct 1963. 6'0". LHB. RMF. Brother of P.M. (Somerset). Debut 1983. Glos debut 1984. Blue 1984-85. HS 82 v Somerset (Taunton) 1985. BB 2-44 v Kent (Cambridge) 1983.

SCOTT, Alastair Martin Gordon (Seaford Head CS; Queens). b Guildford 31 Mar 1966. 5'10". RHB. LM. Debut/blue 1985. HS 5*. BB 5-68 v Notts (Camb) 1985.

SIDDIQI, Shah Naweed (City of London S; St. Bartholomew's Hospital; Hughes Hall). b London 13 Sep 1959. 5'11". RHB. OB. Debut 1984. HS 52 v Sussex (Cambridge) 1984. BB 5-90 v Warwicks (Cambridge) 1984.

CAMBRIDGE UNIVERSITY 1985

RESULTS SUMMARY

	Played	Won	Lost	Drawn
All First-Class Matches	9	0	1	8

FIRST-CLASS AVERAGES

CAMBRIDGE UNIVERSITY – BATTING AND FIELDING

	M	I	NO	HS	Runs	Avge	100	50	Ct/St
†T.A. Cotterell	9	12	4	69*	289	36.12	—	1	1
†P.G.P. Roebuck	9	15	3	82	343	28.58	—	1	4
†A.E. Lea	8	15	2	47*	298	22.92	—	—	3
†D.J. Fell	9	16	1	109*	332	22.13	1	1	4
A.D.H. Grimes	6	3	1	22*	43	21.50	—	—	1
†C.C. Ellison	7	6	0	51	109	18.16	—	1	1
†C.R. Andrew	8	15	1	66	253	18.07	—	2	4
†S.R. Gorman	9	15	5	43	177	17.70	—	—	3
†J.E. Davidson	4	4	2	22	25	12.50	—	—	2
†A.G. Davies	9	13	2	43*	124	11.27	—	—	11/2
M.S. Ahluwalia	4	7	1	31	55	9.16	—	—	3
†D.G. Price	6	9	1	29	60	7.50	—	—	1
†A.M.G. Scott	9	7	4	5*	12	4.00	—	—	2

Also batted (1 match): D.W. Browne 10 (1 ct), S.N. Siddiqi 0.

CAMBRIDGE UNIVERSITY – BOWLING

	O	M	R	W	Avge	Best	5 wI	10 wM
A.M.G. Scott	243.3	34	879	25	35.16	5-68	1	—
C.C. Ellison	223.5	58	591	13	45.46	3.76	—	—
C.R. Andrew	80.2	10	279	6	46.50	3-101	—	—
A.D.H. Grimes	130	28	480	9	53.33	3-99	—	—
T.A. Cotterell	232.4	54	742	11	67.45	3-53	—	—

Also Bowled: J.E. Davidson 80-12-254-4; S.R. Gorman 117.4-17-465-3; A.E. Lea 2-0-9-0; D.G. Price 1-0-7-0; S.N. Siddiqi 2-0-12-0.

†Blue 1985

CAMBRIDGE UNIVERSITY RECORDS

FIRST-CLASS CRICKET

Highest Total	For	703-9d v Sussex; Hove	1890
	V	703-3d by W. Indians; Cambridge	1950
Lowest Total	For	30 v Yorkshire; Cambridge	1928
	V	32 by Oxford U; Lord's	1878
Highest Innings	For	254* K.S. Duleepsinhji v Middlesex; Cambridge	1927
	V	304* E. de C. Weekes for W. Indians; Cambridge	1950

Highest Partnerships

1st	349	J.G. Dewes/D.S. Sheppard v Sussex; Hove	1950
2nd	429*	J.G. Dewes/G.H.G. Doggart v Essex; Cambridge	1949
3rd	284	E.T. Killick/G.C. Grant v Essex; Cambridge	1929
4th	275	R. de W.K. Winlaw/J.H. Human v Essex; Cambridge	1934
5th	220	R. Subba Row/F.C.M. Alexander v Notts; Nottingham	1953
6th	245	J.L. Bryan/C.T. Ashton v Surrey; The Oval	1921
7th	289	G. Goonesena/G.W. Cook v Oxford U; Lord's	1957
8th	145	H. Ashton/A.E.R. Gilligan v F. Foresters; Cambridge	1920
9th	200	G.W. Cook/C.S. Smith v Lancashire; Liverpool	1957
10th	177	A.E.R. Gilligan/J.H. Naumann v Sussex; Hove	1919

Best Bowling (Innings)	For	10-69 S.M.J. Woods v C.I. Thornton's XI; Cambridge	1890
	V	10-38 S.E. Butler for Oxford U; Lord's	1871
Best Bowling (Match)	For	15-88 S.M.J. Woods v C.I. Thornton's XI; Cambridge	1890
	V	15-95 S.E. Butler for Oxford U; Lord's	1871

Most Runs – Season	1581	D.S. Sheppard	(av 79.05)	1952
Most Runs – Career	4310	J.M. Brearley	(av 38.48)	1961-1968
Most 100s – Season	7	D.S. Sheppard		1952
Most 100s – Career	14	D.S. Sheppard		1950-1952
Most Wkts – Season	80	O.S. Wheatley	(av 17.63)	1958
Most Wkts – Career	208	G. Goonesena	(av 21.82)	1954-1957

UNIVERSITY MATCH RECORDS

Highest Total	432-9d		1936
Lowest Total	39		1858
Highest Innings	211	G. Goonesena	1957
Best Bowling (Innings)	8-44	G.E. Jeffery	1873
Best Bowling (Match)	13-73	A.G. Steel	1878
Hat-Tricks	F.C. Cobden (1870), A.G. Steel (1879), P.H. Morton (1880), J.F. Ireland (1911), R.G.H. Lowe (1926)		
Match Double	No instance		

OXFORD UNIVERSITY

BRETTELL, James Gordon (Cheltenham C; Lincoln). b Woking, Surrey 19 Dec 1962. 6'0". RHB, SLA. Debut 1984. HS 0*. BB 2-87 v Worcs (Oxford) 1985.

BRISTOWE, William Robert (Charterhouse; St. Edmund Hall). b Woking 17 Nov 1963. 5'11". RHB, OB. Debut 1984. Blue 1984-85. HS 42* v Yorks (Oxford) 1985.

CARR, John Donald (Repton S; Worcester). b St. John's Wood, London 15 Jun 1963. 5'11". RHB, OB. Son of D.B. (Derbyshire, OU and England 1945-63). OU and Middlesex debuts 1983. Blue 1983-84-85. Secretary 1984. Hertfordshire 1982-84. HS 123 OU v Lancs (Oxford) 1984. BB 6-61 Middlesex v Glos (Lord's) 1985.

DENNY, Christopher Mark (St Dunstan's C; Christ Church). b Farnborough, Kent 22 Apr 1964. 6'2". RHB, SLA. Debut 1985. HS 19 v Hants (Oxford) 1985.

FRANKS, Jonathan **Guy** (Stamford S; St. Edmund Hall). b Stamford, Lincs 23 Sep 1962. 5'11". RHB, WK. Debut 1983. Blue 1984-85. HS 42* v Middx (Oxford) 1984.

HAGAN, David Andrew (Trinity S, Leamington Spa; St. Edmund Hall). b Wide Open, Northumb 25 Jun 1966. 5'9". RHB, OB. Debut 1985. HS 46 v Worcs (Oxford) 1985.

HARRISON, Dominic Stephen (Ampleforth C; University). b Tittensor, Staffs 15 Jan 1963. 5'9". RHB, WK. Debut 1983. HS 8.

LAWRENCE, Mark Philip (Manchester GS; Merton). b Warrington, Cheshire 6 May 1962. 5'9". LHB, SLA. Debut 1982. Blue 1984-85. HS 18 v Middlesex (Oxford) 1982. BB 3-79 v Kent (Oxford) 1984.

MacLARNON, Patrick Craig (Loughborough GS; St. Peter's). b Nottingham 24 Sep 1963. 6'2". RHB, RM. Debut/blue 1985. HS 56 v Warwicks (Oxford) 1985. BB 1-18.

MILLER, Andrew John Trevor (Haileybury C; St. Edmund Hall). b Chesham, Bucks 30 May 1963. 5'11". LHB, RM. Debut 1982. Blue 1983-84-85. Captain 1985. Middlesex debut 1983. HS 128* OU v CU (Lord's) 1984. BB 1-4. Awards: BHC 2.

PATEL, Tikendra **('Tiku')** (Vandyke Upper S; Queen's). b Ahmedabad, India 9 Oct 1965. 5'8". RHB, OB. Debut 1985. Beds 1983. HS 47 v Hants (Oxford) 1985.

QUINLAN, Jeremy David (Sherborne S; St. Peter's). b Watford, Herts 18 Apr 1965. 6'2". RHB, RM. Debut/blue 1985. HS 22*/BB 4-76 v Leics (Oxford) 1985.

RUTNAGUR, Richard Sohrab (Westminster S; New). b Bombay, India 9 Aug 1964. 5'9". RHB, RM. Son of D.J. (Cricket Correspondent). Debut/blue 1985. HS 66 v Kent (Oxford) 1985. BB 5-112 v Zimbabweans (Oxford) 1985.

TAYLOR, Darren Philip (Burnley GS; Christ Church). b Burnley, Lancs 15 Feb 1965. 5'9". RHB, WK. Debut 1985. HS 5* (ending a sequence of 0, 0, 0, 0, 0*).

THORNE, David Anthony (Coventry S; Keble). b Coventry 12 Dec 1964. 5'11". RHB, LM. Warwickshire debut 1983. OU debut 1984. Blue 1984-85. Secretary 1985. **Captain 1986**. HS 124 v Zimbabweans (Oxford) 1985. BB 5-39 v CU (Lord's) 1984.

TOOGOOD, Giles John (N. Bromsgrove HS; Lincoln). b West Bromwich 19 Nov 1961. 5'11" RHB, RMF. Debut 1982. Blue 1982-83-84-85. Captain 1983. HS 149/BB 8-52 (10-93 match) v CU (Lord's) 1985. First Englishman to do Varsity match double.

TOOLEY, Christopher Donald Michael (St. Dunstan's C; Magdalen) b Bromley, Kent 19 Apr 1964. 6'1". RHB, RM. Debut/blue 1985. HS 66 v Hants (Oxford) 1985.

OXFORD UNIVERSITY 1985

RESULTS SUMMARY

	Played	Won	Lost	Drawn
All First-Class Matches	11	0	4	7

FIRST-CLASS AVERAGES

OXFORD UNIVERSITY – BATTING AND FIELDING

	M	I	NO	HS	Runs	Avge	100	50	Ct/St
†D.A. Thorne	11	18	3	124	849	56.60	1	8	8
†J.D. Carr	6	9	1	115	415	51.87	2	2	3
†G.J. Toogood	9	15	1	149	507	36.21	1	2	4
†A.J.T. Miller	10	17	3	78	462	33.00	—	3	3
†J.G. Franks	3	4	1	35	71	23.66	—	—	4/1
†W.R. Bristowe	5	8	1	42*	156	22.28	—	—	3
†R.S. Rutnagur	11	15	2	66	246	18.92	—	2	3
†P.C. MacLarnon	7	10	1	56	168	18.66	—	1	3
D.A. Hagan	5	10	1	46	148	16.44	—	—	4
†C.D.M. Tooley	11	16	0	66	257	16.06	—	1	2
T. Patel	9	17	4	47	159	12.23	—	—	5
†J.D. Quinlan	7	6	2	22*	34	8.50	—	—	1
C.M. Denny	4	6	1	19	28	5.60	—	—	3
D.S. Harrison	4	5	2	6	12	4.00	—	—	4/2
†M.P. Lawrence	11	9	3	9*	20	3.33	—	—	2
D.P. Taylor	4	6	2	5*	5	1.25	—	—	1/2

Also batted (4 matches): J.G. Brettell 0, 0* (1 ct).

OXFORD UNIVERSITY – BOWLING

	O	M	R	W	Avge	Best	5 wI	10 wM
G.J. Toogood	209.2	44	691	18	38.38	8-52	1	1
R.S. Rutnagur	189	25	728	15	48.53	5-112	1	—
D.A. Thorne	196.1	34	664	13	51.07	4-64	—	—
M.P. Lawrence	341.5	65	1154	20	57.70	3-99	—	—
J.D. Carr	184	48	462	8	57.75	4-65	—	—
J.D. Quinlan	189	37	635	10	63.50	4-76	—	—

Also bowled: J.G. Brettell 62.4-14-266-4; W.R. Bristowe 1-0-5-0; D.A. Hagan 1-0-6-0; P.C. MacLarnon 60.3-10-229-1.

†Blue 1985

OXFORD UNIVERSITY RECORDS

FIRST-CLASS CRICKET

Highest Total	For	651 v Sussex; Hove	1895
	V	679-7d by Australians; Oxford	1938
Lowest Total	For	12 v MCC; Oxford	1877
	V	24 by MCC; Oxford	1846
Highest Innings	For	281 K.J. Key v Middlesex; Chiswick Park	1887
	V	338 W.W. Read for Surrey; The Oval	1888

Highest Parternships

1st	338	T. Bowring/H. Teesdale v Gentlemen; Oxford	1908
2nd	226	W.G. Keighley/H.A. Pawson v Cambridge U; Lord's	1947
3rd	273	F.C. de Saram/N.S. Mitchell-Innes v Glos; Oxford	1934
4th	276	P.G.T. Kingsley/N.M. Ford v Surrey; The Oval	1930
5th	256*	A.A. Baig/C.A. Fry v F. Foresters; Oxford	1959
6th	270	D.R. Walsh/S.A. Westley v Warwicks; Oxford	1969
7th	340	K.J. Key/H. Philipson v Middlesex; Chiswick Park	1887
8th	160	H. Philipson/A.C.M. Croome v MCC; Lord's	1889
9th	157	H.M. Garland-Wells/C.K.H. Hill-Wood v Kent; Oxford	1928
10th	149	F.H. Hollins/B.A. Collins v MCC; Oxford	1901

Best Bowling	For	10-38	S.E. Butler v Cambridge U; Lord's	1871
(Innings)	V	10-49	W.G. Grace for MCC; Oxford	1886
Best Bowling	For	15-65	B.J.T. Bosanquet v Sussex; Oxford	1900
(Match)	V	16-225	J.E. Walsh for Leics; Oxford	1953

Most Runs – Season	1307	Nawab of Pataudi, sr	(av 93.35)	1931
Most Runs – Career	3319	N.S. Mitchell-Innes	(av 47.41)	1934-1937
Most 100s – Season	6	Nawab of Pataudi, sr		1931
Most 100s – Career	9	A.M. Crawley		1927-1930
		Nawab of Pataudi, sr		1928-1931
		N.S. Mitchell-Innes		1934-1937
		M.P. Donnelly		1946-1947
Most Wkts – Season	70	I.A.R. Peebles	(av 18.15)	1930
Most Wkts – Career	182	R.H.B. Bettington	(av 19.38)	1920-1923

UNIVERSITY MATCH RECORDS

Highest Total	503		1900
Lowest Total	32		1878
Highest Innings	238*	Nawab of Pataudi, sr	1931
Best Bowling (Innings)	10-38	S.E. Butler	1871
Best Bowling (Match)	15-95	S.E. Butler	1871
Hat-Tricks	No instance		
Match Double	160 and 11-66	P.R. le Couteur	1910
	149 and 10-93	G.J. Toogood	1985

FIRST-CLASS AVERAGES 1985

These averages include performances in all first-class matches played in the United Kingdom and Ireland in 1985. 'Cap' denotes the season in which the player was awarded a 1st XI cap by the county he represented in 1985.

Team abbreviations: A – Australia; CU – Cambridge University; D – Derbyshire; DBC – D.B. Close's XI; Eng – England; Ex – Essex; Gm – Glamorgan; Gs – Gloucestershire; H – Hampshire; Ire –Ireland; K – Kent; La – Lancashire; Le – Leicestershire; M – Middlesex; MCC – Marylebone CC; MC – Minor Counties; Nh – Northamptonshire; Nt – Nottinghamshire; OU – Oxford University; RW – Rest of the World XI; Sc – Scotland; Sm – Somerset; Sy – Surrey; Sx – Sussex; Wa – Warwickshire; Wo – Worcestershire; Y – Yorkshire; Z – Zimbabwe. Daggers (†) signify left-handed batsmen.

BATTING AND FIELDING

	Cap	*M*	*I*	*NO*	*HS*	*Runs*	*Avge*	*100*	*50*	*Ct/St*
†Abrahams, J. (La)	1982	25	39	4	101*	932	26.62	1	4	15
Acfield, D.L. (Ex)	1970	25	21	11	14	80	8.00	—	—	6
Afford, J.A. (Nt)	—	3	1	0	2	2	2.00	—	—	2
Agnew, J.P. (Eng/Le)	1984	16	15	3	36	121	10.08	—	—	3
Ahluwalia, M.S. (CU)	—	4	7	1	31	55	9.16	—	—	3
Allott, P.J.W. (Eng/La/MCC)	1981	19	21	6	78	272	18.13	—	1	6
Amiss, D.L. (Wa)	1965	26	44	5	140	1555	39.87	5	7	24
Anderson, I.S. (D)	1985	19	35	3	95	876	27.37	—	7	16
†Andrew, C.R.S(CU)	—	8	15	1	66	253	18.07	—	2	4
Andrew, S.J.W. (H)	—	12	5	4	6*	9	9.00	—	—	5
Arnold, K.A. (MC)	—	1	—	—	—	—	—	—	—	1
Asif Din (Wa)	—	6	11	2	89	325	36.11	—	2	2
Aslett, D.G. (K)	1983	13	23	1	174	732	33.27	2	1	5
Athey, C.W.J. (Gs/MCC)	1985	24	38	7	170	1442	46.51	5	7	26
Atkinson, J.C.M. (Sm)	—	6	5	1	79	167	41.75	—	1	—
Atkinson, S.R. (MC)	—	1	1	0	63	63	63.00	—	1	1
Bail, P.A.C. (Sm)	—	5	9	2	78*	127	18.14	—	1	—
Bailey, R.J. (Nh/MCC)	1985	26	38	7	107*	1194	38.51	2	7	6
Bainbridge, P. (Gs)	1981	24	38	9	151*	1644	56.68	4	11	10
Bairstow, D.L. (Y/DBC)	1973	26	35	10	122*	1181	47.24	3	3	45/13
Balderstone, J.C. (Le)	1973	25	40	5	134	1271	36.31	2	6	10
Banks, D.A. (Wo)	—	6	7	2	76	196	39.20	—	2	2
Baptiste, E.A.E. (K)	1983	23	36	5	82	972	31.35	—	6	12
Barclay, J.R.T. (Sx)	1976	22	17	6	37*	257	23.36	—	—	12
†Barlow, G.D. (M)	1976	20	32	4	141	1343	47.96	6	2	6
Barnett, K.J. (D)	1982	25	41	2	134*	1568	40.20	4	7	13
Barrett, B.J. (Wo)	—	1	—	—	—	—	—	—	—	—
Barwick, S.R. (Gm)	—	22	15	5	29	57	5.70	—	—	4
Benjamin, W.K.R. (RW)	—	1	2	1	15	15	15.00	—	—	—
Bennett, M.J. (A)	—	11	10	3	23	111	15.85	—	—	6
†Benson, M.R. (K)	1981	24	43	3	162	1501	37.52	3	11	15
Bent, P. (Wo)	—	1	1	0	14	14	14.00	—	—	—
Billington, D.J. (Le)	—	1	1	0	19	19	19.00	—	—	1
Birch, J.D. (Nt)	1981	14	23	7	68*	409	25.56	—	2	5
Blackett, M. (Le)	—	2	4	2	28*	41	20.50	—	—	—

	Cap	M	I	NO	HS	Runs	Avge	100	50	Ct/St
Blakey, R.J. (Y)	—	14	22	2	90	518	25.90	—	2	12
Boon, D.C. (A)	—	15	20	5	206*	832	55.46	3	3	13
†Booth, P.A. (Y)	—	4	2	0	4	4	2.00	—	—	2
Booth, S.C. (Sm)	—	11	8	3	28	78	15.60	—	—	13
†Border, A.R. (A)	—	14	21	2	196	1355	71.31	8	1	13
Botham, I.T. (Eng/Sm)	1976	19	27	5	152	1530	69.54	5	9	17
Boycott, G. (Y)	1963	21	34	12	184	1657	75.31	6	9	10
Boyd-Moss, R.J. (Nh)	1984	20	31	3	121	766	27.35	2	2	6
Brandes, E.A. (Z)	—	3	4	1	19	30	10.00	—	—	—
Brassington, A.J. (Gs)	1978	3	2	2	3*	3	—	—	—	6
Brettell, J.G. (OU)	—	4	2	1	0*	0	0.00	—	—	1
Briers, N.E. (Le)	1981	23	29	4	129	576	23.04	1	1	7
Bristowe, W.R. (OU)	—	5	8	1	42*	156	22.28	—	—	3
†Broad, B.C. (Nt)	1984	25	47	3	171	1786	40.59	2	14	15
Brown, A. (Sc)	—	1	1	0	57	57	57.00	—	1	1/2
†Brown, A.M. (D)	—	2	3	0	74	93	31.00	—	1	3
Brown, K.R. (M)	—	8	11	2	102	298	33.11	1	1	8
Brown, R.D. (Z)	—	5	8	0	27	113	14.12	—	—	1
Browne, D.W. (CU)	—	1	1	0	10	10	10.00	—	—	1
Bullen, C.K. (Sy)	—	3	4	0	19	53	13.25	—	—	2
Butchart, I.P. (Z)	—	6	8	1	82	134	19.14	—	1	1
†Butcher, A.R. (Sy)	1975	26	46	3	126	1407	32.72	2	5	12
Butcher, I.P. (Le)	1984	25	39	3	120	1192	33.11	1	8	20
Butcher, R.O. (M)	1979	26	38	6	120	1210	37.81	1	9	24
Capel, D.J. (Nh)	—	23	30	6	81	599	24.95	—	5	5
Carr, J.D. (M/OU)	—	11	16	1	115	474	31.60	2	2	6
Carrick, P. (Y)	1976	24	25	2	92	540	23.47	—	3	16
Chadwick, M.R. (La)	—	12	17	1	132	410	25.62	1	1	5
†Childs, J.H. (Ex)	—	6	4	1	6	17	5.66	—	—	1
Chivers, I.J. (H)	—	1	—	—	—	—	—	—	—	—
Clift, P.B. (Le)	1976	22	26	5	106	495	23.57	1	1	10
†Clinton, G.S. (Sy)	1980	18	32	6	123	1225	47.11	3	7	13
†Close, D.B. (DBC)	—	1	2	2	22*	42	—	—	—	2
Cobb, R.A. (Le)	—	16	23	4	78	601	31.63	—	4	11
Cohen, M.F. (Ire)	—	1	2	0	22	31	15.50	—	—	—
Connor, C.A. (H)	—	17	9	4	36	65	13.00	—	—	9
Cook, G. (Nh)	1975	24	38	4	126	1295	38.08	1	9	19
Cook, N.G.B. (Le)	1982	18	16	4	45	152	12.66	—	—	8
Coombs, R.V.J. (Sm)	—	4	3	0	1	1	0.33	—	—	—
†Cooper, K.E. (Nt)	1980	22	16	4	46	139	11.58	—	—	4
Corlett, S.C. (Ire)	—	1	1	0	12	12	12.00	—	—	—
Cotterell, T.A. (CU)	—	9	12	4	69*	289	36.12	—	1	1
Cowans, N.G. (Eng/M/MCC/DBC)	1984	23	17	4	22*	130	10.00	—	—	5
Cowdrey, C.S. (K)	1979	20	36	3	159	1079	32.69	2	4	20
Cowdrey, G.R. (K)	—	6	9	2	53	242	34.57	—	2	5
Cowley, N.G. (H)	1978	13	14	4	51	213	21.30	—	1	4
Crowe, M.D. (RW)	—	1	2	0	7	13	6.50	—	—	—
Curran, K.M. (Gs)	1985	26	34	3	83	762	24.58	—	5	8
Curtis, T.S. (Wo)	1984	26	45	2	126*	1365	31.74	1	12	11
Daniel, W.W. (M)	1977	22	15	5	19*	48	4.80	—	—	7
Davidson, I.C. (La)	—	1	2	0	13	13	6.50	—	—	2
Davidson, J.E. (CU)	—	4	4	2	22	25	12.50	—	—	2
Davies, Alec G. (Sy)	—	1	1	1	26*	26	—	—	—	3

	Cap	M	I	NO	HS	Runs	Avge	100	50	Ct/St
Davies, Andrew G. (CU)	—	9	13	2	43*	124	11.27	—	—	11/2
Davies, T. (Gm)	1985	26	25	8	75	503	29.58	—	2	44/5
†Davis, M.R. (Sm)	—	18	20	6	40*	315	22.50	—	—	8
Davison, B.F. (Gs)	1985	24	35	7	111	984	35.14	1	5	9
De Freitas, P.A.J. (Le)	—	9	12	3	30*	117	13.00	—	—	2
De Grandhomme, L.L. (Z)	—	5	6	1	59	157	31.40	—	1	2
Dennis, S.J. (Y)	1983	2	—	—	—	—	—	—	—	1
Denny, C.M. (OU)	—	4	6	1	19	28	5.60	—	—	3
Derrick, J. (Gm)	—	14	15	2	52	160	12.30	—	1	2
†Dilley, G.R. (K)	1980	17	19	5	31	153	10.92	—	—	1
D'Oliveira, D.B. (Wo)	1985	26	44	2	139	1244	29.61	2	7	21
Donald, W.A. (Sc)	—	1	2	1	19*	35	35.00	—	—	2
Doshi, D.R. (RW)	—	1	2	1	0*	0	0.00	—	—	—
Doughty, R.J. (Sy)	—	11	12	2	65	239	23.90	—	2	8
Downton, P.R. (Eng/M)	1981	22	29	7	104	856	38.90	1	7	57/5
†Dredge, C.H. (Sm)	1978	15	13	7	31	124	20.66	—	—	7
Duers, K.G. (Z)	—	3	2	0	1	1	0.50	—	—	—
Duthie, P.G. (Sc)	—	1	1	0	1	1	1.00	—	—	2
Dyer, R.I.H.B. (Wa)	—	26	46	3	109*	1242	28.88	2	8	19
East, D.E. (Ex)	1982	26	32	6	131	889	34.19	2	4	72/4
Edmonds, P.H. (Eng/M/MCC/DBC)	1974	23	23	6	29*	221	13.00	—	—	22
Elder, J.W.G. (Ire)	—	1	1	1	11*	11	—	—	—	1
Ellcock, R.M. (Wo)	—	1	1	0	3	3	3.00	—	—	—
Ellis, R.G.P. (Gs)	—	1	2	0	20	23	11.50	—	—	2
Ellison, C.C. (CU)	—	7	6	0	51	109	18.16	—	1	1
†Ellison, R.M. (Eng/K)	1983	18	26	6	98	539	26.95	—	3	4
Emburey, J.E. (Eng/M/MCC/DBC)	1977	25	25	4	68	581	27.66	—	4	22
Evans, K.P. (Nt)	—	3	3	0	13	24	8.00	—	—	1
†Fairbrother, N.H. (La)	1985	25	39	4	164*	1395	39.85	3	7	12
Fell, D.J. (CU)	—	9	16	1	109*	332	22.13	1	1	4
Fell, M.A. (D)	—	5	8	0	27	98	12.25	—	—	—
Feltham, M.A. (Sy)	—	1	2	0	27	35	17.50	—	—	—
†Felton, N.A. (Sm)	—	18	27	0	112	922	34.14	1	7	3
Ferguson, S.A.R. (Sm)	—	1	1	0	8	8	8.00	—	—	—
Ferreira, A.M. (Wa)	1983	25	38	10	101*	805	28.75	1	2	14
Ferris, G.J.F. (Le)	—	10	9	6	22*	29	9.66	—	—	—
Finney, R.J. (D)	1985	25	37	9	82	381	13.60	—	1	3
Fletcher, K.W.R. (Ex)	1963	23	28	7	78*	688	32.76	—	7	11
Fletcher, S.D. (Y)	—	14	10	7	15*	36	12.00	—	—	3
Folley, I. (La)	—	21	27	8	69	262	13.78	—	1	9
Foster, N.A. (Eng/Ex)	1983	15	14	2	63	196	16.33	—	1	9
†Fowler, G. (La/MCC)	1981	16	25	0	88	428	17.12	—	1	4
Fowler, W.P. (D)	—	10	14	1	79	266	20.46	—	2	3
Franks, J.G. (OU)	—	3	4	1	35	71	23.66	—	—	4/1
Fraser, A.R.C. (M)	—	2	1	0	1	1	1.00	—	—	—
Fraser-Darling, C.D. (Nt)	—	2	4	1	23*	33	11.00	—	—	4
French, B.N. (Nt/MCC)	1980	25	34	8	52*	439	16.88	—	1	65/7
Gard, T. (Sm)	1983	26	26	4	47	294	13.36	—	—	31/7
Garner, J. (Sm)	1979	15	11	3	22	92	11.50	—	—	4
Garnham, M.A. (Le)	—	23	26	4	100	542	24.63	1	1	53/7
Gatting, M.W. (Eng/M/DBC)	1977	23	34	5	160	1650	56.89	3	13	20

	Cap	M	I	NO	HS	Runs	Avge	100	50	Ct/St
†Gifford, N. (Wa)	1983	24	25	8	26	132	7.76	—	—	9
Gilbert, D.R. (A)	—	10	8	3	12	39	7.80	—	—	2
†Gladwin, C. (Ex)	1984	13	22	2	92*	500	25.00	—	2	4
Goldie, C.F.E. (H)	—	1	—	—	—	—	—	—	—	1/1
Gooch, G.A. (Eng/Ex/MCC)	1975	21	33	2	202	2208	71.22	7	9	25
Gorman, S.R. (CU)	—	9	15	5	43	177	17.70	—	—	3
†Gould, I.J. (Sx)	1981	24	25	8	101	616	36.23	1	4	35/4
†Gower, D.I. (Eng/Le/MCC)	1977	21	29	2	215	1477	54.70	6	3	10
Graveney, D.A. (Gs)	1976	24	25	11	53*	266	19.00	—	1	17
Gray, A.H. (Sy)	1985	19	10	1	20	48	5.33	—	—	3
Green, A.M. (Sx)	1985	25	43	4	133	1646	42.20	3	10	16
Greenidge, C.G. (H)	1972	19	32	2	204	1236	41.20	2	8	16
Greig, I.A. (Sx)	1981	15	16	4	43	264	22.00	—	—	13
Griffiths, B.J. (Nh)	1978	13	9	4	12	17	3.40	—	—	2
Grimes, A.D.H. (CU)	—	6	3	1	22*	43	21.50	—	—	1
†Hadlee, R.J. (Nt)	1978	19	29	11	73*	592	32.88	—	5	17
Hagan, D.A. (OU)	—	5	10	1	46	148	16.44	—	—	4
Halliday, M. (Ire)	—	1	1	—	47	47	47.00	—	—	1
Harden, R.J. (Sm)	—	12	17	5	107	366	30.50	1	1	9
Hardie, B.R. (Ex)	1974	26	45	7	162	1374	36.15	4	4	22
†Hardy, J.J.E. (H)	—	16	25	4	107*	742	35.33	1	3	4
Harper, R.A. (Nh/RW)	—	24	28	7	127	763	36.33	1	3	22
Harrison, D.S. (OU)	—	4	5	2	6	12	4.00	—	—	4/2
†Harrison, G.D. (Ire)	—	1	1	—	10	10	10.00	—	—	—
Hartley, P.J. (Y)	—	12	11	3	35	159	19.87	—	—	1
Hartley, S.N. (Y)	1981	17	20	2	108*	554	30.77	1	3	7
Hassan, B. (Nt)	1970	3	5	1	34	109	27.25	—	—	4
Hayes, K.A. (La)	—	5	7	0	117	310	44.28	1	2	3
Hayhurst, A.N. (La)	—	1	1	0	17	17	17.00	—	—	—
Hayward, R.E. (Sm)	—	9	12	3	100*	278	30.88	1	1	3
Hemmings, E.E. (Nt)	1980	21	22	5	56*	297	17.47	—	1	7
†Henderson, S.P. (Gm)	—	7	12	4	111	306	38.25	1	1	3
Henriksen, S. (La)	—	1	2	2	10*	10	—	—	—	1
Herbert, R. (MC)	—	1	1	0	43	43	43.00	—	—	1
Hick, G.A. (Z/Wo)	—	17	25	1	230	1265	52.70	4	3	12
Hilditch, A.M.J. (A)	—	17	27	0	119	829	30.70	1	4	7
Hill, A. (D)	1976	10	14	3	120	333	30.27	1	1	3
†Hinks, S.G. (K)	1985	26	48	3	117	1536	34.13	1	10	23
Hoffman, D.S. (Wa)	—	17	15	4	13*	39	3.54	—	—	3
Holding, M.A. (D)	1983	12	19	1	80	413	22.94	—	3	6
Holland, R.G. (A)	—	13	10	1	35	59	6.55	—	—	5
Holmes, G.C. (Gm)	1985	27	40	3	112	1129	30.51	2	7	10
Hopkins, J.A. (Gm)	1977	23	34	2	114*	794	24.81	1	4	8
Houghton, D.L. (Z)	—	6	8	1	104	231	33.00	1	—	3
Howarth, G.P. (Sy)	1974	2	4	1	53	58	19.33	—	1	—
Hughes, D.P. (La)	1970	10	16	2	75*	411	29.35	—	3	9
Hughes, S.P. (M)	1981	12	11	6	30*	94	18.80	—	—	6
Humpage, G.W. (Wa)	1976	25	42	6	159	1360	37.77	2	6	76/4
†Humphries, D.J. (Wo)	1978	1	1	1	62*	62	—	—	1	2
Hussain, M. (Wo)	—	1	1	0	4	4	4.00	—	—	—
Illingworth, R.K. (Wo)	—	20	20	8	39*	165	13.75	—	—	8
Imran Khan (Sx)	1978	14	21	8	117*	890	68.46	1	6	—

	Cap	M	I	NO	HS	Runs	Avge	100	50	Ct/St
Inchmore, J.D. (Wo)	1976	17	9	2	24	100	14.28	—	—	4
Jackson, P.B. (Ire)	—	1	1	0	28	28	28.00	—	—	—
†James, K.D. (H)	—	8	11	4	124	268	38.28	1	—	6
James, S.P. (Gm)	—	1	—	—	—	—	—	—	—	—
Jarvis, K.B.S. (K)	1977	19	18	5	7	41	3.15	—	—	5
Jarvis, M.P. (Z)	—	4	3	1	6	10	5.00	—	—	1
Jarvis, P.W. (Y)	—	14	16	2	28	151	10.78	—	—	6
Javed Miandad (Gm)	1980	20	29	6	200*	1441	62.65	4	8	13
†Jefferies, S.T. (La)	—	4	7	0	93	274	39.14	—	3	—
Jesty, T.E. (Sy)	1985	24	36	8	141*	1216	43.42	4	5	19
Johnson, G.W. (K)	1970	11	16	4	30*	237	19.75	—	—	5
Johnson, P. (Nt)	—	21	34	4	118	933	31.10	1	6	13
†Jones, A.L. (Gm)	1983	19	27	2	80	636	25.44	—	4	11
†Jones, A.N. (Sx)	—	12	9	5	26	83	20.75	—	—	1
Jones, A.P. (Sm)	—	3	4	2	1*	3	1.50	—	—	1
Joseph, R.F. (Nh)	—	2	1	1	26*	26	—	—	—	—
†Kallicharran, A.I. (Wa)	1972	21	35	2	152*	1052	31.87	2	6	6
Kapil Dev (Wo)	—	12	21	2	100	816	42.94	1	5	11
Ker, J.E. (Sc)	—	1	1	0	4	4	4.00	—	—	—
Kimber, S.J.S. (Wo)	—	2	1	1	14	14	—	—	—	1
Knott, A.P.E. (K)	1965	19	24	5	87*	379	19.94	—	2	53/1
Lamb, A.J. (Eng/Nh/MCC)	1978	19	26	4	122*	903	41.04	2	5	14
Lampitt, S.R. (Wo)	—	1	1	0	0	0	0.00	—	—	—
Lanchbury, R.J. (MC)	—	1	1	0	0	0	0.00	—	—	—
Larkins, W. (Nh/DBC)	1976	26	42	0	163	1549	36.88	3	4	19
Lawrence, D.V. (Gs)	1985	25	26	5	41	259	12.33	—	—	11
†Lawrence, M.P. (OU)	—	11	9	3	9*	20	3.33	—	—	2
Lawson, G.F. (A)	—	13	13	2	53	154	14.00	—	1	1
Lea, A.E. (Cu)	—	8	15	2	47*	298	22.92	—	—	3
Lenham, N.J. (Sx)	—	11	16	2	89	473	33.78	—	3	4
Le Roux, G.S. (Sx)	1981	18	16	4	61	421	35.08	—	2	1
Lethbridge, C. (Wa)	—	3	3	1	47	84	42.00	—	—	—
Lever, J.K. (Ex)	1970	23	23	9	24*	193	13.78	—	—	8
Lilley, A.W. (Ex)	—	16	26	2	68*	516	21.50	—	4	7
†Lloyd, C.H. (La)	1969	4	7	1	131	288	48.00	1	1	3
†Lloyd, T.A. (Wa)	1980	18	34	2	160	1230	38.43	2	8	5
†Lloyds, J.W. (Gs)	1985	25	33	6	101	818	30.29	1	5	25
†Lord, G.J. (Wa)	—	8	11	1	199	271	27.10	1	—	—
Love, J.D. (Y)	1980	21	28	5	106	937	40.73	1	6	8
Luckhurst, B.W. (K)	1963	1	2	1	9*	10	10.00	—	—	—
Lynch, M.A. (Sy)	1982	25	39	7	145	1714	53.56	7	6	36
McBrine, A. (Ire)	—	1	1	0	24	24	24.00	—	—	—
McDermott, C.J. (A)	—	16	14	3	53*	183	16.63	—	1	2
McEwan, K.S. (Ex)	1974	26	42	4	121	1293	34.02	3	6	17
McEwan, S.M. (Wo)	—	10	8	5	13*	25	8.33	—	—	1
McFarlane, L.L. (Gm)	—	13	6	2	8	12	3.00	—	—	4
MacLarnon, P.C. (OU)	—	7	10	1	56	168	18.66	—	1	3
McPate, W.A. (Sc)	—	1	1	0	14	14	14.00	—	—	—
Maher, B.J.M. (D)	—	14	18	6	46	150	12.50	—	—	19/2
Makinson, D.J. (La)	—	15	21	9	58*	372	31.00	—	1	2
Malcolm, D.E. (D)	—	1	1	0	0	0	0.00	—	—	—
Mallender, N.A. (Nh/DBC)	1984	24	25	8	52*	267	15.70	—	1	6
Malone, S.J. (Gm)	—	9	6	1	2	4	0.80	—	—	2

	Cap	M	I	NO	HS	Runs	Avge	100	50	Ct/St
Marks, V.J. (Sm)	1979	26	34	5	82	885	30.51	—	7	8
Marples, C. (D)	—	11	15	5	34	114	11.40	—	—	23/1
Marsh, S.A. (K)	—	3	4	1	31	59	19.66	—	—	9/3
Marshall, M.D. (H)	1981	22	33	2	66	768	24.77	—	5	10
Martindale, D.J.R. (Nt)	—	9	14	3	104*	317	28.81	1	1	6
Maru, R.J. (H)	—	23	19	9	62	227	22.70	—	1	15
†Matthews, G.R.J. (A)	—	10	12	3	51*	216	24.00	—	1	3
Mattocks, D.E. (MC)	—	1	1	1	1*	1	—	—	—	4
Maynard, C. (La)	—	19	27	5	43	266	12.09	—	—	42/8
Maynard, M.P. (Gm)	—	4	3	0	102	198	66.00	1	1	1
Medlycott, K.T. (Sy)	—	2	3	1	5	11	5.50	—	—	—
Mendis, G.D. (Sx)	1980	25	43	6	143*	1756	47.45	6	6	8
Merry, W.G. (MC)	—	1	—	—	—	—	—	—	—	—
Metcalfe, A.A. (Y)	—	6	12	0	109	257	21.41	1	1	1
Metson, C.P. (M)	—	8	9	3	14*	59	9.83	—	—	18
†Miller, A.J.T. (OU/M)	—	12	20	4	78	506	31.62	—	3	3
Miller, G. (D)	1976	21	31	5	105	744	28.61	1	4	27
Moir, D.G. (D)	1985	8	9	0	46	178	19.77	—	—	7
Monkhouse, G. (Sy)	1984	16	14	8	47	203	33.83	—	—	8
Monkhouse, S. (Wa)	—	1	2	1	5	7	7.00	—	—	—
Moores, P. (Sx)	—	1	—	—	—	—	—	—	—	1
†Morris, H. (Gm)	—	15	18	4	62	375	26.78	—	1	4
Morris, J.E. (D)	—	18	27	1	109*	722	27.76	1	3	5
Mortensen, O.H. (D)	—	13	15	7	16*	39	4.87	—	—	4
†Morton, W. (Wa)	—	2	1	0	3	3	3.00	—	—	3
Moxon, M.D. (Y/MCC/DBC)	1984	23	36	1	168	1447	41.34	4	6	11
Munton, T.A. (Wa)	—	1	—	—	—	—	—	—	—	—
Murphy, A.J. (La)	—	2	3	1	2*	3	1.50	—	—	—
Mushtaq Mohammad (RW)	—	1	2	0	16	25	12.50	—	—	1
Neale, P.A. (Wo)	1978	25	42	10	152*	1411	44.09	3	7	5
Needham, A. (Sy)	1985	25	37	5	138	1223	38.21	3	5	12
Newell, M. (Nt)	—	7	13	0	74	309	23.76	—	3	4
Newman, P.G. (D)	—	20	29	3	115	604	23.23	1	3	2
Newport, P.J. (Wo)	—	18	26	10	36	338	21.12	—	—	2
Nicholas, M.C.J. (H/MCC)	1982	26	41	5	146	1419	39.41	3	8	19
North, P.D. (Gm)	—	1	1	1	0*	0	—	—	—	—
O'Donnell, S.P. (A)	—	11	16	5	100*	448	40.72	1	—	5
†Old, C.M. (Wa)	1984	7	7	2	41	122	24.40	—	—	1
Oldham, S. (Y)	—	2	2	1	6	8	8.00	—	—	1
†Ollis, R.L. (Sm)	—	15	20	1	55	325	17.10	—	1	6
Ontong, R.C. (Gm)	1979	26	30	7	130	1121	48.73	2	8	12
Ormrod, J.A. (La)	1984	4	7	0	23	54	7.71	—	—	3
O'Shaughnessy, S.J. (La)	1985	13	23	2	63	275	13.09	—	1	10
Ottley, D.G. (MC)	—	1	1	0	47	47	47.00	—	—	—
Palmer, G.V. (Sm)	—	8	11	3	45*	164	20.50	—	—	2
Parker, P.W.G. (Sx)	1979	16	28	4	105	818	34.08	1	5	14
Parks, R.J. (H)	1982	25	24	9	53*	377	25.13	—	2	58/4
†Parsons, G.J. (Le)	1984	16	16	4	32	170	14.16	—	—	—
Patel, D.N. (Wo)	1979	26	42	3	88	1042	26.71	—	5	17
Patel, H.V. (Wo)	—	1	1	0	39	39	39.00	—	—	—
Patel, T. (OU)	—	9	17	4	47	159	12.23	—	—	5
Paterson, G.A. (Z)	—	6	9	0	92	320	35.55	—	2	—

	Cap	M	I	NO	HS	Runs	Avge	100	50	Ct/St
Patterson, B.P. (La)	—	16	15	5	22	38	3.80	—	—	4
Pauline, D.B. (Sy)	—	13	18	2	77	392	24.50	—	3	4
Payne, I.R. (Gs)	—	7	6	1	37	106	21.20	—	—	4
†Penn, C. (K)	—	8	7	2	50	102	20.40	—	1	9
Phillip, N. (Ex)	1978	4	7	0	50	129	18.42	—	1	3
Phillips, R.B. (A/RW)	—	8	9	2	39	180	25.71	—	—	14/2
†Phillips, W.B. (A)	—	14	22	3	128	899	47.31	1	6	20/1
†Pick, R.A. (Nt)	—	13	15	5	63	250	25.00	—	1	3
Pickles, C.S. (Y)	—	6	3	1	31*	52	26.00	—	—	3
Pierson, A.R.K. (Wa)	—	12	14	7	17*	90	12.85	—	—	3
Pigott, A.C.S. (Sx)	1982	9	3	2	10*	10	10.00	—	—	7
Plumb, S.G. (MC)	—	1	1	0	21	21	21.00	—	—	1
Pocock, P.I. (Sy)	1967	24	18	6	41	183	15.25	—	—	2
Pont, I.L. (Ex)	—	6	5	2	12	48	16.00	—	—	—
Pont, K.R. (Ex)	1976	10	15	3	62*	294	24.50	—	2	4
Popplewell, N.F.M. (Sm)	1983	18	30	2	172	1064	38.00	1	7	10
Potter, L. (K)	—	13	15	2	58	245	18.84	—	2	10
Price, D.G. (CU)	—	6	9	1	29	60	7.50	—	—	1
Price, M.R. (Gm)	—	14	11	4	36	136	19.42	—	—	2
Prichard, P.J. (Ex)	—	21	34	4	95	779	25.96	—	5	14
Pridgeon, A.P. (Wo)	1980	1	—	—	—	—	—	—	—	—
Pringle, D.R. (Ex)	1982	23	31	4	121*	654	24.22	1	1	18
Prior, J.A. (Ire)	—	1	2	1	19	33	33.00	—	—	2
Pycroft, A.J. (Z)	—	4	6	2	110*	245	61.25	1	—	2
Quinlan, J.D. (OU)	—	7	6	2	22*	34	8.50	—	—	1
Radford, N.V. (Wo)	1985	24	25	7	57*	306	17.00	—	1	4
Radley, C.T. (M/DBC)	1967	27	38	12	200	1375	52.88	3	8	12
Randall, D.W. (Nt)	1973	25	47	7	117	2151	53.77	5	14	24
Rea, M.P. (Ire)	—	1	2	0	39	44	22.00	—	—	—
Reeve, D.A. (Sx)	—	17	15	5	56	170	17.00	—	1	6
Rhodes, S.J. (Wo)	—	26	34	13	58*	538	25.61	—	1	54/3
Rice, C.E.B. (Nt)	1975	20	33	8	171*	1394	55.76	4	6	21
Richards, C.J. (Sy)	1978	22	27	12	75*	665	44.33	—	3	41/7
Richards, I.V.A. (Sm)	1974	19	24	0	322	1836	76.50	9	6	9
†Riddell, N.A. (MC)	—	1	1	0	23	23	23.00	—	—	2
Ripley, D. (Nh)	—	14	14	4	27	83	8.30	—	—	21/4
Ritchie, G.M. (A)	—	16	23	3	155	1097	54.85	4	4	7
Roberts, B. (D)	—	25	42	4	100*	1128	29.68	2	2	22
Roberts, M.L. (Gm)	—	1	1	0	0	0	0.00	—	—	—
Robinson, P.E. (Y)	—	13	16	1	79	450	30.00	—	3	2
Robinson, R.T. (Eng/Nt/MCC)	1983	18	31	4	175	1619	59.96	6	9	13
†Roebuck, P.G.P. (CU)	—	9	15	3	82	343	28.58	—	1	4
Roebuck, P.M. (Sm)	1978	22	33	5	132*	1255	44.82	2	7	10
Romaines, P.W. (Gs)	1983	20	34	4	114*	667	22.23	1	4	10
Roope, G.R.J. (MC)	—	1	1	0	61	61	61.00	—	1	3
†Rose, B.C. (Sm)	1975	5	9	1	81*	196	24.50	—	1	2
Rose, G.D. (M)	—	2	2	0	15	19	9.50	—	—	—
Russell, A.B. (Sc)	—	1	1	0	51	51	51.00	—	1	—
Russell, P.E. (D)	1975	3	3	2	3*	5	5.00	—	—	—
†Russell, R.C. (Gs)	1985	23	23	4	34	253	13.31	—	—	59/6
Rutnagur, R.S. (OU)	—	11	15	2	66	246	18.92	—	2	3
†Sadiq Mohammad (RW)	—	1	2	0	65	89	44.50	—	1	—
Sainsbury, G.E. (Gs)	—	6	5	3	8*	11	5.50	—	—	2

	Cap	M	I	NO	HS	Runs	Avge	100	50	Ct/St
Saxelby, K. (Nt)	1984	18	13	4	29*	78	8.66	—	—	1
Scothern, M. (Wo)	—	1	—	—	—	—	—	—	—	—
Scott, A.M.G. (CU)	—	9	7	4	5*	12	4.00	—	—	2
Scott, C.W. (Nt)	—	2	1	1	39*	39	—	—	—	5
†Shah, A.H. (Z)	—	4	6	1	40	95	19.00	—	—	1
Sharma, R. (D)	—	7	12	2	41*	209	20.90	—	—	6
Sharp, G. (Nh)	1973	11	13	1	25	111	9.25	—	—	16/3
†Sharp, K. (Y/DBC)	1982	20	34	4	96	750	25.00	—	3	15
Shaw, C. (Y)	—	17	13	5	12	57	7.12	—	—	5
Shepherd, J.N. (Gs)	1983	1	—	—	—	—	—	—	—	—
Siddiqi, S.N. (CU)	—	1	1	0	0	0	0.00	—	—	—
Sidebottom, A. (Eng/Y/MCC)	1980	11	11	3	55	196	24.50	—	1	2
Simmons, J. (La)	1971	21	30	4	101	485	18.65	1	2	18
Simpson, D.J. (Sc)	—	1	2	1	6	7	7.00	—	—	1
†Slack, W.N. (M)	1981	26	43	8	201*	1900	54.28	4	11	27
Small, G.C. (Wa)	1982	21	27	8	31*	285	15.00	—	—	7
Smith, C.L. (H)	1981	23	39	4	143*	2000	57.14	7	11	12
†Smith, D.M. (Wo)	1984	19	28	4	112	1113	46.37	3	7	11
Smith, I. (Gm)	—	6	5	0	12	27	5.40	—	—	1
Smith, K.D. (Wa)	1978	5	9	1	42	120	15.00	—	—	1
Smith, L.K. (Wo)	—	1	1	0	28	28	28.00	—	—	—
Smith, P.A. (Wa)	—	24	37	3	93	815	23.97	—	5	9
Smith, R.A. (H)	1985	26	44	8	140*	1533	42.58	3	7	14
Smith, T.S. (MC)	—	1	1	0	9	9	9.00	—	—	1
Snodgrass, D.L. (Sc)	—	1	1	0	12	12	12.00	—	—	1
Standing, D.K. (Sx)	—	1	2	0	7	10	5.00	—	—	—
Stanworth, J. (La)	—	6	10	2	50*	70	8.75	—	1	6/3
Steele, J.F. (Gm)	1984	11	12	3	100	283	31.44	1	—	11
Stephenson, F.D. (RW)	—	1	2	0	40	40	20.00	—	—	1
Stephenson, J.P. (Ex)	—	1	2	0	10	14	7.00	—	—	1
Stevenson, A. (Sc)	—	1	1	0	9	9	9.00	—	—	—
Stevenson, G.B. (Y)	1978	4	6	2	35*	99	24.75	—	—	1
Stewart, A.J. (Sy)	1985	23	36	4	158	1009	31.53	1	5	28/1
Stirling, D.A. (RW)	—	1	2	0	20	23	11.50	—	—	—
Storie, A.C. (Nh)	—	7	12	2	106	407	40.70	1	3	3
Stovold, A.W. (Gs)	1976	22	37	2	112	694	19.82	2	2	20
Streak, D.H. (Z)	—	3	3	1	29	72	36.00	—	—	1
Such, P.M. (Nt)	—	14	12	4	8	18	2.25	—	—	7
Swallow, I.G. (Y)	—	10	11	2	25*	101	11.22	—	—	4
Swan, R.G. (Sc)	—	1	1	0	2	2	2.00	—	—	—
Sykes, J.F. (M)	—	11	13	3	126	275	27.50	1	1	10
Tavaré, C.J. (K)	1978	23	40	6	150*	1225	36.02	3	4	20
Taylor, D.P. (OU)	—	4	6	2	5*	5	1.25	—	—	1/2
Taylor, L.B. (Eng/Le)	1981	20	18	9	20*	89	9.88	—	—	6
Taylor, N.R. (K)	1982	16	25	7	120*	843	46.83	3	3	6
Taylor, N.S. (Sy)	—	7	8	3	21*	57	11.40	—	—	1
Tedstone, G.A. (Wa)	—	1	1	0	22	22	22.00	—	—	1/1
Terry, V.P. (H)	1983	25	41	2	148*	1284	32.92	2	10	34
†Thomas, D.J. (Sy/MCC)	1982	12	12	3	25*	116	12.88	—	—	2
Thomas, J.G. (Gm)	—	16	16	2	60*	268	19.14	—	1	6
Thomson, J. (Sc)	—	1	1	1	0*	0	—	—	—	—
Thomson, J.R. (A)	—	11	11	6	28*	82	16.40	—	—	2
Thorne, D.A. (OU/Wa)	—	12	20	3	124	849	49.94	1	8	8

	Cap	M	I	NO	HS	Runs	Avge	100	50	Ct/St
Tomlins, K.P. (M)	1983	9	15	1	58	354	25.28	—	1	6
Toogood, G.J. (OU)	—	9	15	1	149	507	36.21	1	2	4
Tooley, C.D.M. (OU)	—	11	16	0	66	257	16.06	—	1	2
Topley, T.D. (Sy/Ex)	—	5	4	2	9*	15	7.50	—	—	2
Traicos, A.J. (Z)	—	6	5	2	27*	57	19.00	—	—	7
Tremlett, T.M. (H)	1983	24	29	14	102*	450	30.00	1	—	5
†Turner, D.R. (H)	1970	7	9	2	49*	202	28.85	—	—	2
Turner, M.S. (Sm)	—	10	12	6	24*	143	23.83	—	—	2
Turner, S. (Ex)	1970	5	7	0	35	78	11.14	—	—	—
†Turner, S.J. (Sm)	—	1	1	1	9*	9	—	—	—	2/2
Twizell, P.H. (Gs)	—	1	—	—	—	—	—	—	—	—
Underwood, D.L. (K/MCC)	1964	25	25	9	16*	124	7.75	—	—	7
Varey, D.W. (La)	—	22	34	3	112	960	30.96	1	2	5
Viswanath, G.R. (RW)	—	1	2	0	7	7	3.50	—	—	—
†Walker, A. (Nh)	—	12	14	8	18*	83	13.83	—	—	6
Wall, S. (Wa)	—	12	16	5	28	128	11.63	—	—	5
Waller, A.C. (Z)	—	2	3	1	56*	69	34.50	—	1	2
Waller, C.E. (Sx)	1976	16	9	3	8	37	6.16	—	—	2
Walsh, C.A. (Gs)	1985	21	18	6	37	189	15.75	—	—	4
Walton, K.G. (Z)	—	3	5	1	20*	57	14.25	—	—	2
Ward, D.M. (Sy)	—	6	10	3	143*	279	39.85	1	—	2
†Waring, I.C. (Sx)	—	1	—	—	—	—	—	—	—	—
Warke, S.J.S. (Ire)	—	1	2	1	144*	209	209.00	1	1	—
Warner, A.E. (D)	—	15	20	2	60	314	17.44	—	2	2
Waterman, P.A. (Sy)	—	6	2	1	1*	1	1.00	—	—	2
Waterton, S.N.V. (K)	—	4	2	2	16*	22	—	—	—	7/2
Watkinson, M. (La)	—	19	29	1	106	692	24.71	1	4	6
Watson, R.G. (La)	—	1	1	0	18	18	18.00	—	—	—
Wellham, D.M. (A)	—	10	16	4	125*	669	55.75	2	4	1
Wells, A.P. (Sx)	—	23	33	7	102	600	23.07	1	1	12
Wells, C.M. (Sx/MCC)	1982	26	37	6	100*	960	30.96	1	4	7
†Wessels, K.C. (A)	—	16	26	1	156	905	36.20	1	8	9
Weston, M.J. (Wo)	—	19	30	1	132	845	29.13	1	3	5
Wheeler, M.B.H. (Nh)	—	2	—	—	—	—	—	—	—	—
Whitaker, J.J. (Le)	—	25	34	3	109	1103	35.58	3	5	6
Whitticase, P. (Le)	—	3	5	1	55*	149	37.25	—	1	9
†Wild, D.J. (Nh)	—	18	22	4	80	525	29.16	—	2	4
Willey, P. (Eng/Le/MCC)	1984	23	32	4	147	1292	46.14	3	6	10
Williams, N.F. (M/MCC)	1984	22	21	4	67	378	22.23	—	1	3
Williams, R.G. (Nh)	1979	21	31	3	118	880	31.42	2	4	2
Wills, R.T. (Ire)	—	1	1	0	9	9	9.00	—	—	—
†Wood, G.M. (A)	—	16	25	3	172	691	31.40	2	—	6
Wright, A.J. (Gs)	—	9	16	3	47*	249	19.15	—	—	2
†Wright, J.G. (D)	1977	11	16	2	177*	797	56.92	2	4	6
Wyatt, J.G. (Sm)	—	17	26	0	145	816	31.38	2	2	7
Young, B.A. (RW)	—	1	2	0	14	14	7.00	—	—	—
†Younis Ahmed (Gm)	1985	22	30	8	177	1421	64.59	5	4	3
Zaheer Abbas (Gs)	1975	1	1	0	38	38	38.00	—	—	1

BOWLING

A key to the abbreviated categories of bowler will be found on page 72.

	Cat	O	M	R	W	Avge	Best	5 wI	10 wM
Abrahams, J. (La)	**OB**	31.2	10	99	4	24.75	3-46	—	—
Acfield, D.L. (Ex)	**OB**	588.4	130	1674	41	40.82	6-81	1	—
Afford, J.A. (Nt)	**SLA**	25	5	77	2	38.50	1-25	—	—
Agnew, J.P. (Eng/Le)	**RF**	445.4	89	1512	55	27.49	9-70	3	1
Allott, P.J.W. (Eng/La/MCC)	**RFM**	560.2	167	1328	58	22.89	6-71	3	—
Anderson, I.S. (D)	**OB**	3	1	9	0	—	—	—	—
Andrew, C.R. (CU)	**OB**	80.2	10	279	6	46.50	3-101	—	—
Andrew, S.J.W. (H)	**RMF**	284	53	992	30	33.06	6-43	1	—
Arnold, K.A. (MC)	**RFM**	34	8	108	5	21.60	5-57	1	—
Asif Din (Wa)	**LB**	5.2	2	7	1	7.00	1-2	—	—
Aslett, D.G. (K)	**LB**	17.1	1	78	1	78.00	1-44	—	—
Athey, C.W.J. (Gs/MCC)	**RM**	50.1	6	212	9	23.55	3-33	—	—
Atkinson, J.C.M. (Sm)	**RMF**	65	9	250	2	125.00	1-36	—	—
Bail, P.A.C. (Sm)		4	2	4	0	—	—	—	—
Bailey, R.J. (Nh/MCC)	**OB**	3	0	16	0	—	—	—	—
Bainbridge, P. (Gs)	**RM**	200	46	570	19	30.00	5-60	1	—
Balderstone, J.C. (Le)	**SLA**	15	3	68	1	68.00	1-1	—	—
Baptiste, E.A.E. (K)	**RFM**	562	116	1661	58	28.63	6-42	2	—
Barclay, J.R.T. (Sx)	**OB**	300.4	55	913	31	29.45	6-78	2	—
Barlow, G.D. (M)	**RM**	3	0	14	0	—	—	—	—
Barnett, K.J. (D)	**LB**	173.4	33	514	17	30.23	6-115	1	—
Barrett, B.J. (Wo)	**RFM**	18	7	40	1	40.00	1-40	—	—
Barwick, S.R. (Gm)	**RMF**	473.4	96	1376	36	38.22	7-43	1	—
Benjamin, W.K.R. (RW)	**RF**	21	5	61	3	20.33	2-31	—	—
Bennett, M.J. (A)	**SLA**	266.4	62	766	16	47.87	4-39	—	—
Benson, M.R. (K)	**OB**	20.2	0	138	1	138.00	1-4	—	—
Birch, J.D. (Nt)	**RM**	17	3	47	0	—	—	—	—
Boon, D.C. (A)	**RM**	6	0	33	0	—	—	—	—
Booth, P.A. (Y)	**SLA**	117.1	40	288	6	48.00	3-86	—	—
Booth, S.C. (Sm)	**SLA**	390.2	112	1138	28	40.64	4-88	—	—
Border, A.R. (A)	**SLA**	13	2	38	0	—	—	—	—
Botham, I.T. (Eng/Sm)	**RFM**	406.2	67	1376	44	31.27	5-109	1	—
Boycott, G. (Y)	**RM**	10	2	29	0	—	—	—	—
Boyd-Moss, R.J. (Nh)	**SLA**	125.4	30	380	10	38.00	3-48	—	—
Brandes, E.A. (Z)	**RFM**	47.4	3	190	3	63.33	2-46	—	—
Brettell, J.G. (OU)	**SLA**	62.4	14	266	4	66.50	2–87	—	—
Briers, N.E. (Le)	**RM**	88	18	303	8	37.87	4-29	—	—
Bristowe, W.R. (OU)	**OB**	1	0	5	0	—	—	—	—
Broad, B.C. (Nt)	**RM**	15.3	3	58	3	19.33	1-1	—	—
Brown, K.R. (M)		1	1	0	0	—	—	—	—
Bullen, C.K. (Sy)	**OB**	28	11	75	2	37.50	2-36	—	—
Butchart, I.P. (Z)	**RM**	167	42	547	20	27.35	5-65	1	—
Butcher, A.R. (Sy)	**SLA**	158	35	449	10	44.90	3-43	—	—
Butcher, I.P. (Le)	**RM**	2	1	5	0	—	—	—	—
Butcher, R.O. (M)	**RM**	19	5	46	2	23.00	1-13	—	—
Capel, D.J. (Nh)	**RM**	384.3	63	1299	41	31.68	7-62	1	—
Carr, J.D. (M/OU)	**OB**	249.1	65	616	17	36.23	6-61	1	—
Carrick, P. (Y)	**SLA**	712.3	184	1923	65	29.58	7-99	2	1

	Cat	O	M	R	W	Avge	Best	5 wI	10 wM
Chadwick, M.R. (La)	RM	5	0	20	0	—	—	—	—
Childs, J.H. (Ex)	SLA	197	64	528	5	105.60	2-129	—	—
Chivers, I.J. (H)	OB	22	5	72	1	72.00	1-5	—	—
Clift, P.B. (Le)	RM	595.3	169	1446	47	30.76	5-38	1	—
Clinton, G.S. (Sy)	RM	6	0	46	0	—	—	—	—
Close, D.B. (DBC)	OB	6	1	33	2	16.50	2-33	—	—
Connor, C.A. (H)	RFM	467.5	91	1467	35	41.91	4-62	—	—
Cook, G. (Nh)	SLA	1	0	6	0	—	—	—	—
Cook, N.G.B. (Le)	SLA	558.1	186	1332	30	44.40	4-59	—	—
Coombs, R.V.J. (Sm)	SLA	93	27	268	16	16.75	5-58	1	—
Cooper, K.E. (Nt)	RFM	604.3	187	1566	61	25.67	7-10	2	—
Corlett, S.C. (Ire)	RM	24.2	7	56	4	14.00	4-56	—	—
Cotterell, T.A. (CU)	SLA	232.4	54	742	11	67.45	3-53	—	—
Cowans, N.G. (Eng/M/MCC/DBC)	RF	474.2	85	1676	73	22.95	6-31	6	—
Cowdrey, C.S. (K)	RM	210.1	29	756	15	50.40	3-5	—	—
Cowley, N.G. (H)	OB	247.5	60	699	25	27.96	3-17	—	—
Crowe, M.D. (RW)	RMF	—							
Curran, K.M. (Gs)	RFM	469.5	104	1419	61	23.26	5-35	2	—
Daniel, W.W. (M)	RF	575.1	90	2111	79	26.72	7-62	2	—
Davidson, I.C. (La)	OB	10	3	24	2	12.00	2-24	—	—
Davidson, J.E. (CU)	RMF	80	12	254	4	63.50	3-22	—	—
Davis, M.R. (Sm)	LFM	366	60	1249	24	52.04	4-83	—	—
De Freitas, P.A.J. (Le)	RFM	234.2	43	703	27	26.03	5-39	1	—
De Grandhomme, L.L. (Z)	OB	46	9	148	4	37.00	3-79	—	—
Dennis, S.J. (Y)	LFM	33.2	4	86	3	28.66	2-37	—	—
Derrick, J. (Gm)	RM	226.1	39	706	14	50.42	4-60	—	—
Dilley, G.R. (K)	RF	350.2	71	1075	32	33.59	5-53	2	—
D'Oliveira, D.B. (Wo)	OB	16	1	55	1	55.00	1-1	—	—
Donald, W.A. (Sc)	RM	18	3	63	1	63.00	1-47	—	—
Doshi, D.R. (RW)	SLA	32	6	104	3	34.66	2-75	—	—
Doughty, R.J. (Sy)	RFM	223.5	36	867	34	25.50	6-33	1	—
Downton, P.R. (Eng/M)	OB	8	6	5	0	—	—	—	—
Dredge, C.H. (Sm)	RMF	317.4	73	929	25	37.16	5-95	1	—
Duers, K.G. (Z)	RFM	66	13	235	4	58.75	3-75	—	—
Duthie, P.G. (Sc)	RM	32	11	72	2	36.00	1-25	—	—
Edmonds, P.H. (Eng/M/MCC/DBC)	SLA	850.1	243	1942	76	25.55	6-87	2	—
Elder, J.W.G. (Ire)	RFM	15	5	27	2	13.50	2-27	—	—
Ellcock, R.M (Wo)	RF	28	0	91	0	—	—	—	—
Ellis, R.G.P. (Gs)	RM/OB	3	1	7	1	7.00	1-7	—	—
Ellison, C.C. (CU)	RMF	223.5	58	591	13	45.46	3-76	—	—
Ellison, R.M. (Eng/K)	RFM	432.1	113	1118	65	17.20	7-87	5	2
Emburey, J.E. (Eng/M/MCC/DBC)	OB	797.1	230	1737	59	29.44	6-35	2	—
Evans, K.P. (Nt)	RMF	30	8	69	1	69.00	1-26	—	—
Fairbrother, N.H. (La)	LM	26	7	75	1	75.00	1-3	—	—
Feltham, M.A. (Sy)	RM	11	1	74	0	—	—	—	—
Ferreira, A.M. (Wa)	RMF	673.3	129	2167	77	28.14	5-41	2	1
Ferris, G.J.F. (Le)	RF	231.3	32	826	15	55.06	3-84	—	—
Finney, R.J. (D)	LM	449.3	81	1453	53	27.41	7-61	4	—
Fletcher, K.W.R. (Ex)	LB	4	0	35	1	35.00	1-35	—	—

	Cat	O	M	R	W	Avge	Best	5 wI	10 wM
Fletcher, S.D. (Y)	RMF	345.5	48	1253	26	48.19	4-91	—	—
Folley, I. (La)	SLA	453.3	113	1286	41	31.36	6-8	1	—
Foster, N.A. (Eng/Ex)	RFM	436.5	87	1434	52	27.57	5-40	4	—
Fraser, A.R.C. (M)	RFM	43.5	10	119	8	14.87	4-48	—	—
Fraser-Darling C.D. (Nt)	RFM	19	3	88	0	—	—	—	—
Garner, J. (Sm)	RF	295.4	75	739	31	23.83	5-46	1	—
Gatting, M.W. (Eng/M/DBC)	RM	92.5	17	293	11	26.63	3-55	—	—
Gifford, N. (Wa)	SLA	611.5	188	1541	46	33.50	5-128	1	—
Gilbert, D.R. (A)	RFM	253.2	42	885	21	42.14	4-41	—	—
Gladwin, C (Ex)	RM	3	0	12	0	—	—	—	—
Gooch, G.A. (Eng/Ex/MCC)	RM	284.2	66	773	29	26.65	5-46	1	—
Gorman, S.R. (CU)	OB	117.4	17	465	3	155.00	1-27	—	—
Gould, I.J. (Sx)		4	0	75	0	—	—	—	—
Gower, D.I. (Eng/Le/MCC)	OB	2.1	0	16	0	—	—	—	—
Graveney, D.A. (Gs)	SLA	410.1	133	1013	41	24.70	4-91	—	—
Gray, A.H. (Sy)	RF	524	99	1816	79	22.98	8-40	6	1
Green, A.M. (Sx)	RM	53.3	10	153	3	51.00	2-20	—	—
Greenidge, C.G. (H)	RM	4	1	16	0	—	—	—	—
Greig, I.A. (Sx)	RMF	283	58	931	25	37.24	5-80	1	—
Griffiths, B.J. (Nh)	RFM	313.4	76	918	32	28.68	6-76	1	—
Grimes, A.D.H. (CU)	RM	130	28	480	9	53.33	3-99	—	—
Hadlee, R.J. (Nt)	RFM	473.5	136	1026	59	17.38	8-41	2	—
Hagan, D.A. (OU)	OB	1	0	6	0	—	—	—	—
Halliday, M. (Ire)	OB	27	10	64	4	16.00	4-64	—	—
Harden, R.J. (Sm)	LM	12.3	5	33	2	16.50	1-4	—	—
Hardie, B.R. (Ex)	RM	6	1	35	1	35.00	1-10	—	—
Harper, R.A. (Nh/RW)	OB	775.3	192	2107	58	36.32	5-94	1	—
Harrison, G.D. (Ire)	RFM	6	3	11	0	—	—	—	—
Hartley, P.J. (Y)	RMF	315.5	40	1175	31	37.90	5-75	2	—
Hartley, S.N. (Y)	RM	96.3	16	349	9	38.77	4-51	—	—
Hayhurst, A.N. (La)	RM	13	4	37	3	12.33	3-37	—	—
Hemmings, E.E. (Nt)	OB	716.3	171	2103	55	38.23	6-51	2	—
Henderson, S.P. (Gm)	RM	8	2	31	0	—	—	—	—
Henriksen, S. (La)	RFM	12	1	44	1	44.00	1-44	—	—
Herbert, R. (MC)	OB	36	5	90	3	30.00	3-76	—	—
Hick, G.A. (Z/Wo)	OB	146	27	501	8	62.62	2-34	—	—
Hilditch, A.M.J. (A)	RM	7	2	29	0	—	—	—	—
Hinks, S.G. (K)	RM	33	1	120	1	120.00	1-18	—	—
Hoffman, D.S. (Wa)	RMF	326.4	55	1160	29	40.00	4-100	—	—
Holding, M.A. (D)	RF	354.5	67	1124	50	22.48	6-65	3	1
Holland, R.G. (A)	LB	376	94	1017	29	35.06	5-51	2	—
Holmes, G.C. (Gm)	RM	347.3	86	1041	27	38.55	4-49	—	—
Hopkins, J.A. (Gm)		6	1	22	0	—	—	—	—
Hughes, D.P. (La)	SLA	21	12	26	1	26.00	1-26	—	—
Hughes, S.P. (M)	RFM	266.2	43	932	24	38.83	5-64	1	—
Illingworth, R.K. (Wo)	SLA	406.5	116	1046	37	28.27	7-50	2	1
Imran Khan (Sx)	RF	422.1	114	1040	51	20.39	5-49	2	—
Inchmore, J.D. (Wo)	RFM	338.5	71	844	33	25.57	4-42	—	—
James, K.D. (H)	LMF	177.4	43	635	15	42.33	6-22	1	—

	Cat	O	M	R	W	Avge	Best	5 wI	10 wM
Jarvis, K.B.S. (K)	RFM	530.4	115	1674	51	32.82	5-43	2	—
Jarvis, M.P. (Z)	LFM	110	13	392	10	39.20	3-37	—	—
Jarvis, P.W. (Y)	RFM	371.5	53	1330	44	30.22	7-105	3	—
Javed Miandad (Gm)	LB	27.3	2	120	3	40.00	2-67	—	—
Jefferies, S.T. (La)	LFM	116.1	13	379	12	31.58	4-64	—	—
Jesty, T.E. (Sy)	RM	144.2	28	517	14	36.92	2-32	—	—
Johnson, G.W. (K)	OB	156.3	24	501	11	45.54	5-78	1	—
Johnson, P. (Nt)	RM	26	4	152	1	152.00	1-112	—	—
Jones, A.L. (Gm)		1	0	24	0	—	—	—	—
Jones, A.N. (Sx)	RFM	246	37	848	20	42.40	5-39	1	—
Jones, A.P. (Sm)	RMF	37	4	142	3	47.33	1-9	—	—
Joseph, R.F. (Nh)	RFM	38	5	143	4	35.75	3-73	—	—
Kallicharran, A.I. (Wa)	OB	11.4	0	56	0	—	—	—	—
Kapil Dev (Wo)	RFM	304.5	83	805	37	21.75	4-56	—	—
Ker, J. E. (Sc)	RM	20	8	35	1	35.00	1-21	—	—
Kimber, S.J.S. (Wo)	RMF	20	2	72	3	24.00	3-40	—	—
Lamb, A.J. (Eng/Nh/MCC)	RM	4	1	17	0	—	—	—	—
Lampitt, S.R. (Wo)	RM	1	0	1	0	—	—	—	—
Lanchbury, R.J. (MC)	RM	2	0	6	0	—	—	—	—
Larkins, W. (Nh/DBC)	RM	83	16	284	1	284.00	1-34	—	—
Lawrence, D.V. (Gs)	RF	544.5	66	2093	85	24.62	7-48	5	—
Lawrence, M.P. (OU)	SLA	341.5	65	1154	20	57.70	3-99	—	—
Lawson, G.F. (A)	RF	347	61	1165	31	37.58	5-103	1	—
Lea, A.E. (CU)	LB	2	0	9	0	—	—	1	—
Le Roux, G.S. (Sx)	RFM	402.2	72	1132	40	28.30	6-46	2	—
Lethbridge, C. (Wa)	RMF	65	7	263	5	52.60	2-43	—	—
Lever, J.K. (Ex)	LFM	720.3	188	1995	77	25.90	6-47	6	—
Lilley, A.W. (Ex)	RM	29.4	0	184	3	61.33	3-116	—	—
Lloyd, T.A. (Wa)	RM	31	1	127	4	31.75	3-62	—	—
Lloyds, J.W. (Gs)	OB	180.1	42	575	21	27.38	5-37	1	—
Lord, G.J. (Wa)	SLA	5	0	19	0	—	—	—	—
Love, J.D. (Y)	RM	1	0	8	1	8.00	1-8	—	—
Lynch, M.A. (Sy)	RM/OB	6	1	46	0	—	—	—	—
McBrine, A. (Ire)	SLA	16	8	28	0	—	—	—	—
McDermott, C.J. (A)	RF	421.5	49	1609	51	31.54	8-141	3	—
McEwan, S.M. (Wo)	RFM	178	29	635	16	39.68	3-47	—	—
McFarlane, L.L. (Gm)	RFM	259	42	1008	16	63.00	4-100	—	—
MacLarnon, P.C. (OU)	RM	60.3	10	229	1	229.00	1-18	—	—
McPate, W.A. (Sc)	RFM	14	4	38	0	—	—	—	—
Makinson, D.J. (La)	LFM	366	68	1079	32	33.71	5-60	1	—
Malcolm, D.E. (D)	RF	17	2	82	3	27.33	3-82	—	—
Mallender, N.A. (Nh/DBC)	RFM	521.4	98	1533	49	31.28	5-83	1	—
Malone, S.J. (Gm)	RMF	174.1	23	654	13	50.30	5-38	1	—
Marks, V.J. (Sm)	OB	812.4	197	2421	72	33.62	8-17	4	2
Marshall, M.D. (H)	RF	688.1	193	1680	95	17.68	7-59	5	—
Martindale, D.J.R. (Nt)	OB	2	0	8	0	—	—	—	—
Maru, R.J. (H)	SLA	704.5	197	1923	73	26.34	5-16	3	—
Matthews, G.R.J. (A)	OB	159.4	34	521	12	43.41	3-76	—	—
Maynard, M.P. (Gm)	RM	0.1	0	4	0	—	—	—	—
Medlycott, K.T. (Sy)	SLA	24	12	39	1	39.00	1-17	—	—
Mendis, G.D. (Sx)	RM	4	0	65	1	65.00	1-65	—	—

	Cat	O	M	R	W	Avge	Best	5 wI	10 wM
Merry, W.G. (MC)	RMF	33	7	123	2	61.50	2-64	—	—
Metcalfe, A.A. (Y)	OB	3	0	4	0	—	—	—	—
Miller, G. (D)	OB	385.2	77	1204	28	43.00	6-110	1	—
Moir, D.G. (D)	SLA	186	48	517	12	43.08	3-102	—	—
Monkhouse, G. (Sy)	RMF	383.4	78	1068	40	26.70	5-61	1	—
Monkhouse, S. (Wa)	LFM	17	2	61	1	61.00	1-61	—	—
Morris. H. (Gm)	RM	3	0	32	0	—	—	—	—
Morris, J.E. (D)	RM	5.1	0	55	0	—	—	—	—
Mortensen, O.H. (D)	RFM	340	75	1026	33	31.09	5-87	1	—
Morton, W. (Wa)	SLA	46	7	159	2	79.50	2-98	—	—
Moxon, M.D. (Y/MCC/DBC)	RM	44	5	185	5	37.00	1-13	—	—
Munton, T.A. (Wa)	RFM	9	0	35	0	—	—	—	—
Murphy, A.J. (La)	RMF	56.2	15	207	6	34.50	3-84	—	—
Mushtaq Mohammad (RW)	LB	2	0	5	0	—	—	—	—
Needham, A. (Sy)	OB	351.4	76	1017	23	44.21	5-42	1	—
Newell, M. (Nt)	LB	12	2	62	1	62.00	1-38	—	—
Newman, P.G. (D)	RFM	400.5	76	1315	42	31.30	4-29	—	—
Newport, P.J. (Wo)	RFM	362.2	57	1214	46	26.39	5-18	3	—
Nicholas, M.C.J. (H/MCC)	RM	129	25	464	8	58.00	2-22	—	—
North, P.D. (Gm)	RM	27	7	60	1	60.00	1-60	—	—
O'Donnell, S.P. (A)	RMF	242.4	47	819	12	68.25	3-37	—	—
Old, C.M (Wa)	RFM	153.2	38	466	13	35.84	6-68	1	—
Oldham, S. (Y)	RFM	39	11	102	4	25.50	2-13	—	—
Ollis, R.L. (Sm)	RM	4	1	8	0	—	—	—	—
Ontong, R.C. (Gm)	OB	586.5	145	1777	64	27.76	8-67	4	1
O'Shaughnessy, S.J. (La)	RM	142	21	521	15	34.73	4-68	—	—
Ottley, D.G. (MC)		2	1	1	0	—	—	—	—
Palmer, G.V. (Sm)	RMF	167	19	683	7	97.57	2-53	—	—
Parker, P.W.G. (Sx)	RM	1	0	12	0	—	—	—	—
Parsons, G.J. (Le)	RMF	356.2	75	1010	23	43.91	6-11	1	—
Patel, D.N. (Wo)	OB	442	117	1244	34	36.58	3-33	—	—
Patterson, B.P. (La)	RFM	364.3	59	1144	41	27.90	7-49	3	1
Pauline, D.B. (Sy)	RM	161.4	32	567	16	35.43	5-52	1	—
Payne, I.R. (Gs)	RM	64	13	214	4	53.50	3-68	—	—
Penn, C. (K)	RFM	124.4	17	466	14	33.28	4-63	—	—
Phillip, N. (Ex)	RFM	75.3	14	242	6	40.33	4-55	—	—
Pick, R.A. (Nt)	RMF	290	52	1096	26	42.15	4-51	—	—
Pickles, C.S. (Y)	RM	126.3	30	385	6	64.16	2-31	—	—
Pierson, A.R.K. (Wa)	OB	155	30	587	8	73.37	3-92	—	—
Pigott, A.C.S. (Sx)	RFM	184.4	39	633	19	33.31	3-22	—	—
Plumb, S.G. (MC)	RM	10	1	31	0	—	—	—	—
Pocock, P.I. (Sy)	OB	576.2	131	1632	48	34.00	7-42	1	—
Pont, I.L. (Ex)	RFM	115.5	15	485	19	25.52	5-103	1	—
Pont, K.R. (Ex)	RM	115	24	398	9	44.22	2-43	—	—
Popplewell, N.F.M. (Sm)	RM	27.5	2	157	0	—	—	—	—
Potter, L. (K)	LM	258.3	67	772	21	36.76	4-87	—	—
Price, D.G. (CU)	OB	1	0	7	0	—	—	—	—
Price, M.R. (Gm)	SLA	258.4	63	697	17	41.00	4-97	—	—

	Cat	O	M	R	W	Avge	Best	5 wI	10 wM
Pridgeon, A.P. (Wo)	RM	9	2	14	1	14.00	1-14	—	—
Pringle, D.R. (Ex)	RMF	604.1	146	1556	53	29.35	6-42	1	—
Prior, J.A. (Ire)	RM	6	4	8	0	—	—	—	—
Quinlan, J.D. (OU)	RM	189	37	635	10	63.50	4-76	—	—
Radford, N.V. (Wo)	RFM	779.4	130	2493	101	24.68	6-45	4	—
Radley, C.T. (M/DBC)	LB	13	3	43	2	21.50	2-38	—	—
Randall, D.W. (Nt)	RM	28	2	174	5	34.80	3-103	—	—
Reeve, D.A. (Sx)	RM	475.5	107	1424	48	29.66	5-24	2	—
Rice, C.E.B. (Nt)	RMF	284	82	779	25	31.16	4-24	—	—
Richards, C.J. (Sy)	OB	27	2	120	4	30.00	2-42	—	—
Richards, I.V.A. (Sm)	OB	183	48	494	7	70.57	2-55	—	—
Ritchie, G.M. (A)	RM	6.3	0	33	1	33.00	1-22	—	—
Roberts, B. (D)	RM	20	1	106	0	—	—	—	—
Robinson, R.T. (Eng/Nt/MCC)	RM	1	0	8	0	—	—	—	—
Roebuck, P.M. (Sm)	OB	16	3	47	0	—	—	—	—
Romaines, P.W. (Gs)		10	0	42	3	14.00	3-42	—	—
Rose, B.C. (Sm)	LM	1	0	8	0	—	—	—	—
Rose, G.D. (M)	RM	45.1	8	142	9	15.77	6-41	1	—
Russell, P.E. (D)	RM/OB	89.5	22	243	4	60.75	2-34	—	—
Rutnagur, R.S. (OU)	RM	189	25	728	15	48.53	5-112	1	—
Sainsbury, G.E. (Gs)	LMF	178	59	481	27	17.81	7-38	2	—
Saxelby, K. (Nt)	RMF	429	103	1385	36	38.47	6-64	2	1
Scothern, M. (Wo)	RFM	16	6	42	1	42.00	1-42	—	—
Scott, A.M.G. (CU)	LM	243.3	34	879	25	35.16	5-68	1	—
Shah, A.H. (Z)	RM	28	7	106	0	—	—	—	—
Sharp, G. (Nh)	SLA	1	0	2	0	—	—	—	—
Sharp, K. (Y/DBC)	OB	35	11	89	1	89.00	1-15	—	—
Shaw, C. (Y)	RFM	417	95	1286	32	40.18	5-76	1	—
Shepherd, J.N. (Gs)	RM	14	3	41	0	—	—	—	—
Siddiqi, S.N. (CU)	RM	2	0	12	0	—	—	—	—
Sidebottom, A. (Eng/Y/MCC)	RMF	268.4	38	916	26	35.23	4-70	—	—
Simmons, J. (La)	OB	543.1	155	1427	37	38.56	4-55	—	—
Slack, W.N. (M)	RM	9	1	29	0	—	—	—	—
Small, G.C. (Wa)	RFM	592.3	114	1850	69	26.81	5-24	5	—
Smith, C.L. (H)	OB	66	6	297	4	74.25	1-16	—	—
Smith, I. (Gm)	RM	44.4	11	154	1	154.00	1-39	—	—
Smith, P.A. (Wa)	RFM	237.2	24	1143	26	43.96	4-25	—	—
Smith, R.A. (H)	LB	27.4	8	76	4	19.00	2-11	—	—
Smith, T.S. (MC)	SLA	61	26	137	7	19.57	5-79	1	—
Steele, J.F. (Gm)	SLA	215.1	60	581	11	52.81	3-6	—	—
Stephenson, F.D. (RW)	RFM	14	4	38	1	38.00	1-24	—	—
Stevenson, A. (Sc)	OB	46	12	109	4	27.25	4-66	—	—
Stevenson, G.B. (Y)	RMF	72.4	10	252	6	42.00	3-39	—	—
Stewart, A.J. (Sy)		6	0	43	0	—	—	—	—
Stirling, D.A. (RW)	RFM	19	5	60	3	20.00	2-39	—	—
Storie, A.C. (Nh)	RM	18	6	51	0	—	—	—	—
Streak, D.H. (Z)	RFM	20.3	4	69	3	23.00	2-27	—	—
Such, P.M. (Nt)	OB	405.1	105	1152	32	36.00	5-73	1	—
Swallow, I.G. (Y)	OB	225	46	670	12	55.83	4-53	—	—
Sykes, J.F. (M)	OB	191.5	42	575	13	44.23	3-58	—	—
Taylor, L.B. (Eng/Le)	RFM	566.5	141	1376	60	22.93	5-45	3	—

	Cat	O	M	R	W	Avge	Best	5 wI	10 wM
Taylor, N.R. (K)	**OB**	64	9	220	6	36.66	2-20	—	—
Taylor, N.S. (Sy)	**RFM**	149	22	579	18	32.16	7-44	1	—
Thomas, D.J. (Sy/MCC)	**LFM**	361.4	62	1186	32	37.06	5-51	1	—
Thomas, J.G. (Gm)	**RF**	340.3	51	1232	39	31.58	4-47	—	—
Thomson, J. (Sc)	**SLA**	56	12	143	3	47.66	3-89	—	—
Thomson, J.R. (A)	**RF**	241.3	33	988	29	34.06	6-44	2	—
Thorne, D.A. (OU/Wa)	**LM**	196.1	34	664	13	51.07	4-64	—	—
Tomlins, K.P. (M)	**RM**	2	0	9	0	—	—	—	—
Toogood, G.J. (OU)	**RMF**	209.2	44	691	18	38.38	8-52	1	1
Topley, T.D. (Sy/Ex)	**RMF**	161.1	37	464	17	27.29	4-57	—	—
Traicos, A.J. (Z)	**OB**	167.1	48	439	8	54.87	2-33	—	—
Tremlett, T.M. (H)	**RMF**	665.5	181	1620	75	21.60	5-42	2	—
Turner, M.S. (Sm)	**RFM**	185.5	30	648	13	49.84	4-74	—	—
Turner, S. (Ex)	**RMF**	121.5	25	321	11	29.18	4-36	—	—
Twizell, P.H. (Gs)	**RFM**	28	6	98	2	49.00	2-65	—	—
Underwood, D.L. (K/MCC)	**LM**	807	290	1802	67	26.89	6-56	1	1
Walker, A. (Nh)	**RFM**	251.4	51	786	23	34.17	4-38	—	—
Wall, S. (Wa)	**RMF**	301.1	44	973	28	34.75	4-59	—	—
Waller, C.E. (Sx)	**SLA**	381.5	117	882	20	44.10	7-61	1	—
Walsh, C.A. (Gs)	**RF**	560.3	124	1706	85	20.07	7-51	4	1
Warner, A.E. (D)	**RFM**	267.3	40	1013	24	42.20	5-51	1	—
Waterman, P.A. (Sy)	**RFM**	115	25	382	12	31.83	3-22	—	—
Watkinson, M. (La)	**RMF**	420.1	94	1228	39	31.48	5-109	1	—
Wells, C.M. (Sx/MCC)	**RM**	537.4	144	1457	38	38.34	4-76	—	—
Wessels, K.C. (A)	**RM/OB**	32	9	79	0	—	—	—	—
Weston, M.J. (Wo)	**RM**	273.5	72	777	19	40.89	3-37	—	—
Wheeler, M.B.H. (Nh)	**RMF**	34	3	117	1	117.00	1-87	—	—
Wild, D.J. (Nh)	**RM**	82.5	7	368	2	184.00	1-58	—	—
Willey, P. (Eng/Le/MCC)	**OB**	399.3	117	1017	36	28.25	6-43	3	—
Williams, N.F. (M/MCC)	**RFM**	490.2	69	1784	58	30.75	5-15	2	—
Williams, R.G. (Nh)	**OB**	312.2	75	979	24	40.79	5-34	1	—
Wright, J.G. (D)	**RM**	6	0	42	0	—	—	—	—
Wyatt, J.G. (Sm)	**RM**	10	0	59	1	59.00	1-40	—	—
Younis Ahmed (Gs)	**SLA**	74.4	22	178	2	89.00	1-38	—	—

FIRST-CLASS CAREER RECORDS

Compiled by Brian Heald and Geoffrey Saulez

The following career records are for all players who appeared in first-class cricket during the 1985 season. Some players who did not appear for their counties in 1985, but who are likely to do so in 1986, are also included.

BATTING AND FIELDING

'1000' denotes instances of 1000 or more runs in a season. Where such aggregates have been achieved outside the United Kingdom they are shown after a plus sign.

	M	*I*	*NO*	*HS*	*Runs*	*Avge*	*100*	*1000*	*Ct/St*
Abrahams, J.	216	333	44	201*	8225	28.46	10	3	142
Acfield, D.L.	401	398	202	42	1625	8.29	—	—	132
Afford, J.A.	6	1	0	2	2	2.00	—	—	3
Agnew, J.P.	98	95	18	56	733	9.51	—	—	26
Ahluwalia, M.S.	4	7	1	31	55	9.16	—	—	3
Alderman, T.M.	120	138	64	52*	647	8.74	—	—	108
Allott, P.J.W.	134	135	36	78	1436	14.50	—	—	40
Amiss, D.L.	607	1048	117	262*	40673	43.68	96	21+1	398
Anderson, I.S.	112	181	24	112	3870	24.64	2	1	94
Andrew, C.R.	17	33	2	101*	658	21.22	1	—	6
Andrew, S.J.W.	19	11	8	6*	21	7.00	—	—	6
Arnold, K.A.	1	—	—	—	—	—	—	—	1
Asif Din	71	112	13	102	2568	25.93	1	—	40
Aslett, D.G.	77	136	12	221*	4642	37.43	11	2	52
Athey, C.W.J.	213	358	32	170	10057	30.84	20	4	202/2
Atkinson, J.C.M.	6	5	1	79	167	41.75	—	—	—
Atkinson, S.R.	1	1	0	63	63	63.00	—	—	1
Bail, P.A.C.	5	9	2	78*	127	18.14	—	—	—
Bailey, R.J.	56	91	16	114	2709	36.12	5	2	26
Bainbridge, P.	148	255	43	151*	7169	33.81	11	5	72
Bairstow, D.L.	383	543	107	145	11466	26.29	7	3	815/129
Balderstone, J.C.	376	596	60	181*	18624	34.74	31	11	207
Banks, D.A.	19	29	3	100	691	26.57	1	—	8
Baptiste, E.A.E.	100	144	23	136*	3381	27.94	2	—	52
Barclay, J.R.T.	272	431	44	119	9641	24.91	9	4	215
Barlow, G.D.	246	398	58	177	12193	35.86	25	7	134
Barnett, K.J.	161	252	24	144	7759	34.03	15	3	96
Barrett, B.J.	1	—	—	—	—	—	—	—	—
Barwick, S.R.	69	63	28	29	339	9.68	—	—	18
Benjamin, W K.R.	1	2	1	15	15	15.00	—	—	—
Bennett, M.J.	44	53	14	59*	914	23.43	—	—	41
Benson, M.R.	107	185	18	162	6341	37.97	15	4	55
Bent, P.	1	1	0	14	14	14.00	—	—	—
Billington, D.J.	1	1	0	19	19	19.00	—	—	1
Birch, J.D.	182	275	45	125	6265	27.23	5	2	134
Blackett, M.	2	4	2	28*	41	20.50	—	—	—

	M	I	NO	HS	Runs	Avge	100	1000	Ct/St
Blakey, R.J.	14	22	2	90	518	25.90	—	—	12
Boon, D.C.	73	120	11	227	4548	41.72	12	—	55
Boon, T.J.	59	100	12	144	2383	27.07	4	1	19
Booth, PUAU	16	18	4	26	82	5.85	—	—	4
Booth, S.C.	33	34	15	42	202	10.63	—	—	33
Border, A.R.	159	267	41	200	11821	52.30	33	1+4	151
Botham, I.T.	269	414	31	228	13437	35.08	29	4	246
Boycott, G.	596	994	161	261*	47434	56.94	149	23+3	260
Boyd-Moss, R.J.	118	202	16	139	5658	30.41	11	2	51
Brandes, E.A.	3	4	1	19	30	10.00	—	—	—
Brassington, A.J.	127	155	46	35	881	8.08	—	—	215/48
Brettell, J.G.	5	4	2	0*	0	0.00	—	—	2
Briers, N.E.	188	294	30	201*	7248	27.45	10	3	74
Bristowe, W.R.	10	16	4	42*	260	21.66	—	—	5
Broad, B.C.	139	250	18	171	8288	35.72	11	5	65
Brown, A.	7	10	0	57	167	16.70	—	—	10/3
Brown, A.M.	2	3	0	74	93	31.00	—	—	3
Brown, K.R.	9	12	2	102	304	30.40	1	—	9
Brown, R.D.	47	89	5	200*	2081	24.77	4	—	47/10
Browne, D.W.	1	1	0	10	10	10.00	—	—	1
Bullen, C.K.	4	4	0	19	53	13.25	—	—	2
Burrows, D.A.	1	1	0	0	0	0.00	—	—	—
Butchart, I.P.	24	39	6	89	671	20.33	—	—	15
Butcher, A.R.	274	465	43	216*	14100	33.41	28	7	126
Butcher, I.P.	74	122	8	139	3752	32.91	9	2	61
Butcher, R.O.	202	316	31	197	9027	31.67	13	3	229/1
Capel, D.J.	72	106	21	109*	2419	28.45	1	—	33
Carr, J.D.	29	40	5	123	1009	28.82	4	—	20
Carrick, P.	287	358	66	131*	6366	21.80	3	—	148
Chadwick, M.R.	20	33	1	132	705	22.03	1	—	8
Childs, J.H.	171	155	73	34*	552	6.73	—	—	64
Chivers, I.J.	1	—	—	—	—	—	—	—	—
Clarke, S.T.	176	195	33	100*	2479	15.30	1	—	100
Clift, P.B.	280	398	86	106*	7301	23.40	2	—	139
Clinton, G.S.	168	284	35	192	8027	32.23	14	4	59
Close, D.B.	785	1223	173	198	34968	33.30	52	20	813/1
Cobb, R.A.	60	91	5	78	1936	22.51	—	—	37
Cohen, M.F.	3	4	0	22	31	7.75	—	—	1
Connor, C.A.	38	32	13	36	130	6.84	—	—	16
Cook, G.	366	644	47	172	18913	31.68	27	10	367/3
Cook, N.G.B.	172	174	51	75	1455	11.82	—	—	100
Coombs, R.V.J.	4	3	0	1	1	0.33	—	—	—
Cooper, K.E.	181	173	40	46	1252	9.41	—	—	58
Corlett, S.C.	31	43	7	60	546	15.16	—	—	24
Cotterell, T.A.	29	40	8	69*	617	19.28	—	—	6
Cowans, N.G.	101	98	16	66	660	8.04	—	—	39
Cowdrey, C.S.	189	281	41	159	7453	31.05	10	3	174
Cowdrey, G.R.	7	10	2	53	249	31.12	—	—	6
Cowley, N.G.	221	316	46	109*	5980	22.14	2	1	85
Crowe, M.D.	101	167	22	190	6603	45.53	20	1+1	112
Curran, K.M.	45	64	8	96	1363	24.33	—	—	14
Curtis, T.S.	86	149	16	129	4174	31.38	4	2	43

	M	*I*	*NO*	*HS*	*Runs*	*Avge*	*100*	*1000*	*Ct/St*
Daniel, W.W.	232	211	92	53*	1380	11.59	—	—	55
Davidson, I.C.	1	2	0	13	13	6.50	—	—	2
Davidson, J.E.	4	4	2	22	25	12.50	—	—	2
Davies, Alec G.	1	1	1	26*	26	—	—	—	3
Davies, Andrew G.	21	31	7	69	449	18.70	—	—	25/4
Davies, T.	76	93	23	75	1459	20.84	—	—	133/19
Davis, M.R.	60	63	19	60*	683	15.52	—	—	23
Davison, B.F.	456	745	78	189	26923	40.36	53	13+1	330
De Freitas, P.A.J.	9	12	3	30*	117	13.00	—	—	2
De Grandhomme, L.L.	15	23	7	60	428	26.75	—	—	12
Dennis, S.J.	49	51	20	53*	313	10.09	—	—	13
Denny, C.M.	4	6	1	19	28	5.60	—	—	3
Derrick, J.	29	35	12	69*	563	24.47	—	—	12
Dilley, G.R.	131	138	47	81	1358	14.92	—	—	54
D'Oliveira, D.B.	76	126	8	139	3105	26.31	3	1	53
Donald, W.A.	7	12	2	45	192	19.20	—	—	3
Doshi, D.R.	234	250	69	44	1407	7.77	—	—	62
Doughty, R.J.	25	31	9	65	453	20.59	—	—	10
Downton, P.R.	194	233	47	104	4149	22.30	1	—	424/56
Dredge, C.H.	174	197	65	56*	1873	14.18	—	—	77
Duers, K.G.	9	7	4	4*	10	3.33	—	—	2
Duthie, P.G.	2	3	0	34	65	21.66	—	—	2
Dyer, R.I.H.B.	60	106	9	109*	2752	28.37	3	2	34
East, D.E.	116	150	23	131	2703	21.28	2	—	297/24
Edmonds, P.H.	341	436	74	142	7028	19.41	3	—	313
Elder, J.W.G.	9	9	3	11*	36	6.00	—	—	7
Ellcock, R.M.	26	34	8	45*	340	13.07	—	—	4
Ellis, R.G.P.	40	73	3	105*	2020	28.85	2	—	21
Ellison, C.C.	18	19	6	51	214	16.46	—	—	6
Ellison, R.M.	83	111	30	108	2070	25.55	1	—	34
Emburey, J.E.	271	321	70	133	5284	21.05	2	—	242
Evans, K.P.	6	7	0	42	72	10.28	—	—	4
Fairbrother, N.H.	65	104	10	164*	3355	35.69	4	2	39
Falkner, N.J.	1	1	1	101*	101	—	1	—	—
Fell, D.J.	9	16	1	109*	332	22.13	1	—	4
Fell, M.A.	20	35	0	108	506	14.45	1	—	13
Feltham, M.A.	14	17	5	44	241	20.08	—	—	5
Felton, N.A.	47	75	2	173*	2143	29.35	3	—	13
Ferguson, S.A.R.	1	1	0	8	8	8.00	—	—	—
Ferreira, A.M.	186	287	56	112*	6202	26.84	3	—	92
Ferris, G.J.F.	30	31	16	26	113	7.53	—	—	3
Finney, R.J.	70	110	17	82	1677	18.03	—	—	13
Fletcher, K.W.R.	674	1090	158	228*	35701	38.30	62	20	597
Fletcher, S.D.	25	19	10	28*	85	9.44	—	—	3
Folley, I.	67	79	25	69	712	13.18	—	—	21
Foster, N.A.	70	77	22	63	1049	19.07	—	—	29
Fowler, G.	135	223	9	226	7703	35.99	21	4	63/5
Fowler, W.P.	65	107	14	116	2258	24.27	2	—	43
Franks, J.G.	16	24	3	42*	339	16.14	—	—	14/2
Fraser, A.R.C.	3	1	0	1	1	1.00	—	—	—
Fraser-Darling, C.D.	3	4	1	23*	33	11.00	—	—	5
French, B.N.	199	260	52	98	3805	18.29	—	—	455/50

	M	I	NO	HS	Runs	Avge	100	1000	Ct/St
Gard, T.	90	99	19	51*	1121	14.01	—	—	146/33
Garner, J.	174	187	48	104*	2375	17.08	1	—	108
Garnham, M.A.	75	104	18	100	2083	24.22	1	—	160/23
Gatting, M.W.	258	398	66	258	15512	46.72	36	7+1	237
Gifford, N.	641	740	234	89	6781	13.40	—	—	311
Gilbert, D.R.	30	29	21	38*	138	17.25	—	—	6
Gladwin, C.	49	82	5	162	2419	31.41	1	1	22
Goldie, C.F.E.,	23	24	3	77	302	14.38	—	—	35/9
Gooch, G.A.	313	526	45	227	21171	44.01	54	9+1	297
Gorman, S.R.	9	15	5	43	177	17.70	—	—	3
Gould, I.J.	207	270	42	128	5398	23.67	2	—	417/66
Gower, D.I.	268	422	38	215	15590	40.59	34	6	169
Graveney, D.A.	289	390	106	119	5353	18.84	2	—	151
Gray, A.H.	33	29	4	41*	292	11.68	—	—	10
Green, A.M.	89	156	9	133	4431	30.14	3	2	49
Greenidge, C.G.	406	695	59	273*	28461	44.75	65	14+1	414
Greig, I.A.	138	182	23	147*	4003	25.17	4	—	88
Griffiths, B.J.	167	132	48	16	272	3.23	—	—	34
Grimes, A.D.H.	13	14	3	22*	101	9.18	—	—	3
Hadlee, R.J.	262	368	68	210*	8737	29.12	9	1	154
Hagan, D.A.	5	10	1	46	148	16.44	—	—	4
Halliday, M.	11	10	4	47	122	20.33	—	—	5
Harden, R.J.	12	17	5	107	366	30.50	1	—	9
Hardie, B.R.	287	466	58	162	13953	34.19	18	10	263
Hardy, J.J.E.	29	45	10	107*	1255	35.85	1	—	13
Harper, R.A.	80	100	12	127	1966	22.34	1	—	87
Harrison, D.S.	5	7	2	8	21	4.20	—	—	5/2
Harrison, G.D.	3	4	1	86	149	49.66	—	—	—
Hartley, P.J.	15	15	4	35	190	17.27	—	—	2
Hartley, S.N.	109	164	23	114	3524	24.99	4	—	44
Hassan, B.	332	549	54	182*	14394	29.07	15	5	308/1
Hayes, K.A.	43	70	4	152	1578	23.90	2	—	15
Hayhurst, A.N.	1	1	0	17	17	17.00	—	—	—
Hayward, R.E.	42	66	13	102	1424	26.86	3	—	22
Hemmings, E.E.	343	458	100	127*	7145	19.95	1	—	157
Henderson, S.P.	70	116	17	209*	2611	26.37	4	—	46
Henriksen, S.	1	2	2	10*	10	—	—	—	1
Herbert, R.	7	10	1	43	105	12.77	—	—	6
Hick, G.A.	30	49	5	230	1926	43.77	4	1	28
Hilditch, A.M.J.	81	142	3	230	5270	37.91	8	—	61
Hill, A.	234	407	41	160*	10918	29.83	15	4	88
Hinks, S.G.	42	76	4	117	1986	27.58	1	1	29
Hoffman, D.S.	17	15	4	13*	39	3.54	—	—	3
Holding, M.A.	144	181	26	80	2367	15.27	—	—	59
Holland, R.G.	62	62	14	40	449	9.35	—	—	35
Holmes, G.C.	102	162	27	112	3564	26.40	3	2	40
Hopkins, J.A.	262	460	29	230	12099	28.07	17	7	181/1
Houghton, D.L.	48	86	5	104	2282	28.17	1	—	91/13
Howarth, G.P.	332	575	42	183	17126	32.13	32	4	226
Hughes, D.P.	354	463	84	153	8612	22.72	8	2	242
Hughes, S.P.	77	75	35	41*	368	9.20	—	—	22
Humpage, G.W.	248	409	51	254	13238	36.97	25	8	472/56
Humphries, D.J.	175	252	46	133*	5116	24.83	4	—	294/60

	M	I	NO	HS	Runs	Avge	100	1000	Ct/St
Hussain, M.	1	1	0	4	4	4.00	—	—	—
Illingworth, R.K.	77	91	25	55	975	14.77	—	—	30
Imran Khan	310	483	79	170	14464	35.80	23	4	97
Inchmore, J.D.	209	238	51	113	3082	16.48	1	—	69
Jackson, P.B.	5	6	1	46	134	26.80	—	—	11/1
James, K.D.	29	33	10	124	605	26.30	1	—	9
James, S.P.	1	—	—	—	—	—	—	—	—
Jarvis, K.B.S.	224	168	70	19	316	3.22	—	—	55
Jarvis, M.P.	10	11	3	8	39	4.87	—	—	2
Jarvis, P.W.	35	38	11	37	337	12.48	—	—	13
Javed Miandad	314	505	82	311	22534	53.27	63	5+8	291/3
Jefferies, S.T.	83	112	19	93	2491	26.78	—	—	25
Jesty, T.E.	390	620	83	248	17186	32.00	31	8	232/1
Johnson, G.W.	390	605	78	168	12922	24.51	11	3	316
Johnson, P.	51	83	8	133	2282	30.42	4	—	29/1
Jones, A.L.	147	257	20	132	6119	25.81	5	2	97
Jones, A.N.	38	36	17	35	229	12.05	—	—	5
Jones, A.P.	3	4	2	1*	3	1.50	—	—	1
Joseph, R.F.	26	36	21	26*	128	8.53	—	—	4
Kallicharran, A.I.	448	739	77	243*	29771	44.97	78	11+1	286
Kapil Dev	173	250	26	193	6933	30.95	9	—	119
Ker, J.E.	9	13	5	50	151	18.87	—	—	3
Kimber, S.J.S.	2	1	1	14*	14	—	—	—	1
Knott, A.P.E.	511	745	134	156	18105	29.63	17	2	1211/133
Lamb, A.J.	246	414	70	178	16402	47.68	41	6	184
Lampitt, S.R.	1	1	0	0	0	0.00	—	—	—
Lanchbury, R.J.	14	23	3	50*	357	17.85	—	—	2
Larkins, W.	287	494	27	252	16214	34.71	37	8	148
Lawrence, D.V.	54	60	13	41	416	8.85	—	—	14
Lawrence, M.P.	24	25	8	18	89	5.23	—	—	7
Lawson, G.F.	104	132	29	57	1459	14.16	—	—	44
Lea, A.E.	17	33	2	119	693	22.35	1	—	5
Lenham, N.J.	12	17	2	89	504	33.60	—	—	5
Le Roux, G.S.	182	218	61	83	3932	25.04	—	—	62
Lethbridge, C.	50	58	13	87*	1033	22.95	—	—	16
Lever, J.K.	469	482	183	91	3310	11.07	—	—	177
Lilley, A.W.	47	74	4	100*	1691	24.15	1	—	23
Lloyd, C.H.	483	722	95	242*	30885	49.25	78	10+4	377
Lloyd, T.A.	165	294	32	208*	9652	36.83	17	5	92
Lloyds, J.W.	126	196	27	132*	4868	28.80	6	—	110
Lord, G.J.	15	20	1	199	445	23.42	1	—	4
Love, J.D.	179	287	43	170*	7806	31.99	12	2	93
Luckhurst, B.W.	389	662	77	215	22303	38.12	48	14	391
Lynch, M.A.	165	278	32	145	8603	34.97	21	4	136
McBrine, A.	1	1	0	24	24	24.00	—	—	—
McDermott, C.J.	32	35	7	53*	482	17.21	—	—	7
McEwan, K.S.	382	631	56	218	23135	40.23	61	12	335/7
McEwan, S.M.	10	8	5	13*	25	8.33	—	—	1
McFarlane, L.L.	56	42	20	15*	127	5.77	—	—	13

	M	I	NO	HS	Runs	Avge	100	1000	Ct/St
Mackintosh, K.S.	33	33	17	31	303	18.93	—	—	14
MacLarnon, P.C.	7	10	1	56	168	18.66	—	—	3
McPate, W.A.	3	4	2	14	31	15.50	—	—	—
Maher, B.J.M.	41	55	16	66	501	12.84	—	—	68/7
Makinson, D.J.	19	26	11	58*	390	26.00	—	—	2
Malcolm, D.E.	8	9	1	23	40	5.00	—	—	4
Mallender, N.A.	128	146	43	88	1360	13.20	—	—	48
Malone, S.J.	57	46	15	23	182	5.87	—	—	13
Marks, V.J.	241	360	56	134	8816	29.00	4	1	103
Marples, C.	11	15	5	34	114	11.40	—	—	23/1
Marsh, S.A.	11	14	3	48	180	16.36	—	—	26/3
Marshall, M.D.	197	253	28	116*	5075	22.55	4	—	79
Martindale, D.J.R.	9	14	3	104*	317	28.81	1	—	6
Maru, R.J.	56	55	16	62	620	15.89	—	—	51
Matthews, G.R.J.	44	64	14	103	1820	36.40	1	—	24
Mattocks, D.E.	1	1	1	1*	1	—	—	—	4
Maynard, C.	98	124	22	85	1879	18.42	—	—	157/25
Maynard, M.P.	4	3	0	102	198	66.00	1	—	1
Medlycott, K.T.	8	9	6	117*	139	46.33	1	—	—
Mendis, G.D.	206	363	33	209*	11621	35.21	23	6	91/1
Merry, W.G.	28	17	11	14*	42	7.00	—	—	6
Metcalfe, A.A.	16	27	0	122	602	22.29	2	—	7
Metson, C.P.	21	27	9	96	397	22.05	—	—	47/2
Middleton, T.C.	1	2	0	10	15	7.50	—	—	—
Miller, A.J.T.	36	63	8	128*	1781	32.38	2	1	6
Miller, G.	297	442	72	130	10188	27.53	2	—	231
Moir, D.G.	72	86	11	107	1168	15.57	1	—	64
Monkhouse, G.	65	74	29	100*	996	22.13	1	—	29
Monkhouse, S.	1	2	1	5	7	7.00	—	—	—
Moores, P.	12	15	3	45	215	17.91	—	—	19/6
Morris, H.	40	60	14	114*	1379	29.98	1	—	14
Morris, J.E.	44	77	3	135	2049	27.68	4	—	13
Mortensen, O.H.	39	46	26	40*	178	8.90	—	—	13
Morton, W.	12	11	2	13*	50	5.55	—	—	9
Moxon, M.D.	79	136	5	168	4813	36.74	11	2	50
Munton, T.A.	1	—	—	—	—	—	—	—	—
Murphy, A.J.	2	3	1	2*	3	1.50	—	—	—
Mushtaq Mohammad	502	843	104	303*	31091	42.07	72	12+3	347
Neale, P.A.	223	383	51	163*	11925	35.91	19	7	85
Needham, A.	80	115	15	138	2364	23.64	4	1	36
Newell, M.	11	20	1	76	418	22.00	—	—	10
Newman, P.G.	83	98	16	115	1253	15.28	1	—	18
Newport, P.J.	35	46	17	41*	635	21.89	—	—	5
Nicholas, M.C.J.	148	253	30	206*	7561	33.90	16	4	97
North, P.D.	1	1	1	0*	0	—	—	—	—
O'Donnell, S.P.	18	25	6	130	976	51.36	3	—	6
Old, C.M.	378	462	91	116	7756	20.30	6	—	214
Oldham, S.	129	98	41	50	648	11.36	—	—	38
Ollis, R.L.	37	60	4	99*	1016	18.14	—	—	19
Ontong, R.C.	273	455	54	204*	11896	29.66	18	5	132
Ormrod, J.A.	500	846	95	204*	23205	30.89	32	13	399
O'Shaughnessy, S.J.	81	131	20	159*	3001	27.03	5	1	32

	M	I	NO	HS	Runs	Avge	100	1000	Ct/St
Ottley, D.G.	8	10	1	47	156	17.33	—	—	3
Palmer, G.V.	35	46	7	78	615	15.76	—	—	25
Parker, P.W.G.	220	371	52	215	11069	34.69	25	6	146
Parks, R.J.	132	147	36	89	1922	17.31	—	—	309/39
Parsons, G.J.	132	167	38	76	2441	18.92	—	—	40
Patel, D.N.	214	337	22	197	8905	28.26	14	5	129
Patel, H.V.	1	1	0	39	39	39.00	—	—	—
Patel, T.	9	17	4	47	159	12.23	—	—	5
Paterson, G.A.	18	31	1	92	655	21.83	—	—	2
Patterson, B.P.	29	29	7	22	81	3.68	—	—	6
Pauline, D.B.	49	76	6	115	1803	25.75	1	—	18
Payne, I.R.	36	43	6	43	444	12.00	—	—	34
Penn, C.	29	31	8	115	497	21.60	1	—	22
Phillip, N.	230	334	37	134	7013	23.61	1	—	75
Phillips, R.B.	77	114	25	111*	2605	29.26	1	—	230/14
Phillips, W.B.	66	118	10	260	4378	40.53	9	0+1	87/3
Pick, R.A.	31	33	12	63	430	20.47	—	—	6
Pickles, C.S.	6	3	1	31*	52	26.00	—	—	3
Pierson, A.R.K.	12	14	7	17*	90	12.85	—	—	3
Pigott, A.C.S.	98	106	23	63	1238	14.91	—	—	42
Plumb, S.G.	4	6	1	37*	118	23.60	—	—	2
Pocock, P.I.	533	565	147	75*	4774	11.42	—	—	179
Pont, I.L.	10	12	3	16	80	8.88	—	—	1
Pont, K.R.	191	292	43	125*	6416	25.76	7	—	91
Popplewell, N.F.M.	143	214	27	172	5070	27.11	4	2	110
Potter, L.	54	90	8	165*	2413	29.42	4	—	32
Price, D.G.	13	20	1	49	299	15.73	—	—	4
Price, M.R.	17	13	4	36	144	16.00	—	—	2
Prichard, P.J.	41	63	6	100	1667	29.24	1	—	24
Pridgeon, A.P.	188	195	75	67	1032	9.38	—	—	62
Pringle, D.R.	137	199	39	127*	4619	28.86	7	—	76
Prior, J.A.	5	8	1	87	219	31.28	—	—	3
Pycroft, A.J.	49	89	11	133	3102	39.76	4	—	38
Quinlan, J.D.	7	6	2	22*	34	8.50	—	—	1
Radford, N.V.	98	110	27	76*	1507	18.15	—	—	40
Radley, C.T.	525	834	125	200	25276	35.65	44	16	497
Randall, D.W.	349	596	55	209	20599	38.07	37	10	255
Rea, M.P.	1	2	0	39	4	22.00	—	—	—
Reeve, D.A.	55	57	14	119	848	19.72	1	—	27
Rhodes, S.J.	29	36	14	58*	579	26.31	—	—	57/3
Rice, C.E.B.	377	607	94	246	21122	41.17	40	11	301
Richards, C.J.	212	269	66	117*	5029	24.77	3	—	404/57
Richards, I.V.A.	359	572	38	322	26841	50.26	86	11+3	329/1
Riddell, N.A.	2	3	0	23	57	19.00	—	—	2
Ripley, D.	28	35	7	61*	364	13.00	—	—	47/16
Ritchie, G.M.	79	125	11	196	5144	45.12	13	1+1	56
Roberts, B.	60	100	11	100*	2652	29.79	2	1	51
Roberts, M.L.	1	1	0	0	0	0.00	—	—	—
Robinson, P.E.	28	40	6	92	1206	35.47	—	—	9
Robinson, R.T.	138	238	31	207	8597	41.53	18	3	69
Roebuck, P.G.P.	20	34	8	82	711	27.34	—	—	7

	M	I	NO	HS	Runs	Avge	100	1000	Ct/St
Roebuck, P.M.	228	375	54	159	11245	35.03	15	5	110
Rolls, L.M.	1	—	—	—	—	—	—	—	—
Romaines, P.W.	95	172	12	186	4924	30.77	10	2	38
Roope, G.R.J.	402	645	129	171	19098	37.01	26	8	602/2
Rose, B.C.	253	421	45	205	12392	32.95	23	8	120
Rose, G.D.	2	2	0	15	19	9.50	—	—	—
Russell, A.B.	1	1	0	51	51	51.00	—	—	—
Russell, P.E.	170	210	46	72	2020	12.31	—	—	124
Russell, R.C.	73	89	21	64*	1355	19.92	—	—	142/35
Rutnagur, R.S.	11	15	2	66	246	18.92	—	—	3
Sadiq Mohammad	386	682	40	203	24046	37.45	50	7+3	326
Sainsbury, G.E.	54	50	28	13	123	5.59	—	—	11
Saxelby, K.	81	84	23	59*	749	12.27	—	—	11
Scothern, M.	1	—	—	—	—	—	—	—	—
Scott, A.M.G.	9	7	4	5*	12	4.00	—	—	2
Scott, C.W.	9	9	3	78	190	31.66	—	—	18/2
Shah, A.H.	12	21	1	105	452	22.60	1	—	5
Sharma, R.	7	12	2	41*	209	20.90	—	—	6
Sharp, G.	306	396	81	98	6254	19.85	—	—	565/90
Sharp, K.	146	245	19	173	6995	30.96	11	1	72
Shaw, C.	20	18	7	17	89	8.09	—	—	5
Shepherd, J.N.	422	611	106	170	13353	26.44	10	2	290
Siddiqi, S.N.	7	13	0	52	219	16.84	—	—	1
Sidebottom, A.	158	178	43	124	3183	23.57	1	—	38
Simmons, J.	386	484	121	112	8438	23.24	6	—	302
Simpson, D.J.	2	4	1	9	19	6.33	—	—	1
Slack, W.N.	155	262	31	248*	9113	39.45	16	5	123
Small, G.C.	113	139	34	57*	1372	13.06	—	—	32
Smith, C.L.	138	244	25	193	8924	40.74	25	4	81
Smith, D.M.	177	274	57	189*	7426	34.22	13	3	119
Smith, I.	6	5	0	12	27	5.40	—	—	1
Smith, K.D.	197	346	29	140	8734	27.55	9	4	70
Smith, L.K.	1	1	0	28	28	28.00	—	—	—
Smith, P.A.	70	111	11	114	2696	26.96	1	1	27
Smith, R.A.	71	123	19	140*	3871	37.22	8	1	33
Smith, T.S.	1	1	0	9	9	9.00	—	—	1
Snodgrass, D.L.	2	2	0	12	18	9.00	—	—	3
Standing, D.K.	7	12	4	60	262	32.75	—	—	3
Stanworth, J.	19	26	7	50*	178	9.36	—	—	24/4
Steele, J.F.	367	588	80	195	14772	29.07	21	6	404
Stephenson, F.D.	30	45	4	165	918	22.39	1	—	19
Stephenson, J.P.	1	2	0	10	14	7.00	—	—	1
Stevenson, A.W.J.	1	1	0	9	9	9.00	—	—	—
Stevenson, G.B.	185	226	33	115*	3905	20.23	2	—	73
Stewart, A.J.	50	78	11	158	2139	31.92	2	1	65/2
Stirling, D.A.	39	53	17	47	635	17.63	—	—	7
Storie, A.C.	7	12	2	106	407	40.70	1	—	3
Stovold, A.W.	271	487	26	212*	13986	30.33	17	6	258/45
Streak, D.H.	13	17	5	29	225	18.75	—	—	5
Such, P.M.	47	46	17	16	63	2.17	—	—	26
Swallow, I.G.	23	23	7	34*	256	16.00	—	—	14
Swan, R.G.	6	11	1	66	205	20.50	—	—	3
Sykes, J.F.	12	14	3	126	279	25.36	1	—	10

	M	I	NO	HS	Runs	Avge	100	1000	Ct/St
Tavaré, C.J.	254	432	46	168*	14685	32.04	28	9	248
Taylor, D.P.	4	6	2	5*	5	1.25	—	—	1/12
Taylor, J.P.	3	2	0	11	11	5.50	—	—	2
Taylor, L.B.	158	135	60	47	762	10.16	—	—	39
Taylor, N.R.	106	184	28	155*	5458	34.98	14	3	60
Taylor, N.S.	18	15	5	21*	73	7.30	—	—	5
Tedstone, G.A.	18	23	6	67*	310	18.23	—	—	29/7
Terry, V.P.	82	135	16	175*	4234	35.57	11	3	77
Thomas, D.J.	121	160	32	119	2502	19.54	2	—	43
Thomas, J.G.	73	91	13	84	1177	15.08	—	—	32
Thomson, J.	3	3	2	1*	1	1.00	—	—	2
Thomson, J.R.	175	207	60	61	1960	13.33	—	—	60
Thorne, D.A.	26	43	9	124	1217	35.79	1	—	18
Tomlins, K.P.	84	123	14	146	2883	26.44	4	—	63
Toogood, G.J.	31	54	6	149	1372	28.58	2	—	11
Tooley, C.D.M.	11	16	0	66	257	16.06	—	—	2
Topley, T.D.	5	4	2	9*	15	7.50	—	—	2
Traicos, A.J.	89	124	55	43	945	13.69	—	—	75
Trembath, C.R.	4	4	3	17*	33	33.00	—	—	1
Tremlett, T.M.	135	181	39	102*	2988	21.04	1	—	57
Turner, D.R.	359	590	55	181*	15637	29.22	24	7	174
Turner, M.S.	11	14	6	24*	144	18.00	—	—	2
Turner, S.	359	509	100	121	9339	22.83	4	—	217
Turner, S.J.	6	7	4	27*	84	28.00	—	—	14/5
Twizell, P.H.	1	—	—	—	—	—	—	—	—
Underwood, D.L.	629	664	186	111	4754	9.94	1	—	256
Varey, D.W.	52	90	9	156*	2166	26.74	2	—	19
Viswanath, G.R.	293	464	43	247	17230	40.92	43	0+5	219
Walker, A.	31	33	15	19	165	9.16	—	—	13
Wall, S.	19	25	9	28	175	10.93	—	—	6
Waller, A.C.	4	7	2	75	204	40.80	—	—	2
Waller, C.E.	227	266	111	51*	1481	9.55	—	—	133
Walsh, C.A.	63	72	21	37	539	10.56	—	—	15
Walton, K.G.	8	15	1	37	207	14.78	—	—	7
Ward, D.M.	6	10	3	143	279	39.85	1	—	2
Waring, I.C.	1	—	—	—	—	—	—	—	—
Warke, S.J.S.	4	6	1	144*	375	75.00	1	—	3
Warner, A.E.	43	59	11	67	794	16.54	—	—	12
Waterman, P.A.	11	6	3	6*	7	2.33	—	—	4
Waterton, S.N.V.	25	28	5	50	386	16.78	—	—	43/10
Watkinson, M.	52	78	11	106	1528	22.80	1	—	15
Watson, R.G.	2	3	0	18	33	11.00	—	—	—
Wellham, D.M.	68	110	18	136*	4271	46.42	11	0+1	29
Wells, A.P.	71	112	21	127	2621	28.80	3	1	36
Wells, C.M.	142	221	33	203	6118	32.54	11	3	39
Wessels, K.C.	166	289	23	254	13133	49.37	33	2+3	114
Weston, M.J.	89	150	7	145*	3609	25.23	3	1	38
Wheeler, M.B.H.	2	—	—	—	—	—	—	—	—
Whitaker, J.J.	54	82	9	160	2505	34.31	5	2	30
Whitticase, P.	11	14	3	55*	184	16.72	—	—	27
Wild, D.J.	52	77	11	144	1783	27.01	2	—	13

	M	I	NO	HS	Runs	Avge	100	1000	Ct/St
Willey, P.	427	699	99	227	18371	30.61	34	6	177
Williams, N.F.	91	98	23	67	1522	20.29	—	—	24
Williams, R.G.	205	331	40	175*	8931	30.69	15	6	75
Wills, R.T.	5	7	0	48	121	17.28	—	—	—
Wood, G.M.	150	258	18	173*	8687	36.19	20	0+1	107
Wright, A.J.	51	91	10	139	1999	24.67	1	—	21
Wright, J.G.	251	434	30	190	16641	41.19	40	6+1	151
Wyatt, J.G.	39	66	2	145	1834	28.65	3	—	16
Young, B.A.	13	23	4	65*	368	19.36	—	—	26
Younis Ahmed	435	723	112	221*	24543	40.16	43	13	235
Zaheer Abbas	445	746	89	274	34285	52.18	107	11+6	262

BOWLING

'100wS' denotes instances of 100 or more wickets in a season.

	Runs	Wkts	Avge	Best	5wI	10wM	100wS
Abrahams, J.	2571	51	50.41	3-27	—	—	—
Acfield, D.L.	25888	917	28.23	8-55	33	4	—
Afford, J.A.	333	9	37.00	2-49	—	—	—
Agnew, J.P.	8163	271	30.12	9-70	11	2	—
Alderman, T.M.	11253	458	24.56	7-28	25	4	—
Allott, P.J.W.	9555	363	26.32	8-48	18	—	—
Amiss, D.L.	718	18	39.88	3-21	—	—	—
Anderson, I.S.	1290	20	64.50	4-35	—	—	—
Andrew, C.R.	847	12	70.58	3-77	—	—	—
Andrew, S.J.W.	1522	41	37.12	6-43	1	—	—
Arnold, K.A.	108	5	21.60	5-57	1	—	—
Asif Din	1852	34	54.47	5-100	1	—	—
Aslett, D.G.	731	11	66.45	4-119	—	—	—
Athey, C.W.J.	1326	30	44.20	3-3	—	—	—
Atkinson, J.C.M.	250	2	125.00	1-36	—	—	—
Bail, P.A.C.	4	0	—	—	—	—	—
Bailey, R.J.	96	4	24.00	3.33			
Bainbridge, P.	5486	141	38.90	6-59	3	—	—
Bairstow, D.L.	247	6	41.16	3-82	—	—	—
Balderstone, J.C.	8017	308	26.02	6-25	5	—	—
Banks, D.A.	17	0	—	—	—	—	—
Baptiste, E.A.E.	6937	254	27.31	6-42	7	—	—
Barclay, J.R.T.	9871	324	30.46	6-61	9	1	—
Barlow, G.D.	68	3	22.66	1-6	—	—	—
Barnett, K.J.	2132	38	56.10	6-115	1	—	—
Barrett, B.J.	40	1	40.00	1-40	—	—	—
Barwick, S.R.	4321	136	31.77	8-42	5	—	—
Benjamin, W.K.R.	61	3	20.33	2-31	—	—	—
Bennett, M.J.	3361	112	30.00	6-32	5	—	—
Benson, M.R.	210	1	210.00	1-4	—	—	—
Birch, J.D.	1903	38	50.07	6-64	1	—	—
Boon, D.C.	100	2	50.00	1-12	—	—	—
Boon, T.J.	57	0	—	—	—	—	—
Booth, P.A.	1109	23	48.21	3-22	—	—	—

	Runs	Wkts	Avge	Best	5wI	10wM	100wS
Booth, S.C.	3159	87	36.31	4-26	—	—	—
Border, A.R.	1868	54	34.59	4-61	—	—	—
Botham, I.T.	22957	896	25.62	8-34	50	7	1
Boycott, G.	1459	45	32.42	4-14	—	—	—
Boyd-Moss, R.J.	1879	43	43.69	5-27	1	—	—
Brandes, E.A.	190	3	63.33	2-46	—	—	—
Brassington, A.J.	10	0	—	—	—	—	—
Brettell, J.G.	340	5	68.00	2-87	—	—	—
Briers, N.E.	910	30	30.33	4-29	—	—	—
Bristowe, W.R.	5	0	—	—	—	—	—
Broad, B.C.	845	16	52.81	2-14	—	—	—
Brown, K.R.	0	0	—	—	—	—	—
Bullen, C.K.	104	2	52.00	2-36	—	—	—
Burrows, D.A.	76	0	—	—	—	—	—
Butchart, I.P.	1095	34	32.20	5-65	1	—	—
Butcher, A.R.	4503	113	39.84	6-48	1	—	—
Butcher, I.P.	20	1	20.00	1-2	—	—	—
Butcher, R.O.	122	2	61.00	1-13	—	—	—
Capel, D.J.	2642	66	40.03	7-62	2	—	—
Carr, J.D.	1977	48	41.18	6-61	3	—	—
Carrick, P.	21230	720	29.48	8-33	35	5	—
Chadwick, M.R.	20	0	—	—	—	—	—
Childs, J.H.	13996	426	32.85	9-56	21	2	—
Chivers, I.J.	72	1	72.00	1-5	—	—	—
Clarke, S.T.	13974	692	20.19	7-34	42	6	—
Clift, P.B.	19234	771	24.94	8-17	23	2	—
Clinton, G.S.	173	4	43.25	2-8	—	—	—
Close, D.B.	30876	1170	26.38	8-41	43	3	2
Cobb, R.A.	5	0	—	—	—	—	—
Connor, C.A.	3416	97	35.21	7-37	1	—	—
Cook, G.	675	14	48.21	3-47	—	—	—
Cook, N.G.B.	13640	467	29.20	7-63	19	2	—
Coombs, R.V.J.	268	16	16.75	5-58	1	—	—
Cooper, K.E.	11867	432	27.46	8.44	14	—	—
Corlett, S.C.	2182	74	29.48	7-82	4	—	—
Cotterell, T.A.	2574	41	62.78	5-89	1	—	—
Cowans, N.G.	7307	288	25.37	6-31	14	—	—
Cowdrey, C.S.	3973	97	40.95	3-5	—	—	—
Cowdrey, G.R.	22	1	22.00	1-22	—	—	—
Cowley, N.G.	11791	352	33.49	6-48	4	—	—
Crowe, M.D.	2985	100	29.85	5-18	4	—	—
Curran, K.M.	2474	106	23.33	5-35	2	—	—
Curtis, T.S.	194	4	48.50	2-58	—	—	—
Daniel, W.W.	16791	771	21.77	9-61	31	7	—
Davidson, I.C.	24	2	12.00	2-24	—	—	—
Davidson, J.E.	254	4	63.50	3-22	—	—	—
Davis, M.R.	4172	127	32.85	7-55	4	1	—
Davison, B.F.	2660	82	32.43	5-52	1	—	—
De Freitas, P.A.J.	703	27	26.03	5-39	1	—	—
De Grandhomme, L L	820	23	35.65	3-56	—	—	—
Dennis, S.J.	4238	139	30.48	5-35	4	—	—
Derrick, J.	1178	22	53.54	4-60	—	—	—

	Runs	Wkts	Avge	Best	5wI	10wM	100wS
Dilley, G.R.	8797	302	29.12	6-66	11	1	—
D'Oliveira, D.B.	658	15	43.86	2-50	—	—	—
Donald, W.A.	127	2	63.50	1-46	—	—	—
Doshi, D.R.	23325	889	26.23	7-29	42	6	1
Doughty, R.J.	1806	57	31.68	6-33	2	—	—
Downton, P.R.	5	0	—	—	—	—	—
Dredge, C.H.	11962	405	29.53	6-37	12	—	—
Duers, K.G.	790	27	29.25	8-102	2	—	—
Duthie, P.G.	145	3	48.22	1-25	—	—	—
Dyer, R.I.H.B.	41	0	—	—	—	—	—
East, D.E.	11	0	—	—	—	—	—
Edmonds, P.H.	28209	1129	24.98	8-53	47	9	—
Elder, J.W.G.	337	14	24.07	3-56	—	—	—
Ellcock, R.M.	2011	63	31.92	4-34	—	—	—
Ellis, R.G.P.	271	5	54.20	2-40	—	—	—
Ellison, C.C.	1058	25	42.32	4-36	—	—	—
Ellison, R.M.	5059	206	24.55	7-87	7	2	—
Emburey, J.E.	21371	893	23.93	7-36	45	8	1
Evans, K.P.	242	3	80.66	2-31	—	—	—
Fell, M.A.	157	1	157.00	1-20	—	—	—
Feltham, M.A.	1130	34	33.23	5-62	1	—	—
Felton, N.A.	4	0	—	—	—	—	—
Ferreira, A.M.	15346	520	29.51	8-38	18	2	—
Ferris, G.J.F.	2476	82	30.19	7-42	3	1	—
Finney, R.J.	4233	146	28.99	7-61	7	—	—
Fletcher, K.W.R.	2287	51	44.84	5-41	1	—	—
Fletcher, S.D.	1910	48	39.79	4-24	—	—	—
Folley, I.	3581	109	32.85	6-8	3	—	—
Foster, N.A.	6612	256	25.82	6-30	13	1	—
Fowler, G.	94	2	47.00	2-43	—	—	—
Fowler, W.P.	1242	19	65.36	2-4	—	—	—
Fraser, A.R.C.	243	9	27.00	4-48	—	—	—
Fraser-Darling, C.D.	143	3	47.66	2-14	—	—	—
French, B.N.	22	0	—	—	—	—	—
Gard, T.	8	0	—	—	—	—	—
Garner, J.	13508	731	18.47	8-31	42	7	—
Gatting, M.W.	3025	115	26.30	5-34	2	—	—
Gifford, N.	45097	1935	23.30	8-28	89	14	4
Gilbert, D.R.	2783	76	36.61	5-56	2	—	
Gladwin, C.	71	0	—	—	—	—	—
Gooch, G.A.	5322	169	31.49	7-14	3	—	—
Gorman, S.R.	465	3	155.00	1-27	—	—	—
Gould, I.J.	110	0	—	—	—	—	—
Gower, D.I.	209	4	52.25	3-47	—	—	—
Graveney, D.A.	18159	635	28.59	8.85	28	4	—
Gray, A.H.	2993	125	23.94	8-40	9	2	—
Green, A.M.	808	19	42.52	2-20	—	—	—
Greenidge, C.G.	472	17	27.76	5-49	1	—	—
Greig, I.A.	8743	301	29.04	7-43	8	2	—
Griffiths, B.J.	12158	423	28.74	8-50	13	—	—
Grimes, A.D.H.	907	12	75.58	3-99	—	—	—

	Runs	Wkts	Avge	Best	5wI	10wM	100wS
Hadlee, R.J.	20426	1092	18.70	8-41	61	8	2
Hagan, D.A.	6	0	—	—	—	—	—
Halliday, M.	658	31	21.22	5-39	1	—	—
Harden, R.J.	33	2	16.50	1-4	—	—	—
Hardie, B.R.	115	3	38.33	2-39	—	—	—
Hardy, J.J.E.	3	0	—	—	—	—	—
Harper, R.A.	6703	234	28.64	6-57	13	1	—
Harrison, G.D.	65	2	32.50	2-30	—	—	—
Hartley, P.J.	1390	33	42.12	5-75	2	—	—
Hartley, S.N.	1901	42	45.26	4-51	—	—	—
Hassan, B.	407	6	67.83	3-33	—	—	—
Hayes, K.A.	537	17	31.58	6-58	1	—	—
Hayhurst, A.N.	37	3	12.33	3-37	—	—	—
Hayward, R.E.	55	0	—	—	—	—	—
Hemmings, E.E.	28738	987	29.11	10-175	47	11	—
Henderson, S.P.	216	3	72.00	2-48	—	—	—
Henriksen, S.	44	1	44.00	1-44	—	—	—
Herbert, R.	238	6	39.66	3-64	—	—	—
Hick, G.A.	1009	18	56.05	3-39	—	—	—
Hilditch, A.M.J.	91	0	—	—	—	—	—
Hill, A.	343	8	42.87	3-5	—	—	—
Hinks, S.G.	178	3	59.33	1-18	—	—	—
Hoffman, D.S.	1160	29	40.00	4-100	—	—	—
Holding, M.A.	12338	527	23.41	8-92	29	4	—
Holland, R.G.	6557	211	31.07	9-83	7	2	—
Holmes, G.C.	2329	56	41.58	5-86	1	—	—
Hopkins, J.A.	90	0	—	—	—	—	—
Houghton, D.L.	0	0	—	—	—	—	—
Howarth, G.P.	3593	112	32.08	5-32	1	—	—
Hughes, D.P.	18254	610	29.92	7-24	20	2	—
Hughes, S.P.	5921	208	28.46	6-32	7	—	—
Humpage, G.W.	444	10	44.10	2-13	—	—	—
Illingworth, R.K.	5559	160	34.74	7-50	5	1	—
Imran Khan	23575	1074	21.85	8-58	59	11	—
Inchmore, J.D.	14215	497	28.60	8-58	18	1	—
James, K.D.	1585	51	31.07	6-22	2	—	—
Jarvis, K.B.S.	17392	594	29.27	8-97	18	3	—
Jarvis, M.P.	730	19	38.42	3-37	—	—	—
Jarvis, P.W.	3108	87	35.72	7-105	5	—	—
Javed Miandad	6363	191	33.31	7-39	6	—	—
Jefferies, S.T.	7696	283	27.19	8-46	10	2	
Jesty, T.E.	15582	569	27.38	7-75	18	—	—
Johnson, G.W.	17601	567	31.04	7-76	23	3	—
Johnson, P.	175	3	58.33	1-0	—	—	—
Jones, A.L.	152	1	152.00	1-60	—	—	—
Jones, A.N.	2333	74	31.52	5-99	2	—	—
Jones, A.P.	142	3	47.33	1-9	—	—	—
Joseph, R.F.	2070	44	47.04	6-114	1	—	—
Kallicharran, A.I.	3443	75	45.90	5-45	1	—	—
Kapil Dev	14733	552	26.69	9-83	29	3	—
Ker, J.E.	348	12	29.00	3-45	—	—	—

	Runs	Wkts	Avge	Best	5wI	10wM	100wS
Kimber, S.J.S.	72	3	24.00	3-40	—	—	—
Knott, A.P.E.	87	2	43.50	1-5	—	—	—
Lamb, A.J.	122	5	24.40	1-1	—	—	—
Lampitt, S.R.	1	0	—	—	—	—	—
Lanchbury, R.J.	6	0	—	—	—	—	—
Larkins, W.	1644	39	42.15	5-59	1	—	—
Lawrence, D.V.	4397	135	32.57	7-48	8	—	—
Lawrence, M.P.	2425	35	69.28	3-79	—	—	—
Lawson, G.F.	9639	378	25.50	8-112	18	2	—
Lea, A.E.	101	2	50.50	2-27	—	—	—
Le Roux, G.S.	13632	654	20.84	8-107	31	3	—
Lethbridge, C.	2996	77	38.90	5-68	1	—	—
Lever, J.K.	36827	1549	23.77	8-37	79	12	4
Lilley, A.W.	205	5	41.00	3-116	—	—	—
Lloyd, C.H.	4104	114	36.00	4-48	—	—	—
Lloyd, T.A.	867	13	66.69	3-62	—	—	—
Lloyds, J.W.	5242	156	33.60	7-88	7	1	—
Lord, G.J.	31	0	—	—	—	—	—
Love, J.D.	241	2	120.50	1-8	—	—	—
Luckhurst, B.W.	2744	64	42.87	4-32	—	—	—
Lynch, M.A.	709	15	47.26	3-6	—	—	—
McBrine, A.	28	0	—	—	—	—	—
McDermott, C.J.	3204	106	30.22	8-141	4	—	—
McEwan, K.S.	309	4	77.25	1-0	—	—	—
McEwan S.M.	635	16	39.68	3-47	—	—	—
McFarlane, L.L.	4140	102	40.58	6-59	1	—	—
Mackintosh, K.S.	2092	59	35.45	6-61	1	—	—
MacLarnon, P.C.	229	1	229.00	1-18	—	—	—
McPate, W.A.	153	3	51.00	2-70	—	—	—
Makinson, D.J.	1392	39	35.69	5-60	1	—	—
Malcolm, D.E.	756	19	39.78	3-78	—	—	—
Mallender, N.A.	9285	318	29.19	7-27	8	1	—
Malone, S.J.	4236	118	35.89	7-55	3	1	—
Marks, V.J.	18894	577	32.74	8-17	28	3	—
Marshall, M.D.	15831	867	18.25	8-71	56	8	1
Martindale, D.J.R.	8	0	—	—	—	—	—
Maru, R.J.	4353	143	30.44	7-79	5	—	—
Matthews, G.R.J.	3221	80	40.26	5-32	1	—	—
Maynard, C.	8	0	—	—	—	—	—
Maynard, M.P.	4	0	—	—	—	—	—
Medlycott, K.T.	225	8	28.12	2-15	—	—	—
Mendis, G.D.	76	1	76.00	1-65	—	—	—
Merry, W.G.	1677	51	32.88	4-24	—	—	—
Metcalfe, A.A.	10	0	—	—	—	—	—
Miller, A.J.T.	4	1	4.00	1-4	—	—	—
Miller, G.	19504	739	26.39	8-70	34	6	—
Moir, D.G.	6678	199	33.55	6-60	9	1	—
Monkhouse, G.	4093	159	25.74	7-51	2	—	—
Monkhouse, S.	61	1	61.00	1-61	—	—	—
Morris, H.	100	1	100.00	1-45	—	—	—
Morris, J.E.	128	1	128.00	1-35	—	—	—
Mortensen, O.H.	3201	117	27.35	6-27	4	1	—

	Runs	Wkts	Avge	Best	5wI	10wM	100wS
Morton, W.	924	25	36.96	4-40	—	—	—
Moxon, M.D.	844	15	56.26	3-26	—	—	—
Munton, T.A.	35	0	—	—	—	—	—
Murphy, A.J.	207	6	34.50	3-84	—	—	—
Mushtaq Mohammad	22790	936	24.34	7-18	39	2	—
Neale, P.A.	201	1	201.00	1-15	—	—	—
Needham, A.	4202	103	40.79	6-30	5	—	—
Newell, M.	76	1	76.00	1-38	—	—	—
Newman, P.G.	6481	196	33.06	7-104	2	—	—
Newport, P.J.	2259	76	29.72	5-18	4	—	—
Nicholas, M.C.J.	1770	44	40.32	5-45	1	—	—
North, P.D.	60	1	60.00	1-60	—	—	—
O'Donnell, S.P.	1394	27	51.62	4-118	—	—	—
Old, C.M.	25081	1070	23.44	7-20	39	2	—
Oldham, S.	8919	273	32.67	7-78	4	—	—
Ollis, R.L.	10	0	—	—	—	—	—
Ontong, R.C.	18812	632	29.76	8-67	25	3	—
Ormrod, J.A.	1094	25	43.76	5-27	1	—	—
O'Shaughnessy, S.J.	3229	98	32.94	4-66	—	—	—
Ottley, D.G.	1	0	—	—	—	—	—
Palmer, G.V.	2601	57	45.63	5-38	1	—	—
Parker, P.W.G.	553	10	55.30	2-21	—	—	—
Parks, R.J.	0	0	—	—	—	—	—
Parsons, G.J.	9438	314	30.05	9-72	7	1	—
Patel, D.N.	12011	334	35.96	7-46	12	—	—
Patterson, B.P.	2683	82	32.71	7-49	5	1	—
Pauline, D.B.	595	16	36.18	5-52	1	—	—
Payne, I.R.	1341	30	44.70	5-13	1	—	—
Penn, C.	1400	31	45.16	4-63	—	—	—
Phillip, N.	17032	688	24.75	7-33	30	2	—
Phillips, R.B.	11	0	—	—	—	—	—
Phillips, W.B.	3	0	—	—	—	—	—
Pick, R.A.	2369	58	40.84	5-25	2	1	—
Pickles, C.S.	385	6	64.16	2-31	—	—	—
Pierson, A.R.K.	587	8	73.37	3-92	—	—	—
Pigott, A.C.S.	6996	249	28.09	7-74	10	1	—
Plumb, S.G.	91	2	45.50	2-47	—	—	—
Pocock, P.I.	41553	1577	26.34	9-57	60	7	1
Pont, I.L.	787	22	35.77	5-103	1	—	—
Pont, K.R.	3087	92	33.55	5-17	2	—	—
Popplewell, N.F.M.	4441	103	43.11	5-33	1	—	—
Potter, L.	1531	43	35.60	4-63	—	—	—
Price, D.G.	7	0	—	—	—	—	—
Price, M.R.	806	19	42.42	4-97	—	—	—
Prichard, P.J.	5	0	—	—	—	—	—
Pridgeon, A.P.	14240	418	34.06	7-35	8	1	—
Pringle, D.R.	8868	313	28.33	7-32	9	1	—
Prior, J.A.	119	3	39.66	2-7	—	—	—
Pycroft, A.J.	47	1	47.00	1-0	—	—	—
Quinlan, J.D.	635	10	63.50	4-76	—	—	—

	Runs	Wkts	Avge	Best	5wI	10wM	100wS
Radford, N.V.	8676	308	28.16	6-41	11	1	1
Radley, C.T.	160	8	20.00	2-38	—	—	—
Randall, D.W.	359	11	32.63	3-15	—	—	—
Reeve, D.A.	4077	145	28.11	5-22	3	—	—
Rice, C.E.B.	16460	742	22.18	7-62	20	1	—
Richards, C.J.	164	4	41.00	2-42	—	—	—
Richards, I.V.A.	6919	161	42.97	5-88	1	—	—
Ritchie, G.M.	72	3	24.00	1-4	—	—	—
Roberts, B.	1966	54	36.40	4-32	—	—	—
Robinson, P.E.	12	0	—	—	—	—	—
Robinson, R.T.	102	2	51.00	1-22	—	—	—
Roebuck, P.G.P.	269	6	44.83	2-44	—	—	—
Roebuck, P.M.	2069	42	49.26	6-50	1	—	—
Rolls, L.M.	49	0	—	—	—	—	—
Romaines, P.W.	59	3	19.66	3-42	—	—	—
Roope, G.R.J.	8395	225	37.31	5-14	4	—	—
Rose, B.C.	232	6	38.66	3-9	—	—	—
Rose, G.D.	142	9	15.77	6-41	1	—	—
Russell, P.E.	10351	339	30.53	7-46	5	—	—
Rutnagur, R.S.	728	15	48.53	5-112	1	—	—
Sadiq Mohammad	7455	234	31.85	7-34	8	—	—
Sainsbury, G.E.	4282	141	30.36	7-38	7	—	—
Saxelby, K.	5608	184	30.47	6-64	5	1	—
Scothern, M.	42	1	42.00	1-42	—	—	—
Scott, A.M.G.	879	25	35.16	5-68	1	—	—
Shah, A.H.	192	1	192.00	1-38	—	—	—
Sharp, G.	70	1	70.00	1-47	—	—	—
Sharp, K.	410	8	51.25	2-13	—	—	—
Shaw, C.	1463	37	39.54	5-76	1	—	—
Shepherd, J.N.	31976	1155	27.28	8-40	54	2	—
Siddiqi, S.N.	102	5	20.40	5-90	1	—	—
Sidebottom, A.	9460	390	24.25	7-18	14	2	—
Simmons, J.	23909	859	27.83	7-59	33	4	—
Slack, W.N.	491	18	27.27	3-17	—	—	—
Small, G.C.	8816	283	31.15	7-68	9	—	—
Smith, C.L.	1958	35	55.94	3-35	—	—	—
Smith, D.M.	1485	28	53.03	3-40	—	—	—
Smith, I.	154	1	154.00	1-39	—	—	—
Smith, K.D.	3	0	—	—	—	—	—
Smith, P.A.	3362	77	43.66	4-25	—	—	—
Smith, R.A.	123	4	30.75	2-11	—	—	—
Smith, T.S.	137	7	19.57	5-79	1	—	—
Snodgrass, D.L.	80	3	26.66	2-30	—	—	—
Standing, D.K.	32	0	—	—	—	—	—
Steele, J.F.	15210	575	26.45	7-29	16	—	—
Stephenson, F.D.	2471	109	22.66	6-19	6	1	—
Stevenson, A.W.J.	109	4	27.25	4-66	—	—	—
Stevenson, G.B.	13933	484	28.78	8-57	18	2	—
Stewart, A.J.	43	0	—	—	—	—	—
Stirling, D.A.	3029	96	31.55	6-75	2	—	—
Storie, A.C.	51	0	—	—	—	—	—
Stovold, A.W.	86	2	43.00	1-0	—	—	—
Streak, D.H.	647	16	40.43	4-81	—	—	—

	Runs	Wkts	Avge	Best	5wI	10wM	100wS
Such, P.M.	3593	119	30.19	6-123	5	—	—
Swallow, I.G.	1372	29	47.31	4-52	—	—	—
Swan, R.G.	0	0	—	—	—	—	—
Sykes, J.F.	629	14	44.92	3-58	—	—	—
Tavaré, C.J.	293	2	146.50	1-20	—	—	—
Taylor, J.P.	188	2	94.00	2-92	—	—	—
Taylor, L.B.	11163	461	24.21	7-28	15	1	—
Taylor, N.R.	508	11	46.18	2-20	—	—	—
Taylor, N.S.	1553	50	31.60	7-44	2	—	—
Terry, V.P.	39	0	—	—	—	—	—
Thomas, D.J.	9423	284	33.17	6-36	6	1	—
Thomas, J.G.	5622	191	29.43	5-56	6	1	—
Thomson, J.	297	7	42.42	4-46	—	—	—
Thomson, J.R.	16479	633	26.03	7-27	26	3	—
Thorne, D.A.	1418	80	47.26	5-39	1	—	—
Tomlins, K.P.	326	4	81.50	2-28	—	—	—
Toogood, G.J.	912	21	43.42	8-52	1	1	—
Topley, T.D.	464	17	27.29	4-57	—	—	—
Traicos, A.J.	7119	217	32.80	6-66	7	—	—
Trembath, C.R.	444	11	40.36	5-91	1	—	—
Tremlett, T.M.	6712	291	23.06	6-82	7	—	—
Turner, D.R.	332	9	36.88	2-7	—	—	—
Turner, M.S.	733	13	56.38	4-74	—	—	—
Turner, S.	21213	819	25.90	6-26	27	1	—
Twizell, P.H.	98	2	49.00	2-65	—	—	—
Underwood, D.L.	47327	2368	19.98	9-28	151	47	10
Varey, D.W.	4	0	—	—	—	—	—
Viswanath, G.R.	723	15	48.20	2-21	—	—	—
Walker, A.	2482	72	34.47	4-38	—	—	—
Wall, S.	1518	37	41.02	4-59	—	—	—
Waller, C.E.	18312	630	29.06	7-61	22	1	—
Walsh, C.A.	5788	231	25.05	7-51	12	1	—
Warner, A.E.	2960	85	34.82	5-27	2	—	—
Waterman, P.A.	727	18	40.38	3-22	—	—	—
Watkinson, M.	3431	104	32.99	6-39	4	—	—
Wellham, D.M.	11	1	11.00	1-11	—	—	—
Wells, A.P.	42	0	—	—	—	—	—
Wells, C.M.	5482	166	33.02	5-25	2	—	—
Wessels, K.C.	256	5	51.02	1-0	—	—	—
Weston, M.J.	1537	41	37.48	4-44	—	—	—
Wheeler, M.B.H.	117	1	117.00	1-87	—	—	—
Whitaker, J.J.	88	0	—	—	—	—	—
Wild, D.J.	1313	21	62.62	3-15	—	—	—
Willey, P.	18886	639	29.55	7-37	25	3	—
Williams, N.F.	7324	245	29.89	7-55	4	1	—
Williams, R.G.	9295	273	34.04	7-73	7	—	—
Wood, G.M.	132	5	26.40	3-18	—	—	—
Wright, A.J.	3	0	—	—	—	—	—
Wright, J.G.	226	2	113.00	1-4	—	—	—
Wyatt, J.G.	63	2	31.50	1-0	—	—	—
Younis Ahmed	1817	41	44.31	4-10	—	—	—
Zaheer Abbas	1059	28	37.82	5-15	1	—	—

TEST CAREER RECORDS

These individual career records include all official Test matches played before 7 January 1986. The following series in 1985-86 are NOT included: New Zealand v Australia, West Indies v England, Sri Lanka v Pakistan. Records for Australia, New Zealand, India, Pakistan and Sri Lanka are compiled by **Brian Heald.**

ENGLAND

BATTING AND FIELDING

	M	*I*	*NO*	*HS*	*Runs*	*Avge*	*100*	*50*	*Ct/St*
J.P. Agnew	3	4	3	5	10	10.00	—	—	—
P.J.W. Allott	13	18	3	52*	213	14.20	—	1	4
I.T. Botham	79	125	3	208	4409	36.13	13	20	92
N.G. Cowans	19	29	7	36	175	7.95	—	—	9
C.S. Cowdrey	5	6	1	38	96	19.20	—	—	5
P.R. Downton	21	31	6	74	576	23.04	—	4	54/3
P.H. Edmonds	33	39	6	64	652	19.75	—	2	31
R.M. Ellison	7	8	1	41	89	12.71	—	—	2
J.E. Emburey	28	39	8	57	456	14.70	—	1	18
N.A. Foster	9	12	2	18*	78	7.80	—	—	3
G. Fowler	21	37	0	201	1307	35.32	3	8	10
M.W. Gatting	41	70	10	207	2246	37.43	4	13	35
G.A. Gooch	48	84	4	196	3027	37.83	5	17	40
D.I. Gower	76	129	11	215	5385	45.63	12	25	55
A.J. Lamb	38	64	6	137*	2211	38.12	7	9	41
P.I. Pocock	25	37	4	33	206	6.24	—	—	15
R.T. Robinson	11	18	3	175	934	62.26	3	3	5
A. Sidebottom	1	1	0	2	2	2.00	—	—	—
L.B. Taylor	2	1	1	1*	1	—	—	—	1
P. Willey	21	40	6	102*	962	28.29	2	4	3

BOWLING

	Balls	*Runs*	*Wkts*	*Avge*	*Best*	*5wI*	*10wM*
J.P. Agnew	552	373	4	93.25	2-51	—	—
P.J.W. Allott	2223	1084	26	41.69	6-61	1	—
I.T. Botham	18391	9046	343	26.37	8-34	25	4
N.G. Cowans	3452	2003	51	39.27	6-77	2	—
C.S. Cowdrey	366	288	4	72.00	2-65	—	—
P.H. Edmonds	8232	2866	88	32.56	7-66	2	—
R.M. Ellison	1559	674	27	24.96	6-77	2	1
J.E. Emburey	6473	2240	75	29.86	6-33	3	—
N.A. Foster	1974	985	27	36.48	6-104	3	1
G. Fowler	18	11	0	—	—	—	—
M.W. Gatting	332	167	2	83.50	1-14	—	—
G.A. Gooch	1185	450	10	45.00	2-12	—	—
D.I. Gower	30	15	1	15.00	1-1	—	—
A.J. Lamb	24	22	1	22.00	1-6	—	—
P.I. Pocock	6650	2976	67	44.41	6-79	3	—
R.T. Robinson	6	0	0	—	—	—	—
A. Sidebottom	112	65	1	65.00	1-65	—	—
L.B. Taylor	381	178	4	44.50	2-34	—	—
P. Willey	1067	441	6	73.50	2-73	—	—

TEST CAREER RECORDS
AUSTRALIA

BATTING AND FIELDING

	M	I	NO	HS	Runs	Avge	100	50	Ct/St
T.M. Alderman	22	33	15	23	113	6.27	—	—	17
M.J. Bennett	3	5	2	23	71	23.66	—	—	5
D.C. Boon	13	24	1	131	754	32.78	2	4	8
A.R. Border	78	138	23	196	5909	51.38	16	31	85
R.J. Bright	20	33	7	33	360	13.84	—	—	11
J. Dyson	30	58	7	127*	1359	26.64	2	5	10
D.R. Gilbert	6	10	4	12*	41	6.83	—	—	—
A.M.J. Hilditch	18	34	0	119	1073	31.55	2	6	13
R.M. Hogg	38	58	13	52	439	9.75	—	1	7
R.G. Holland	11	15	4	10	35	3.18	—	—	5
D.W. Hookes	23	41	3	143*	1306	34.36	1	8	12
K.J. Hughes	70	124	6	213	4415	37.41	9	22	50
M.G. Hughes	1	1	0	0	0	0.00	—	—	1
R.B. Kerr	2	4	0	17	31	7.75	—	—	1
G.F. Lawson	36	59	10	57*	743	15.16	—	3	7
C.J. McDermott	12	18	1	36	171	10.05	—	—	3
G.R. Marsh	3	6	1	92	176	35.20	—	—	1
G.R.J. Matthews	11	19	2	115	577	33.94	2	2	5
S.P. O'Donnell	6	10	3	48	206	29.42	—	—	4
W.B. Phillips	24	43	2	159	1350	32.92	2	6	50
C.G. Rackemann	5	5	0	12	16	3,20	—	—	2
B.A. Reid	3	4	0	13	20	5.00	—	—	—
G.M. Ritchie	20	37	3	146	1210	35.58	3	5	10
S.J. Rixon	13	24	3	54	394	18.76	—	2	42/5
J.R. Thomson	51	73	20	49	679	12.81	—	—	20
S.R. Waugh	2	4	0	13	26	6.50	—	—	—
D.M. Wellham	5	9	0	103	239	26.55	1	—	2
K.C. Wessels	24	42	1	179	1761	42.95	4	9	18
G.M. Wood	53	101	5	172	3109	32.38	8	13	38
G.N. Yallop	39	70	3	268	2756	41.13	8	9	23

BOWLING

	Balls	Runs	Wkts	Avge	Best	5wI	10wM
T.M. Alderman	5373	2597	79	32.87	6-128	5	—
M.J. Bennett	665	325	6	54.16	3-79	—	—
A.R. Border	1583	625	15	41.66	3-20	—	—
R.J. Bright	4647	1751	43	40.72	7-87	3	1
D.R. Gilbert	1239	609	13	46.84	3-48	—	—
R.M. Hogg	7633	3503	123	28.47	6-74	6	2
R.G. Holland	2889	1352	34	39.76	6-54	3	2
D.W. Hookes	96	41	1	41.00	1-4	—	—
K.J. Hughes	85	28	0	—	—	—	—
M.G. Hughes	228	123	1	123.00	1-123	—	—
G.F. Lawson	8405	4250	145	29.31	8-112	10	2
C.J. McDermott	2696	1586	46	34.47	8-141	2	—
G.R.J. Matthews	1615	769	15	51.26	3-110	—	—
S.P. O'Donnell	940	504	6	84.00	3-37	—	—

C.G. Rackemann	936	540	23	23.47	6-86	3	1
B.A. Reid	800	325	11	29.54	4-100	—	—
G.M. Ritchie	6	10	0	—	—	—	—
J.R. Thomson	10535	5601	200	28.00	6-46	8	—
S.R. Waugh	108	69	2	34.50	2-36	—	—
K.C. Wessels	90	42	0	—	—	—	—
G.N. Yallop	192	116	1	116.00	1-21	—	—

TEST CAREER RECORDS

WEST INDIES

BATTING AND FIELDING

	M	*I*	*NO*	*HS*	*Runs*	*Avge*	*100*	*50*	*Ct/St*
C.G. Butts	1	1	0	9	9	9.00	—	—	—
W.W. Davis	11	12	4	77	157	19.62	—	1	7
P.J.L. Dujon	33	44	4	139	1764	44.10	4	8	108/2
J. Garner	51	60	13	60	609	12.95	—	1	37
H.A. Gomes	49	75	10	143	2841	43.70	9	12	15
C.G. Greenidge	66	111	13	223	4816	49.14	12	26	62
R.A. Harper	14	17	2	39*	203	13.53	—	—	19
D.L. Haynes	54	88	7	184	3234	39.92	7	20	33
M.A. Holding	55	71	10	69	786	12.88	—	5	18
C.H. Lloyd	110	175	14	242*	7515	46.67	19	39	90
A.L. Logie	13	17	1	130	493	30.81	1	3	7
M.D. Marshall	40	48	3	92	800	17.77	—	5	19
I.V.A. Richards	77	116	7	291	5889	54.02	19	25	77
R.B. Richardson	15	22	1	185	967	46.04	4	3	19
C.A. Walsh	6	7	4	18*	44	14.66	—	—	2

BOWLING

	Balls	*Runs*	*Wkts*	*Avge*	*Best*	*5wI*	*10wM*
C.G. Butts	282	113	0	—	—	—	—
W.W. Davis	2100	1082	32	33.81	4-19	—	—
J. Garner	11769	4792	220	21.78	6-56	6	—
H.A. Gomes	2215	867	13	66.69	2-20	—	—
C.G. Greenidge	26	4	0	—	—	—	—
R.A. Harper	2548	966	34	28.41	6-57	1	—
D.L. Haynes	18	8	1	8.00	1-2	—	—
M.A. Holding	11842	5414	233	23.23	8-92	13	2
C.H. Lloyd	1716	622	10	62.20	2-13	—	—
A.L. Logie	7	4	0	—	—	—	—
M.D. Marshall	8864	4157	188	22.11	7.53	13	2
I.V.A. Richards	2812	1023	19	53.84	2-20	—	—
R.B. Richardson	12	0	0	—	—	—	—
C.A. Walsh	1028	507	16	31.68	3-55	—	—

TEST CAREER RECORDS
NEW ZEALAND

BATTING AND FIELDING

	M	*I*	*NO*	*HS*	*Runs*	*Avge*	*100*	*50*	*Ct/St*
S.L. Boock	26	37	8	37	192	6.62	—	—	13
B.P. Bracewell	6	12	2	8	24	2.40	—	—	1
J.G. Bracewell	15	24	6	83*	303	16.83	—	1	15
V.R. Brown	2	3	1	36*	51	25.50	—	—	3
B.L. Cairns	43	65	8	64	928	16.28	—	2	30
E.J. Chatfield	25	33	21	21*	129	10.75	—	—	6
J.V. Coney	43	72	12	174*	2166	36.10	2	13	50
J.J. Crowe	23	38	2	128	1009	28.02	2	5	30
M.D. Crowe	26	43	2	188	1422	34.68	3	5	31
B.A. Edgar	33	58	3	161	1786	32.47	3	11	14
E.J. Gray	4	8	0	25	86	10.75	—	—	2
R.J. Hadlee	60	100	12	103	2199	24.98	1	11	31
G.P. Howarth	47	83	5	147	2531	32.44	6	11	29
P.E. McEwan	4	7	1	40*	96	16.00	—	—	5
J.F. Reid	16	27	2	180	1246	49.84	6	2	8
K.R. Rutherford	4	7	0	5	12	1.71	—	—	1
I.D.S. Smith	28	41	9	113*	763	23.84	1	2	74/5
M.C. Snedden	11	12	2	32	147	14.70	—	—	2
D.A. Stirling	4	7	1	16	64	10.66	—	—	—
G.B. Troup	13	17	6	13*	45	4.09	—	—	2
J.G. Wright	44	76	2	141	2315	31.28	4	9	23

BOWLING

	Balls	*Runs*	*Wkts*	*Avge*	*Best*	*5wI*	*10wM*
S.L. Boock	5620	2102	65	32.33	7-87	4	—
B.P. Bracewell	1036	585	14	41.78	3-110	—	—
J.G. Bracewell	3009	1290	37	34.86	5-75	1	—
V.R. Brown	342	176	1	176.00	1-17	—	—
B.L. Cairns	10628	4280	130	32.92	7-74	6	1
E.J. Chatfield	5898	2392	77	31.06	6-73	3	1
J.V. Coney	2445	785	24	32.70	3-28	—	—
J.J. Crowe	18	9	0	—	—	—	—
M.D. Crowe	1011	500	12	41.66	2-25	—	—
B.A. Edgar	18	3	0	—	—	—	—
E.J. Gray	642	311	8	38.87	3-73	—	—
R.J. Hadlee	15309	6743	299	22.55	9-52	24	6
G.P. Howarth	614	271	3	90.33	1-13	—	—
P.E. McEwan	36	13	0	—	—	—	—
J.F. Reid	12	7	0	—	—	—	—
K.R. Rutherford	58	48	1	48.00	1-38	—	—
I.D.S. Smith	18	5	0	—	—	—	—
M.C. Snedden	1878	930	24	38.75	3-21	—	—
D.A. Stirling	638	420	10	42.00	4-88	—	—
G.B. Troup	2721	1214	36	33.72	6-95	1	1
J.G. Wright	30	5	0	—	—	—	—

TEST CAREER RECORDS
INDIA

BATTING AND FIELDING

	M	I	NO	HS	Runs	Avge	100	50	Ct/St
M. Amarnath	54	91	9	138	3680	44.87	10	10	38
M. Azharuddin	9	14	2	122	664	55.33	3	2	8
R.M.H. Binny	21	33	3	83*	675	22.50	—	4	8
A.D. Gaekwad	40	70	4	201	1985	30.07	2	10	15
S.M. Gavaskar	112	195	16	236*	9192	51.35	32	39	97
Kapil Dev	74	110	9	126*	3051	30.20	3	17	32
S.M.H. Kirmani	88	124	22	102	2759	27.04	2	12	160/38
Madan Lal	38	60	16	74	1000	22.75	—	5	15
A. Malhotra	7	10	1	72*	226	25.11	—	1	2
Maninder Singh	15	18	6	15	61	5.08	—	—	5
S.M. Patil	29	47	4	174	1588	36.93	4	7	12
M. Prabhakar	2	4	1	35*	86	28.66	—	—	—
L.S. Rajput	2	4	0	61	105	26.25	—	1	1
C. Sharma	10	12	6	54	173	28.83	—	1	3
G. Sharma	2	2	1	10*	11	11.00	—	—	1
R.J. Shastri	40	61	8	142	1924	36.30	5	8	17
L. Sivaramakrishnan	9	9	1	25	130	16.25	—	—	9
K. Srikkanth	14	23	1	116	766	34.81	1	5	9
D.B. Vengsarkar	82	134	14	159	4625	38.54	9	25	57
S. Viswanath	3	5	0	20	31	6.20	—	—	11
N.S. Yadav	26	32	10	43	355	16.13	—	—	8

BOWLING

	Balls	Runs	Wkts	Avge	Best	5wI	10wM
M. Amarnath	3401	1678	30	55.93	4-63	—	—
M. Azharuddin	6	8	0	—	—	—	—
R.M.H. Binny	2051	1157	27	42.85	3-18	—	—
A.D. Gaekwad	334	187	2	93.50	1-4	—	—
S.M. Gavaskar	350	187	1	187.00	1-34	—	—
Kapil Dev	16007	8054	281	28.66	9-83	19	2
S.M.H. Kirmani	19	13	1	13.00	1-9	—	—
Madan Lal	5872	2798	68	41.14	5-23	4	—
A. Malhotra	18	3	0	—	—	—	—
Maninder Singh	3087	1272	22	57.81	4-85	—	—
S.M. Patil	645	240	9	26.66	2-26	—	—
M. Prabhakar	174	102	1	102.00	1-68	—	—
C. Sharma	1545	944	22	42.90	5-118	1	—
G. Sharma	516	167	3	55.66	3-115	—	—
R.J. Shastri	9649	3603	93	38.74	5-75	2	—
L. Sivaramakrishnan	2367	1145	26	44.03	6-64	3	1
K. Srikkanth	48	21	0	—	—	—	—
D.B. Vengsarkar	47	36	0	—	—	—	—
N.S. Yadav	6199	2670	75	35.60	5-99	2	—

TEST CAREER RECORDS
PAKISTAN

BATTING AND FIELDING

	M	I	NO	HS	Runs	Avge	100	50	Ct/St
Abdul Qadir	36	42	4	54	579	15.23	—	2	11
Anil Dalpat	9	12	1	52	167	15.18	—	1	22/3
Ashraf Ali	5	5	3	65	206	103.00	—	2	9/2
Azeem Hafeez	18	21	5	24	134	8.37	—	—	1
Imran Khan	54	79	12	123	2092	31.22	2	8	16
Iqbal Qasim	41	46	14	56	380	11.87	—	1	32
Jalaluddin	6	3	2	2	3	3.00	—	—	—
Javed Miandad	71	111	17	280*	5350	56.91	14	28	62/1
Manzoor Elahi	2	3	1	26	49	24.50	—	—	2
Mohsin Kamal	2	2	1	4*	4	4.00	—	—	—
Mohsin Khan	42	69	6	200	2611	41.44	7	0	31
Mudassar Nazar	55	86	7	231	3352	42.43	8	15	38
Qasim Omar	20	33	1	210	1346	42.06	3	4	14
Ramiz Raja	3	5	1	52	86	21.50	—	1	4
Rashid Khan	4	6	3	59	155	51.66	—	1	2
Salim Malik	27	36	6	119*	1268	42.26	5	6	29
Salim Yousuf	3	4	1	27	67	22.33	—	—	16/3
Shoaib Mohammad	6	9	1	80	213	26.62	—	1	4
Tahir Naqqash	15	19	5	57	300	21.42	—	1	3
Tausif Ahmed	11	8	4	18	52	13.00	—	—	4
Wasim Akram	5	6	4	8*	18	9.00	—	—	1
Wasim Raja	57	92	14	125	2821	36.16	4	18	20
Zaheer Abbas	78	124	11	274	5062	44.79	12	20	34

BOWLING

	Balls	Runs	Wkts	Avge	Best	5wI	10wM
Abdul Qadir	9392	4281	123	34.80	7-142	9	2
Azeem Hafeez	4351	2204	63	34.98	6-46	4	—
Imran Khan	13275	5587	249	22.43	8-58	17	4
Iqbal Qasim	10785	3995	137	29.16	7-49	5	2
Jalaluddin	1197	537	11	48.81	3-77	—	—
Javed Miandad	1446	672	17	39.52	3-74	—	—
Manzoor Elahi	138	76	1	76.00	1-74	—	—
Mohsin Kamal	366	213	6	35.50	3-50	—	—
Mohsin Khan	86	30	0	—	—	—	—
Mudassar Nazar	4320	1863	49	38.02	6-32	1	—
Qasim Omar	6	0	0	—	—	—	—
Rashid Khan	738	360	8	45.00	3-129	—	—
Salim Malik	122	61	3	20.33	1-3	—	—
Shoaib Mohammad	18	8	0	—	—	—	—
Tahir Naqqash	2800	1398	34	41.11	5-40	2	—
Tausif Ahmed	2582	1028	35	29.37	5-54	1	—
Wasim Akram	1185	484	20	24.20	5-56	2	1
Wasim Raja	4082	1826	51	35.80	4-50	—	—
Zaheer Abbas	370	132	3	44.00	2-21	—	—

TEST CAREER RECORDS
SRI LANKA

BATTING AND FIELDING

	M	*I*	*NO*	*HS*	*Runs*	*Avge*	*100*	*50*	*Ct/St*
F.S. Ahangama	3	3	1	11	11	5.50	—	—	1
A.L.F. De Mel	13	23	4	34	253	13.31	—	—	8
E.A.R. De Silva	1	1	1	1*	1	—	—	—	1
P.A. De Silva	7	13	1	122	437	36.41	2	1	1
R.L. Dias	15	28	1	109	1107	41.00	3	7	6
A.P. Gurusinghe	1	2	0	17	29	14.50	—	—	2
B.R. Jurangpathy	1	2	0	1	1	0.20	—	—	—
R.S. Madugalle	18	34	4	103	933	31.10	1	6	8
L.R.D. Mendis	16	31	1	124	1091	36.36	4	6	5
A. Ranatunga	15	28	1	111	875	32.40	1	6	7
R.J. Ratnayake	10	16	2	56	187	13.35	—	1	5
J.R. Ratnayeke	11	21	5	36	240	15.00	—	—	1
S.A.R. Silva	7	13	2	111	333	30.27	2	—	30/1
C.D.U.S. Weerasinghe	1	1	0	3	3	3.00	—	—	—
S. Wettimuny	17	32	1	190	1046	33.74	2	5	8
R.G.C.E. Wijesuriya	4	7	2	8	22	4.40	—	—	1

BOWLING

	Balls	*Runs*	*Wkts*	*Avge*	*Best*	*5wI*	*10wM*
F.S. Ahangama	810	348	18	19.33	5-52	1	—
A.L.F. De Mel	2880	1802	48	37.54	6-109	3	—
E.A.R. De Silva	162	38	0	—	—	—	—
P.A. De Silva	30	22	0	—	—	—	—
B.R. Jurangpathy	24	24	0	—	—	—	—
R.S. Madugalle	72	32	0	—	—	—	—
A. Ranatunga	858	368	7	52.57	2-17	—	—
R.J. Ratnayake	2105	1139	34	33.50	6-85	2	—
J.R. Ratnayeke	1876	984	27	36.44	8-83	2	—
C.D.U.S. Weerasinghe	114	36	0	—	—	—	—
S. Wettimuny	12	21	0	—	—	—	—
R.G.C.E. Wijesuriya	586	294	1	294.00	1-68	—	—

ONE-DAY INTERNATIONALS CAREER RECORDS

These One-day International career records for players contracted to play county cricket in 1986 are complete to 24 August 1985 and are compiled by **Victor Isaacs**.

BATTING AND FIELDING

	M	*I*	*NO*	*HS*	*Runs*	*Avge*	*100*	*50*	*Ct/St*
J.P. Agnew	3	1	1	2*	2	—	—	—	1
T.M. Alderman (Aus)	23	9	3	9*	27	4.50	—	—	12
P.J.W. Allott	13	6	1	8	15	3.00	—	—	2
D.L. Amiss	18	18	0	137	859	47.72	4	1	2
C.W.J. Athey	2	2	0	51	83	41.50	—	1	1
R.J. Bailey	1	1	1	41*	41	—	—	—	—
D.L. Bairstow	21	20	6	23*	206	14.71	—	—	17/4
E.A.E. Baptiste (WI)	29	10	2	28*	119	14.87	—	—	4
G.D. Barlow	6	6	1	80*	149	29.80	—	1	4
A.R. Border (Aus)	114	106	16	127*	2898	32.20	3	18	31
I.T. Botham	75	66	8	72	1248	21.51	—	5	27
G. Boycott	36	34	4	105	1082	36.06	1	9	5
A.R. Butcher	1	1	0	14	14	14.00	—	—	—
R.O. Butcher	3	3	0	52	58	19.33	—	1	—
S.T. Clarke (WI)	10	8	2	20	60	10.00	—	—	4
G. Cook	6	6	0	32	106	17.66	—	—	2
N.G.B. Cook	1	—	—	—	—	—	—	—	1
N.G. Cowans	23	8	3	4*	13	2.60	—	—	5
C.S. Cowdrey	3	3	1	46*	51	25.50	—	—	—
K.M. Curran (Zim)	6	6	0	73	212	35.33	—	2	—
W.W. Daniel (WI)	18	5	4	16*	49	49.00	—	—	5
G.R. Dilley	18	11	3	31*	96	12.00	—	—	1
P.R. Downton	11	9	3	44*	165	27.50	—	—	7/1
P.H. Edmonds	23	16	6	20	100	10.00	—	—	3
R.M. Ellison	9	9	4	24	59	11.80	—	—	2
J.E. Emburey	8	7	1	18	31	5.16	—	—	3
K.W.R. Fletcher	24	22	3	131	757	39.84	1	5	4
N.A. Foster	16	8	3	24	42	8.40	—	—	6
G. Fowler	24	24	2	81*	714	32.45	—	4	3/2
B.N. French	3	2	0	7	11	5.50	—	—	3/1
J. Garner (WI)	76	31	13	37	195	10.83	—	—	17
M.W. Gatting	42	39	10	115*	902	31.10	1	4	12
N. Gifford	2	1	0	0	0	0.00	—	—	1
G.A. Gooch	40	39	2	117*	1335	36.08	3	9	16
I.J. Gould	18	14	2	42	155	12.91	—	—	15/3
D.I. Gower	77	74	7	158	2427	36.22	7	8	30
C.G. Greenidge (WI)	68	68	7	115	2912	47.73	6	19	23
R.J. Hadlee (NZ)	75	61	7	79	952	17.62	—	1	22
R.A. Harper (WI)	18	4	2	45*	71	35.50	—	—	7
E.E. Hemmings	5	2	0	3	4	2.00	—	—	1
M.A. Holding (WI)	87	35	9	64	215	8.26	—	1	26
G.W. Humpage	3	2	0	6	11	5.50	—	—	2
Imran Khan (Pak)	55	45	14	102*	1023	33.00	1	3	18
Javed Miandad (Pak)	75	72	14	119*	2155	37.15	2	13	26
T.E. Jesty	10	10	4	52*	127	21.16	—	1	5

	M	I	NO	HS	Runs	Avge	100	50	Ct/St
A.I. Kallicharran (WI)	31	28	4	78	826	34.41	—	6	8
Kapil Dev (Ind)	61	57	8	175*	1336	27.26	1	6	21
A.J. Lamb	43	42	8	118	1569	46.14	3	9	11
W. Larkins	6	6	0	34	84	14.00	—	—	2
J.K. Lever	22	11	4	27*	56	8.00	—	—	6
C.H. Lloyd (WI)	87	69	19	102	1977	39.54	1	11	40
T.A. Lloyd	3	3	0	49	101	33.66	—	—	—
J.D. Love	3	3	0	43	61	20.33	—	—	1
V.J. Marks	33	24	3	44	285	13.57	—	—	8
M.D. Marshall (WI)	60	32	12	56*	339	16.95	—	1	8
G. Miller	25	18	2	46	136	8.50	—	—	4
M.D. Moxon	5	5	0	70	132	26.40	—	1	4
C.M. Old	32	25	7	51*	338	18.77	—	1	8
P.I. Pocock	1	1	0	4	4	4.00	—	—	—
D.R. Pringle	9	7	2	34*	78	15.60	—	—	5
C.T. Radley	4	4	1	117*	250	83.33	1	1	—
D.W. Randall	49	45	5	88	1067	26.67	—	5	25
C.J. Richards	3	2	0	3	3	1.50	—	—	1
I.V.A. Richards (WI)	98	89	15	189*	4071	55.01	8	27	44
R.T. Robinson	7	7	0	37	97	13.85	—	—	1
B.C. Rose	2	2	0	54	99	49.50	—	1	1
C.L. Smith	4	4	0	70	109	27.25	—	1	—
G.B. Stevenson	4	4	3	28*	43	43.00	—	—	2
C.J. Tavaré	29	28	2	83*	720	27.69	—	4	7
D.L. Underwood	26	13	4	17	53	5.88	—	—	6
C.A. Walsh (WI)	4	—	—	—	—	—	—	—	—
C.M. Wells	2	2	0	17	22	11.00	—	—	—
P. Willey	22	20	1	64	487	25.63	—	5	4
J.G. Wright (NZ)	71	70	1	84	1767	25.60	—	11	28

BOWLING

	Balls	Runs	Wkts	Avge	Best	4W
J.P. Agnew	126	120	3	40.00	3-38	—
T.M. Alderman (Aus)	1290	803	29	27.69	5-17	1
P.J.W. Allott	819	552	15	36.80	3-41	—
R.J. Bailey	36	25	0	—	—	—
E.A.E. Baptiste (WI)	1476	989	27	36.63	2-10	—
A.R. Border (Aus)	900	717	20	35.85	3-21	—
I.T. Botham	3936	2639	100	26.39	4-56	1
G. Boycott	168	105	5	21.00	2-14	—
S.T. Clarke (WI)	524	245	13	18.84	3-22	—
N.G.B. Cook	48	34	1	34.00	1-34	—
N.G. Cowans	1282	913	23	39.66	3-44	—
C.S. Cowdrey	52	55	2	27.50	1-3	—
K.M. Curran (Zim)	350	274	5	54.80	3-65	—
W.W. Daniel (WI)	912	595	23	25.86	3-27	—
G.R. Dilley	972	595	18	33.05	4-45	1
P.H. Edmonds	1168	687	20	34.35	3-39	—
R.M. Ellison	414	289	8	36.12	3-42	—
J.E. Emburey	435	262	5	52.40	2-22	—
N.A. Foster	834	600	14	42.85	3-44	—
J. Garner (WI)	4184	2102	116	18.12	5-31	4
M.W. Gatting	248	212	6	35.33	3-32	—
N. Gifford	120	50	4	12.50	4-23	1
G.A. Gooch	889	682	18	37.88	2-12	—
D.I. Gower	3	5	0	—	—	—
C.G. Greenidge (WI)	60	45	1	45.00	1-21	—
R.J. Hadlee (NZ)	4017	2148	100	21.48	5-25	4
R.A. Harper (WI)	924	602	24	25.08	3-34	—
E.E. Hemmings	249	175	5	35.00	3-11	—
M.A. Holding (WI)	4734	2613	122	21.41	5-26	5
Imran Khan (Pak)	2123	1152	56	20.57	6-14	1
Javed Miandad (Pak)	352	209	5	41.80	2-22	—
T.E. Jesty	108	93	1	93.00	1-23	—
A.I. Kallicharran (WI)	105	64	3	21.33	2-10	—
Kapil Dev (Ind)	3200	1929	79	24.41	5-43	1
W. Larkins	12	21	0	—	—	—
J.K. Lever	1152	713	24	29.70	4-29	1
C.H. Lloyd (WI)	358	210	8	26.25	2-4	—
V.J. Marks	1772	1076	44	24.45	5-20	2
M.D. Marshall (WI)	3252	1783	70	25.47	4-34	1
G. Miller	1268	813	25	32.52	3-27	—
C.M. Old	1755	999	45	22.20	4-8	2
P.I. Pocock	60	20	0	—	—	—
D.R. Pringle	492	401	12	33.41	3-21	—
D.W. Randall	2	2	1	2.00	1-2	—
I.V.A. Richards (WI)	3160	2348	62	37.87	3-27	—
C.L. Smith	36	28	2	14.00	2-8	—
G.B. Stevenson	192	125	7	17.85	4-33	1
C.J. Tavaré	12	3	0	—	—	—
D.L. Underwood	1278	734	32	22.93	4-44	1
C.A. Walsh (WI)	240	198	4	49.50	2-52	—
P. Willey	936	594	12	49.50	3-33	—
J.G. Wright (NZ)	24	8	0	—	—	—

CRICKET RECORDS
FIRST-CLASS CRICKET

UPDATED TO THE END OF THE 1°85 ENGLISH SEASON

TEAM RECORDS

Highest Innings Totals

1107	Victoria v New South Wales	Melbourne	1926-27
1059	Victoria v Tasmania	Melbourne	1922-23
951-7d	Sind v Baluchistan	Karachi	1973-74
918	New South Wales v South Australia	Sydney	1900-01
912-8d	Holkar v Mysore	Indore	1945-46
910-6d	Railways v Dera Ismail Khan	Lahore	1964-65
903-7d	England v Australia	The Oval	1938
887	Yorkshire v Warwickshire	Birmingham	1896
849	England v West Indies	Kingston	1929-30

There have been 22 instances of a team scoring over 800 runs in an innings, the most recent being by Sind in 1973-74 (above).

Highest Second Innings Total

770	New South Wales v South Australia	Adelaide	1920-21

Highest Fourth Innings Total

654-5	England v South Africa	Durban	1938-39

Highest Match Aggregate

2376	Bombay v Maharashtra	Poona	1948-49

Record Margin of Victory

Innings and 851 runs: Railways v Dera Ismail Khan at Lahore 1964-65

Most Runs in a Day

721	Australians v Essex	Southend	1948

Most Hundreds in an Innings

6	Holkar v Mysore	Indore	1945-46
5	New South Wales v South Australia	Sydney	1900-01
5	Australia v West Indies	Kingston	1954-55

Lowest Innings Totals

12	†Oxford University v MCC and Ground	Oxford	1877
12	Northamptonshire v Gloucestershire	Gloucester	1907
13	Auckland v Canterbury	Auckland	1877-78
13	Nottinghamshire v Yorkshire	Nottingham	1901
14	Surrey v Essex	Chelmsford	1983
15	MCC v Surrey	Lord's	1839
15	†Victoria v MCC	Melbourne	1903-04
15	†Northamptonshire v Yorkshire	Northampton	1908
15	Hampshire v Warwickshire	Birmingham	1922

†*Batted one man short*

There have been 26 instances of a team being dismissed for under 20, the most recent being by Surrey in 1983 (above).

Lowest Match Aggregate by One Team

34 (16 and 18)	Border v Natal	East London	1959-60

Lowest Completed Match Aggregate by Both Teams

105	MCC v Australians	Lord's	1878

Fewest Runs in an Uninterrupted Day's Play

95	Australians (80) v Pakistan (15-2)	Karachi	1956-57

Tied Matches

Before 1948 a match was considered to be tied if the scores were level after the fourth innings, even if the side batting last had wickets in hand when play ended. Law 22 was amended in 1948 and since then a match has been tied only when the scores are level after the fourth innings has been completed. There have been 46 tied first-class matches, five of which would not have qualified under the current law. The most recent are:

Victoria (230-5d/245) v New Zealanders (301-9d/174-3d), Melbourne	1982-83
Muslim Commercial Bank (229/238) v Railways (149/318), Sialkot	1983-84
Kent (92/243) v Sussex (143/192), Hastings	1984
Northamptonshire (124/330) v Kent (250-6d/204-5d), Northampton	1984

BATTING RECORDS

Highest Individual Innings

499†	Hanif Mohammad, Karachi v Bahawalpur; Karachi	1958-59
452*	D.G. Bradman, New South Wales v Queensland; Sydney	1929-30
443*	B.B. Nimbalkar, Maharashtra v Kathiawar; Poona	1948-49
437	W.H. Ponsford, Victoria v Queensland; Melbourne	1927-28
429	W.H. Ponsford, Victoria v Tasmania; Melbourne	1922-23
428	Aftab Baloch, Sind v Baluchistan; Karachi	1973-74
424	A.C. MacLaren, Lancashire v Somerset; Taunton	1895
385	B. Sutcliffe, Otago v Canterbury; Christchurch	1952-53
383	C.W. Gregory, New South Wales v Queensland; Brisbane	1906-07
369	D.G. Bradman, South Australia v Tasmania; Adelaide	1935-36
365*	C. Hill, South Australia v. New South Wales; Adelaide	1900-01
365*	G.St. A. Sobers, West Indies v Pakistan; Kingston	1957-58

364	L. Hutton, England v Australia; Oval	1938
359*	V.M. Merchant, Bombay v Maharashtra; Bombay	1943-44
359	R.B. Simpson, New South Wales v Queensland; Brisbane	1963-64
357*	R. Abel, Surrey v Somerset; Oval	1899
357	D.G. Bradman, South Australia v Victoria; Melbourne	1935-36
356	B.A. Richards, South Australia v Western Australia; Perth	1970-71
355	B. Sutcliffe, Otago v Auckland; Dunedin	1949-50
352	W.H. Ponsford, Victoria v New South Wales; Melbourne	1926-27
350	Rashid Israr, Habib Bank v National Bank; Lahore	1976-77

†In 16 hours 10 minutes – the longest first-class innings.
There have been 94 triple hundreds in first-class cricket, the most recent being 322 by I.V.A. Richards for Somerset v Warwickshire at Taunton in 1985.

Most Hundreds in Successive Innings

6	C.B. Fry	Sussex and Rest of England	1901
6	D.G. Bradman	South Australia and D.G. Bradman's XI	1938-39
6	M.J. Procter	Rhodesia	1970-71
5	E. de C. Weekes	West Indians (in New Zealand)	1955-56

Two Double Hundreds in a Match

244	202*	A.E. Fagg	Kent v Essex	Colchester	1938

Double Hundred and Hundred in a Match Most Times

4	Zaheer Abbas	Gloucestershire	1976-81

Two Hundreds in a Match Most Times

8	Zaheer Abbas	Gloucestershire and PIA	1976-82
7	W.R. Hammond	Gloucestershire, England and MCC	1927-45

Most Hundreds in a Season

18	D.C.S. Compton	1947
16	J.B. Hobbs	1925
15	W.R. Hammond	1938

Most Hundreds in a Career

(*The season in which his 100th hundred was scored is given in brackets*)

197	J.B. Hobbs (1923)	122	T.W. Graveney (1964)
170	E.H. Hendren (1928-29)	117	D.G. Bradman (1947-48)
167	W.R. Hammond (1935)	107	A. Sandham (1935)
153	C.P. Mead (1927)	107	M.C. Cowdrey (1973)
149	H. Sutcliffe (1932)	107	Zaheer Abbas (1982-83)
149	G. Boycott (1977)	104	T.W. Hayward (1913)
145	F.E. Woolley (1929)	103	J.H. Edrich (1977)
129	L. Hutton (1951)	103	G.M. Turner (1982)
126	W.G. Grace (1895)	102	E. Tyldesley (1934)
123	D.C.S. Compton (1952)	102	L.E.G. Ames (1950)

Most Runs in a Month

1294	(avge 92.42)	L. Hutton	Yorkshire	June 1949

Most Runs in a Season

Runs			*I*	*NO*	*HS*	*Avge*	*100*	*Season*
3816	D.C.S. Compton	Middlesex	50	8	246	90.85	18	1947
3539	W.J. Edrich	Middlesex	52	8	267*	80.43	12	1947
3518	T.W. Hayward	Surrey	61	8	219	66.37	13	1906

The feat of scoring 3000 runs in a season has been achieved on 28 occasions, the most recent instance being by W.E. Alley (3019) in 1961. The highest aggregate in a season since 1969, when the number of County Championship matches was substantially reduced, is 2559 by G.A. Gooch in 1984.

1000 Runs in a Season Most Times

28 W.G. Grace (Gloucestershire), F.E. Woolley (Kent)

Highest Batting Average in a Season

(*Qualification: 12 innings*)

Avge			*I*	*NO*	*HS*	*Runs*	*100*	*Season*
115.66	D.G. Bradman	Australians	26	5	278	2429	13	1938
102.53	G. Boycott	Yorkshire	20	5	175*	1538	6	1979
102.00	W.A. Johnston	Australians	17	16	28*	102	—	1953
100.12	G. Boycott	Yorkshire	30	5	233	2503	13	1971

Fastest Hundred

35 min	P.G.H. Fender, Surrey v Northamptonshire; Northampton	1920
35 min	S.J. O'Shaughnessy, Lancashire v Leicestershire; Manchester	1983

Fastest Double Hundred

113 min	R.J. Shastri	Bombay v Baroda	Bombay	1984-85

Fastest Triple Hundred

181 min	D.C.S. Compton, MCC v North-Eastern Transvaal; Benoni	1948-49

Most Sixes in an Innings

15	J.R. Reid, Wellington v N. Districts; Wellington	1962-63
13	Majid Khan, Pakistanis v Glamorgan; Swansea	1967
13	C.G. Greenidge, D.H. Robins' XI v Pakistanis; Eastbourne	1974
13	C.G. Greenidge, Hampshire v Sussex; Southampton	1975
13	G.W. Humpage, Warwickshire v Lancashire; Southport	1982
13	R.J. Shastri, Bombay v Baroda; Bombay	1984-85

Most Sixes in a Match

17	W.J. Stewart	Warwickshire v Lancashire	Blackpool	1959

Most Sixes in a Season

80	I.T. Botham	Somerset and England	1985

Most Boundaries in an Innings

68	P.A. Perrin	Essex v Derbyshire	Chesterfield	1904

Most Runs off One Over

36	G.St. A. Sobers	Nottinghamshire v Glamorgan	Swansea	1968
36	R.J. Shastri	Bombay v Baroda	Bombay	1984-85

Both batsmen hit all six balls of an over (bowled by M.A. Nash and Tilak Raj respectively) for six.

Most Runs in a Day

345	C.G. Macartney, Australians v Nottinghamshire; Nottingham	1921

There have been 16 instances of a batsman scoring 300 or more runs in a day, the most recent being by I.V.A. Richards (322) in 1985.

Highest Partnerships

First Wicket

561	Waheed Mirza/Mansoor Akhtar, Karachi Whites v Quetta; Karachi	1976-77
555	H. Sutcliffe/P. Holmes, Yorkshire v Essex; Leyton	1932
554	J.T. Brown/J. Tunnicliffe, Yorkshire v Derbyshire; Chesterfield	1898

Second Wicket

465*	J.A. Jameson/R.B. Kanhai, Warwickshire v Glos; Birmingham	1974
455	K.V. Bhandarkar/B.B. Nimbalkar, Maharashtra v Kathiawar; Poona	1948-49
451	D.G. Bradman/W.H. Ponsford, Australia v England; The Oval	1934

Third Wicket

456	Aslam Ali/Khalid Irtiza, United Bank v Multan; Karachi	1975-76
451	Mudassar Nazar/Javed Miandad, Pakistan v India; Hyderabad	1982-83
445	P.E. Whitelaw/W.N. Carson, Auckland v Otago; Dunedin	1936-37
434	J.B. Stollmeyer/G.E. Gomez, Trinidad v British Guiana; Port-of-Spain	1946-47
424*	W.J. Edrich/D.C.S. Compton, Middlesex v Somerset; Lord's	1948

Fourth Wicket

577	V.S. Hazare/Gul Mahomed, Baroda v Holkar; Baroda	1946-47
574*	C.L. Walcott/F.M.M. Worrell, Barbados v Trinidad; Port-of-Spain	1945-46
502*	F.M.M. Worrell/J.D.C. Goddard, Barbados v Trinidad; Bridgetown	1943-44
470	A.I. Kallicharran/G.W. Humpage, Warwickshire v Lancashire; Southport	1982

Fifth Wicket

405	D.G. Bradman/S.G. Barnes, Australia v England; Sydney	1946-47
397	W. Bardsley/C. Kelleway, NSW v South Australia; Sydney	1920-21
393	E.G. Arnold/W.B. Burns, Worcestershire v Warwicks; Birmingham	1909

Sixth Wicket

487*	G.A. Headley/C.C. Passailaigue, Jamaica v Ld Tennyson's XI; Kingston	1931-32
428	W.W. Armstrong/M.A. Noble, Australians v Sussex; Hove	1902
411	R.M. Poore/E.G. Wynyard, Hampshire v Somerset; Taunton	1899

Seventh Wicket

347	D.St. E. Atkinson/C.C. Depeiza, West Indies v Australia; Bridgetown	1954-55
344	K.S. Ranjitsinhji/W. Newham, Sussex v Essex; Leyton	1902
340	K.J. Key/H. Philipson, Oxford U v Middlesex; Chiswick Park	1887

Eighth Wicket

433	A. Sims/V.T. Trumper, Australians v Canterbury; Christchurch	1913-14
292	R. Peel/Lord Hawke, Yorkshire v Warwickshire; Birmingham	1896
270	V.T. Trumper/E.P. Barbour, NSW v Victoria, Sydney	1912-13

Ninth Wicket

283	J. Chapman/A. Warren, Derbyshire v Warwicks; Blackwell	1910
251	J.W.H.T. Douglas/S.N. Hare, Essex v Derbyshire; Leyton	1921
245	V.S. Hazare/N.D. Nagarwalla, Maharashtra v Baroda; Poona	1939-40

Tenth Wicket

307	A.F. Kippax/J.E.H. Hooker, NSW v Victoria; Melbourne	1928-29
249	C.T. Sarwate/S.N. Bannerjee, Indians v Surrey; The Oval	1946
235	F.E. Woolley/A. Fielder, Kent v Worcestershire; Stourbridge	1909

Most Runs in a Career

	Career	*I*	*NO*	*Runs*	*HS*	*Avge*	*100*
J.B. Hobbs	1905-34	1315	106	**61237**	316*	50.65	197
F.E. Woolley	1906-38	1530	84	**58959**	395*	40.77	145
E.H. Hendren	1907-38	1300	166	**57611**	301*	50.80	170
C.P. Mead	1905-36	1340	185	**55061**	280*	47.67	153
W.G. Grace	1865-1908	1493	105	**54896**	344	39.55	126
W.R. Hammond	1920-51	1005	104	**50551**	336*	56.10	167
H. Sutcliffe	1919-45	1088	123	**50138**	313	51.95	149
T.W. Graveney	1948-71/2	1223	159	**47793**	258	44.91	122
G. Boycott	1962-85	994	161	**47434**	261*	56.94	149
T.W. Hayward	1893-1914	1138	96	**43551**	315*	41.79	104
M.C. Cowdrey	1950-76	1130	134	**42719**	307	42.89	107
A. Sandham	1911-37/8	1000	79	**41284**	325	44.82	107
D.L. Amiss	1960-85	1048	117	**40673**	262*	43.68	96
L. Hutton	1934-60	814	91	**40140**	364	55.51	129
M.J.K. Smith	1951-75	1091	139	**39832**	204	41.84	69
W. Rhodes	1898-1930	1527	237	**39763**	267*	30.82	58
J.H. Edrich	1956-78	979	104	**39790**	310*	45.47	103
R.E.S. Wyatt	1923-57	1141	157	**39405**	232	40.04	85
D.C.S. Compton	1936-64	839	88	**38942**	300	51.85	123
E. Tyldesley	1909-36	961	106	**38874**	256*	45.46	102
J.T. Tyldesley	1895-1923	933	62	**37896**	295*	40.70	86
J.W. Hearne	1909-36	1025	116	**37252**	285*	40.98	96
L.E.G. Ames	1926-51	951	95	**37248**	295	43.51	102
D. Kenyon	1946-67	1159	59	**37002**	259	33.63	74
W.J. Edrich	1934-58	964	92	**36965**	267*	42.39	86
J.M. Parks	1949-76	1227	172	**36673**	205*	34.76	51
D. Denton	1894-1920	1161	70	**36440**	221	33.40	69
G.H. Hirst	1891-1929	1214	151	**36272**	341	34.12	60
A. Jones	1957-83	1168	72	**36049**	204*	32.89	56
W.G. Quaife	1894-1928	1203	185	**36016**	255*	35.37	72
R.E. Marshall	1945/6-72	1053	59	**35725**	228*	35.94	68
K.W.R. Fletcher	1962-85	1090	158	**35701**	228*	38.30	62
G. Gunn	1902-32	1061	82	**35208**	220	35.96	62

LEADING CURRENT PLAYERS

These career records list in order of success in each department of the game the leading current players who are available for first-class county cricket in 1986. All figures are to the end of the 1985 English season.

BATTING AND BOWLING

An order of merit based on the highest career averages. with batting and bowling qualifications of 100 innings and 100 wickets respectively.

BATSMEN	*Runs*	*Avge*	BOWLERS	*Wkts*	*Avge*
G. Boycott	47434	56.94	M.D. Marshall	867	18.25
Javed Miandad	22534	53.27	J. Garner	731	18.47
A.R. Border	11821	52.30	R.J. Hadlee	1092	18.70
I.V.A. Richards	26841	50.26	D.L. Underwood	2368	19.98
C.H. Lloyd	30885	49.25	S.T. Clarke	692	20.19
A.J. Lamb	16402	47.68	G.S. Le Roux	654	20.84
M.W. Gatting	15512	46.72	W.W. Daniel	771	21.77
A.I. Kallicharran	29771	44.97	Imran Khan	1074	21.85
C.G. Greenidge	28461	44.75	C.E.B. Rice	742	22.18
G.A. Gooch	21171	44.01	T.M. Tremlett	291	23.06
D.L. Amiss	40673	43.68	N. Gifford	1935	23.30
R.T. Robinson	8597	41.53	K.M. Curran	106	23.33
J.G. Wright	16641	41.19	M.A. Holding	527	23.41
C.E.B. Rice	21122	41.17	C.M. Old	1070	23.44
C.L. Smith	8924	40.74	J.K. Lever	1549	23.77
D.I. Gower	15590	40.59	J.E. Emburey	893	23.93
B.F. Davison	26923	40.36	A.H. Gray	125	23.94
Younis Ahmed	24543	40.16	L.B. Taylor	461	24.21
W.N. Slack	9113	39.45	A. Sidebottom	390	24.25
K.W.R. Fletcher	35701	38.30	R.M. Ellison	206	24.55
D.W. Randall	20599	38.07	T.M. Alderman	458	24.56
M.R. Benson	6341	37.97	P.B. Clift	771	24.94
D.G. Aslett	4642	37.43	P.H. Edmonds	1129	24.98

WICKET-KEEPING AND FIELDING

The following wicket-keepers and fielders have most dismissals and catches in the field respectively.

WICKET-KEEPERS	*Total*	*Ct*	*St*	FIELDERS	*Ct*
D.L. Bairstow	944	815	129	K.W.R. Fletcher	597
G.W. Humpage	528	472	56	C.T. Radley	497
B.N. French	505	455	50	C.G. Greenidge	414
I.J. Gould	483	417	66	J.F. Steele	404
P.R. Downton	480	424	56	D.L. Amiss	398
C.J. Richards	461	404	57	C.H. Lloyd	377
R.J. Parks	348	309	39	G. Cook	367
D.E. East	321	297	24	B.F. Davison	330

MOST WICKETS IN A CAREER

	Career	Runs	Wkts	Avge	100w
W. Rhodes	1898-1930	69993	**4187**	16.71	23
A.P. Freeman	1914-36	69577	**3776**	18.42	17
C.W.L. Parker	1903-35	63821	**3278**	19.46	16
J.T. Hearne	1888-1923	54342	**3061**	17.75	15
T.W.J. Goddard	1922-52	59116	**2979**	19.84	16
W.G. Grace	1865-1908	51545	**2876**	17.92	10
A.S. Kennedy	1907-36	61044	**2874**	21.24	15
D. Shackleton	1948-69	53303	**2857**	18.65	20
G.A.R. Lock	1946-71	54710	**2844**	19.23	14
F.J. Titmus	1949-82	63313	**2830**	22.37	16
M.W. Tate	1912-37	50567	**2784**	18.16	13+1
G.H. Hirst	1891-1929	51300	**2739**	18.72	15
C. Blythe	1899-1914	42136	**2506**	16.81	14
W.E. Astill	1906-39	57781	**2431**	23.76	9
D.L. Underwood	1963-85	47327	**2368**	19.98	10
J.C. White	1909-37	43759	**2356**	18.57	14
W.E. Hollies	1932-57	48656	**2323**	20.94	14
F.S. Trueman	1949-69	42154	**2304**	18.29	12
J.B. Statham	1950-68	36995	**2260**	16.36	13
R.T.D. Perks	1930-55	53770	**2233**	24.07	16
J. Briggs	1879-1900	35390	**2221**	15.93	12
D.J. Shepherd	1950-72	47298	**2218**	21.32	12
E.G. Dennett	1903-26	42568	**2147**	19.82	12
T. Richardson	1892-1905	38794	**2105**	18.42	10
T.E. Bailey	1945-67	48170	**2082**	23.13	9
R. Illingworth	1951-83	42023	**2072**	20.28	10
F.E. Woolley	1906-38	41066	**2068**	19.85	8
G. Geary	1912-38	41339	**2063**	20.03	11
D.V.P. Wright	1932-57	49305	**2056**	23.98	10
J.A. Newman	1906-30	51211	**2032**	25.20	9
A. Shaw	1864-97	24496	**2021**	12.12	9
S. Haigh	1895-1913	32091	**2012**	15.94	11

ALL-ROUND RECORDS

The 'Double' Event

3000 runs and 100 wickets: J.H. Parks, 1937.
2000 runs and 200 wickets: G.H. Hirst, 1906.
2000 runs and 100 wickets: F.E. Woolley (4), J.W. Hearne (3), G.H. Hirst (2), W. Rhodes (2), T.E. Bailey, D.E. Davies, W.G. Grace, G.L. Jessop, V.W.C. Jupp, James Langridge, F.A. Tarrant, C.L. Townsend, L. F. Townsend.
1000 runs and 200 wickets: M.W. Tate (3), A.E. Trott (2), A.S. Kennedy.
Most 'Doubles': W. Rhodes (16), G.H. Hirst (14), V.W.C. Jupp (10).
'Double' in first season: D.B. Close, 1949. At the age of 18, Close is the youngest player ever to perform this feat.
The feat of scoring 1000 runs and taking 100 wickets has been achieved on 303 occasions, the last instance being R.J. Hadlee in 1984.

BOWLING RECORDS

All Ten Wickets in an Innings

This feat has been achieved on 71 occasions at first-class level.
Three Times: A.P. Freeman (1929, 1930, 1931)
Twice: V.E. Walker (1859, 1865); H. Verity (1931, 1932); J.C. Laker (1956).

Instances since 1945:

W.E Hollies, Warwickshire v Nottinghamshire	Birmingham	1946
J.M. Sims, East v West	Kingston/Thames	1948
J.K.R. Graveney, Gloucestershire v Derbyshire	Chesterfield	1949
T.E. Bailey, Essex v Lancashire	Clacton	1949
R. Berry, Lancashire v Worcestershire	Blackpool	1953
S.P. Gupte, Bombay v Pakistan Services	Bombay	1954-55
J.C. Laker, Surrey v Australians	Oval	1956
K. Smales, Nottinghamshire v Gloucestershire	Stroud	1956
G.A.R. Lock, Surrey v Kent	Blackheath	1956
J.C. Laker, England v Australia	Manchester	1956
P.M. Chatterjee, Bengal v Assam	Jorhat	1956-57
J.D. Bannister, Warwickshire v Combined Services	Birmingham	1959
A.J.G. Pearson, Cambridge U v Leicestershire	Loughborough	1961
N.I. Thomson, Sussex v Warwickshire	Worthing	1964
P.J. Allan, Queensland v Victoria	Melbourne	1965-66
I.J. Brayshaw, Western Australia v Victoria	Perth	1967-68
Shahid Mahmood, Karachi Whites v Khairpur	Karachi	1969-70
E.E. Hemmings, International XI v W. Indians	Kingston	1982-83
P. Sunderam, Rajasthan v Vidarbha	Jodhpur	1985-86

Most Wickets in a Match

19	J.C. Laker	England v Australia	Manchester	1956

Most Wickets in a Season

W		*Season*	*M*	*O*	*M*	*R*	*Avge*
304	A.P. Freeman	1928	37	1976.1	423	5489	18.05
298	A.P. Freeman	1933	33	2039	651	4549	15.26

NB. The feat of taking 250 wickets in a season has been achieved on 12 occasions, the last instance being by A.P. Freeman in 1933 as above. 200 or more wickets in a season have been taken on 59 occasions, the last instance being by G.A.R. Lock (212 wkts, avge 12.02) in 1957.

The most wickets taken in a season since the reduction of County Championship matches in 1969 are as follows.

W		*Season*	*M*	*O*	*M*	*R*	*Avge*
134	M.D. Marshall	1982	22	822	225	2108	15.73
131	L.R. Gibbs	1971	23	1024.1	295	2475	18.89
121	R.D. Jackman	1980	23	746.2	220	1864	15.40

NB. 100 wickets in a season have been taken on 37 occasions since 1969.

Most Hat-tricks in a Career

7 D.V.P. Wright.
6 T.W.J. Goddard, C.W.L. Parker.
5 S. Haigh, V.W.C. Jupp, A.E.G. Rhodes, F.A. Tarrant.

WICKET-KEEPING RECORDS

Most Dismissals in an Innings

8 (8 ct)	A.T.W. Grout, Queensland v W. Australia; Brisbane	1959-60
8 (8 ct)	D.E. East, Essex v Somerset; Taunton	1985

Most Dismissals in a Match

12 (8 ct, 4 st)	E. Pooley, Surrey v Sussex; Oval	1868
12 (9 ct, 3 st)	D. Tallon, Queensland v NSW; Sydney	1938-39
12 (9 ct, 3 st)	H.B. Taber, NSW v S. Australia; Adelaide	1968-69

Most Catches in a Match

11	A. Long, Surrey v Sussex; Hove	1964
11	R.W. Marsh, W. Australia v Victoria; Perth	1975-76
11	D.L. Bairstow, Yorkshire v Derbyshire; Scarborough	1982

Most Dismissals in a Season

127 (79 ct, 48 st) L.E.G. Ames 1929

Most Dismissals in a Career

	Career	*Dismissals*	*Ct*	*St*
R.W. Taylor	1960-84	**1646**	1471	175
J.T. Murray	1952-75	**1527**	1270	257
H. Strudwick	1902-27	**1468**	1215	253
A.P.E. Knott	1965-85	**1344**	1211	133
F.H. Huish	1895-1914	**1328**	952	376
D. Hunter	1889-1909	**1327**	955	372
B. Taylor	1949-73	**1294**	1082	212
H.R. Butt	1890-1912	**1262**	971	291
J.H. Board	1891-1915	**1206**	852	354
H. Elliott	1920-47	**1206**	904	302
J.M. Parks	1949-76	**1182**	1089	93
R. Booth	1951-70	**1122**	946	176
L.E.G. Ames	1926-51	**1113**	698	415
G. Duckworth	1923-47	**1090**	751	339
H.W. Stephenson	1948-64	**1084**	752	332
J.G. Binks	1955-69	**1071**	895	176
T.G. Evans	1939-69	**1066**	816	250
A. Long	1960-80	**1046**	922	124
G.O. Dawkes	1937-61	**1042**	896	146
R.W. Tolchard	1965-83	**1037**	912	125
W.L. Cornford	1921-47	**1000**	656	344

FIELDING RECORDS
Most Catches

Innings: 7 M.J. Stewart, Surrey v Northants; Northampton 1957
7 A.S. Brown, Glos v Notts; Nottingham 1966
Match: 10 W.R. Hammond, Glos v Surrey; Cheltenham 1928
Season: 78 W.R. Hammond (1928); 77 M.J. Stewart (1957)
Career: 1018 F.E. Woolley; 877 W.G. Grace; 830 G.A.R. Lock; 819 W.R. Hammond; 813 D.B. Close; 786 J.G. Langridge; 755 E.H. Hendren, C.A. Milton

TEST CRICKET RECORDS

Records include all official Test matches played before 7 January 1986. The following series played in 1985-86 are NOT included: New Zealand v Australia, West Indies v England, Sri Lanka v Pakistan.

HIGHEST INNINGS TOTALS

903-7d	England v Australia (Oval)	1938
849	England v West Indies (Kingston)	1929-30
790-3d	West Indies v Pakistan (Kingston)	1957-58
758-8d	Australia v West Indies (Kingston)	1954-55
729-6d	Australia v England (Lord's)	1930
701	Australia v England (Oval)	1934
695	Australia v England (Oval)	1930
687-8d	West Indies v England (Oval)	1976
681-8d	West Indies v England (Port-of-Spain)	1953-54
674-6	Pakistan v India (Faisalabad)	1984-85
674	Australia v India (Adelaide)	1947-48
668	Australia v West Indies (Bridgetown)	1954-55
659-8d	Australia v England (Sydney)	1946-47
658-8d	England v Australia (Nottingham)	1938
657-8d	Pakistan v West Indies (Bridgetown)	1957-58
656-8d	Australia v England (Manchester)	1964
654-5	England v South Africa (Durban)	1938-39
652-8d	West Indies v England (Lord's)	1973
652-7d	England v India (Madras)	1984-85
652	Pakistan v India (Faisalabad)	1982-83
650-6d	Australia v West Indies (Bridgetown)	1964-65

The highest innings for the countries not mentioned above are:

644-7d	India v West Indies (Kanpur)	1978-79
622-9d	South Africa v Australia (Durban)	1969-70
553-7d	New Zealand v Australia (Brisbane)	1985-86
491-7d	Sri Lanka v England (Lord's)	1984

LOWEST INNINGS TOTALS

26	New Zealand v England (Auckland)	1954-55
30	South Africa v England (Port Elizabeth)	1895-96
30	South Africa v England (Birmingham)	1924
35	South Africa v England (Cape Town)	1898-99
36	Australia v England (Birmingham)	1902
36	South Africa v Australia (Melbourne)	1931-32
42	Australia v England (Sydney)	1887-88
42	New Zealand v Australia (Wellington)	1945-46
42†	India v England (Lord's) †*Batted one man short*	1974
43	South Africa v England (Cape Town)	1888-89
44	Australia v England (Oval)	1896
45	England v Australia (Sydney)	1886-87
45	South Africa v Australia (Melbourne)	1931-32
47	South Africa v England (Cape Town)	1888-89
47	New Zealand v England (Lord's)	1958

The lowest innings for the countries not mentioned above are:

62	Pakistan v Australia (Perth)	1981-82
76	West Indies v Pakistan (Dacca)	1958-59
93	Sri Lanka v New Zealand (Wellington)	1982-83

HIGHEST INDIVIDUAL INNINGS

365*	G.St A. Sobers, West Indies v Pakistan (Kingston)	1957-58
364	L. Hutton, England v Australia (Oval)	1938
337	Hanif Mohammad, Pakistan v West Indies (Bridgetown)	1957-58
336*	W.R. Hammond, England v New Zealand (Auckland)	1932-33
334	D.G. Bradman, Australia v England (Leeds)	1930
325	A. Sandham, England v West Indies (Kingston)	1929-30
311	R.B. Simpson, Australia v England (Manchester)	1964
310*	J.H. Edrich, England v New Zealand (Leeds)	1965
307	R.M. Cowper, Australia v England (Melbourne)	1965-66
304	D.G. Bradman, Australia v England (Leeds)	1934
302	L.G. Rowe, West Indies v England (Bridgetown)	1973-74
299*	D.G. Bradman, Australia v South Africa (Adelaide)	1931-32
291	I.V.A. Richards, West Indies v England (Oval)	1976
287	R.E. Foster, England v Australia (Sydney)	1903-04
285*	P.B.H. May, England v West Indies (Birmingham)	1957
280*	Javed Miandad, Pakistan v India (Hyderabad)	1982-83
278	D.C.S. Compton, England v Pakistan (Nottingham)	1954
274	R.G. Pollock, South Africa v Australia (Durban)	1969-70
274	Zaheer Abbas, Pakistan v England (Birmingham)	1971
270*	G.A. Headley, West Indies v England (Kingston)	1934-35
270	D.G. Bradman, Australia v England (Melbourne)	1936-37
268	G.N. Yallop, Australia v Pakistan (Melbourne)	1983-84
266	W.H. Ponsford, Australia v England (Oval)	1934
262*	D.L. Amiss, England v West Indies (Kingston)	1973-74
261	F.M.M. Worrell, West Indies v England (Nottingham)	1950
260	C.C. Hunte, West Indies v Pakistan (Kingston)	1957-58
259	G.M. Turner, New Zealand v West Indies (Georgetown)	1971-72
258	T.W. Graveney, England v West Indies (Nottingham)	1957
258	S.M. Nurse, West Indies v New Zealand (Christchurch)	1968-69
256	R.B. Kanhai, West Indies v India (Calcutta)	1958-59
256	K.F. Barrington, England v Australia (Manchester)	1964
255*	D.J. McGlew, South Africa v New Zealand (Wellington)	1952-53
254	D.G. Bradman, Australia v England (Lord's)	1930
251	W.R. Hammond, England v Australia (Sydney)	1928-29
250	K.D. Walters, Australia v New Zealand (Christchurch)	1976-77
250	S.F.A.F. Bacchus, West Indies v India (Kanpur)	1978-79

The highest individual innings for other countries are:

236*	S.M. Gavaskar, India v West Indies (Madras)	1983-84
190	S. Wettimuny, Sri Lanka v England (Lord's)	1984

MOST RUNS IN A SERIES

Runs		*Series*	*T*	*I*	*NO*	*HS*	*Avge*	*100*	*50*
974	D.G. Bradman (A v E)	1930	5	7	0	334	139.14	4	—
905	W.R. Hammond (E v A)	1928-29	5	9	1	251	113.12	4	—
834	R.N. Harvey (A v SA)	1952-53	5	9	0	205	92.66	4	3
829	I.V.A. Richards (WI v E)	1976	4	7	0	291	118.42	3	2
827	C.L. Walcott (WI v A)	1954-55	5	10	0	155	82.70	5	2
824	G.St A. Sobers (WI v P)	1957-58	5	8	2	365*	137.33	3	3
810	D.G. Bradman (A v E)	1936-37	5	9	0	270	90.00	3	1
806	D.G. Bradman (A v SA)	1931-32	5	5	1	299*	201.50	4	—
779	E.de C. Weekes (WI v I)	1948-49	5	7	0	194	111.28	4	2
774	S.M. Gavaskar (I v WI)	1970-71	4	8	3	220	154.80	4	3
761	Mudassar Nazar (P v I)	1982-83	6	8	2	231	126.83	4	1
758	D.G. Bradman (A v E)	1934	5	8	0	304	94.75	2	1
753	D.C.S. Compton (E v SA)	1947	5	8	0	208	94.12	4	2

RECORD WICKET PARTNERSHIPS

1st	413	V. Mankad/Pankaj Roy, I v NZ (Madras)	1955-56
2nd	451	W.H. Ponsford/D.G. Bradman, A v E (Oval)	1934
3rd	451	Mudassar Nazar/Javed Miandad, P v I (Hyderabad)	1982-83
4th	411	P.B.H. May/M.C. Cowdrey, E v WI (Birmingham)	1957
5th	405	S.G. Barnes/D.G. Bradman, A v E (Sydney)	1946-47
6th	346	J.H.W. Fingleton/D.G. Bradman, A v E (Melbourne)	1936-37
7th	347	D.St E. Atkinson/C.C. Depeiza, WI v A (Bridgetown)	1954-55
8th	246	L.E.G. Ames/G.O.B. Allen, E v NZ (Lord's)	1931
9th	190	Asif Iqbal/Intikhab Alam, P v E (Oval)	1967
10th	151	B.F. Hastings/R.O. Collinge, NZ v P (Auckland)	1972-73

WICKET PARTNERSHIPS OF OVER 300

451	2nd	W.H. Ponsford/D.G. Bradman, A v E (Oval)	1934
451	3rd	Mudassar Nazar/Javed Miandad, P v I (Hyderabad)	1982-83
446	2nd	C.C. Hunte/G.St A. Sobers, WI v P (Kingston)	1957-58
413	1st	V. Mankad/Pankaj Roy, I v NZ (Madras)	1955-56
411	4th	P.B.H. May/M.C. Cowdrey, E v WI (Birmingham)	1957
405	5th	S.G. Barnes/D.B. Bradman, A v E (Sydney)	1946-47
399	4th	G.St A. Sobers/F.M.M. Worrell, WI v E (Bridgetown)	1959-60
397	3rd	Qasim Omar/Javed Miandad, P v SL (Faisalabad)	1985-86
388	4th	W.H. Ponsford/D.G. Bradman, A v E (Leeds)	1934
387	1st	G.M. Turner/T.W. Jarvis, NZ v WI (Georgetown)	1971-72
382	2nd	L. Hutton/M. Leyland, E v A (Oval)	1938
382	1st	W.M. Lawry/R.B. Simpson, A v WI (Bridgetown)	1964-65
370	3rd	W.J. Edrich/D.C.S. Compton, E v SA (Lord's)	1947
369	2nd	J.H. Edrich/K.F. Barrington, E v NZ (Leeds)	1965
359	1st	L. Hutton/C. Washbrook, E v SA (Johannesburg)	1948-49
351	2nd	G.A. Gooch/D.I. Gower, E v A (Oval)	1985
350	4th	Mushtaq Mohammad/Asif Iqbal, P v NZ (Dunedin)	1972-73
347	7th	D.St E. Atkinson/C.C. Depeiza, WI v A (Bridgetown)	1954-55
346	6th	J.H.W. Fingleton/D.G. Bradman, A v E (Melbourne)	1936-37
344*	2nd	S.M. Gavaskar/D.B. Vengsarkar, I v WI (Calcutta)	1978-79
341	3rd	E.J. Barlow/R.G. Pollock, SA v A (Adelaide)	1963-64
338	3rd	E.de C. Weekes/F.M.M. Worrell, WI v E (Port-of-Spain)	1953-54
336	4th	W.M. Lawry/K.D. Walters, A v WI (Sydney)	1968-69
331	2nd	R.T. Robinson/D.I. Gower, E v A (Birmingham)	1985
323	1st	J.B. Hobbs/W. Rhodes, E v A (Melbourne)	1911-12
319	3rd	A. Melville/A.D. Nourse, SA v E (Nottingham)	1947
316†	3rd	G.R. Viswanath/Yashpal Sharma, I v E (Madras)	1981-82
308	7th	Waqar Hasan/Imtiaz Ahmed, P v NZ (Lahore)	1955-56
308	3rd	R.B. Richardson/I.V.A. Richards, WI v A (St. John's)	1983-84
303	3rd	I.V.A. Richards/A.I. Kallicharran, WI v E (Nottingham)	1976
301	2nd	A.R. Morris/D.G. Bradman, A v E (Leeds)	1948

†415 runs were added for this wicket in two separate partnerships. D.B. Vengsarkar retired hurt and was replaced by Yashpal Sharma after 99 runs had been added.

HIGHEST RUN AGGREGATES

Runs			*Tests*	*Inns*	*NO*	*HS*	*Avge*	*100*	*50*
9192	S.M. Gavaskar	(I)	112	195	16	236*	51.35	32	39
8114	G. Boycott	(E)	108	193	23	246*	47.72	22	42
8032	G.St A. Sobers	(WI)	93	160	21	365*	57.78	26	30
7624	M.C. Cowdrey	(E)	114	188	15	182	44.06	22	38
7515	C.H. Lloyd	(WI)	110	175	14	242*	46.67	19	39
7249	W.R. Hammond	(E)	85	140	16	336*	58.45	22	24
7110	G.S. Chappell	(A)	87	151	19	247*	53.86	24	31
6996	D.G. Bradman	(A)	52	80	10	334	99.94	29	13
6971	L. Hutton	(E)	79	138	15	364	56.67	19	33
6806	K.F. Barrington	(E)	82	131	15	256	58.67	20	35
6227	R.B. Kanhai	(WI)	79	137	6	256	47.53	15	28
6149	R.N. Harvey	(A)	79	137	10	205	48.41	21	24
6080	G.R. Viswanath	(I)	91	155	10	222	41.93	14	35
5909	A.R. Border	(A)	78	138	23	196	51.38	16	31
5889	I.V.A. Richards	(WI)	77	116	7	291	54.02	19	25
5807	D.C.S. Compton	(E)	78	131	15	278	50.06	17	28
5410	J.B. Hobbs	(E)	61	102	7	211	56.94	15	28
5385	D.I. Gower	(E)	76	129	11	215	45.63	12	25
5357	K.D. Walters	(A)	74	125	14	250	48.26	15	33
5350	Javed Miandad	(P)	71	111	17	280*	56.91	14	28
5345	I.M. Chappell	(A)	75	136	10	196	42.42	14	26
5234	W.M. Lawry	(A)	67	123	12	210	47.15	13	27
5138	J.H. Edrich	(E)	77	127	9	310*	43.54	12	24
5062	Zaheer Abbas	(P)	78	124	11	274	44.79	12	20
4882	T.W. Graveney	(E)	79	123	13	258	44.38	11	20
4869	R.B. Simpson	(A)	62	111	7	311	46.81	10	27
4816	C.G. Greenidge	(WI)	66	111	13	223	49.14	12	26
4737	I.R. Redpath	(A)	66	120	11	171	43.45	8	31
4625	D.B. Vengsarkar	(I)	82	134	14	159	38.54	9	25
4555	H. Sutcliffe	(E)	54	84	9	194	60.73	16	23
4537	P.B.H. May	(E)	66	106	9	285*	46.77	13	22
4502	E.R. Dexter	(E)	62	102	8	205	47.89	9	27

NINE OR TEN WICKETS IN AN INNINGS

10-53	J.C. Laker, England v Australia (Manchester)	1956
9-28	G.A. Lohmann, England v South Africa (Johannesburg)	1895-96
9-37	J.C. Laker, England v Australia (Manchester)	1956
9-52	R.J. Hadlee, New Zealand v Australia (Brisbane)	1985-86
9-69	J.M. Patel, India v Australia (Kanpur)	1959-60
9-83	Kapil Dev, India v West Indies (Ahmedabad)	1983-84
9-86	Sarfraz Nawaz, Pakistan v Australia (Melbourne)	1978-79
9-95	J.M. Noreiga, West Indies v India (Port-of-Spain)	1970-71
9-102	S.P. Gupte, India v West Indies (Kanpur)	1958-59
9-103	S.F. Barnes, England v South Africa (Johannesburg)	1913-14
9-113	H.J. Tayfield, South Africa v England (Johannesburg)	1956-57
9-121	A.A. Mailey, Australia v England (Melbourne)	1920-21

FIFTEEN OR MORE WICKETS IN A MATCH

19-90	J.C. Laker, England v Australia (Manchester)	1956
17-159	S.F. Barnes, England v South Africa (Johannesburg)	1913-14
16-137	R.A.L. Massie, Australia v England (Lord's)	1972
15-28	J. Briggs, England v South Africa (Cape Town)	1888-89
15-45	G.A. Lohmann, England v South Africa (Port Elizabeth)	1895-96
15-99	C. Blythe, England v South Africa (Leeds)	1907
15-104	H. Verity, England v Australia (Lord's)	1934
15-123	R.J. Hadlee, New Zealand v Australia (Brisbane)	1985-86
15-124	W. Rhodes, England v Australia (Melbourne)	1903-04

HAT-TRICKS

F.R. Spofforth	Australia v England (Melbourne)	1878-79
W. Bates	England v Australia (Melbourne)	1882-83
J. Briggs	England v Australia (Sydney)	1891-92
G.A. Lohmann	England v South Africa (Port Elizabeth)	1895-96
J.T. Hearne	England v Australia (Leeds)	1899
H. Trumble	Australia v England (Melbourne)	1901-02
H. Trumble	Australia v England (Melbourne)	1903-04
T.J. Matthews (2)*	Australia v South Africa (Manchester)	1912
M.J.C. Allom†	England v New Zealand (Christchurch)	1929-30
T.W.J. Goddard	England v South Africa (Johannesburg)	1938-39
P.J. Loader	England v West Indies (Leeds)	1957
L.F. Kline	Australia v South Africa (Cape Town)	1957-58
W.W. Hall	West Indies v Pakistan (Lahore)	1958-59
G.M. Griffin	South Africa v England (Lord's)	1960
L.R. Gibbs	West Indies v Australia (Adelaide)	1960-61
P.J. Petherick	New Zealand v Pakistan (Lahore)	1976-77

**In each innings.*   *†Four wickets in five balls.*

MOST WICKETS IN A SERIES

Wkts		*Series*	*Tests*	*Balls*	*Mdns*	*Runs*	*Avge*	*5 wI*	*10 wM*
49	S.F. Barnes (E v SA)	1913-14	4	1356	56	536	10.93	7	3
46	J.C. Laker (E v A)	1956	5	1703	127	442	9.60	4	2
44	C.V. Grimmet (A v SA)	1935-36	5	2077	140	642	14.59	5	3
42	T.M. Alderman (A v E)	1981	6	1950	76	893	21.26	4	—
41	R.M. Hogg (A v E)	1978-79	6	1740	60	527	12.85	5	2
40	Imran Khan (P v I)	1982-83	6	1339	69	558	13.95	4	2
39	A.V. Bedser (E v A)	1953	5	1591	58	682	17.48	5	1
39	D.K. Lillee (A v E)	1981	6	1870	81	870	22.30	2	1
38	M.W. Tate (E v A)	1924-25	5	2528	62	881	23.18	5	1
37	W.J. Whitty (A v SA)	1910-11	5	1395	55	632	17.08	2	—
37	H.J. Tayfield (SA v E)	1956-57	5	2280	105	636	17.18	4	1
36	A.E.E. Vogler (SA v E)	1909-10	5	1349	33	783	21.75	4	1
36	A.A. Mailey (A v E)	1920-21	5	1465	27	946	26.27	4	2
35	G.A. Lohmann (E v SA)	1895-96	3	520	38	203	5.80	4	2
35	B.S. Chandrasekhar (I v E)	1972-73	5	1747	83	662	18.91	4	—

HIGHEST WICKET AGGREGATES

Wkts			*Tests*	*Balls*	*Runs*	*Avge*	*5wI*	*10wM*
355	D.K. Lillee	(A)	70	18467	8493	23.92	23	7
343	I.T. Botham	(E)	79	18391	9046	26.37	25	4
325	R.G.D. Willis	(E)	90	17357	8190	25.20	16	—
309	L.R. Gibbs	(WI)	79	27115	8989	29.09	18	2
307	F.S. Trueman	(E)	67	15178	6625	21.57	17	3
299	R.J. Hadlee	(NZ)	60	15309	6743	22.55	24	6
297	D.L. Underwood	(E)	86	21862	7674	25.83	17	6
281	Kapil Dev	(I)	74	16007	8054	28.66	19	2
266	B.S. Bedi	(I)	67	21364	7637	28.71	14	1
252	J.B. Statham	(E)	70	16056	6261	24.84	9	1
249	Imran Khan	(P)	54	13275	5587	22.43	17	4
248	R. Benaud	(A)	63	19108	6704	27.03	16	1
246	G.D. McKenzie	(A)	60	17681	7328	29.78	16	3
242	B.S. Chandrasekhar	(I)	58	15963	7199	29.74	16	2
236	A.V. Bedser	(E)	51	15918	5876	24.89	15	5
235	G.St A. Sobers	(WI)	93	21599	7999	34.03	6	—
233	M.A. Holding	(WI)	55	11842	5414	23.23	13	2
228	R.R. Lindwall	(A)	61	13650	5251	23.03	12	—
220	J. Garner	(WI)	51	11769	4792	21.78	6	—
216	C.V. Grimmett	(A)	37	14513	5231	24.21	21	7
202	A.M.E. Roberts	(WI)	47	11136	5174	25.61	11	2
202	J.A. Snow	(E)	49	12021	5387	26.66	8	1
200	J.R. Thomson	(A)	51	10535	5601	28.00	8	—

MOST WICKET-KEEPING DISMISSALS IN AN INNINGS

7 (7 ct)	Wasim Bari, Pakistan v New Zealand (Auckland)	1978-79
7 (7 ct)	R.W. Taylor, England v India (Bombay)	1979-80
6 (6 ct)	A.T.W. Grout, Australia v South Africa (Johannesburg)	1957-58
6 (6 ct)	D.T. Lindsay, South Africa v Australia (Johannesburg)	1966-67
6 (6 ct)	J.T. Murray, England v India (Lord's)	1967
6 (6 ct)	R.W. Marsh, Australia v England (Brisbane)	1982-83
6 (6 ct)	S.A.R. Silva, Sri Lanka v India (Colombo)	1985-86
6 (5 ct, 1 st)	S.M.H. Kirmani, India v New Zealand (Christchurch)	1975-76

MOST WICKET-KEEPING DISMISSALS IN A MATCH

10 (10 ct)	R.W. Taylor, England v India (Bombay)	1979-80

MOST WICKET-KEEPING DISMISSALS IN A SERIES

28 (28 ct)	R.W. Marsh, Australia v England	1982-83
26 (23 ct, 3 st)	J.H.B. Waite, South Africa v New Zealand	1961-62
26 (26 ct)	R.W. Marsh, Australia v West Indies (6 Tests)	1975-76
24 (22 ct, 2 st)	D.L. Murray, West Indies v England	1963
24 (24 ct)	D.T. Lindsay, South Africa v Australia	1966-67
24 (21 ct, 3 st)	A.P.E. Knott, England v Australia (6 Tests)	1970-71

HIGHEST WICKET-KEEPING DISMISSAL AGGREGATES

Total			*Tests*	*Ct*	*St*
355	R.W. Marsh	Australia	96	343	12
269	A.P.E. Knott	England	95	250	19
228	Wasim Bari	Pakistan	81	201	27
219	T.G. Evans	England	91	173	46
198	S.M.H. Kirmani	India	88	160	38
189	D.L. Murray	West Indies	62	181	8
187	A.T.W. Grout	Australia	51	163	24
174	R.W. Taylor	England	57	167	7
141	J.H.B. Waite	South Africa	50	124	17
130	W.A.S. Oldfield	Australia	54	78	52
114†	J.M. Parks	England	46	103	11
110	P.J.L. Dujon	West Indies	33	108	2

†Including two catches taken in the field.

MOST CATCHES IN AN INNINGS (FIELDERS)

5	V.Y. Richardson, Australia v South Africa (Durban)	1935-36
5	Yajurvindra Singh, India v England (Bangalore)	1976-77

MOST CATCHES IN A MATCH (FIELDERS)

7	G.S. Chappell, Australia v England (Perth)	1974-75
7	Yajurvindra Singh, India v England (Bangalore)	1976-77

MOST CATCHES IN A SERIES (FIELDERS)

15	J.M. Gregory, Australia v England	1920-21

HIGHEST AGGREGATE OF CATCHES (FIELDERS)

Total			*Tests*
122	G.S. Chappell	Australia	87
120	M.C. Cowdrey	England	114
110	W.R. Hammond	England	85
110	R.B. Simpson	Australia	62
109	G.St A. Sobers	West Indies	93
105	I.M. Chappell	Australia	75

MOST TEST APPEARANCES

England	M.C. Cowdrey	114
Australia	R.W. Marsh	96
South Africa	J.H.B. Waite	50
West Indies	C.H. Lloyd	110
New Zealand	B.E. Congdon	61
India	S.M. Gavaskar	112
Pakistan	Wasim Bari	81
Sri Lanka	R.S. Madugalle	18

BATTING RECORDS

Highest Individual Innings

189*	I.V.A. Richards, West Indies v England	Manchester	1984
175*	Kapil Dev, India v Zimbabwe	Tunbridge Wells	1983
171*	G.M. Turner, New Zealand v East Africa	Birmingham	1975
158	D.I. Gower, England v New Zealand	Brisbane	1982-83
153*	I.V.A. Richards, West Indies v Australia	Melbourne	1979-80

Hundred On Debut

103	D.L. Amiss, England v Australia	Manchester	1972
148	D.L. Haynes, West Indies v Australia	St. Johns	1977-78

Highest Partnerships For Each Wicket

1st	188	K. Srikkanth/R.J. Shastri, I v E	Cuttack	1984-85
2nd	221	C.G. Greenidge/I.V.A. Richards WI v I	Jamshedpur	1983-84
3rd	224*	D.M. Jones/A.R. Border, A v SL	Adelaide	1984-85
4th	157*	R.B. Kerr/D.M. Jones, A v E	Melbourne	1984-85
5th	152	I.V.A. Richards/C.H. Lloyd, WI v SL	Brisbane	1984-85
6th	144	Imran Khan/Shahid Mahboob, P v SL	Leeds	1983
7th	108	Ramiz Raja/Anil Dalpat, P v NZ	Christchurch	1984-85
8th	68	B.E. Congdon/B.L. Cairns, NZ v E	Scarborough	1978
9th	126*	Kapil Dev/S.M.H. Kirmani, I v Z	Tunbridge Wells	1983
10th	106*	I.V.A. Richards/M.A. Holding, WI v E	Manchester	1984

Most Runs in a Career

		I	*NO*	*HS*	*Runs*	*Avge*	*100*	*50*
I.V.A. Richards	WI	89	15	189*	4071	55.01	8	27
D.L. Haynes	WI	92	12	148	3348	41.85	8	19
C.G. Greenidge	WI	68	7	115	2912	47.73	6	19
A.R. Border	A	106	16	127*	2898	32.20	3	18
Zaheer Abbas	P	57	6	123	2464	48.31	7	12
D.I. Gower	E	74	7	158	2427	36.22	7	8
G.S. Chappell	A	71	14	138*	2329	40.85	3	14
Javed Miandad	P	72	14	119*	2155	37.15	2	13
G.M. Wood	A	71	9	114*	2129	34.33	3	11

BOWLING RECORDS

Most Wickets in an Innings

7-51	W.W. Davis, West Indies v Australia	Leeds	1983
6-14	G.J. Gilmour, Australia v England	Leeds	1975
6-14	Imran Khan, Pakistan v India	Sharjah	1984-85
6-15	C.E.H. Croft, West Indies v England	Kingstown	1980-81
6-39	K.H. MacLeay, Australia v England	Nottingham	1983

Hat-Trick

Jalaluddin	Pakistan v Australia	Hyderabad	1982-83

Most Wickets in a Career

		Balls	*Runs*	*Wkts*	*Avge*	*Best*	*4w*
M.A. Holding	WI	4734	2613	122	21.41	5-26	5
J. Garner	WI	4184	2102	116	18.12	5-31	4
D.K. Lillee	A	3593	2145	103	20.82	5-34	6
I.T. Botham	E	3936	2639	100	26.39	4-56	1
R.J. Hadlee	NZ	4017	2148	100	21.48	5-25	4

WICKET-KEEPING RECORDS

Most Dismissals in an Innings

5 (5 ct)	R.G. de Alwis	SL v A	Colombo	1982-83
5 (5 ct)	S.M.H. Kirmani	I v Z	Leicester	1983
5 (5 ct)	R.W. Marsh	A v E	Leeds	1981
5 (3 ct/2 st)	S. Viswanath	I v E	Sydney	1984-85

Most Dismissals in a Career

R.W. Marsh	Australia	123 dismissals (119 ct/4 st) in 91 matches

FIELDING RECORDS

Most Catches in an Innings

4	Salim Malik	P v NZ	Sialkot	1984-85
4	S.M. Gavaskar	I v P	Sharjah	1984-85

Most Catches in a Career

I.V.A. Richards	West Indies	44 in 98 matches
C.H. Lloyd	West Indies	40 in 87 matches

ALL-ROUND RECORDS

Fifty Runs and Four Wickets in a Match

69*/4-42	D.A.G. Fletcher	Z v A	Nottingham	1983

1000 Runs and 100 Dismissals

I.T. Botham	England	1248 Runs	100 Wickets
R.W. Marsh	Australia	1220 Runs	123 Dismissals (119 ct/4 st)

LIMITED-OVERS CRICKET

Updated to 24 August 1985

RESULTS OF ONE-DAY INTERNATIONAL MATCHES 1970-71 TO 1985

(*329 MATCHES*)

		Matches	*E*	*A*	*I*	*NZ*	*P*	*SL*	*WI*	*C*	*EA*	*Z*	*Tied*	*NR*
England	v Australia	33	17	15	—	—	—	—	—	—	—	—	—	1
	v India	15	10	—	5	—	—	—	—	—	—	—	—	—
	v New Zealand	21	10	—	—	8	—	—	—	—	—	—	—	3
	v Pakistan	16	10	—	—	—	6	—	—	—	—	—	—	—
	v Sri Lanka	4	3	—	—	—	—	1	—	—	—	—	—	—
	v West Indies	18	4	—	—	—	—	—	14	—	—	—	—	—
	v Canada	1	1	—	—	—	—	—	—	—	—	—	—	—
	v East Africa	1	1	—	—	—	—	—	—	—	—	—	—	—
Australia	v India	13	—	8	4	—	—	—	—	—	—	—	—	1
	v New Zealand	21	—	13	—	7	—	—	—	—	—	—	—	1
	v Pakistan	16	—	7	—	—	7	—	—	—	—	—	—	2
	v Sri Lanka	10	—	5	—	—	—	3	—	—	—	—	—	2
	v West Indies	40	—	11	—	—	—	—	28	—	—	—	1	—
	v Canada	1	—	1	—	—	—	—	—	—	—	—	—	—
	v Zimbabwe	2	—	1	—	—	—	—	—	—	—	1	—	—
India	v New Zealand	12	—	—	3	9	—	—	—	—	—	—	—	—
	v Pakistan	15	—	—	8	—	6	—	—	—	—	—	—	1
	v Sri Lanka	5	—	—	4	—	—	1	—	—	—	—	—	—
	v West Indies	12	—	—	3	—	—	—	9	—	—	—	—	—
	v East Africa	1	—	—	1	—	—	—	—	—	—	—	—	—
	v Zimbabwe	2	—	—	2	—	—	—	—	—	—	—	—	—
New Zealand	v Pakistan	12	—	—	—	7	4	—	—	—	—	—	—	1
	v Sri Lanka	12	—	—	—	9	—	3	—	—	—	—	—	—
	v West Indies	10	—	—	—	1	—	—	8	—	—	—	—	1
	v East Africa	1	—	—	—	1	—	—	—	—	—	—	—	—
Pakistan	v Sri Lanka	7	—	—	—	—	5	2	—	—	—	—	—	—
	v West Indies	18	—	—	—	—	3	—	15	—	—	—	—	—
	v Canada	1	—	—	—	—	1	—	—	—	—	—	—	—
Sri Lanka	v West Indies	7	—	—	—	—	—	—	7	—	—	—	—	—
West Indies	v Zimbabwe	2	—	—	—	—	—	—	2	—	—	—	—	—
		329	56	61	30	42	32	10	83	—	—	1	1	13

	Matches	*Won*	*Lost*	*Tied*	*NR*
England	109	56	49	—	4
Australia	136	61	67	1	7
India	75	30	43	—	2
New Zealand	89	42	41	—	6
Pakistan	85	32	49	—	4
Sri Lanka	45	10	33	—	2
West Indies	107	83	22	1	1
Canada	3	—	3	—	—
East Africa	3	—	3	—	—
Zimbabwe	6	1	5	—	—

TEAM RECORDS

Highest Innings Totals

338-5	(60 overs)	Pakistan v Sri Lanka	Swansea	1983
334-4	(60 overs)	England v India	Lord's	1975
333-9	(60 overs)	England v Sri Lanka	Taunton	1983
333-8	(45 overs)	West Indies v India	Jamshedpur	1983-84
330-6	(60 overs)	Pakistan v Sri Lanka	Nottingham	1975

Highest Total Batting Second

297-6	(48.5 overs)	New Zealand v England	Adelaide	1982-83

Highest Match Aggregate

626-14	(120 overs)	Pakistan v Sri Lanka	Swansea	1983

Lowest Innings Totals

(*Excluding Abbreviated Matches*)

45	(40.3 overs)	Canada v England	Manchester	1979
63	(25.5 overs)	India v Australia	Sydney	1980-81
70	(25.2 overs)	Australia v England	Birmingham	1977
74	(29 overs)	New Zealand v Australia	Wellington	1981-82
79	(34.2 overs)	India v Pakistan	Sialkot	1978-79

Lowest Match Aggregate

91-12	(54.2 overs)	England v Canada	Manchester	1979

Largest Margins of Victory

232 runs	Australia beat Sri Lanka	Adelaide	1984-85
202 runs	England beat India	Lord's	1975
10 wickets	India beat East Africa	Leeds	1975
10 wickets	New Zealand beat India	Melbourne	1980-81
10 wickets	West Indies beat Zimbabwe	Birmingham	1983
10 wickets	India beat Sri Lanka	Sharjah	1983-84
10 wickets	West Indies beat New Zealand	Port-of-Spain	1984-85

Tied Match

Australia (222-9) v West Indies (222-5)	Melbourne	1983-84

Smallest Margins of Victory

(*Excluding Abbreviated Matches*)

1 run	New Zealand beat Pakistan	Sialkot	1976-77
1 run	New Zealand beat Australia	Sydney	1980-81
1 wicket	England beat West Indies	Leeds	1973
1 wicket	West Indies beat Pakistan	Birmingham	1975
1 wicket	New Zealand beat West Indies	Christchurch	1979-80
1 wicket	West Indies beat Pakistan	Adelaide	1983-84
1 wicket	Pakistan beat New Zealand	Multan	1984-85

TEXACO TROPHY RECORDS 1972-1985

(Including the Prudential Trophy)

Highest Total: 320-8 England v Australia; Birmingham 1980
Lowest Total: 70 Australia v England; Birmingham 1977
Highest Aggregate: 593 England (320-8) v Australia (273-5); Birmingham 1980
Largest Victories: 9 wkts England beat India; Leeds 1982
132 runs England beat Pakistan; Manchester 1978
Narrowest Victories: 1 wkt England beat West Indies; Leeds 1973
2 runs Australia beat England; Birmingham 1981
Highest Score 189* I.V.A. Richards WI v E Manchester 1984

Hundreds (18)

D.L. Amiss (3)	103	E v A	Manchester	1972
	100	E v NZ	Swansea	1973
	108	E v A	The Oval	1977
G.S. Chappell	125*	A v E	The Oval	1977
R.C. Fredericks	105	WI v E	The Oval	1973
G.A. Gooch (3)	108	E v A	Birmingham	1980
	115	E v A	Birmingham	1985
	117*	E v A	Lord's	1985
D.I. Gower (2)	114*	E v P	The Oval	1978
	102	E v A	Lord's	1985
A.J. Lamb	118	E v P	Nottingham	1982
D. Lloyd	116*	E v P	Nottingham	1974
Majid Khan	109	P v E	Nottingham	1974
C.T. Radley	117*	E v NZ	Manchester	1978
I.V.A. Richards (2)	119*	WI v E	Scarborough	1976
	189*	WI v E	Manchester	1984
G.M. Wood (2)	108	A v E	Leeds	1981
	114*	A v E	Lord's	1985

Fastest Hundred: 88 balls – Majid Khan, P v E; Nottingham 1974
Fastest Fifties: 35 balls – R.O. Butcher, E v A; Birmingham 1980
35 balls – Kapil Dev, I v E; Leeds 1982

Highest Partnership for Each Wicket

1st	161	D.L. Amiss/J.M. Brearley, E v A; The Oval	1977
2nd	202	G.A. Gooch/D.I. Gower, E v A; Lord's	1985
3rd	159	A.J. Lamb/D.I. Gower, E v I; The Oval	1982
4th	116	G.A. Gooch/I.T. Botham, E v A; Manchester	1985
5th	74	A.R. Border/M.F. Kent, A v E; Lord's	1981
6th	86	K.J. Hughes/R.W. Marsh, A v E; The Oval	1980
7th	77	A.W. Greig/A.P.E. Knott, E v A; Lord's	1972
8th	68	B.E. Congdon/B.L. Cairns, NZ v E; Scarborough	1978
9th	47	A.J. Lamb/N.A. Foster, E v WI; Manchester	1984
10th	106*	I.V.A. Richards/M.A. Holding, WI v E; Manchester	1984

Most Wickets	5-18 G.J. Cosier, A v E; Birmingham	1977
	5-20 G.S. Chappell, A v E; Birmingham	1977
	5-28 B.L. Cairns, NZ v E; Scarborough	1978
	5-31 M. Hendrick, E v A; The Oval	1980
	5-50 V.A. Holder, WI v E; Birmingham	1976

Most Economical Bowling

O	*M*	*R*	*W*		
11	4	12	1	L.R. Gibbs, WI v E; The Oval	1973
11	4	12	2	C.M. Old, E v WI; Leeds	1980

Most Expensive Bowling

O	*M*	*R*	*W*		
11	0	84	0	B.L. Cairns, NZ v E; Manchester	1978

Most Wicket-Keeping Dismissals

5 (5 ct)	R.W. Marsh, A v E; Leeds	1981

Most Catches in the Field

3	A.W. Greig, E v WI; Leeds	1973
3	B.S. Bedi, I v E; Leeds	1974

RESULTS SUMMARY 1972-1985

	Played	*Won*	*Lost*	*No Result*
ENGLAND	38	22	15	1
AUSTRALIA	14	6	8	—
WEST INDIES	10	7	3	—
NEW ZEALAND	4	—	3	1
INDIA	4	—	4	—
PAKISTAN	6	2	4	—

1986 TEXACO TROPHY VENUES
55-OVERS MATCH RECORDS

THE OVAL, LONDON

Highest Total	280-3		Kent v Surrey	1976
Lowest Total	94		Camb U v Surrey	1974
Highest Score	125*	G.S. Chappell	Aus v England	1977
Best Bowling	5-21	B.D. Julien	Kent v Surrey	1973
	5-21	P.H.L. Wilson	Surrey v Comb U	1979

OLD TRAFFORD, MANCHESTER

Highest Total	314-5		Worcs v Lancs	1980
Lowest Total	68		Glam v Lancs	1973
Highest Score	189*	I.V.A. Richards	W. Indies v England	1984
Best Bowling	6-10	C.E.H. Croft	Lancs v Scotland	1982

HEADINGLEY, LEEDS

Highest Total	276-4		Warwicks v Yorks	1984
Lowest Total	109		Minor C (N) v Yorks	1974
Highest Score	108	G.M. Wood	Aus v England	1981
Best Bowling	5-50	G.B. Stevenson	Yorks v Worcs	1982

THE 1986 SEASON

Tours by first India and then New Zealand highlight the 1986 fixture list. Each will be playing a three-match rubber against England, with Cornhill Insurance continuing the sponsorship which they began in 1978. For the first time the opening Tests of both series will be at Lord's.

India, reigning world champions of limited-overs cricket, will be especially anxious to achieve a Test victory. In 42 matches since defeating Keith Fletcher's England team at Bombay in December 1981, they have won only once and been beaten 12 times. Perhaps even more remarkable is the fact that Kapil Dev is still looking for his first victory after leading India in 20 Tests.

Two rising stars will be making their first appearances in England. Mohammed Azharuddin, who announced his arrival at international level by uniquely scoring hundreds in each of his first three Tests, and the 20-year-old leg-spinner, Laxman Sivaramakrishnan, who played havoc with both batsmen and copy-takers by taking 19 wickets in his first two Tests against England. 'Siva' will be hoping that the three gods whose names he bears provide more favourable weather and pitches than those responsible for Bob Holland's welfare managed last season.

Also on display for the first time will be India's dashing opening batsman, Krishnamachari Srikkanth, and lively new-ball bowler, Chetan Sharma. Sunil Gavaskar will be looking forward to the Third Test at Edgbaston and his 115th Test cap – a world record to add to his tallies of runs (9,192) and hundreds (32).

After their historic 2-1 victory in Australia, New Zealand will undoubtedly fancy their chances of winning a series in England for the first time. Much will depend on Richard Hadlee retaining the form and fitness which accounted for 33 wickets in that short rubber. His knowledge of English batsmen and pitches is second to none and the Second Test will be played at Trent Bridge, his adopted home ground. Not since Alec

Bedser's day has one bowler carried a national attack to such an extent.

Their batting has plenty of depth with John Wright, Martin Crowe and Jeremy Coney well-versed in English conditions. Although he will be making his first visit here, John Reid (unrelated to his famous namesake), enjoyed considerable success on recent visits to Pakistan and Australia, confirming his temperament and application in a succession of long innings. On such Barringtonian performances are Test match victories based.

ENGLAND v INDIA

1930 TO 1984-85

Season	*Captains* *England*	*India*	*P*	*E W*	*I W*	*D*
1932	D.R. Jardine	C.K. Nayudu	1	1	—	—
1933-34	D.R. Jardine	C.K. Nayudu	3	2	—	1
1936	G.O.B. Allen	Maharaja of Vizianagram	3	2	—	1
1946	W.R. Hammond	Nawab of Pataudi sr	3	1	—	2
1951-52	N.D. Howard[1]	V.S. Hazare	5	1	1	3
1952	L. Hutton	V.S. Hazare	4	3	—	1
1959	P.B.H. May[2]	D.K. Gaekwad[3]	5	5	—	—
1961-62	E.R. Dexter	N.J. Contractor	5	—	2	3
1963-64	M.J.K. Smith	Nawab of Pataudi jr	5	—	—	5
1967	D.B. Close	Nawab of Pataudi jr	3	3	—	—
1971	R. Illingworth	A.L. Wadekar	3	—	1	2
1972-73	A.R. Lewis	A.L. Wadekar	5	1	2	2
1974	M.H. Denness	A.L. Wadekar	3	3	—	—
1976-77	A.W. Greig	B.S. Bedi	5	3	1	1
1979	J.M. Brearley	S. Venkataraghavan	4	1	—	3
1979-80	J.M. Brearley	G.R. Viswanath	1	1	—	—
1981-82	K.W.R. Fletcher	S.M. Gavaskar	6	—	1	5
1982	R.G.D. Willis	S.M. Gavaskar	3	1	—	2
1984-85	D.I. Gower	S.M. Gavaskar	5	2	1	2
	At Lord's		10	8	—	2
	At Manchester		7	3	—	4
	At The Oval		7	2	1	4
	At Leeds		4	3	—	1
	At Nottingham		1	1	—	—
	At Birmingham		3	3	—	—
	At Bombay		9	2	2	5
	At Calcutta		8	1	2	5
	At Madras		8	3	3	2
	At Delhi		7	3	—	4
	At Kanpur		6	1	—	5
	At Bangalore		2	—	1	1
	In England		32	20	1	11
	In India		40	10	8	22
	Totals		72	30	9	33

The Maharaja of Porbandar captained the 1932 Indian touring team but he did not play in the inaugural Test match.

The following deputised for the official touring captain or were appointed for only a minor portion of a home series:

[1]D.B. Carr (5th). [2]M.C. Cowdrey (4th and 5th). [3]Pankaj Roy (2nd).

HIGHEST INNINGS TOTALS

England	in England	633-5d	Birmingham	1979
	in India	652-7d	Madras	1984-85
India	in England	510	Leeds	1967
	in India	553-8d	Kanpur	1984-85

LOWEST INNINGS TOTALS

England	in England	101	The Oval	1971
	in India	102	Bombay	1981-82
India	in England	42	Lord's	1974
	in India	83	Madras	1976-77

HIGHEST MATCH AGGREGATE

1371 for 28 wickets	Madras	1984-85

LOWEST MATCH AGGREGATE

482 for 31 wickets	Lord's	1936

HIGHEST INDIVIDUAL INNINGS

England	in England	246*	G. Boycott, Leeds	1967
		217	W.R. Hammond, The Oval	1936
		205*	J. Hardstaff, jr, Lord's	1946
		214*	D. Lloyd, Birmingham	1974
		200*	D.I. Gower, Birmingham	1979
		208	I.T. Botham, The Oval	1982
	in India	207	M.W. Gatting, Madras	1984-85
		201	G. Fowler, Madras	1984-85
India	in England	221	S.M. Gavaskar, The Oval	1979
	in India	222	G.R. Viswanath, Madras	1981-82
		203*	Nawab of Pataudi jr, Delhi	1963-64

107 hundreds have been scored in this series (England 59, India 48).

HUNDRED IN EACH INNINGS

No instance

HUNDRED ON DEBUT IN SERIES

England	136	B.H. Valentine	Bombay	1933-34
	137*	A.J. Watkins	Delhi	1951-52
	175	T.W. Graveney	Bombay	1951-52
	100	M.J.K. Smith	Manchester	1959
	246*	G. Boycott	Leeds	1967
	109	B.L. D'Oliveira	Leeds	1967
	200*	D.I. Gower	Birmingham	1979
India	118	L. Amarnath	Bombay	1933-34
	112	A.A. Baig	Manchester	1959
	105	Hanumant Singh	Delhi	1963-64
	110	M. Azharuddin	Calcutta	1984-85

HIGHEST AGGREGATE OF RUNS IN A SERIES

England	in England	403	I.T. Botham	1982
	in India	594	K.F. Barrington	1961-62
India	in England	542	S.M. Gavaskar	1979
	in India	586	V.L. Manjrekar	1961-62

RECORD WICKET PARTNERSHIPS – ENGLAND

1st	178	G. Fowler/R.T. Robinson	Madras	1984-85
2nd	241	G. Fowler/M.W. Gatting	Madras	1984-85
3rd	169	R. Subba Row/M.J.K. Smith	The Oval	1959
4th	266	W.R. Hammond/T.S. Worthington	The Oval	1936
5th	254	K.W.R. Fletcher/A.W. Greig	Bombay	1972-73
6th	171	I.T. Botham/R.W. Taylor	Bombay	1979-80
7th	125	D.W. Randall/P.H. Edmonds	Lord's	1982
8th	168	R. Illingworth/P. Lever	Manchester	1971
9th	83	K.W.R. Fletcher/N. Gifford	Madras	1972-73
10th	70	P.J.W. Allott/R.G.D. Willis	Lord's	1982

RECORD WICKET PARTNERSHIPS – INDIA

1st	213	S.M. Gavaskar/C.P.S. Chauhan	The Oval	1979
2nd	192	F.M. Engineer/A.L. Wadekar	Bombay	1972-73
3rd	316	G.R. Viswanath/Yashpal Sharma	Madras	1981-82
4th	222	V.S. Hazare/ V.L. Manjrekar	Leeds	1952
5th	214	M. Azharuddin/R.J. Shastri	Calcutta	1984-85
6th	130	S.M.H. Kirmani/Kapil Dev	The Oval	1982
7th	235	R.J. Shastri/S.M.H. Kirmani	Bombay	1984-85
8th	128	R.J. Shastri/S.M.H. Kirmani	Delhi	1981-82
9th	104	R.J. Shastri/Madan Lal	Delhi	1981-82
10th	51	R.G. Nadkarni/B.S. Chandrasekhar	Calcutta	1963-64
		S.M.H. Kirmani/C. Sharma	Madras	1984-85

BEST INNINGS BOWLING ANALYSIS

England	in England	8-31	F.S. Trueman	Manchester	1952
	in India	7-46	J.K. Lever	Delhi	1976-77
India	in England	6-35	L. Amar Singh	Lord's	1936
	in India	8-55	M.H. Mankad	Madras	1951-52

BEST MATCH BOWLING ANALYSIS

England	in England	11-93	A.V. Bedser	Manchester	1946
	in India	13-106	I.T. Botham	Bombay	1979-80
India	in England	8-114	B.S. Chandrasekhar	The Oval	1971
	in India	12-108	M.H. Mankad	Madras	1951-52

HIGHEST WICKET AGGREGATE IN A SERIES

England	in England	29	F.S. Trueman	1952
	in India	29	D.L. Underwood	1976-77
India	in England	17	S.P. Gupte	1959
	in India	35	B.S. Chandrasekhar	1972-73

ENGLAND v NEW ZEALAND

1929-30 TO 1983-84

Season	*Captains* *England*	*New Zealand*	*P*	*E W*	*NZ W*	*D*
1929-30	A.H.H. Gilligan	T.C. Lowry	4	1	—	3
1931	D.R. Jardine	T.C. Lowry	3	1	—	2
1932-33	D.R. Jardine[1]	M.L. Page	2	—	—	2
1937	R.W.V. Robins	M.L. Page	3	1	—	2
1946-47	W.R. Hammond	W.A. Hadlee	1	—	—	1
1949	F.G. Mann[2]	W.A. Hadlee	4	—	—	4
1950-51	F.R. Brown	W.A. Hadlee	2	1	—	1
1954-55	L. Hutton	G.O. Rabone	2	2	—	—
1958	P.B.H. May	J.R. Reid	5	4	—	1
1958-59	P.B.H. May	J.R. Reid	2	1	—	1
1962-63	E.R. Dexter	J.R. Reid	3	3	—	—
1965	M.J.K. Smith	J.R. Reid	3	3	—	—
1965-66	M.J.K. Smith	B.W. Sinclair[3]	3	—	—	3
1969	R. Illingworth	G.T. Dowling	3	2	—	1
1970-71	R. Illingworth	G.T. Dowling	2	1	—	1
1973	R. Illingworth	B.E. Congdon	3	2	—	1
1974-75	M.H. Denness	B.E. Congdon	2	1	—	1
1977-78	G. Boycott	M.G. Burgess	3	1	1	1
1978	J.M. Brearley	M.G. Burgess	3	3	—	—
1983	R.G.D. Willis	G.P. Howarth	4	3	1	—
1983-84	R.G.D. Willis	G.P. Howarth	3	—	1	2
	At Lord's		9	5	—	4
	At The Oval		7	4	—	3
	At Manchester		4	2	—	2
	At Leeds		5	3	1	1
	At Birmingham		2	2	—	—
	At Nottingham		4	3	—	1
	At Christchurch		11	5	1	5
	At Wellington		5	2	1	2
	At Auckland		11	3	—	8
	At Dunedin		2	1	—	1
	In England		31	19	1	11
	In New Zealand		29	11	2	16
	Total		60	30	3	27

The following deputised for the official touring captain or were appointed for only a minor portion of a home series:
[1]R.E.S. Wyatt (2nd). [2]F.R. Brown (3rd and 4th). [3]M.E. Chapple (1st).

HIGHEST INNINGS TOTALS

England	in England	546-4d	Leeds	1965
	in New Zealand	593-6d	Auckland	1974-75
New Zealand	in England	551-9d	Lord's	1973
	in New Zealand	537	Wellington	1983-84

LOWEST INNINGS TOTALS

England	in England	187	Manchester	1937
	in New Zealand	64	Wellington	1977-78
New Zealand	in England	47	Lord's	1958
	in New Zealand	26	Auckland	1954-55

HIGHEST MATCH AGGREGATE

1293 for 34 wickets	Lord's	1931

LOWEST MATCH AGGREGATE

390 for 30 wickets	Lord's	1958

HIGHEST INDIVIDUAL INNINGS

England	in England	310*	J.H. Edrich, Leeds	1965
		206	L. Hutton, The Oval	1949
	in New Zealand	336*	W.R. Hammond, Auckland	1932-33
		227	W.R. Hammond Christchurch	1932-33
		216	K.W.R. Fletcher, Auckland	1974-75
New Zealand	in England	206	M.P. Donnelly, Lord's	1949
	in New Zealand	174*	J.V. Coney, Wellington	1983-84

91 hundreds have been scored in this series (England 65, New Zealand 26).

HUNDRED IN EACH INNINGS

New Zealand	122	102	G.P. Howarth	Auckland	1977-78

HUNDRED ON DEBUT IN SERIES

England	137	L.E.G. Ames	Lord's	1931
	122	G.O.B. Allen	Lord's	1931
	117	H. Sutcliffe	The Oval	1931
	114	J. Hardstaff jr	Lord's	1937
	121	J.D.B. Robertson	Lord's	1949
	103	R.T. Simpson	Manchester	1949
	100	P.E. Richardson	Birmingham	1958
	104*	C.A. Milton	Leeds	1958
	126	K.F. Barrington	Auckland	1962-63
	131*	P.H. Parfitt	Auckland	1962-63
	125	B.R. Knight	Auckland	1962-63
	310*	J.H. Edrich	Leeds	1965
	138*	D.L. Amiss	Nottingham	1973
	139	A.W. Greig	Nottingham	1973
	111	D.I. Gower	The Oval	1978
	109	C.J. Tavaré	The Oval	1983
	105	G. Fowler	The Oval	1983
	102*	A.J. Lamb	The Oval	1983
New Zealand	117	J.E. Mills	Wellington	1929-30

HIGHEST AGGREGATE OF RUNS IN A SERIES

England	in England	469	L. Hutton	1949
	in New Zealand	563	W.R. Hammond	1932-33
New Zealand	in England	462	M.P. Donnelly	1949
	in New Zealand	341	C.S. Dempster	1929-30

RECORD WICKET PARTNERSHIPS – ENGLAND

1st	223	G. Fowler/C.J. Tavaré	The Oval	1983
2nd	369	J.H. Edrich/K.F. Barrington	Leeds	1965
3rd	245	J. Hardstaff jr/W.R. Hammond	Lord's	1937
4th	266	M.H. Denness/K.W.R. Fletcher	Auckland	1974-75
5th	242	W.R. Hammond/L.E.G. Ames	Christchurch	1932-33
6th	240	P.H. Parfitt/B.R. Knight	Auckland	1962-63
7th	149	A.P.E. Knott/P. Lever	Auckland	1970-71
8th	246	L.E.G. Ames/G.O.B. Allen	Lord's	1931
9th	163*	M.C. Cowdrey/A.C. Smith	Wellington	1962-63
10th	59	A.P.E. Knott/N. Gifford	Nottingham	1973

RECORD WICKET PARTNERSHIPS – NEW ZEALAND

1st	276	C.S. Dempster/J.E. Mills	Wellington	1929-30
2nd	131	B. Sutcliffe/J.R. Reid	Christchurch	1950-51
3rd	190	B.E. Congdon/B.F. Hastings	Lord's	1973
4th	154	J.G. Wright/J.J. Crowe	Auckland	1983-84
5th	177	B.E. Congdon/V. Pollard	Nottingham	1973
6th	117	M.G. Burgess/V. Pollard	Lord's	1973
7th	104	B. Sutcliffe/V. Pollard	Birmingham	1965
8th	104	D.A.R. Moloney/A.W. Roberts	Lord's	1937
9th	118	J.V. Coney/B.L. Cairns	Wellington	1983-84
10th	57	F.L.H. Mooney/J. Cowie	Leeds	1949

BEST INNINGS BOWLING ANALYSIS

England	in England	7-32	D.L. Underwood, Lord's	1969
	in New Zealand	7-75	F.S. Trueman, Christchurch	1962-63
New Zealand	in England	7-74	B.L. Cairns, Leeds	1983
	in New Zealand	7-143	B.L. Cairns, Wellington	1983-84

BEST MATCH BOWLING ANALYSIS

England	in England	12-101	D.L. Underwood, The Oval	1969
	in New Zealand	12-97	D.L. Underwood, Christchurch	1970-71
New Zealand	in England	10-140	J. Cowie, Manchester	1937
	in New Zealand	10-100	R.J. Hadlee, Wellington	1977-78

HIGHEST WICKET AGGREGATE IN A SERIES

England	in England	34	G.A.R. Lock	1958
	in New Zealand	17	K. Higgs	1965-66
			D.L. Underwood	1970-71
			I.T. Botham	1977-78
New Zealand	in England	21	R.J. Hadlee	1983
	in New Zealand	15	R.O. Collinge	1977-78
			R.J. Hadlee	1977-78

FIRST-CLASS UMPIRES 1986

***BIRD, Harold Dennis ('Dickie')** (Raley SM, Barnsley), b Barnsley, Yorkshire 19 Apr 1933. RHB, RM. Yorkshire 1956-59. Leicestershire 1960-64 (cap 1960). 1000 runs (1): 1028 (1960). HS 181* Yorks v Glam (Bradford) 1959. F-c career: 93 matches; 3314 runs @ 20.71, 2 hundreds. Appointed 1970. Umpired 32 Tests (1973 to 1985).

***BIRKENSHAW, Jack** (Rothwell GS), b Rothwell, Yorkshire 13 Nov 1940. LHB, OB. Yorkshire 1958-60. Leicestershire 1961-80 (cap 1965; benefit of £13,000 in 1974). Worcestershire 1981. Tests: 5 (1972-73 to 1973-74); 148 runs @ 21.14, HS 64 v Ind (Kanpur) 1972-73; 13 wickets @ 36.07, BB 5-57 v Pak (Karachi) 1972-73. Tours: WI 1969-70 (DN), 1973-74; Ind/Pak/SL 1967-68 (Int XI), 1972-73. HS 131 Leics v Surrey (Guildford) 1969. BB 8-94 Leics v Somerset (Taunton) 1972. F-c career: 490 matches; 12,780 runs @ 23.57, 4 hundreds; 1073 wickets @ 27.28. Appointed 1982. Promoted to Test panel 1986.

***CONSTANT, David** John, b Bradford-on-Avon, Wiltshire 9 Nov 1941. LHB, SLA. Kent 1961-63. Leicestershire 1965-68. HS 80 Leics v Glos (Bristol) 1966. F-c career: 61 matches; 1517 runs @ 19.20; 1 wicket @ 36.00. Appointed 1969. Umpired 30 Tests (1971 to 1985).

COOK, Cecil ('Sam'), b Tetbury, Gloucestershire 23 Aug 1921. RHB, SLA. Gloucestershire 1946-64 (cap 1946; benefit of £3067 in 1957; testimonial 1964). Took a wicket with his first ball in first-class cricket. Tests: 1 (1947); 4 runs, 0 wickets v SA (Nottingham). HS 35* v Sussex (Hove) 1957. BB 9-42 v Yorks (Bristol) 1947. F-c career: 506 matches; 1965 runs @ 5.39; 1782 wickets @ 20.52. Appointed 1971.

DUDLESTON, Barry (Stockport S), b Bebington, Cheshire 16 Jul 1945. RHB, SLA. Leicestershire 1966-80 (cap 1969; benefit of £25,000 in 1980). Gloucestershire 1981-83. Rhodesia 1976-80. 1000 (8); most – 1374 (1970). HS 202 Leics v Derbys (Leicester) 1979. BB 4-6 Leics v Surrey (Leicester) 1972. F-c career: 295 matches; 14,747 runs @ 32.48, 32 hundreds; 47 wickets @ 29.04. Appointed 1984.

EVANS, David Gwilliam Lloyd, b Lambeth, London 27 Jul 1933. RHB, WK. Glamorgan 1956-69 (cap 1959; benefit of £3500 in 1969). HS 46* v Oxford U (Oxford) 1961. F-c career: 270 matches; 2875 runs @ 10.53; 558 dismissals (502 ct, 56 st). Appointed 1971. Umpired 9 Tests (1981 to 1985).

HAMPSHIRE, John Harry (Oakwood THS, Rotherham), b Thurnscoe, Yorkshire 10 Feb 1941. RHB, LB. Son of John (Yorks 1937); brother of A.W. (Yorks 1975). Yorkshire 1961-81 (cap 1963; benefit of £28,425 in 1976; captain 1979-80). Derbyshire 1982-84 (cap 1982). Tasmania 1967-69, 1977-79. Tests: 8 (1969 to 1975); HS 107 v WI (Lord's) 1969 on debut (only player to score hundred at Lord's on debut in Tests. Tours: Aus 1970-71; SA 1972-73 (DHR), 1974-75 (DHR); WI 1964-65 (Cavs); NZ 1970-71; Pak 1967-68 (Cwlth XI); SL 1969-70; Zim 1980-81 (Leics). 1000 runs (15); most – 1596 (1978). HS 183* Yorks v Sussex (Hove) 1971. BB 7-52 Yorks v Glam (Cardiff) 1963. F-c career: 577 matches; 28,059 runs @ 34.55, 43 hundreds; 30 wickets @ 54.56; 445 ct. Appointed 1985.

HARRIS, John Humphrey, b Taunton 13 Feb 1936. LHB, RFM. Somerset 1952-59. Suffolk 1960-62. Devon 1975. HS 41 v Worcs (Taunton) 1957. BB 3-29 v Worcs (Bristol) 1959. F-c career: 15 matches: 154 runs @ 11.00; 19 wickets @ 32.57. Appointed 1983.

HOLDER, John Wakefield (Combermere S, Barbados), b St. George, Barbados 19 Mar 1945. RHB, RFM. Hampshire 1968-72. HS 33 v Sussex (Hove) 1971. BB 7-79 v Glos (Gloucester) 1972. F-c career: 47 matches; 374 runs @ 10.68; 139 wickets @ 24.56. Appointed 1983.

JAMESON, John Alexander (Taunton S), b Bombay, India 30 Jun 1941. RHB, RM/OB, WK. Brother of T.E.N. (Cambridge U and Warwicks 1970). Warwickshire 1960-76 (cap 1964; benefit of £13,500 in 1974). Tests: 4 (1971 to 1973-74); 214 runs @ 26.75, HS 82 v Ind (Oval) 1971; 1 wkt. Tours: Rhodesia 1972-73 (Int Wand); WI 1973-74. 1000 runs (11); most – 1948 (1973). HS 240* v Glos (Birmingham) 1974, sharing world record 2nd wicket partnership of 465 (unbroken) with R.B. Kanhai. BB 4-22 v Oxford U (Oxford) 1971. F-c career: 361 matches; 18,941 runs @ 33.34; 33 hundreds; 89 wickets @ 42.49. Appointed 1984.

JONES, Allan Arthur (St. John's C, Horsham), b Horley, Surrey 9 Dec 1947. RHB, RFM. Sussex 1966-69. Somerset 1970-75 (cap 1972). Northern Transvaal 1972-73. Middlesex 1976-79 (cap 1976). Orange Free State 1976-77. Glamorgan 1980-81. HS 33 Middx v Kent (Canterbury) 1978. BB 9-51 Somerset v Sussex (Hove) 1972. F-c career: 214 matches; 799 runs @ 5.39; 549 wickets @ 28.07. Appointed 1985.

JULIAN, Raymond (Wigston SM), b Cosby, Leicestershire 23 Aug 1936. RHB, WK. Leicestershire 1953-71 (cap 1961). HS 51 v Worcs (Worcester) 1962. F-c career: 192 matches; 2581 runs @ 9.73; 421 dismissals (382 ct, 39 st). Appointed 1972.

KITCHEN, Mervyn John (Backwell SM, Nailsea), b Nailsea, Somerset 1 Aug 1940. LHB, RM. Somerset 1960-79 (cap 1966; testimonial of £6000 in 1973). Tour: Rhodesia 1972-73 (Int Wand). 1000 runs (7); most – 1730 (1968). HS 189 v Pakistanis (Taunton) 1967. BB 1-4. F-c career: 354 matches; 15,230 runs @ 26.25, 17 hundreds; 2 wickets @ 54.50. Appointed 1982.

LEADBEATER, Barrie (Harehills SS), b Harehills, Leeds 14 Aug 1943. RHB, RM. Yorkshire 1966-79 (cap 1969; joint benefit sharing £33,846 with G.A. Cope in 1980). Tour: WI 1969-70 (DN). HS 140* v Hants (Portsmouth) 1976. F-c career: 147 matches; 5373 runs @ 25.34, 1 hundred; 1 wicket @ 5.00. Appointed 1981.

LYONS, Kevin James (Lady Mary's HS), b Cardiff 18 Dec 1946. RHB, RM. Glamorgan 1967-77. Tour: WI 1969-70 (Glam). HS 92 v Cambridge U (Cambridge) 1972. F-c career: 62 matches: 1673 runs @ 19.68; 2 wickets @ 126.00. Appointed 1985.

***MEYER, Barrie** John (Boscombe SS), b Bournemouth 21 Aug 1932. RHB, WK. Gloucestershire 1957-71 (cap 1958; benefit 1971). HS 63 v Indians (Cheltenham) 1959, 63 v Oxford U (Bristol) 1962, and 63 v Sussex (Bristol) 1964. F-c career: 406 matches; 5367 runs @ 14.16; 826 dismissals (707 ct, 119 st). Soccer for Bristol Rovers, Plymouth Argyle, Newport County and Bristol City. Appointed 1973. Umpired in 17 Tests (1978 to 1985).

OSLEAR, Donald Osmund, b Cleethorpes, Lincolnshire 3 Mar 1929. No appearances at first-class level. Soccer for Grimsby Town, Hull City and Oldham Athletic. Also played Ice Hockey. Appointed 1975. Umpired in 5 Tests (1980 to 1984).

***PALMER, Kenneth** Ernest (Southbroom SM, Devizes), b Winchester 22 Apr 1937. RHB, RFM. Brother of Roy (Somerset 1965-70) and father of G.V. (Somerset 1982-). Somerset 1955-69 (cap 1958; testimonial of £4000 in 1968). Tours: WI 1963-64 (Cavs); Pak 1963-64 (Cwlth XI). Tests: 1 (1964-65; while coaching in South Africa); 10 runs; 1 wicket. 1000 runs (1): 1036 (1961). 100 wickets (4); most – 139 (1963). HS 125* v Northants (Northampton) 1961. BB 9-57 v Notts (Nottingham) 1963. F-c career: 314 matches; 7761 runs @ 20.64, 2 hundreds; 866 wickets @ 21.34. Appointed 1972. Umpired in 11 Tests (1978 to 1985).

PALMER, Roy (Southbroom SM), b Devizes, Wiltshire 12 Jul 1942. RHB, RFM. Brother of K.E. (above). Somerset 1965-70. HS 84 v Leics (Taunton) 1967. BB 6-45 v Middx (Lord's) 1967. F-c career: 74 matches; 1037 runs @ 13.29; 172 wickets @ 31.62. Appointed 1980.

†**PLEWS, Nigel** Trevor, b Nottingham 5 Sep 1934. Former policeman (Fraud Squad). No first-class appearances. Appointed 1982.

***SHEPHERD, David** Robert (Barnstaple GS; St. Luke's C, Exeter), b Bideford, Devon 27 Dec 1940. RHB, RM. Gloucestershire 1965-79 (cap 1969; joint benefit with J. Davey 1978). Scored 108 on debut (v OU). Devon 1959-64. 1000 runs (2); most – 1079 (1970). HS 153 v Middx (Bristol) 1968. F-c career: 282 matches; 10,672 runs @ 24.47, 12 hundreds; 2 wickets @ 53.00. Appointed 1981. Umpired 2 Tests 1985.

WHITE, Robert Arthur (Chiswick GS), b Fulham, London 6 Oct 1936. LHB, OB. Middlesex 1958-65 (cap 1963). Nottinghamshire 1966-80 (cap 1966; benefit of £11,000 in 1974). 1000 runs (1): 1355 (1963). HS 116* Notts v Surrey (Oval) 1967. BB 7-41 Notts v Derbys (Ilkeston) 1971. F-c career; 413 matches; 12,452 runs @ 23.18, 5 hundreds; 693 wickets @ 30.50. Appointed 1983.

***WHITEHEAD, Alan** Geoffrey Thomas, b Butleigh, Somerset 28 Oct 1940. LHB, SLA. Somerset 1957-61. HS 15 v Hants (Southampton) 1959, and 15 v Leics (Leicester) 1960. BB 6-74 v Sussex (Eastbourne) 1959. F-c career: 38 matches; 137 runs @ 5.70; 67 wickets @ 34.41. Appointed 1970. Umpired 2 Tests (1982 and 1985).

WIGHT, Peter Bernard, b Georgetown, British Guiana 25 Jun 1930. RHB, OB. Brother of G.L. (West Indies), H.A. and N. (all British Guiana). British Guiana 1950-51. Somerset 1953-65 (cap 1954; benefit of £5000 in 1963). Canterbury 1963-64. 1000 runs (10); most – 2375 (1960). HS 222* v Kent (Taunton) 1959. BB 6-29 v Derbys (Chesterfield) 1957. F-c career: 333 matches 17,773 runs @ 33.09, 28 hundreds; 68 wickets @ 33.26. Appointed 1966.

RESERVE LIST

M.J. HARRIS, M. HENDRICK, D. LLOYD, H.J. RHODES and D.S. THOMPSETT.

* On Test Match Panel for 1986.
† Added to Test Match Panel for Texaco Trophy internationals
See page 73 for key to abbreviations.

PRINCIPAL FIXTURES 1986

**Including play on Sunday*

Saturday 19 April

Other Matches
The Parks: Oxford U v Somerset
Fenners: Cambridge v Leics

Wednesday 23 April

The Parks: Oxford U v Glos
Fenners: Cambridge U v Essex
Lord's: MCC v Middx

Saturday 26 April

Britannic Assurance Championship
*Bristol: Glos v Glam
*Leicester: Leics v Kent
Lord's: Middx v Derbys
*Trent Bridge: Notts v Hants
*Taunton: Somerset v Yorks
*Hove: Sussex v Lancs
*Edgbaston: Warwicks v Essex
*Worcester: Worcs v Surrey
Other Match
Fenners: Cambridge U v Northants

Wednesday 30 April

Britannic Assurance Championship
Chesterfield: Derbys v Somerset
Southampton: Hants v Glam
Canterbury: Kent v Northants
Old Trafford: Lancs v Leics
The Oval: Surrey v Notts
Other Matches
The Parks: Oxford U v Middx
Fenners: Cambridge U v Warwicks

Saturday 3 May

Benson & Hedges Cup
Chesterfield: Derbys v Leics
Bristol: Glos v Somerset
Old Trafford: Lancs v Yorks
Lord's: Middx v Surrey
Hove: Sussex v Essex
†Slough: Minor Counties v Northants
The Parks: Combined U v Hants
Glasgow (Titwood): Scotland v Worcs

Sunday 4 May

John Player League
Chelmsford: Essex v Warwicks
Cardiff: Glam v Hants
Canterbury: Kent v Glos
Old Trafford: Lancs v Sussex
Leicester: Leics v Derbys
Lord's: Middx v Notts
Bradford: Yorks v Somerset
Tourist Match
Arundel: Lavinia, Duchess of Norfolk XI v India (one day)

Tuesday 6 May

Tourist Match
Worcs v India

Wednesday 7 May

Britannic Assurance Championship
Chelmsford: Essex v Kent
Old Trafford: Lancs v Hants
Lord's: Middx v Leics
Northampton: Northants v Glos
Taunton: Somerset v Glam
The Oval: Surrey v Warwicks
Headingley: Yorks v Sussex
Other Match
The Parks: Oxford U v Notts

Saturday 10 May

Benson & Hedges Cup
Swansea: Glam v Sussex
Southampton: Hants v Middx
Canterbury: Kent v Surrey
Leicester: Leics v Warwicks
Northampton: Northants v Derbys
Trent Bridge: Notts v Yorks
Taunton: Somerset v Essex
Perth: Scotland v Lancs
Tourist Match
*Cheltenham Town CC: Glos v India

Sunday 11 May

John Player League
Derby: Derbys v Sussex
Swansea: Glam v Leics
Southampton: Hants v Northants
Trent Bridge: Notts v Warwicks

†will continue or start on Sunday, if necessary

Taunton: Somerset v Middx
The Oval: Surrey v Yorks
Worcester: Worcs v Kent

Tuesday 13 May

Benson & Hedges Cup
Chelmsford: Essex v Glos
Northampton: Northants v Leics
Trent Bridge: Notts v Scotland
Taunton: Somerset v Glam
The Oval: Surrey v Hants
Worcester: Worcs v Lancs
Walsall: Minor Counties v Warwicks
Fenners: Combined U v Kent

Thursday 15 May

Benson & Hedges Cup
Derby: Derbys v Minor Counties
Chelmsford: Essex v Glam
Bristol: Glos v Sussex
Southampton: Hants v Kent
Lord's: Middx v Combined U
Edgbaston: Warwicks v Northants
Worcester: Worcs v Notts
Headingley: Yorks v Scotland
Tourist Match
The Oval: Surrey v India (one day)

Saturday 17 May

Benson & Hedges Cup
Swansea: Glam v Glos
Canterbury: Kent v Middx
Liverpool: Lancs v Notts
Leicester: Leics v Minor Counties
The Oval: Surrey v Combined U
Hove: Sussex v Somerset
Edgbaston: Warwicks v Derbys
Headingley: Yorks v Worcs
Britannic Assurance Championship
Northampton: Northants v Essex
Tourist Match
*Southampton: Hants v India

Sunday 18 May

John Player League
Leek CC: Derbys v Warwicks
Swindon: Glos v Essex
Leicester: Leics v Lancs
Lord's: Middx v Kent
Trent Bridge: Notts v Sussex
The Oval: Surrey v Glam
Headingley: Yorks v Worcs

Wednesday 21 May

Britannic Assurance Championship
Chelmsford: Essex v Yorks
Lord's: Middx v Glam
Trent Bridge: Notts v Leics
Taunton: Somerset v Glos
Hove: Sussex v Surrey
Edgbaston: Warwicks v Northants
Worcester: Worcs v Lancs
Tourist Match
Canterbury: Kent v India
Other Match
Fenners: Cambridge U v Hants

Saturday 24 May

Britannic Assurance Championship
*Derby: Derbys v Notts
Cardiff: Glam v Somerset
Bournemouth: Hants v Glos
Lord's: Middx v Sussex
Northampton: Northants v Leics
Edgbaston: Warwicks v Worcs
Headingley: Yorks v Lancs

Saturday 24 May

TEXACO TROPHY
The Oval: ENGLAND v INDIA
(First One-day International)

Sunday 25 May

John Player League
Cardiff: Glam v Somerset
Canterbury: Kent v Surrey
Northampton: Northants v Leics
Hove: Sussex v Glos
Edgbaston: Warwicks v Worcs
Sheffield: Yorks v Essex

Monday 26 May

TEXACO TROPHY
Old Trafford: ENGLAND v INDIA
(Second One-day International)

Wednesday 28 May

Benson & Hedges Cup Quarter-finals
Tourist Match
Venue: Ireland v India (two days)

Thursday 3 July

CORNHILL INSURANCE TEST SERIES
Edgbaston: ENGLAND v INDIA (Third Test Match)

Saturday 5 July

Britannic Assurance Championship
Derby: Derbys v Kent
Cardiff: Glam v Glos
Old Trafford: Lancs v Essex
Uxbridge: Middx v Warwicks
Taunton: Somerset v Hants
The Oval: Surrey v Northants
Worcester: Worcs v Notts
Middlesbrough: Yorks v Leics
Tourist Match
*Hove: Sussex v New Zealand

Sunday 6 July

John Player League
Derby: Derbys v Kent
Cardiff: Glam v Glos
Old Trafford: Lancs v Essex
Lord's: Middx v Warwicks
Tring: Northants v Surrey
Taunton: Somerset v Hants
Worcester: Worcs v Notts
Middlesbrough: Yorks v Leics

Wednesday 9 July

NatWest Bank Trophy (Second Round)
Southampton or St Albans: Hants or Herts v Worcs or Oxfordshire
Taunton or Dean Park: Somerset or Dorset v Lancs or Cumberland
Reading (Courage's) or Bristol: Berks or Glos v Leics or Ireland
Exmouth or Trent Bridge: Devon or Notts v Scotland or Kent
Hove or Bury St Edmonds: Sussex or Suffolk v Staffs or Glam
Edgbaston or Darlington (Feetham's): Warwicks or Durham v Northumberland or Essex
Derby or Truro: Derbys or Cornwall v Cheshire or Surrey
Headingley or Wisbech: Yorks or Cambridgeshire v Northants or Middx

Tourist Match
Norwich (Lakenham): Minor Counties v New Zealand

Saturday 12 July

Lord's: BENSON & HEDGES CUP FINAL
Tourist Matches
*Scarborough: Yorks v India
*Edgbaston (or Old Trafford): Warwicks (or Lancs if Warwicks in B & H Final) v New Zealand

Sunday 13 July

John Player League
Chelmsford: Essex v Somerset
Leicester: Leics v Middx
Finedon: Northants v Derbys
Trent Bridge: Notts v Glos
Hove: Sussex v Glam

Wednesday 16 July

Britannic Assurance Championship
Southend: Essex v Leics
Neath: Glam v Worcs
Bristol: Glos v Sussex
Lord's: Middx v Somerset
Northampton: Northants v Lancs
Worksop: Notts v Yorks
The Oval: Surrey v Kent
Edgbaston: Warwicks v Derbys
TEXACO TROPHY
Headingley: ENGLAND v NEW ZEALAND (First One-day International)

Friday 18 July

TEXACO TROPHY
Old Trafford: ENGLAND v NEW ZEALAND (Second One-day International)

Saturday 19 July

Britannic Assurance Championship
Derby: Derbys v Middx
Southend: Essex v Worcs
Swansea: Glam v Northants
Bristol: Glos v Somerset
Portsmouth: Hants v Warwicks
Canterbury: Kent v Lancs
Leicester: Leics v Sussex

*Headingley: Yorks v Surrey
Tourist Match
*Trent Bridge: Notts v New Zealand
Other Match
Venue: Ireland v MCC (three days)

Sunday 20 July

John Player League
Derby: Derbys v Middx
Southend: Essex v Worcs
Neath: Glam v Northants
Bristol: Glos v Somerset
Portsmouth: Hants v Warwicks
Canterbury: Kent v Lancs
Leicester: Leics v Sussex

Wednesday 23 July

Britannic Assurance Championship
Portsmouth: Hants v Derbys
Southport: Lancs v Notts
Leicester: Leics v Glam
The Oval: Surrey v Essex
Hove: Sussex v Worcs
Scarborough: Yorks v Kent

Thursday 24 July

CORNHILL INSURANCE TEST SERIES
Lord's: ENGLAND v NEW ZEALAND
(First Test Match)

Saturday 26 July

Britannic Assurance Championship
Abergavenny: Glam v Derbys
Northampton: Northants v Middx
Guildford: Surrey v Sussex
Edgbaston: Warwicks v Lancs
Worcester: Worcs v Glos
Sheffield: Yorks v Notts

Sunday 27 July

John Player League
Ebbw Vale: Glam v Derbys
Southampton: Hants v Leics
Northampton: Northants v Kent
Taunton: Somerset v Lancs
Guildford: Surrey v Sussex
Worcester: Worcs v Glos
Hull (or Scarborough): Yorks v Notts

Wednesday 30 July

NatWest Bank Trophy Quarter-finals

Thursday 31 July

Jesmond: An England XI v Rest of the World XI (one day)

Friday 1 August

Jesmond: An England XI v Rest of the World XI (one day)

Saturday 2 August

Britannic Assurance Championship
Cheltenham: Glos v Hants
Canterbury: Kent v Leics
Old Trafford: Lancs v Yorks
Lord's: Middx v Northants
Weston-super-Mare: Somerset v Worcs
Eastbourne: Sussex v Essex
Tourist Match
*Derby: Derbys v New Zealand
Other Match
*Headingley: England Young Cricketers v Sri Lanka Young Cricketers
(First 'Test Match') (four days)

Sunday 3 August

John Player League
Cheltenham: Glos v Hants
Canterbury: Kent v Leics
Old Trafford: Lancs v Yorks
Lord's: Middx v Northants
Trent Bridge: Notts v Glam
Weston-super-Mare: Somerset v Worcs
Eastbourne: Sussex v Essex
Edgbaston: Warwicks v Surrey

Wednesday 6 August

Britannic Assurance Championship
Chelmsford: Essex v Middx
Cheltenham: Glos v Notts
Canterbury: Kent v Hants
Leicester: Leics v Yorks
Northampton: Northants v Glam
Weston-super-Mare: Somerset v Warwicks
The Oval: Surrey v Lancs
Eastbourne: Sussex v Derbys

Thursday 7 August

CORNHILL INSURANCE TEST SERIES
Trent Bridge: ENGLAND v NEW ZEALAND
(Second Test Match)

Saturday 9 August

Britannic Assurance Championship
Buxton: Derbys v Lancs
Cheltenham: Glos v Middx
Southampton: Hants v Sussex
Leicester: Leics v Essex
Wellingborough School: Northants v Somerset
The Oval: Surrey v Worcs
Edgbaston: Warwicks v Kent
Bradford: Yorks v Glam
Other Match
*Chelmsford: England Young Cricketers v Sri Lanka Young Cricketers
(First 'One-day International')

Sunday 10 August

John Player League
Buxton: Derbys v Lancs
Cheltenham: Glos v Middx
Bournemouth: Hants v Sussex
Leicester: Leics v Essex
Wellingborough School: Northants v Somerset
The Oval: Surrey v Worcs
Edgbaston: Warwicks v Kent
Scarborough: Yorks v Glam

Monday 11 August

Lord's: England Young Cricketers v Sri Lanka Young Cricketers
(Second 'One-day International')

Wednesday 13 August

NatWest Bank Trophy Semi-finals
Tourist Match
Old Trafford (or Edgbaston): Lancs (or Warwicks if Lancs in NatWest Semi-final) v New Zealand

Saturday 16 August

Britannic Assurance Championship
Chesterfield: Derbys v Yorks
Colchester: Essex v Northants
Lord's: Middx v Hants
Trent Bridge: Notts v Lancs
Taunton: Somerset v Surrey
Hove: Sussex v Kent
Nuneaton (Griff & Coton): Warwicks v Glos
Worcester: Worcs v Leics
Tourist Match
*Swansea: Glam v New Zealand
Other Match
*Bristol: England Young Cricketers v Sri Lanka Young Cricketers
(Second 'Test Match') (four days)
Venue: Scotland v Ireland (three days)

Sunday 17 August

John Player League
Chesterfield: Derbys v Yorks
Colchester: Essex v Northants
Lord's: Middx v Hants
Trent Bridge: Notts v Lancs
Taunton: Somerset v Surrey
Hove: Sussex v Kent
Edgbaston: Warwicks v Glos
Worcester: Worcs v Leics

Wednesday 20 August

Britannic Assurance Championship
Chesterfield: Derbys v Leics
Colchester: Essex v Glos
Bournemouth: Hants v Worcs
Dartford: Kent v Surrey
Lytham: Lancs v Glam
Northampton: Northants v Notts
Taunton: Somerset v Sussex
Headingley: Yorks v Middx

Thursday 21 August

CORNHILL INSURANCE TEST SERIES
The Oval: ENGLAND v NEW ZEALAND
(Third Test Match)

Saturday 23 August

Britannic Assurance Championship
Chelmsford: Essex v Surrey
Cardiff: Glam v Kent
Bournemouth: Hampshire v Yorks
Old Trafford: Lancs v Glos
Leicester: Leics v Northants
Trent Bridge: Notts v Derbys
Hove: Sussex v Middx
Worcester: Worcs v Warwicks

Sunday 24 August

John Player League
Chelmsford: Essex v Surrey
Bournemouth: Hants v Yorks
Old Trafford: Lancs v Northants

Trent Bridge: Notts v Derbys
Hove: Sussex v Middx
Edgbaston: Warwicks v Somerset
Worcester: Worcs v Glam

Wednesday 27 August

Britannic Assurance Championship
Swansea: Glam v Surrey
Leicester: Leics v Derbys
Lord's: Middx v Lancs
Northampton: Northants v Hants
Trent Bridge: Notts v Kent
Taunton: Somerset v Essex
Edgbaston: Warwicks v Yorks

Saturday 30 August

Britannic Assurance Championship
Derbyshire: Derbys v Hants
Folkestone: Kent v Essex
Leicester: Leics v Somerset
*Hove: Sussex v Notts
Edgbaston: Warwicks v Middx
Other Match
*Trent Bridge: England Young Cricketers v Sri Lanka Young Cricketers (Third 'Test Match') (four days)

Sunday 31 August

John Player League
Heanor: Derbys v Hants
Moreton in Marsh: Glos v Northants
Folkestone: Kent v Essex
Old Trafford: Lancs v Surrey
Leicester: Leics v Somerset
Lord's; Middx v Worcs
Headingley: Yorks v Warwicks
Other Matches
Edgbaston: Warwick Under-25 Final (one day)
Scarborough: D.B. Close's XI v New Zealand (three days)

Wednesday 3 September

Britannic Assurance Championship
Derby: Derbys v Northants
Cardiff: Glam v Notts
Folkestone: Kent v Warwicks
The Oval: Surrey v Glos
Worcester: Worcs v Somerset
Other Match
Scarborough: ASDA CRICKET CHALLENGE
Essex v Lancs (one day)

Thursday 4 September

ASDA CRICKET CHALLENGE
Hants v Yorks (one day)

Friday 5 September

ASDA CRICKET CHALLENGE FINAL (one day)

Saturday 6 September

Lord's: NatWest Bank Trophy Final

Sunday 7 September

John Player League
Cardiff: Glam v Middx
Bristol: Glos v Lancs
Canterbury: Kent v Notts
The Oval: Surrey v Hants
Hove: Sussex v Yorks
Worcester: Worcs v Derbys

Wednesday 10 September

Britannic Assurance Championship
Old Trafford: Lancs v Somerset
Trent Bridge: Notts v Essex
Hove: Sussex v Hants
Worcester: Worcs v Glam
Scarborough: Yorks v Northants

Saturday 13 September

Britannic Assurance Championship
Chelmsford: Essex v Glam
Bristol: Glos v Worcs
Southampton: Hants v Lancs
Canterbury: Kent v Middx
Trent Bridge: Notts v Northants
Taunton: Somerset v Derbys
The Oval: Surrey v Leics
Edgbaston: Warwicks v Sussex

Sunday 14 September

John Player League
Chelmsford: Essex v Glam
Southampton: Hants v Lancs
Canterbury: Kent v Yorks
Trent Bridge: Notts v Northants
Taunton: Somerset v Derbys
The Oval: Surrey v Leics
Edgbaston: Warwicks v Sussex

MINOR COUNTIES FIXTURES 1986

(E) *Eastern Division* (W) *Western Division*

MAY		**KNOCKOUT**, *Qualifying Round*
Sun 25	Cambridge (Trinity)	Cambridgeshire v Norfolk
		Cumberland v Cheshire
	Longton	Staffordshire v Buckinghamshire
		CHAMPIONSHIP
Sun 25	Sleaford	(E) Lincolnshire v Bedfordshire
	Jesmond	(E) Northumberland v Hertfordshire
Mon 26	Falkland CC, Newbury	(W) Berkshire v Buckinghamshire
	Sherborne School	(W) Dorset v Wiltshire
Tue 27	Netherfield, Kendal	(E) Cumberland v Hertfordshire
	Hartlepool	(E) Durham v Bedfordshire
	Jesmond	(E) Northumberland v Suffolk
Thu 29	Carlisle	(E) Cumberland v Suffolk
	Burton on Trent	(E) Staffordshire v Hertfordshire
JUNE		
Sun 1	Nantwich	(W) Cheshire v Shropshire
Wed 4	Wisbech	(E) Cambridgeshire v Staffordshire
		KNOCKOUT, *First Round*
Sun 8	Cambridge, Trinity or Horsford	Cambridgeshire or Norfolk v Suffolk
	Jesmond	Northumberland v Lincolnshire
	Christ Church	Oxfordshire v Shropshire
	Sherborne School	Dorset v Wiltshire
	Bovey Tracey	Devon v Cornwall
	Venue to be arranged or Warrington	Cumberland or Cheshire v Durham
	Potter's Bar	Hertfordshire v Bedfordshire
	Bracknell	Berkshire v Staffordshire or Buckinghamshire
		CHAMPIONSHIP
Mon 9	Stockton	(E) Durham v Lincolnshire
Sun 15	Henlow	(E) Bedfordshire v Cumberland
	Watford	(E) Hertfordshire v Norfolk
	Morris Motors	(W) Oxfordshire v Wiltshire
Mon 16	Truro	(W) Cornwall v Cheshire
	Bovey Tracey	(W) Devon v Shropshire
	Jesmond	(E) Northumberland v Staffordshire
Tue 17	Dunstable	(E) Bedfordshire v Norfolk
	Peterborough	(E) Cambridgeshire v Cumberland
Wed 18	Falmouth	(W) Cornwall v Shropshire
	Sidmouth	(W) Devon v Cheshire
	Darlington	(E) Durham v Staffordshire
Sun 22		**KNOCKOUT**, *Quarter-Finals*
		CHAMPIONSHIP
Sun 29	Sherborne School	(W) Dorset v Berkshire
	Chester-le-Street	(E) Durham v Cumberland
	St Albans	(E) Hertfordshire v Lincolnshire
	Bridgnorth	(W) Shropshire v Buckinghamshire
	Frome C.C.	(W) Somerset II v Wiltshire

JULY		
Tue 1	Oxton, Birkenhead	(W) Cheshire v Buckinghamshire
Sun 6		**KNOCKOUT**, *Semi-Finals*
		CHAMPIONSHIP
Sun 6	Bradford College	(W) Berkshire v Oxfordshire
	St Austell	(W) Cornwall v Somerset II
	Burghley Park	(E) Lincolnshire v Cambridgeshire
		MCCA Representative Match (Three days)
Wed 9	Lakenham, Norwich	Minor Counties v New Zealand
JULY		**CHAMPIONSHIP**
Sun 13	Southill Park	(E) Bedfordshire v Hertfordshire
	Bletchley Town	(W) Buckinghamshire v Somerset II
	Bowdon	(W) Cheshire v Berkshire
	Jesmond	(E) Northumberland v Durham
	St Edward's School	(W) Oxfordshire v Cornwall
	Leek	(E) Staffordshire v Norfolk
Tue 15	Wardown Park	(E) Bedfordshire v Cambridgeshire
	Kendal	(E) Cumberland v Norfolk
	Wellington	(W) Shropshire v Berkshire
	Devizes	(W) Wiltshire v Cornwall
Wed 16	Exmouth	(W) Devon v Somerset II
Thu 17	Fenner's	(E) Cambridgeshire v Suffolk
Sun 20		**KNOCKOUT FINAL**
		CHAMPIONSHIP
Sun 20	Lincoln Lindum	(E) Lincolnshire v Staffordshire
	Banbury XX	(W) Oxfordshire v Somerset II
Mon 21	High Wycombe	(W) Buckinghamshire v Cornwall
	Dorchester	(W) Dorset v Devon
	Bishops Stortford	(E) Hertfordshire v Suffolk
Wed 23	Finchampstead	(W) Berkshire v Cornwall
Thu 24	Slough	(W) Buckinghamshire v Dorset
	Ipswich School	(E) Suffolk v Norfolk
Sun 27	Kidmore End	(W) Berkshire v Somerset II
	Sherborne School	(W) Dorset v Cheshire
	Grimsby (Ross)	(E) Lincolnshire v Northumberland
	Stone	(E) Staffordshire v Cumberland
Tue 29	Lakenham	(E) Norfolk v Northumberland
	Christ Church	(W) Oxfordshire v Devon
	Street (Vict. Club)	(W) Somerset II v Cheshire
	Swindon	(W) Wiltshire v Berkshire
Thu 31	Lakenham	(E) Norfolk v Cambridgeshire
	Trowbridge	(W) Wiltshire v Devon
AUGUST		
Sun 3	Knypersley	(E) Staffordshire v Bedfordshire
Mon 4	Lakenham	(E) Norfolk v Lincolnshire
	Taunton	(W) Somerset II v Shropshire
	Mildenhall	(E) Suffolk v Durham
Wed 6	Fenner's	(E) Cambridgeshire v Hertfordshire
	Dean Park	(W) Dorset v Shropshire
	Lakenham	(E) Norfolk v Durham
Sun 10	Bedford, Goldington Bury	(E) Bedfordshire v Northumberland
	Chester, Boughton Hall	(W) Cheshire v Oxfordshire
	Wadebridge	(W) Cornwall v Dorset